States in History

IDEAS is a new Blackwell series which makes available in paperback some of the most adventurous writing in the social and humane sciences in recent years, extending the frontiers of research, crossing disciplinary borders and setting new intellectual standards in international scholarship. Published and forthcoming titles include:

Jean Baechler, John A. Hall and Michael Mann, *Europe and the Rise of Capitalism*

Colin Campbell, *The Romantic Ethic and the Spirit of Modern Consumerism*

William Connolly, *Political Theory and Modernity*

John A. Hall (ed.), *States in History*

Alan Macfarlane, *The Culture of Capitalism*

Derek Sayer, *The Violence of Abstraction*

Michael Peter Smith and Joe R. Feagin, *The Capitalist City*

States in History

Edited by
John A. Hall

Basil Blackwell

© Basil Blackwell Ltd 1986

First published 1986

First published in the USA 1987

First published in paperback 1989

Basil Blackwell Ltd
108 Cowley Road, Oxford OX4 1JF, UK

Basil Blackwell Inc.
3 Cambridge Center, Cambridge, Massachusetts 02142, USA

British Library Cataloguing in Publication Data
A CIP catalogue record for this book is available from the British Library.

Library of Congress Cataloging in Publication Data
States in History.
Includes index.
1. Constitutional history.   2. Comparative
government.   3. State, The.   I. Hall, John A.,
1949–
JF31.S73   1986   320.1   86–11804
ISBN 0–631–14365–3
ISBN 0–631–17136–3 (pbk.)

Typeset by Joshua Associates Limited
Printed in Great Britain by The Camelot Press, Southampton

Contents

Introduction   1
John A. Hall

1   Hunter-Gatherers and the Origin of States   22
    Clive Gamble

2   The Tribe and the State   48
    Patricia Crone

3   Soviets against Wittfogel: or, the Anthropological
    Preconditions of Mature Marxism   78
    Ernest Gellner

4   The Autonomous Power of the State: Its Origins,
    Mechanisms and Results   109
    Michael Mann

5   City-States   137
    Peter Burke

6   States and Economic Development: Reflections on
    Adam Smith   154
    John A. Hall

7   Sharing Public Space: States and Organized Interests
    in Western Europe   177
    Colin Crouch

8   State and Politics in Developed Socialism: Recent
    Developments in Soviet Theory   211
    Karen Dawisha

9   State-Making and Nation-Building   228
    Anthony D. Smith

Contents

10 Patterns of State-Building in Brazil and Argentina   264
    J. G. Merquior

11 Supranationals and the State   289
    Susan Strange

Notes on Contributors   306
Index   307

Introduction

John A. Hall

It is widely agreed that the state is now at the centre of our attention. Given the importance of coercion and violence as forces affecting the historical record, this can only be welcomed as a wholly beneficial development. Indeed it is, at first sight, highly puzzling that the state was once somehow 'off the agenda' and that its salience needed to be rediscovered. This introduction begins by explaining the 'withering away of the state': of course, the explanation says more about hopes entertained by social theorists than it does about actual patterns of social development. A second section describes and evaluates the character of the recent rediscovery of the state. The argument of the book is, of course, that of its title – that states must be considered in their historical contexts – and the final section of this introduction spells out this position. In those final comments, I have also chosen to highlight the advances, conceptual and substantive, made by the various contributors of this volume to the understanding of the behaviour of states.

'The Withering Away of the State'

To discuss the state is to consider the political. There is, of course, a vast history of 'things political'. Each of the world civilizations, for example, has a particular view of the role and duty of states; such views are occasionally considered in this book. However, the hope that the state would 'wither away' is particularly Western and modern. It would not have been comprehensible to the Greeks who regarded the *polis* as the highest expression of communal life. The Greek experience, mediated by the Renaissance, created a tradition of 'civic humanism', interested in the nature of corruption and the possibility of civic virtue; this is a political theory whose influence is by no means finished.[1] But it is fair to say that a rather different and more modern tradition has had greater importance; and it is certainly from this viewpoint that hopes for the 'withering away of the state' derive.

This modern viewpoint is that of classical liberalism, which sees civil society as the fount of all virtue. It is very likely that this viewpoint derives from the decentred but contractualistic civil society, described in my own chapter, established in North-Western Europe after the Fall of Rome. The liberal viewpoint was not one which was necessarily antipolitical.[2] However, it is true that a large part of the liberal interest in politics was negative: the question they asked was how to control political power so that the beneficial workings of civil society could proceed unhindered. But a liberal thinker such as Adam Smith had a lively *positive* appreciation of the necessity of the state to carry out certain key social functions, most notably those of defence, the establishment and maintenance of the rule of law and the protection of property. Even James and John Mill, the advocates of a new democratic era, did not simply trust society as it actally was; they believed that the rule of the wise would need to continue for some considerable time, and that the state should certainly engage in a great deal of social engineering in order to improve society.[3]

Nevertheless, it was the aspect of liberalism that stressed the minimal functions of the state that proved to be most influential. Perhaps this was due to the extraordinary impact of Herbert Spencer, whose thought is relevant here in two ways. First, Spencer entertained in a fully systematic way the notion of the end of the state: as individualism developed and so gained a sense of social responsibility, it became realistic to envisage that it might be so perfected as to allow social life to be guided merely by contractual relationships between free agents.[4] Second, Spencer, as was so often the case, summed up Victorian hopes when he claimed that the spread of commerce would bring in its wake a reign of peace. Wars were created by the remnants of feudal aristocracies, overly represented in the Foreign Offices of various countries, whose style of life, being honorific and militaristic, encouraged war. Once such remnants were removed from office, the spread of commerce would unite the nations of the world through specialization and by

1 Recent interest in the tradition has owed much to the work of J. G. A. Pocock, and in particular to his *The Machiavellian Moment*, Princeton, Princeton University Press, 1975. Modern thinkers influenced, consciously or unconsciously, by this tradition include Jürgen Habermas, Alasdair MacIntyre and Hannah Arendt.

2 I have benefited from the account of liberalism in D. Held, 'Central perspectives on the modern state', in D. Held, J. Anderson, B. Gieben, S. Hall, L. Harris, P. Lewis, N. Parker, B. Tirok, eds, *States and Societies*, Oxford, Martin Robertson, 1983.

3 J. A. Hall, *Liberalism*, London, Granada, 1987, chapters 2–4.

4 J. D. Y. Peel, *Herbert Spencer*, London, Heinemann Educational Books, 1981.

means of increasing prosperity. The development of social relations would mean that states would be deprived of what was, and what was generally recognized to be, their single most important historic function, namely that of preparing for and engaging in war.

It is well known that sustained attack on a particular intellectual position is no bar to unconscious acceptance of many of its key presuppositions. Karl Marx is a prime example of this. He took society-centred analysis to an extreme similar to that of Spencer when he announced that the state would have no reason to exist once the era of class history had been finished: states, deprived of their function would 'wither away'. Ernest Gellner's chapter makes it clear that the key intellectual presupposition at work here is that there is but a single source of evil in human affairs, that of economic exploitation by class, and that there is no ontological basis to political coercion. None of this is, of course, to say that Marx did not offer interesting comments about various states which were in existence, albeit these were fragmentary rather than systematic in nature. But these do not in any way go against the society-centred nature of his general approach. His most important and central point was to reject that part of liberal theory which had seen the state as a source of power in its own right, fit to be controlled so that it could not interfere with the beneficial workings of civil society. He insisted that it was an utter delusion to believe that the restrictions of which liberal political theorists were so proud were in any way real, let alone important. The freedoms established by the bourgeois class were merely formal; this was necessarily so since the state *was* merely the instrument of the bourgeoisie, doing the bidding of the capitalist class. Marx replaced the political problem with the social problem, and his work has been the single most important source of the loss of interest in the state in modern social science.

Scholars of Marx, keen to make his work more relevant to the modern era, have combed his writings to discover more sophisticated statements about the state. They have been successful. Marx was aware of differences in patterns of state-building between various European states, and he had particularly interesting comments to make about the Bonapartist state of Napoleon III.[5] His comments about the latter were sufficiently interesting to allow later theorists to build up a more general Marxist view of the state. A state can, according to this interpretation, gain a measure of autonomy by standing between different social classes. I doubt very much, however, whether this fundamentally challenges the society-centred nature of Marx's general approach. Marx's analysis of

5 K. Marx, *The Eighteenth Brumaire of Louis Bonaparte*, New York, International Publishers, 1963.

the political situation of mid-nineteenth-century France is entirely in terms of class, and allows no room for the autonomous impact of political factors.[6] More importantly, later Marxists are surely right to argue, as against those who believe that Marx's occasional comments could lead to a genuinely political approach, that only a relative autonomy of the state, indeed of the political in general, is compatible with the central tenets, principal aims and chiliastic appeal of Marxism.[7] Gellner's chapter makes this case, and with devastating force, when analysing the problems that the Asiatic Mode of Production causes for the conceptual apparatus of Marxism. Karen Dawisha's description of the Soviet view of the state backs up the general point being made about Marxism. It does so particularly effectively when analysing recent Eastern European attempts to think about the state; Dawisha demonstrates very clearly how hard that task is within the Marxist conceptual apparatus.

If these are the ideological origins of the hope that the state would disappear, it is important to go somewhat further in evaluating Marxism. It is necessary to reject, albeit with regret and fear rather than with joy and exultation, the key sociological presupposition behind this hope. The presupposition in question is that war results merely from a particular type of economic organization, and that peace can be assured if a new type of economic organization takes its place. Here the Marxist tradition, with the partial exception of Friedrich Engels,[8] again entirely apes the liberal tradition it loved to hate. The timetable is, of course, different: peace is dependent upon the establishment of socialism where it will be achieved almost by definition, given that states will by then have withered away. But insofar as modern society witnesses wars, the Marxist argument continues, they are not the result of the autonomous fact of inter-state competition but rather the result of particular economic forces. The pioneer of this view was the maverick liberal John Hobson whose *Imperialism*, celebrated for having influenced both Keynes and Lenin, explained Britain's involvement in the Boer War in terms of the rational but selfish interests of finance capitalists – most of whom, Hobson insisted with a regrettable degree of anti-Semitism, were Jewish.[9] Hobson believed that if capitalism were reconstructed by

6 R. Aron, *Main Currents in Sociological Thought*, vol. I, London, Penguin, 1977, pp. 233–60.

7 B. Badie and P. Birnbaum, *The Sociology of the State*, Chicago, Chicago University Press, 1983, chapter 1, argues that Marx's comments could have led to a sustained appreciation of the state; it was Nicos Poulantzas, above all, who insisted that Marxism could only accommodate the 'relative autonomy' of the state.

8 B. Gallie, *Philosophers of War and Peace*, Cambridge, Cambridge University Press, 1978.

9 J. A. Hobson, *Imperialism*, London, James Nisbet, 1902. For a critical commentary, see Hall, *Liberalism*, chapter 4.

redistributing large profits to the people, the power and influence of finance capitalism would be removed; a reformed market would thereby once again continue to usher in peace. Lenin and Rosa Luxemburg rejected this possibility, and simply expanded the negative side of Hobson's argument when they claimed that capitalism, either in the search for areas in which to invest or as the result of a need for markets, causes wars.

There can be no doubt that the wars of the twentieth century justify the famous declaration of Trotsky that 'war is the locomotive of history'. It is of the utmost importance to establish whether various explanations of these wars as the result of non-political and non-state variables do or do not hold water; the question amounts to being a litmus test of the necessity for studying states as entities in themselves. We can begin by noting the paucity of evidence to suggest that the First World War resulted from the displacement of imperial rivalries, themselves supposedly necessitated by some crisis of capitalism. By and large imperialism was in fact the result of geopolitical rivalry rather than of economic necessity. This was clearly demonstrated by the refusal, to give but one example, of French capitalists to invest in their colonies rather than in Imperial Russia where greater opportunities beckoned.[10] Importantly, the thesis of imperial rivalries causing the First World War fails on chronological grounds simply because 'the scramble for Africa' had been terminated long before the second decade of this century. Such rivalries as there were, and these included those over the arms race as much as those over colonies, had reached remarkably satisfactory conclusions by 1914.

Moreover, the events of 1914 go completely against the grain of Marx's general ethic. The lack of interest he took in states is fundamentally demonstrated by his a priori belief that classes would be transnational phenomena. There is some truth to this claim. A capitalist can sometimes be said to belong to capitalist society rather than to the geographical boundaries of the particular nation-state whose passport he holds. Interestingly, some international capitalists of this type visited various Chancelleries and Foreign Offices in 1914 to argue *against* war; they could do little since the society to which they 'belonged' had no means of coercion of its own, despite its extensive reach. But the outbreak of war showed that there was no truth to the notion that the working class was a single transnational class. Very much to the contrary, the various working classes of the European nations fought, with greater or lesser degrees of willingness, for their different nations.

---

10 R. Aron, *Imperialism and Colonialism*, Montague Burton Lecture, Leeds, Leeds University Press, 1959.

What then were the causes of the First World War? Although this is the type of question upon which total consensus is never likely to be achieved, it can be said with confidence that no explanation which fails to take account of nationalism in the Balkans and, above all, the rivalry endemic to a multipolar system, will carry conviction. That attempts have been made to find further explanations is the result of the enormous losses caused by a war based on industry and fought with citizen armies. The consequences of such a war were, of course, catastrophic; but those who planned the war did not know this in advance; they presumed that the war was as rational a recourse of state activity as it had always been in European history. The war was *normal*, the characteristic product of a multipolar state system.

Recent State Theory

The events of the twentieth century – world wars, nationalism, fascism and the birth of the Soviet Model – clearly demonstrate that the state has not withered away. On reflection, this makes it positively bizarre that much of the theory of modern social science has not paid significant attention to the behaviour of states. But this situation is, as noted, at last being changed, and the two sources of recent work on the state must be examined in turn.

Marxist or Marxisant writers have been at the forefront of recent developments. A key text proved to be Ralph Miliband's *The State in Capitalist Society*, not least because it produced a famous riposte from the most important of Marxist theorists of the state, the late Nicos Poulantzas.[11] Miliband's study centred upon the way in which state personnel were recruited from the dominant social classes, and it was this traditionalist approach that drew Poulantzas's anger. The social background of the elite mattered less, in his view, than did the objective constraints that the management of capitalist society imposed upon it. It is worth pausing for a moment at this statement. Poulantzas certainly went some way beyond Miliband in recognizing that the state could provide certain services for the capitalist class, as a whole and in the long run, that capitalists themselves, anarchically organized and with their eye on the short term, might even oppose. Nevertheless, in the final analysis his theory remained a Marxist one in being consistently society-centred: any autonomy of the state was

---

11 The exchange between Miliband and Poulantzas is available in R. Blackburn, ed., *Ideology in Social Science*, London, Fontana, 1972.

limited by the capitalist mode of production. The state was not fully a force in its own right; it was merely 'relatively' autonomous.

Poulantzas's work is complex and highly abstract; it tends to consider 'the state' rather than particular states located in history. His work is also very diverse; it contains analyses of the Bonapartist and fascist 'balancing acts' as well as completely different definitions of the state, notably in terms of it being an arena of class struggle. There is not enough space here to describe every twist and turn in his intellectual career.[12] Some of the formulae he created to describe state activity are suggestive and are such as to encourage empirical investigation. Nevertheless, criticism may usefully be levelled at the modern Marxist view of the state which he represents since this will serve to advance the argument.

The conception of the state habitually present in writers like Poulantzas is passive. Perhaps a society-centred conceptual apparatus makes this inevitable. This passivity is seen particularly clearly in discussion of the relationship between social classes and the state. The prior existence of social classes is taken for granted. This is extremely unhelpful since it illegitimately rules out of court ways in which the state can be a *prime mover* causing class struggle to take a particular form. More neutral, aseptic studies of class struggle are increasingly stressing that the form of state organization in place in various national states determined the shape that working class organizations then took.[13] One careful account of this sort is Dick Geary's *European Labour Protest 1848–1945*. This begins by noting how similar was the pattern of union recruitment throughout all of Europe; this is explained as the direct and straightforward consequence of industrial capitalist organization. However, this pattern tells us rather little about class struggle. To understand what it was that put workers on the streets, attention must be paid to a different variable:

the major determinant of the forms of political action adopted by the different national labour movements was the role of the state and of the social groups it claimed to represent; for at the level of industrial action clear similarities existed between similar occupations in different countries. Furthermore, it remains true that certain kinds of governmental interference in industrial relations did transform what began as economic protest into political action.[14]

12 For a full account, see B. Jessop, *Nicos Poulantzas: Marxist Theory and Political Strategy*, London, Macmillan, 1985.
13 D. Geary, *European Labour Protest 1848–1945*, London, Methuen, 1984; R. McKibbin, *The Evolution of the Labour Party, 1910–24*, Oxford, Oxford University Press, 1974, conclusion. I have also benefited from listening to talks given by Colin Crouch and Michael Mann.
14 Geary, *European Labour Protest*, p. 60.

The point at issue can be made most clearly by comparing the nature of class struggle in Britain with that in Imperial Germany. The liberal state of Great Britain allowed independent organization and industrial conflict, with the consequence that the state itself was not questioned by the working class. The German position was the reverse of this situation: a repressive state limited industrial organization with the consequence that a genuinely politicized and socialist labour movement was created. Captialism is likely to be under threat to the extent to which states force working classes to become political; if state policy is liberal, it seems, *pace* Marx, that capitalism has little to fear from the organized working class.

There is a more general criticism to be made against modern Marxist theories of the state. Such theories have typically focused on the capitalist state, and very few attempts have been made to consider either states in entirely different historical periods or the states of 'actually existing socialism'. Amongst the various points that a broadening of the range of consideration would bring, one is surely fundamental. When we examine the budgets of very varied types of states in history, the importance of war and the preparation for war becomes quite obvious.[15] In the European sphere since 1945, the modern state *is* largely the 'the best capitalist' 'doing the work of capital'. But it behoves us to remember that these functions are relatively new, and that the task of defending territorial sovereignty has usually seemed more basic. The latter task remains central to most states in the modern world; that Europeans can downplay this is sorry evidence of the extent to which they have become clients of the United States which does provide military protection, albeit, as is natural, largely on its own terms. This is an important point to make in itself; it is also important because it is the necessity of managing state competition that has often provided the opportunity for state elites to gain autonomous power, free from the constraints often imposed upon them by civil society. Two classic instances of this in modern European history have been Prussia and the Soviet Union. In both these cases geopolitical pressures played a significant part in creating an autonomous state in social formations able to play a significant role on the international scene because of their obsessive concentration on military power.

The last argument returns us to the points made in the previous section; it also brings us to the second general approach to the state that has proved of use in recent years. This approach was that pioneered by

15 See various essays, particularly that of Finer, in C. Tilly, ed., *The Formation of National States in Western Europe*, Princeton, Princeton University Press, 1975; M. Mann, 'State and society, 1130–1815: an analysis of English state finances', in M. Zeitlin, ed., *Political Power and Social Theory*, vol. I, Connecticut, J. A. I. Press, 1980.

thinkers of the one country in nineteenth-century Europe which could not ignore the importance of the state. The thinkers in question were German, and they contain amongst their number Ratzenhofer, Schmitt, Oppenheimer, Gumplowicz, Hintze and Max Weber. Such thinkers experienced the activities of their state in nation-building and in war – the two forces being closely related – and were anyway moved to think about the importance of the state because of Germany's insecure geo-political situation. The insights that their perspective brought have already been drawn upon in this introduction, but deserve further atten-tion in their own right.

Otto Hintze's 'Military organization and the organization of the state' represents the views of this group of thinkers in arguing that the char-acter of the state results from the nature of its participation in military struggle.[16] This is a fundamental point beautifully illustrated by the fact that the emergence of a citizen army in classial Greece went hand in hand with the creation of political democracy. Keith Hopkins has also give us a series of analytic studies of Roman history which make the centrality of military organization extremely clear. Most notably, he demonstrates how the spoils of empire, including the capture of slaves, undermined the free citizenry of Rome, despite the fact that they had provided the armies of conquest; this proved to be a sea change in the history of Rome.[17]

When this group of thinkers reflected on what it was that made the state necessary, they tended towards slightly naïve and certainly unpleasant Social Darwinist assumptions. War was seen as 'natural', with the consequence that other questions about the nature and function of the state tended to be forgotten. This generalization holds true even of as sophisticated a thinker as Max Weber. His 'tunnel-vision' in regard to the state can be seen particularly clearly in the nature of his plan for the German constitution after the First World War. What concerned him was that a parliamentary system should take the form in which it could encourage the emergence of a strong leadership, capable of dealing with unimaginative bureaucracies. This was crucial if national power and prestige – values he never questioned – were to be protected. Weber had no conception that a parliamentary system might be desir-able in itself, an institution to foster and protect democracy.[18] All this amounts to saying that this tradition could oversimplify matters, as Michael Mann notes, quite as much as the liberal/Marxist view already

16 O. Hintze, *The Historical Essays of Otto Hintze*, ed. Felix Gilbert, New York, Oxford University Press, 1975.
17 K. Hopkins, *Conquerors and Slaves*, Cambridge, Cambridge University Press, 1978.
18 Held, 'Central perspectives'; J. G. Merquior, *Rousseau and Weber*, London, Routledge & Kegan Paul, 1980.

analysed. Thus it is *not* true to say that state competition by itself results in social change; there are cultures, notably those of classical India and Islam, in which warfare between states was endemic but in which dynamic social change was absent.[19]

The most sophisticated recent state theory has appreciated the importance of both economic and military aspects of state power in the European sphere. What has been offered is a type of combination of both approaches, each of which corrects the defects of the other. A characteristically suggestive and open-minded essay by Otto Hintze, 'Economics and politics in the age of modern capitalism', argues that any periodization of modern European history needs to take into account both the dynamic of capitalism and the consequences of state competition. Hintze notes that much that the state did for reasons of security (the removal of various regional or national autonomies, linking different parts of the territory for logistical reasons, and so on) proved beneficial to capitalism; equally, the spread of capitalism (as in the case of England's successful wars in the eighteenth century) could increase the power of the state.[20] This approach corrects society-centred approaches by demonstrating that economic development is caused by state competition, and that the state, whether seeking to adopt capitalism whilst retaining the traditional power structure or trying to force development by socialist means, tends to be heavily involved in this process. Equally, however, the militarist viewpoint stands corrected by the realization that participation in modern war requires the adoption of modern economic modes of organization.

This dual interest in geopolitical and class bases of power, that is, of military and society-centred approaches, characterizes the most striking single recent work on the state in history, namely Theda Skocpol's *States and Social Revolutions*.[21] Skocpol argued that military competition places great pressure on states to rationalize their societies in order to survive in what Kant termed the 'asocial society of states'. Some states have sufficient co-operation with or control over their societies to make endless adaptation possible, but geopolitical pressure forces other states into fundamental self-questioning. At this point, Skocpol's analysis becomes slightly circular: some states respond to challenge by means of social revolution whilst others stagnate and disappear – as happened to Burgundy and to Poland from the late eighteenth century

19 J. A. Hall, 'War and the rise of the West', in M. Shaw and C. Creighton, eds, *The Sociology of War and Peace*, London, Macmillan, 1986.

20 Hintze, 'Economics and politics in the age of modern capitalism', in idem, *Historical Essays*.

21 T. Skocpol, *States and Social Revolutions*, Cambridge, Cambridge University Press, 1979.

to the Treaty of Versailles. Such circularity does not really matter, however, for Skocpol provides superb examples of the way in which states and societies interact. These analyses are of great theoretical importance, albeit this has not properly been recognized. Merely to combinate the society-centred approach of neo-Marxism with the statist view of the militarist tradition is unsatisfactory, leaving state theory at a very early stage. What Skocpol's work points towards is a genuine convergence between the two approaches such that the interesting questions become those of the ways in which class and state interact. I believe that something like this convergence is now taking place amongst those writing on the state, and this is wholly welcome.

States in History

It is not the purpose of an introduction to tell readers what they should think of the arguments they are about to confront, and no attempt of this type is made here; it is up to readers to make what they will, to take but one example, of Michael Mann's claim that the notion of state 'autonomy' used by Hintze and Skocpol is too limited. Nevertheless, certain arguments deserve highlighting as their covering of new ground renders them hard to assimilate. This process of highlighting naturally falls into three areas.

The origins of the state

The first two chapters in this book were commissioned in order to expand the range of questions concerning the behaviour of states that the social sciences habitually address. The most obvious classic question needing re-assessment is that of the pristine origins of states. This is a topic that has inevitably never ceased to be at the centre of attention of anthropologists and archaeologists. Interestingly, these disciplines have tended to move away from an emphasis on military origins to a reliance upon economic models of causation. But if this debate parallels that in social science generally, views of the origins of the state currently being offered must seem strikingly novel to social scientists.

For it is not in fact the case that social science has *no* sense of the origins of the state; rather it is at the mercy, to adapt Keynes's famous maxim, of the theories of a previous age. In effect this means that Childe's linking of state formation with the neolithic revolution has retained power over our minds despite much doubt cast upon it.

Clive Gamble's chapter explains why this association is no longer taken seriously. Most importantly, he stresses that hunter-gatherers habitually know all about agriculture, but typically choose not to adopt it; this is perfectly rational given that, as Marshall Sahlins stresses so powerfully, their society is leisured and affluent.[22] Moreover, hunter-gatherer society is exceptionally complex; and if we are to believe James Woodburn, it is also highly varied, with a single 'mode of production' being as capable of supporting differing political 'super-structures' as are agrarian and industrial productive systems.[23] The general consequence of these arguments is that entirely novel questions about the origins of states arise, and Gamble is a very sure guide to this conceptual re-evaluation. Once the state is no longer seen as an inevitable and beneficial step, it becomes necessary to ask how social groupings of various sorts could have lost their autonomy in the face of this new source of power. Gamble's own tentative answer is that, in Mann's words, 'exploitation followed function'; once new techniques were pioneered, it became possible to use them to gain power.

Modern social science has paid much obeisance to Weberian injunctions to take the role of ideas in history seriously, but nearly all of this has been ritualistic in character. Very few attempts have been made by sociologists to improve upon Weberian arguments, as is now necessary, given criticism directed at the 'protestant ethic' thesis, decidedly necessary if his central tenet, that the ideas of the world religions mattered, is to be retained. Patricia Crone's account of the creation of Islamic doctrine and the consequent evolution of the Islamic polity is a dazzling exception to this generalization.[24] It represents the most powerful modern vindication of Weber's general position available, albeit Crone's general historical sociology is at present limited to Islam and, importantly, to the effect of Islam upon politics rather than upon attitudes towards work. Crone's general argument in this chapter is that the tribe is an evolutionary dead end, and this despite the ability of nomadic tribesmen occasionally to create vast – but transient – imperial structures. This is not to say that tribesmen have left no impact on the historical record. Tribal egalitarianism was incorporated into relatively immutable Islamic doctrine, and this has

---

22 M. Sahlins, *Stone Age Economics*, London, Tavistock, 1974.

23 J. Woodburn, 'Hunters and gatherers today and the reconstruction of the past', in E. Gellner, ed., *Soviet and Western Anthropology*, London, Duckworth, 1980.

24 P. Crone and M. Cook, *Hagarism*, Cambridge, Cambridge University Press, 1977; P. Crone, *Slaves on Horses*, Cambridge, Cambridge University Press, 1980; P. Crone and M. Hinds, *God's Caliph*, Cambridge, Cambridge University Press, 1986; P. Crone, *Meccan Trade and the Rise of Islam*, forthcoming, Princeton, Princeton University Press; P. Crone, *Roman, Provincial and Islamic Law*, forthcoming.

provided a powerful ideological legacy for contemporary world politics.[25] But there is another characteristic of Crone's argument that deserves highlighting, and this is apparent in the account she offers of the origins of the state in Ancient Sumer. Most modern writers are 'tone deaf' to the psychic power of religion, but Crone has a fully Kierkegaardian appreciation of the 'fear and trembling' involved in religious belief. Acceptance of religion represented an extraordinary change in human perceptions, and Crone suggests that it was made possible by the fact that obedience was given to a divine rather than to a human order. This is a rich and striking interpretation which casts new light on the Durkheimian question of the relation of religion to social cohesion, and it is one full of incidental pleasures such as the appreciation of the role of fishermen rather than of peasants in the transition to the state.

Where the pristine emergence of states is difficult to explain, the secondary emergence of states is a relatively straightforward matter to understand: peoples without states were forced to adopt them, given the superior organizational capacities of states. But this statement should not be interpreted naïvely, so as to allow any simple contrast between a pre-state and a post-state era. More is involved here than simply wishing to stress that the state changes enormously with the industrial revolution. It is important, rather to remember that the state does not monopolize social organization once it is born. This will be made clear for the modern world when emphasis is later placed on the fact that nation-states in the West operate within the larger society of international capitalism. My own chapter describes variations in state forms in the agrarian age, but the warning point in question can be made here in a rather different way. In classical Hindu civilization, most social processes were organized by Brahmans rather than by states, and the latter were consequently – at least to Western eyes – curiously 'free-floating'.[26] More generally, kinship in the agrarian era usually limited the power of the state by fulfilling basic organizational functions, monopoly of which would have increased the power of the state. Only in Latin Christendom, perhaps as the result of the greed and power of the church, was kinship so debilitated as to make for relatively anomic individuals who were excellent fodder for state-building.[27]

25 See E. Gellner, *Muslim Society*, Cambridge, Cambridge University Press, 1981, for an interpretation of why Islam is suited to modern conditions.

26 J. A. Hall, *Powers and Liberties*, Oxford, Blackwell, 1985, chapter 3.

27 J. Goody, *The Development of the Family and Marriage in Europe*, Cambridge, Cambridge University Press, 1983. Some comments on this thesis are offered in Hall, *Powers and Liberties*, chapter 5.

Conceptual distinctions

Discussion of concepts by social scientists has a bad name, and deservedly so since it is often abstract and meretricious. Recent theories of the state have occasionally been of this type, as in the huge, highly complex literature on the 'capitalist state' – literature which simply takes for granted, as noted, that classes, unlike states, have a firm ontological grounding. Nevertheless, genuine conceptual advances have been made, and three of these deserve to be distinguished and highlighted.

The impact of the form of the state. One important reason for studying states is that other social organizations often mould themselves in the image of the state that confronts them. In other words, social processes may well not be autonomous, and this must increase the scepticism shown to society-centred types of social science.

A clear example of the impact of state forms is, as noted, the different ways, principally either industrial or political, in which working classes felt it appropriate to organize themselves in different European states during the nineteenth and twentieth centuries. Colin Crouch's chapter goes well beyond this simple point in analysing the way in which three separate variables serve as historical preconditions to modern corporatism. This chapter is remarkable in advancing well beyond assertions that we need historical understanding to the provision of such understanding – and for the complex variety of all of Europe at that! Other examples of this impact are readily avilable, and one at least may be mentioned. The form of the state in the USA is largely responsible for the absence of corporatism:

such basic (interrelated) features of the U.S. state structure as federalism, the importance of geographic units of representation, nonprogrammatic political parties, fragmented realms of administrative bureaucracy, and the importance of Congress and its specialised committees within the national government's system of divided sovereignty all encourage a proliferation of competing, narrowly specialised, and weakly disciplined interest groups. In short, little about the structure and operations of the American state renders corporatism politically feasible or credible, either for officials or for social groups. Even protest movements in the United States tend to follow issue-specialised and geographically fissiparous patterns. State structures, established interest groups and oppositional groups all may well mirror one another's forms of organisation and scopes of purpose.[28]

28 T. Skocpol, 'Bringing the state back in', in P. Evans, D. Rueschemeyer and T. Skocpol, eds, *Bringing the State Back In*, Cambridge, Cambridge University Press, 1985, pp. 23–4.

Capacity, autonomy and co-operation. Most attention in recent state theory has been directed towards the relations between state and society, that is, to questions about the capacity of states to affect society and the capacity of society to limit the steering room of the state itself. Advances have been made here, but we need to add to them a word about co-operation.

Our understanding of state capacity is much extended by Michael Mann's simple, elegant and profound distinction between the despotic and infrastructural dimensions of state power. This distinction allows us to go some way beyond previous discussions of states in history. One place where this is so is that of our conception of Absolutism. It has long been standard to compare the 'strength' of Absolutist France with the 'weakness' of the British state, but Mann's distinction immediately allows us to see why this is quite wrong. The British state had greater infrastructural powers, being capable above all of extracting really considerable sums in taxation. It seems as if it is infrastructural capacity which really counts since the British state proved itself superior to the French on every occasion bar one in which they came into conflict in the period from Louis XIV to Napoleon. Mann's distinction is at the heart of Merquior's chapter; my own chapter seeks to add some dynamics to the statics of Mann's distinction.

State autonomy cannot be taken for granted; it must first be created and then, since it can be lost, maintained. Mancur Olson has suggested that state autonomy is strongest at the foundation of a nation and that it is compromised thereafter as other social groups organize; and he argues that *The Rise and Decline of Nations* can be explained in terms of this variable – to which he adds interesting, but rather unconvincing, arguments as to how state autonomy can be maintained.[29] Two particular sources of state autonomy are noted by the contributors to the present volume. On the one hand, external challenges, both economic and military, create crises which give state elites at least the chance to gain autonomy from social groups in order to rationalize their society. These challenges were particularly apparent in European history, and they are obviously vital forces of contemporary social reality. On the other hand, state autonomy can be created when key elites have a particularly strong *esprit de corps*. Merquior's analysis of the Brazilian development emphasizes the importance of this sort of background in the Brazilian case, and it is very likely that its presence in South-East Asia in the form of Confucianism explains why states in that area are so successful at promoting economic growth. But if these distinctions are important, they are also obvious and a part of current debate. Mann's chapter goes

29 M. Olson, *The Rise and Decline of Nations*, New Haven, Yale University Press, 1982.

beyond current debate in an important and sustained argument which specifies the origins, mechanisms and results of state autonomy.

It is always tempting to speak of the power of the state in a negative, almost zero-sum manner, and this underlies the notion of the state having autonomy insofar as it can escape social bindings. In a similar vein, Mann speaks of the state's infrastructural power as a capacity to penetrate society. But power has an enabling and cooperative face quite as much as a coercive one, and we should therefore be wary of these formulations. The infrastructural power of the state in part resulted from the provision of services for society. It is impossible to resist the conclusion that the high level of such services in European as compared to Islamic or Chinese history resulted from different power sources pointing in the same direction and co-operating in common endeavours. This point is made in my own chapter.

States in societies. When we think of 'society' we tend, following the classical sociologists, to think of a bounded geographical area ruled over by a state monopolizing violence and within which a set of norms is shared. Such a definition reflects the moment in European history when nation states had perhaps their greatest autonomy, but it is a poor guide even for the period 1870–1914 – and a useless one if we wish to understand the historical record.[30] One great weakness of the definition in question is that 'norms' are not often shared by all social actors, and this is particularly true of the situation 'of pre-industrial imperial rule. But the point to be stressed here is that states themselves often exist in larger societies. This was not true of some ancient empires, most notably those of China and Egypt, which felt they *were* the world, but that it has been true elsewhere is a fact of exceptional importance. The larger societies in question are those of military and economic competition. The former of these was obviously present in late nineteenth- and early twentieth-century Europe, and it has been extended to the globe today – with the important proviso that the rules of this conflict have, in certain delimited senses, changed for the two Superpowers as the result of their possession of nuclear weapons. If the state system was larger than any single nation-state at the turn of this century, so too was capitalist society. Perhaps this was not fully appreciated since development of internal markets and trading with colonies obscured the growth of an international division of labour. Since 1945 that internationalization has gone on apace, and its consequences most certainly affect develop-

---

30 For developments of this argument, see M. Mann, *The Sources of Social Power. Volume One: From the Beginning to 1760 AD*, Cambridge, Cambridge University Press, 1986, and J. A. Hall, 'Theory', in M. Haralambos, ed., *Developments in Sociology*, vol. 2, Ormskirk, Causeway Press, 1986.

mental patterns inside socialist societies despite their desire to withdraw from the world market.

Very few attempts have yet been made to think systematically about the relationships of states to their larger societies, but three avenues of research seem apparent. First, we need to know much more about how larger frames of references come to be established initially, as well as to consider systematically how they are maintained in the longer run. Islam, Neo-Brahmanism and Christianity followed Greek culture in creating networks of interaction larger than any single state; in the modern world, in contrast, the creation of the network of the international market seems to depend, *pace* economists, upon the ability of a leading power to impose itself militarily, as was the case with Britain in the eighteenth century and the United States after 1945. Second, it is noticeable that competition between states inside a larger cultural frame seems to produce, not least in the eyes of several contributors to this book, a particularly dynamic and potent mixture. The clearest single statement of this position in this book is provided by Peter Burke. Burke argues that there is much to recommend the more 'materialist' part of Max Weber's thesis concerning the rise of the West, that is, that part which bases itself upon an appreciation of the autonomy of the European city. This autonomy allowed for social experiments, in economics and in methods of political organization, which had a fundamental impact on the European scene. As this was so, it becomes vital to ask about how this autonomy was achieved. Burke follows Burckhardt in saying that it was the result of a larger system of competing centres of power; that larger system was not so homogenous as to rule out key experiments in interstitial city-states. Finally, we need to complement our understanding of the interrelationships between class and state with a sustained analysis of ways in which the larger shells of international capitalism and international military competition are at once in conflict and in co-operation. The limitations of our current understanding of this area can be demonstrated by a single example. Is it the case that capitalist society is larger than the United States of America? If it is, then one would expect the ending of the American geopolitical role since this can no longer be afforded by a net debtor nation. But American military power may prove sufficient, especially now that it is increasing, to allow it systematically to extract from its clients a military tax – just as did the Roman empire 2,000 years ago. Furthermore, Susan Strange argues in her chapter that American-owned multinationals, whose operation in some ways has harmed the American domestic economy, still probably contribute to the structural strength of the American state, presumably by standing at the forefront of new technologies – which is to say that balance of payments difficulties at any particular moment may not be of vital long-term importance.

Historical patterns and social evolution

All that has been said to this point amounts to a plea for states to be understood in their historical contexts. One of the main tasks that confronts us is, to put the point in a different way, that of understanding the rich and varied mixture of states apparent in human history, and both Crouch and Merquior offer fine demonstrations of the sets of factors that can account for historical variations. Nevertheless, it is possible – and necessary – to go somewhat further than this in an analytic sense, and something can be said about historical patterns and social evolution.

In the course of recorded history, some states which proved themselves 'fitter' than others, have in consequence imposed themselves and have thereby changed the terms under which all states, and particularly new ones, must function. The most obvious case in which this is true is that of the rise of the West. The European system was peculiarly dynamic: power was not held in any single set of hands, and competition, both economic and military, prevented the acceptance of any form of stasis. Although European development combined commerce *and* liberty, European self-congratulation should be strictly limited. Most obviously, Europeans did·not use their power abroad with any respect for liberty. Even more importantly, we cannot help but have doubts about the European legacy given that we now have the advantage of a measure of historical detachment. For the state system created by Europe led to the two world wars and thereby to the destruction of Europe's place in the world. Institutions which were able to create a particular dynamism could not control the forces that they unleashed. Yet these moral questionings are in a sense irrelevant: what matters is that the expansion of Europe destroyed other types of states, and turned the world into a state system in which the old European adage 'adapt or go under' has held sway ever since.

It would, however, be a great mistake to presume that the triumph of the West has resulted in some slavish imitation of the European state, as is made clear in my own chapter. Authoritarianism, whether of left or right, seems to have an 'elective affinity' with forced development, and the commerce plus liberty equation has thereby lost any pretensions to universal validity. We have been prone to forget that capitalism went hand in hand with authority in Imperial Germany and Japan simply because these states were defeated in war; but this was not by any means inevitable, and this combination is very much in evidence in the Third World today. The fact that 'actually existing socialism' has been created as the result of geopolitical pressure and in the wake of military success is much more familiar, albeit the savage irony of society-centred

Marxism inhabiting a supremely statist world – something which is at the heart of Dawisha's chapter – is probably not fully appreciated. Nevertheless, there is imitation of the European system at a deeper level. Historical European states deserve to be considered strong states in being long-lasting and in having the capacity to draw upon considerable levels of social participation. States in the Third World which are successful have developed a similar type of strength, and others need to if they are to survive in a world in which Clausewitzian injunctions retain their force and in which the pressures of economic competition have been greatly intensified. Balance of power politics have always allowed a measure of autonomy for developing states, and the presence of the nuclear umbrellas may allow sufficient room for at least some states to develop such strength since they place a premium upon limiting superpower interference, except in acknowledged areas of geopolitical hegemony.[31]

Anthony Smith's chapter certainly recognizes the importance of a strong state for survival in the modern world, but there is a tinge of pessimism to his views well worth highlighting. Nation-building was once, he argues, believed to be easy and automatic. However, recent history has shown that 'new nations' do not find nation building easy, and Smith explains this in terms of the absence in certain cases of a strong and central ethnic legacy; such a legacy is necessary if nation-building is to be successful. Smith's pessimism largely arises, I suspect, from confronting modern Africa, and it contrasts markedly with Merquior's optimistic analysis of two Latin American states. Both Argentina and Brazil completed their nation-building long ago and both have histories of parliamentary traditions. Merquior's hope is nothing less than that commerce *and* liberty may eventually rule in these countries. One general reflection follows from these two cases. Although there is no doubt that the triumph of the West ruled out of court certain types of state, and imposed upon all the necessity for the creation of strong states, obedience to the functional requirements of the modern world may yet allow very considerable diversity in the world of states. What is needed here, of course, is the development of proper classificatory systems for states in the Third World. Any such classification would have to pay attention to the importance of historical legacies (in Japan, in Islam, and in South-East Asian 'Confucian capitalism'), of successful nation-building, of parliamentary traditions, of geopolitical situation and, of course, of whether industrialization is attempted under the aegis of socialism or inside capitalist society – and this list is certainly not

31 D. Smith, 'Domination and containment', *Comparative Studies in Society and History*, vol. 19, 1977.

complete. We need to investigate, for example, whether the differences between developing states in the capitalist arena is so great as to rule out any similarity of historical development. Is liberalization possible in Brazil and Argentina because of generic features of capitalist development or merely because of the presence of a parliamentary tradition?[32] In other words, is it or is it not likely that Taiwan and South Korea will retain in the longer term their remarkably successful combination of capitalism with authoritarianism?

There is a great deal of sense in talking of historical patterning given that some states have triumphed over others, and have thereby imposed their social patterns. Some such triumphs have most certainly not been the result of any inevitability – there was nothing predetermined about the destruction of Europe's place in world history nor of the form that this destruction took – and the historical patterning mentioned therefore refers very much to the sense of history as accident. Nevertheless, it is noticeable that several of the contributors to this book offer comments of a more systematic nature about social evolution. I think general agreement would be given to the banal but important assertion that once the state had been invented its powers of organization meant that state organization would eventually become necessary throughout the globe. In addition, Gellner and Strange make striking comments about social evolution. But what deserves emphasis here are the two more systematic viewpoints on social evolution put foward in this book. The first of these is that of Mann, who suggests that social evolution occurs by means of a dialectic between multi-power actor civilizations and more centralized and coercive ones. As it happens my own chapter ends with a measure of disagreement from this position, but there is no doubt at all of the importance of Mann's argument. Most theories of social evolution have been rendered virtually meaningless by their failure to specify mechanisms accounting for movement from one stage to another. Marx's conceptualization of class struggle was such a mechanism, but it was one which did not in fact cause social evolution as Marx had hoped. Mann's argument is very important, and one can only hope that it will become the focus of a major debate. Second, it is worth highlighting again Crone's argument about the importance of religion in making the breakthrough to organized social life. Here we have a very different and highly original view of social evolution, albeit one which has not as yet been fully spelled out. An implication of this view is that the key step in social evolution may well prove to be the invention of organized religion, with much that followed it later being of lesser significance.

32 We are now exceptionally well placed to understand the combination of late industrialization with early parliamentarianism: see N. Mouzelis, *Politics in the Semi-Periphery*, London, Macmillan, 1986.

Both these authors appreciate the historical patterning of events, and would not, I think, wish to be seen as evolutionary theorists in any straightforward sense. Indeed, there are good reasons for believing that limitations necessarily bound any theory of social evolution. One reason for this is that the time-scale involved in the recorded history of humanity is insufficient to allow much in the way of evolutionary generalization. More importantly, there are not enough cases at crucial points to produce any elaborate general theory. There were but a handful of world religions, for example, and each differs from the others in so many ways that it is not possible to produce any tight general theory, even if it is our duty to try and generalize as systematically as we can. The same holds true for the emergence of the capitalist dynamic of the West as a whole; this happened once, and every other development is necessarily imitative. The exact form that any theory of social evolution will take in the future depends upon the way in which these considerations are handled. But that it is possible to talk again of such a theory demonstrates much about the rediscovery of nerve on the part of the social sciences – a rediscovery much helped by the interest in states in history.

1

Hunter-Gatherers and the Origin of States

Clive Gamble

Introduction

Most questions about the origins of the state could be answered very simply: discover the origins of *Homo sapiens sapiens*. Once such anatomically modern people have arrived there is no need to invoke mental stature as the brake producing the slow, incremental developments in hominid and human societies over the preceding four million years. From that moment the state is a distinct possibility. Since such people appear in the fossil record at least 40,000 years ago the state is therefore a very long-run phenomenon indeed.[1]

Such a view runs counter to most archaeological accounts where attention is usually focused on the last 5,000 to 10,000 years as the appropriate period for the discussion of state origins and formation. Certainly the archaeology of this period sees some impressive achievements in items of durable material culture, and pyramids *are* difficult to ignore. But being led by the archaeological nose can bias any study of long-run processes even though this smaller, but still immense, time-span may seem sufficient for the exploration of how and why states came into being. For too long, however, we have stubbed our toes on big piles of masonry and called them names, such as states or civilizations, instead of investigating the processes by which such piles were created. Unfortunately the names, and the social typologies they serve, will be with us still for many years, and no doubt even longer in the works of

This paper benefited from the comments of John A. Hall, Paul Rodgers, Stephen Shennan and James Steele. A Visiting Fellowship from the Australian Studies Centre made it possible to consider the Australian evidence at first hand while conversations about the role of negotiators with Harry Lourandos helped shape the argument.

1 The origins of *Homo sapiens sapiens* are still unclear but advanced skulls at Omo in East Africa probably represent the earliest at c.100,000. Europe was colonized c.40,000–35,000 years ago when modern humans replaced Neanderthals. *Homo sapiens sapiens* colonized Australia at least 40,000 years ago.

consumer historians writing for a wider audience.[2] This audience should be aware, however, that while studies into the origins of prehistoric states have demonstrated an enormous variety of cultures and developmental trajectories their eventual convergence has been remarkably similar and limited.[3]

My starting point in this paper will be the hunter-gatherer. These societies are usually omitted from questions of state origins on the grounds of their economies and organizational simplicity. Yet they were the base from which so-called complex social behaviour sprang and which many believe forms the only relevant gestation period for the state. I will argue their case for inclusion in the process by examining the neolithic revolution. From there I shall consider what sets the state apart and the frameworks which are needed to investigate the various forms of control associated with its expansion and consolidation as an enduring idea if not an everlasting entity. In this context the loss of autonomy at many social and political scales, rather than the development of complexity, is seen as the central issue when we start asking how and why state formation took place.

Evolutionary Perspectives

The state as a yardstick for development

For many years the concept, and material reality, of the state provided a safe haven for archaeological procedure and interpretation. At one level of enquiry there was the very practical point that, prior to radiocarbon dating, absolute chronologies were provided by such evidence as kinglists and other early systems of literacy associated with ancient civilizations. While limited, these helped to turn the chronological key on

2 J. M. Roberts, *The Pelican History of the World*, Books 1 and 2, Harmondsworth, Pelican Books, 1980.
3 In a comparative study of state formation in Mexico and Mesopotamia (*The Evolution of Urban Society*, Chicago, Aldine, 1966) R. McAdams concluded that: 'What seems overwhelmingly most important about these differences is how small they bulk, even in aggregate, when considered against the mass of similarities in form and process. In short, the parallels in the Mesopotamian and Mexican "careers to statehood", in the forms that institutions ultimately assumed as well as in the processes leading to them, suggest that both instances are most significantly characterized by a common core of regularly occurring features' (pp. 174–5). Reviews of comparative studies can be found in J. F. Cherry, 'Generalization and the archaeology of the state', in D. Green, C. Haselgrove and M. Spriggs, eds, *Social Organisation and Settlement*, Oxford, British Archaeological Reports, 47, 1978, and N. Yoffee, 'The decline and rise of Mesopotamian civilization: an ethnoarchaeological perspective on the evolution of social complexity', *American Antiquity*, vol. 44, 1979.

immediate prehistoric neighbours and then, by careful scrutiny, on distant associates.

Moreover, following in the tradition of Morgan and Tylor the state represented the culmination of the evolutionary stage of barbarism.[4] According to this classic typology of social evolution savagery was succeeded by barbarism which led, in a small number of areas, to civilization, which then returned these hard-won achievements to societies still at the level of savagery and barbarism. The state, as an instance of civilization, formed a goal towards which regional and national prehistories could aspire.[5] This was either achieved by internal development or as a result of external buffeting and diffusion.

These evolutionary schemes were given archaeological support in the syntheses of prehistoric Europe by Childe.[6] In his view the state was a by-product of the urban revolution,[7] when a creative and innovative burst was held to have radically altered many aspects of social and material life. The check list devised by Childe could then be used to assess the position of a prehistoric culture on the staircase to statehood. The scale and accessibility of Childe's writings, where the investigation of prehistoric sociology was successfully married with the difficult business of prehistoric methodology, places him above his contemporaries. They were generally either so overawed by the mute nature of prehistoric data that they stuck solidly to description, or else too eager to read into the archaeological record the picture of the past they wished to see.[8]

4 L. H. Morgan, *Ancient Society*, New York, World Publishing 1877; E. Tylor, *Anthropology*, London, Macmillan, 1881.

5 The development of the modern Danish state, for example, employed prehistoric objects to symbolize national identity: see K. Kristiansen, 'A social history of Danish archaeology', in G. Daniel, ed., *Towards a History of Archaeology*, London, Thames & Hudson, 1981.

6 V. G. Childe, *The Dawn of European Civilisation*, London, Routledge & Kegan Paul, 1925; *Social Evolution*, London, Watts, 1951; *The Prehistory of European Society*, Harmondsworth, Penguin, 1958.

7 V. G. Childe, 'The urban revolution', *Town Planning Review*, vol. 21 1950.

8 An example of applying this sort of check list is provided by the changed understanding of Mycenaean Greece. The decipherment of linear B in 1952 suddenly elevated this culture from prehistory into at least proto-history if not quite history. Childe had used it in *Social Evolution* in 1951 as an example of advanced barbarism. When editing a reprint of this work in 1963, Wheeler removed Childe's discussion of this example of 'ripe' barbarism and stuck it in an appendix. He felt that this kept faith with Childe's definitions of the evolutionary stages, which it did, and expressed the view that Childe would probably have altered his definition of civilization to incorporate this unexpected development. Throughout his many writings Childe employed a flexible approach to sociological definitions as archaeological evidence suggested improvements and contradictions (see B. McNairn, *The Method and Theory of V. Gordon Childe*, Edinburgh, Edinburgh University Press, 1980). His central analytical concept, however, remained unchanged. This was the linkage of an archaeological culture, defined by constantly

The check list of traits for Childe's urban revolution[9]

1   *Size*: an increase in settlement size towards urban proportions
2   *Surplus*: the centralized accumulation of capital resulting from the imposition of tribute or taxation
3   *Monumental public works*
4   The invention of *writing*
5   Elaboration of exact and predictive *sciences*
6   The appearance and growth of long-distance *trade* in luxuries
7   The emergence of a *class-stratified society* based on the unequal distribution of social surplus
8   *Composition and function of an urban centre*, freeing part of the population from subsistence tasks for full-time craft specialization
9   *State organization* based on residence rather than on kinship. Territorial definitions employed
10   The appearance of *naturalistic art*

So far I have considered the state from the prehistorian's perspective as something to look forward to. From the position of the economic historian casting a glance backwards the state marks the moment when sensible history commenced. For anyone interested in accounting for the European 'miracle' of industrial and social change the first states form a convenient tap-root; sufficiently distant to start the developmental story yet sufficiently familiar in form to require only cursory treatment before turning to a detailed review of the critical historical periods. Hence the period 1400–1800 AD will always be of paramount importance for understanding the origins of the modern world, even though there are some world views that would like to incorporate a greater time depth into the performance of the miracle[10] – to hear some faint echo from barbarism in the industrial clamour.

Neolithic origins

These consumers of reconstructions of the past have little interest, quite understandably, in the complications of archaeological methods and

recurring items in time and space, with a people and a society. Thus the Mycenaeans would always be the Mycenaeans whether they were also a chiefdom, state, urban polity of just heroic barbarians.

9 Childe, 'The urban revolution'; B. McNairn, *The Method and Theory of V. Gordon Childe*; Adams, *The Evolution of Urban Society.*

10 E. L. Jones, *The European Miracle*, Cambridge, Cambridge University Press, 1981, p. 255.

procedures. While they may be vociferously concerned with rival explanations of change in societies in the last 500 years, they will probably accept without question the established view about the origins of these prehistoric states. Here prehistorians have focused on changes in food production, termed by Childe the neolithic revolution.[11] The shift from food procurement to food production, and the sociological inferences based on such a change, has proved to be both a powerful and enduring model. The dramatic nature of this model allowed for little or no continuity between the hunters of savagery and their farming successors – a conclusion based on finding sheep bones and wheat grains as well as houses, pottery and other innovations in material culture, and leading to inferences of sedentism with population growth and the conditions for the emergence of more complex societies. On this evidence the neolithic revolution transformed the world, it made everything possible and was regarded as a great step up on the staircase of progress. The terminology was deliberate since it signified to Childe a transformation as great as that of the industrial revolution where society severed the links with its traditional past.

Consequently it has always been accepted that the domestication of plants and animals was of central importance in the transformation of society to eventual statehood. What had previously been the slow pace of millennia with only minimal change in material culture and basically none in society was now gone. The domestication of the sheep, the cultivation of rice, the planting of maize apparently took the cork out of the evolutionary bottle and unleashed the forces of innovation, rapid change, and directional movement toward greater social complexity: 'the escape from the impasse of savagery was an economic and scientific revolution that made the participants active partners with nature instead of parasites on nature'.[12] As a result societies in the New and Old Worlds expanded like well-blown balloons, driving the last remnants of savagery to the peripheries, where somehow they survived until the present day. One outcome of the model of a neolithic revolution, that serves as both a description and explanation of change, has been to separate the hunters and gatherers of preceding savagery from their ultimately more complex farming successors.

While it is common to oppose the simplicity of hunter-gatherer band societies with the complexity of *all* other types of society, it is also recognized that complex prehistoric societies were extremely varied. A division is often drawn between those judged as pre-state in complexity

11 V. G. Childe, 'Changing methods and aims in prehistory', *Proceedings of the Prehistoric Society*. vol. 1, 1935.
12 V. G. Childe, *What Happened in History*, Harmondsworth, Penguin Books, 1942, p. 55.

and those which, with confidence, can be called states or early states.[13] A great deal of attention has been paid to the problem of classifying these later prehistoric cultures in the surge toward statehood. For example, the introduction of bronze metallurgy provides a marker to distinguish between levels of complexity in Old World cultures but has no global significance in either understanding or identifying the appearance of more complex societies, let alone states.[14] Similarly, changes leading to forms of agricultural intensification are equally erratic when viewed on a world scale.[15] The role and importance of trade in such classifications fares no better, as studies of the extensive networks along the coasts of Papua New Guinea and neighbouring islands have shown.[16]

These millennia of barbarism, more than any other, have seen the application of the social typologies based on the evolutionist theories of White and Steward,[17] and culminating in the work of Service, Sahlins and Fried.[18] They fashioned the evolutionary ladder of band, tribe, chief and state from the organizing principles of ranking and stratification. Following this lead measures have been devised to identify these social types in the past. These include the analysis of cemeteries and mortuary data, examining exchange distributions and estimating the energy investment in buildings and fortifications.[19]

From the perspective of state origins and formations much interest

13 H. J. Claessen and P. Skalník, eds, *The Early State*, The Hague, Paris and New York, Mouton, 1978.

14 Apart from objects made from copper and gold, the more complex metallurgies of bronze and iron are entirely lacking in the New World.

15 The lack of traction animals in Mesoamerica did not hold back the development of civilization and the turkey had to suffice as a source of protein in the absence of such important Old World domesticates as sheep, pigs and cattle.

16 J. Allen, 'Pots and poor princes: a multidimensional approach to the role of pottery trading in coastal Papua', in S. E. van der Leuuw and A. Pritchard, eds, *The Many Dimensions of Pottery*, Amsterdam, Instituut voor Prae- en Protohistorie, 1984; G. Irwin, 'The development of Mailu as a specialized trading and manufacturing centre in Papuan prehistory: the causes and the implications', *Mankind*, vol. 11, 1978.

17 L. White, *The Evolution of Culture*, New York, McGraw Hill, 1959; J. H. Steward, *Theory of Culture Change*, Urbana, University of Illinois Press, 1955.

18 E. R. Service, *Primitive Social Organization: an Evolutionary Perspective*, New York, Random House, 1962; idem, *Origins of the State and Civilization: the Process of Cultural Evolution*, New York, W. W. Norton, 1975; M. Sahlins and E. R. Service, eds, *Evolution and Culture*, Ann Arbor, University of Michigan Press, 1960; M. Fried, *The Evolution of Political Society*, New York, Random House, 1967.

19 C. Renfrew and S. J. Shennan, eds, *Ranking, Resource and Exchange*, Cambridge, Cambridge University Press 1982; J. A. Brown, ed., *Approaches to the Social Dimensions of Mortuary Practices*, SAA Memoir 25, 1971; T. Earle and J. E. Ericson, *Exchange Systems in Prehistory*, New York, Academic Press, 1977; J. A. Sabloff and C. C. Lamberg-Karlovsky, *Ancient Civilisation and Trade*; Albuquerque, University of New Mexico Press, 1975.

has focused on investigating chiefdoms.[20] In particular a methodology has been developed to examine the material correlates of such ranked societies in the archaeological record. At one time it seemed that we might even dig up a chiefdom rather than excavate the Mycenaeans.[21]

Such enthusiasm has, it is to be hoped, now passed. One danger lay in turning the past into nothing more than a pursuit of definitions. In Martin Wobst's phrase, there was a danger of committing ethnography with a shovel;[22] of merely reproducing the present in the past under the tyranny of the ethnographic record and answering questions with definitions, as at the very beginning of this paper. With such limited pursuits there could be little hope for starting to understand why developments in complex behaviour were so varied.

Complex Hunters and Simple Farmers

In this context the use of the term complexity becomes important. It is now common to discuss the concept in terms that can be measured rather than listed on a presence/absence basis. Its investigation is well suited to approaches which model societies as systems where their structural differences are dependent upon the organization and flow of information as the diverse and disparate units, or sub-systems, are integrated. Hence for Flannery complexity is measured via segregation (differentiation) and centralization (the degree of connectedness) in the system.[23]

MacGuire has examined the components of complexity not as a single concept but as variables in cultural evolution.[24] As he points out, the

20 Service, *Origins of the State*, p. 304; R. L. Carneiro, 'The chiefdom: precursor of the state', in G. D. Jones and R. R. Kautz, eds, *The Transition to Statehood in the New World*, Cambridge, Cambridge University Press, 1981.

21 C. Renfrew, 'Monuments, mobilisation and social organisation in neolithic Wessex', in Renfrew, (ed.), *Explanation of Culture Change*, London, Duckworth, 1973; C. Peebles and S. Kus, 'Some archaeological correlates of ranked societies', *American Antiquity* vol. 42, 1977. A recent example of this approach – B. Hayden and A. Cannon, 'The corporate group as an archaeological unit', *Journal of Anthropological Archaeology*, vol. 1, 1982 – has set down the material correlates for recognizing a corporate group in the archaeological record and where little procedural advance seems to have been made from Childe's check list for recognizing the state/civilization.

22 H. M. Wobst, 'The archaeo-ethnology of hunter-gatherers or the tyranny of the ethnographic record in archaeology', *American Antiquity*, vol. 43, 1970.

23 K. V. Flannery, 'The cultural evolution of civilisations', *Annual Review of Ecology and Systematics*, vol. 3, 1972, pp. 409–11, provides a model of state formation where the main measurable trends lies in the increasing capacity for the processing, storage and analysis of information.

24 R. MacGuire, 'Breaking down cultural complexity: inequality and heterogeneity', in M. B. Schiffer, ed., *Advances in Archaeological Method and Theory*, vol. 6, 1983.

concept of complexity includes too much which makes it a lumpen catch-all that explains everything but signifies nothing. His solution is to stress the vertical and horizontal axes in social structure. In this way measures of complexity involve inequality in terms of access to resources and heterogeneity, which refers to the number of social persona in the system.[25] Most importantly, we should not expect these two variables to correlate positively but instead should consider them independently in the process of social change.

It is also important to recognize that on a prehistoric time-scale developments in complexity do not imply the 'success' of a system in either adapting to its environment or maintaining its existing position. A feature of such increasingly complex systems was their repeated collapse.[26] However, while transience was their most notable characteristic their commitment to complexity was permanent.

With such general definitions of complexity, rather than a Childean check list, we need to reconsider whether the so-called simple societies of the hunter and gatherer might have possessed similar organizational principles. If this can indeed be demonstrated then quantum leaps in complexity, such as the invention of agriculture, might not necessarily form such a clear marker for distinguishing between prehistoric societies. In turn this would change the background to the study of state origins.

Unchanging affluence

Hunting and gathering groups have enjoyed a great deal of attention in the last 20 years. The important symposium *Man the Hunter*[27] established a global comparative approach to this socio-economic type that has been investigated in a number of other symposia.[28] In particular, hunters

25 Heterogeneity is assessed in terms of two parameters; nominal (vertical) and graduated (horizontal). In the former, categories are based on divisions such as religion/sex/kin/occupation and are bounded. In the latter, categories are defined by age/power/wealth which are both continuous and rank-ordered. The measure establishes how many individuals have comparable access to resources. The categories in the nominal parameter only become ranked when correlated with the parameter of relative inequality; e.g. all lineages hold land (heterogeneity, nominal parameter) but some hold more than others (inequality, relative parameter) (MacGuire, 'Breaking down cultural complexity', pp. 101–5; P. Blau. *Inequality and Heterogeneity: A Primitive Theory of Social Structure*, New York, Free Press, 1977.

26 T. C. Champion, C. S. Gamble, S. J.Shennan and A. Whittle, *Prehistoric Europe*, London, Academic Press, 1984; S. E. van der Leeuw, ed., *Archaeological Approaches to the Study of Complexity*, Amsterdam, V. I. Cingvla, 1982; J. Friedman and M. J. Rowlands, eds, *The Evolution of Social Systems*, London, Duckworth, 1977.

27 R. B. Lee and I. DeVore, eds, *Man the Hunter*, Chicago, Aldine, 1968.

28 D. Damas, ed., 'Contributions to anthropology: band societies', *National Museum of Canada Bulletin*, vol. 228, 1969; M. Bicchieri, ed., *Hunters and Gatherers Today*, New York,

and gatherers were placed within an ecological framework and variation in aspects of social organization, technology and lifestyles were attributed to the distribution of food resources. This data formed the basis for Lee and DeVore's nomadic style model – the hunters who move around a lot and live in small groups and whose societies are characterized by cycles of fission and fusion.[29] From this model came the view of an unchanging structure for prehistoric hunters and gatherers where any differences could be related to the restless world of climatic change they inhabited.

The novelty of Man the Hunter was, however, to change the nature of their simplicity. Old-style notions of a shifting catch-as-catch-can existence practised by members of the Fourth World was replaced by one of choice and good sense. The discussions contain Sahlins's characterization of hunters and gatherers as the 'original affluent society' – typified by a short working week and few worries, thanks to a naturally well-stocked larder feeding a small population.[30] Following this lead, prehistoric hunters and gatherers were seen as economic savants making perfectly judged decisions, avoiding starvation and crisis with ease.[31] They were resource managers guided by the principle of least effort, the efficient conservation of calories in the pursuit of optimal behaviour.

Perhaps most importantly, the model completely redefined the problem of social, cultural and economic change which everybody knew took place after the end of the last ice age. Rather than escaping from the 'impasse of savagery', the question now became: Why should anyone want to change lots and become a hard-working farmer? Moreover, why follow suit and change to agriculture once it was locally available? Far from seeing the neolithic revolution, in all its diverse global forms, as the best thing before sliced bread, the judgement now had to be that the failures in prehistory were the farmers.[32]

Holt, Rinehart and Winston, 1972. Three important areas have since dominated discussion – the Kalahari, all of Australia and the Arctic. These societies have very different histories of contact with other societies; see   E. Leacock and R. B. Lee, eds, _Politics and History in Band Societies_, Cambridge, Cambridge Univeristy Press, 1982; N. Peterson and M. Langton, eds, _Aborigines, Land and Land Rights_, Canberra, Australian Institute of Aboriginal Studies, 1983; C. Schrire, ed., _Past and Present in Hunter-Gatherer Studies_, New York, Academic Press, 1984.

29 A view that derives from Mauss's brilliant essay on the private and public phases in the yearly cycle of the Eskimo, 'Essai sur les variations saisonnières des sociétés Eskimos: étude de morphologie sociale', _Année Sociologique_, vol. 9, 1904–5.

30 In Lee and DeVore, _Man the Hunter_, pp. 85–9. While this view did much to rehabilitate the general image of hunters and gatherers as surviving on a knife edge and being constantly buffeted by a capricious environment over which they had no control, it did of course go too far. It described the situation for some Kalahari and Arnhem Land groups rather than for all hunters and gatherers.

31 The palaeoeconomy school that was associated with Higgs adopted a definition of economy for use in prehistoric studies as management leading to equilibrium (E. S. Higgs, ed., _Palaeoeconomy_, Cambridge, Cambridge University Press, 1975, p. 4).

[_See opposite page for n. 32_]

This dismal conclusion surfaces in several of the processual explanations concerning the development of more complex behaviour. Where these are related to changes in subsistence, answers have often been sought in terms of external selection on adaptive systems. For example, Binford put forward a marginal zone hypothesis where population pressure on resources resulted from continuing in-migration of population numbers from environmentally more favourable donor areas. This was combined with a squeezing of available land and the resources they contained as sea levels rose and resource zones contracted in the warm-up after the last ice age.[33] Agriculture became a solution that could not be resisted solely on the grounds that it cost too much in terms of extra effort. Furthermore Cohen has argued that the nearly simultaneous appearance of food production in independent centres in the New and Old Worlds can be understood in terms of internal pressure of population on existing food resources, thus precipitating a global food crisis.[34]

Irrespective of the direction from which the selection pressure for change came, the novel scheduling of labour and time budgets in order to integrate diverse resources into a workable exploitation strategy, needed complex systems of organization.[35] Moreover, the superiority of these more complex systems is frequently judged by their unstoppable momentum when released into an 'unsuspecting' continent of simple hunters and gatherers.[36]

Complex prehistoric hunters

How do we go about establishing complexity among prehistoric hunters and gatherers? It would, for example, be very convenient if we could

32 L. R. Binford, *In Pursuit of the Past*, London, Thames & Hudson; 1983. P. Crone, chapter 2 in this volume.

33 L. R. Binford, 'Post-pleistocene adaptations', in S. R. and L. R. Binford, eds, *New Perspectives in Archaeology*, Chicago, Aldine, 1968. This and other models of agricultural origins are well summarized in C. Redman, *The Rise of Civilisation*, San Francisco, W. H. Freeman, 1978.

34 M. N. Cohen, *The Food Crisis in Prehistory*, New Haven, Yale University Press, 1977.

35 K. V. Flannery and M. D. Coe, 'Social and economic systems in formative Mesoamerica', in S. R. and L. R. Binford, *New Perspectives in Archaeology*, pp. 267–83. These processual models which often used an explicitly systemic framework largely replaced the 'event'-orientated accounts of previous workers; for instance, the idea that agriculture arose as a result of settling in to an area and getting to know its resources or that during drought potential domesticates shared the same waterhole as the human group and this suggested the move to husbandry.

36 The wave of advance model, proposed by A. Ammerman and L. L. Cavalli Sforza ('A population model for the diffusion of early farming in Europe', in Renfrew, *Explanation of Culture Change*) as a description of the agricultural colonization of Europe, is still one of the most sophisticated uses of absolute time-rates for studying change provided by radiocarbon dating.

determine relative levels by comparing the ecological complexity of the environments in which they were found.[37] However, the same environment might be exploited in very different ways by local groups of similar size during their annual cycle of production and reproduction. In this instance complexity depends upon the intensity of procurement of basic resources. This level is not fixed by the environment but by the demands of the social system on production.[38] These of course will be very varied and entirely contrary to the view of hunters and gatherers as unchanging.

Alternatively we could accept that an adequate measure of differing levels of complexity among hunters and gatherers is provided by the variables of inequality and heterogeneity discussed above. However, these need to be placed within an operational framework which is provided here by the concept of alliance systems. A network of alliances defines often very diverse social relationships and confirms the authority structures associated with roles and institutions. This is achieved by establishing and maintaining ties of variable commitment and duration through the circulation of people and the exchange of goods and information.[39] In this context an alliance is an achieved social status based to a considerable extent on negotiation.[40]

These alliance systems exist at many spatial and social scales. One way to conceive of them would be as a topological surface of creases, folds, tucks and tears produced by many different forces pulling and pushing the edges in all directions.[41] Thus the concept of alliance systems expects that if these surface conditions can be measured by the variables used above we can then talk of differences in complexity in both space and time. The utility of such a concept is illustrated by MacGuire's point that heterogeneity and inequality are not necessarily in step.[42] Consequently, developments in complexity should not be seen as simple stairways to statehood via a number of revolutionary risers; indeed, the question of change must be kept distinct from the question of variation when comparing either hunter-gatherer systems or these

37 For a full discussion see K. Butzer, *Archaeology as Human Ecology*, Cambridge, Cambridge University Press, 1982.

38 T. Ingold, 'The hunter and his spear: notes on the cultural mediation of social and ecological systems', in A. Sheridan and G. Bailey, eds, *Economic Archaeology*, British Archaeological Reports S96, 1981.

39 B. Bender, 'Gatherer-hunter to farmer: a social perspective', *World Archaeology*, vol. 10, 1978.

40 L. Guemple, 'Kinship and alliance in Belcher Island Eskimo society, in L. Guemple, ed., 'Alliance in Eskimo Society', *Proceedings of the American Ethnological Society 1971 Supplement*, Seattle, University of Washington Press, 1972, p. 56.

41 See C. H. Waddington, *Tools for Thought*, Frogmore, Granada, 1978, for illustrations of epigenetic landscapes.

42 MacGuire, 'Breaking down cultural complexity', p. 93.

with other social systems. Change refers to new premises determining strategies for coping with the constantly shifting conditions while variation deals with alternative solutions under existing premises.

Since alliance systems are regional, even continental, in scale,[43] any discussion of complexity needs to take account of the spatial dimension for the following reasons. In the first place, space provides the analytical framework for investigating organizational complexity among prehistoric hunters. Their patterns of movement form annual ranges for groups and individuals.[44] These spatial units will vary in extent due to the intensity of procurement as well as the structure of resources; they can be probed for information about settlement patterns, the composition of technology and inter-territory contacts as shown by transfers of raw material and finished artifacts. These would of course provide a basis for measuring inequality.

Secondly, in the investigation of local and regional archaeological sequences complexity emerges as part of a process of intensification whereby elements in the system are transformed as a result of coping with stress from both the physical and social environment. These elements can reasonably be expected to include changes in technology, settlement patterns and the organization of time and labour budgets in subsistence production. For example, complex hunters might be expected to show an increase in residential permanence as intricate scheduling of time and labour resources effectively reduces the spatial extent of the annual territory. This would lead to a greater packing of local groups into an area that under a less intensive strategy only supported a single group.[45] Explaining why such developments occured is dependent upon the transformation and reproduction of alliance networks under competitive principles.[46] It was through these networks that all polities ranging from hunters to states obtained the paraphernalia necessary for the process of social reproduction. It was the alliance system which formed the framework for change and transformation

---

43 N. Peterson ed., *Tribes and boundaries in Australia*, Canberra, Australian Institute of Aboriginal Studies, 1976.

44 T. D. Price and J. A. Brown, eds, *Prehistoric Hunter-Gatherers*, New York, Academic Press, 1985; C. Gamble, *The Palaeolithic Settlement of Europe*, Cambridge, Cambridge University Press, 1986.

45 P. Rowley-Conwy, 'Sedentary hunters: the Ertebølle example', in Bailey, ed., *Hunter-gatherer Economy in Prehistory* T. D. Price, 'Complexity in "non-complex" societies', in van der Leeuw, *Archaeological Approaches to the Study of Complexity*, pp. 54–97; Price and Brown, *Prehistoric Hunter-Gatherers*, p. 41.

46 J. Friedman and M. J. Rowlands, 'Notes towards an epigenetic model of the evolution of "civilization",' in Friedman and Rowlands, *The Evolution of Social Systems*.

since its expansion required constant revision of the rules of interaction. They were different not because they possessed alliance systems of different complexity but because the rules structuring those alliance systems were based on different premises.

The argument for complexity can also work in spatially extensive situations. Here intensification results in colonization as a local group used an area's sparse resources for the first time.[47] Such extensions in range are due to developments in the systems of alliances and social contacts needed to sustain populations in harsh, food-poor habitats and may only involve changes in technology on an incidental basis. Here the spatial framework is measuring developments in complexity on a diachronic basis.[48]

Thirdly, at any one point in time there would have been variation in the complexity between the hunter-gatherer groups living in a region.[49] It is now common to talk of a mosaic of such hunter-gatherer societies producing a complex social geography.[50] Bender has emphasized that the characteristic of complexity in these worlds of hunters and gatherers was for shifting emphasis within a regional landscape as power structures emerged at a local level for relatively short periods of time.[51] The regional archaeological evidence includes settlement histories as well as local manifestations of cemeteries,[52] and ceremonial centres marked by artistic codes,[53] prime data for examining social persona and assessing heterogeneity at a local level within a regional system.

Finally, both situations exist either within a world of hunters and gatherers or in a shared world, including the present one, where such systems existed as part of a complex world system. This has been the political map of the world since the emergence of *Homo sapiens sapiens*. Both views of complexity overthrow the idea of uniform and unchanging hunting bands moulded only by the restless environment into a variety of shapes.

47 C. Gamble, 'Interaction and alliance in palaeolithic society', *Man*, vol. 17, 1982.

48 H. M. Wobst, 'Locational relationships in palaeolithic society', *Journal of Human Evolution*, vol. 5, 1976.

49 Bender, 'Gatherer-hunter to farmer'; idem, 'Gatherer-hunter intensification', in Sheridan and Bailey, *Economic Archaeology*.

50 M. W. Conkey, 1985, 'Ritual communication, social elaboration, and the variable trajectories of palaeolithic material culture', in Price and Brown, *Prehistoric Hunter-Gatherers*.

51 B. Bender, 'Prehistoric developments in the American Midcontinent and in Brittany, Northwest France', in Price and Brown, *Prehistoric Hunter-Gatherers*.

52 J. O'Shea and M. Zvelebil, *Journal of Archaeological Anthropology*, vol. 3, 1984.

53 M. A. Jochim, 'Palaeolithic cave art in ecological perspective', in Bailey, *Hunter-Gatherer Economy in Prehistory*.

Australia

A number of these points can be illustrated with a discussion of the Australian evidence. It might seem strange to be discussing the origin of states in a continent where no-one has ever claimed they existed. However, this is an advantage since we are prevented from fitting the evidence to an evolutionary trajectory with known objectives. With a clear palate we can begin to taste complexity.

A dominant view in Australian anthropology and archaeology has been that of the unchanging hunter and gatherer.[54] In an important essay Stanner[55] used a spatial framework to discuss Aboriginal territorial organization. Their spatial domain, he suggested, consisted of an *estate* which was the religious focus of a land-holding local group and a *range* which was not exclusively owned and from which resources were procured. Variation, including spatial size, in estate/range relations could, he argued, be understood by the ecological transformations such territorial relations underwent in the varied environments of Australia.

While many archaeologists have accepted the ethnographically based view of Stanner and others there is mounting evidence that this form of contemporary organization is itself the product of an evolutionary process. Australian prehistorians have shown that the continent was occupied at least 40,000 years ago and probably earlier.[56] This previously unsuspected time-depth is matched by the complicated picture now provided by the physical anthropology of these pleistocene colonizers.[57] However, there is no doubt that all the populations so far identified are *Homo sapiens sapiens.* The unchanging model of hunters and gatherers would only expect, according to this evidence, variation linked to environmental shifts.

Archaeological evidence from many parts of the continent now points to changes beginning some 5,000–4,000 years ago. The evidence takes

54 J. Birdsell, 'Some environmental and cultural factors influencing the structuring of Australian Aboriginal populations', *American Naturalist*, vol. 87, 1953.

55 W. E. H. Stanner, 'Aboriginal territorial organisation: estate, range, domain and regime', *Oceania*, vol. 36, 1965.

56 J. P. White with J. F. O'Connell, *A Prehistory of Australia, New Guinea and Sahul*, Sydney, Academic Press, 1982. The rapid and secure dating of the pleistocene occupation of Australia stands in contrast to the dispute and conjecture that still surrounds the arrival of humans in North America. On the present evidence human occupation in North America is no greater that 12,000 years, making it the New World in prehistory as well as in the fifteenth century AD.

57 White with O'Connell, *A Prehistory of Australia*; R. Jones, 'The fifth continent problems concerning the human colonization of Australia, *Annual Review of Anthropology*, vol. 8, 1979.

the form of extensive drainage systems related to swamp management,[58] the labour-intensive construction of coastal and riverine fish traps,[59] and the use of new plant and arboreal resources.[60] There are changes in stone technology but more important is the associated expansion of settlement which runs against the environmental trend and leads to an increase in the number of findspots in a local region.[61]

The interpretation of this record is debated. Long-term population growth has been put forward as the factor selecting for change and the adoption of novel resources.[62] Alternatively the changes at a regional scale have been interpreted as an intensification in production that came as a response to new levels of social demand, for example the requirement of communion foods to support large group ceremonies.[63] According to this model, population growth is dependent upon these changes. Here the emphasis is on a dynamic model of hunter-gatherer organization and hence developments in complexity, however measured, are expected.[64]

The interest in the Australian evidence hinges on the interpretation that these changes represent new forms of organization which were more complex than any predicted from either the ecological model or the population hypotheses used elsewhere. It is interesting to note

58 H. Lourandos, 'Intensification: a late pleistocene-holocene archaeological sequence from south-western Victoria', *Archaeology in Oceania*, vol. 18, 1983.

59 Idem, 'Intensification and Australian prehistory', in Price and Brown, *Prehistoric Hunter-Gatherers.*

60 J. M. Beaton, 'Fire and water: aspects of Australian Aboriginal management of cycads', *Archaeology in Oceania*, vol. 17, 1982; S. Bowdler, 'Hunters in the highlands: Aboriginal adaptations in the eastern Australian uplands', ibid., vol. 16, 1981.

61 A. Ross, 'Holocene environments and prehistoric site patterning in the Victorian mallee', *Archaeology in Oceania*, vol. 16, 1981; M. J. Morwood, 'The prehistory of the central Queensland Highlands', in *Advances in World Archaeology*, vol. 3, 1984.

62 N. Butlin, *Our Original Aggression*, Sydney, Allen and Unwin, 1983, argues for a dramatic upward revision of population numbers for the Australian continent prior to Cook's arrival. These have always accepted Radcliffe-Brown's guess-estimate of 200,000 persons for the whole continent (J. Beaton, 'Does intensification account for changes in the Australian holocene archaeological record?' *Archaeology in Oceania*, vol. 18, 1983).

63 Lourandos, 'Intensification: a late pleistocene-holocene archaeological sequence from south-western Victoria', and 'Intensification and Australian prehistory'; Bowdler, 'Hunters in the highlands'.

64 There are still many gaps in a regional approach to Australian prehistory and it is not surprising that present syntheses argue for a continent-wide shift to a different order of organization at the 5,000 year marker rather than for diversity at a regional scale. By contrast, the Euopean data base, which has been investigated for much longer and at a very intensive regional and local scale, has produced a synthesis of a structured social mosaic for the late pleistocene-holocene hunters in the continent (Bender, 'Prehistoric developments in the American Midcontinent and in Brittany'; Conkey, 'Ritual communication, social elaboration, and the variable trajectories on palaeolithic material culture'; O. Soffer, 'Patterns of intensification as seen from the upper Palaeolithic of the central Russian plain', in Price and Brown, *Prehistoric Hunter-Gatherers*).

that the changes are not in step with any major shift in the enviroment which might have selected for novel forms of organization.

This conclusion is of course significant if we return to a Near Eastern or New World data base and reconsider the neolithic revolution. For the moment let us forget that pristine states happened in these two geographical areas but retain the model of agricultural development as argued from changes in the archaeological record. From this perspective we would have to put the holocene changes in Australian prehistory into the evolutionary stages of either incipient agriculture or a pre-pottery neolithic or broad spectrum harvesting that are so commonly used to describe the changes in areas which eventually *led to something like states*. Neither should we forget that a number of tropical Aboriginal groups were in contact with Macassan traders long before Captain Cook landed,[65] and that key Pacific plant domesticates have been found in these same areas; and yet the neolithic revolution did not occur.

This discussion of the Australian data emphasizes how the neolithic revolution model was designed to explain a particular set of prehistoric facts. It did this by concentrating upon the artifacts which stood as signposts on the route to complex societies and statehood. It was, however, applied as a global model to describe the conditions necessary to transform society and to usher in complexity. But if we use space rather than artifacts as a framework for investigating questions of complexity then we get a different picture. The revolution has gone. The global impact of intensification on resources, the explosion in population and growth of communities is no longer dependent upon such a rapid or radical transformation. The potential is at least as old as *Homo sapiens sapiens*. The question about state origins comes back to the conditions of failure and their geographical location. 'Why no states?' is every bit as good a question as 'Why no agriculture?'[66]

Complexity and the Early State

In the preceding discussion of the neolithic origins of the state, I hope to have shown that when viewed as changes in complexity the prehistoric picture of state origins is in fact more problematic than previously thought. For example, the Australian evidence shows developments in complexity but without statehood as an end result. Either we conclude that Captain Cook got there too soon or that the

65 D. J. Mulvaney, *The Prehistory of Australia*, Melbourne, Pelican, 1976.
66 Cherry, 'Generalization and the archaeology of the state'; Yoffee, 'The decline and rise of Mesopotamian civilization'.

changes were not associated with any developmental spiral.[67] On the other hand the Australian evidence shows that developments in complexity proceeded independently of food production which, it is often held, was the vital kick which produced *all* complex societies and thence culminated in state organizations. We are then bound to ask what is so different about the state?

The principle features of the early state, irrespective of its many definitions[68] lay in its unpredictability and its transience, but above all in its ability to tie together some paradoxes long enough for them to be recognized. The prehistoric state organized people in subtle ways even though most of the expectations we have about states stress the more obvious methods of coercion and sanctioned force needed to support and define such political systems.[69] The subtlety lay in the use of symbols and the varied means by which control and authority were established.[70] The early state acted as an arena to review the variety of alternative choices while simultaneously suggesting that only limited

67 Yoffee, N. 'Perspectives on 'trends toward social complexity in prehistoric Australia and Papua New Guinea', *Archaeology in Oceania*, vol. 20 1985, p. 47; C. Gamble, 'The mesolithic sandwich: ecological approaches and the archaeological record of the early post glacial', in M. Zvelebil, ed., *Postglacial Adaptations in the Temperate Regions of the Old World*, Cambridge, Cambridge University Press, 1986.

68 Claessen and Skalník, 'The early state: theories and hypotheses', in Claessen and Skalník, *The Early State*, produce a working definition for the early state as an 'organization for the regulation of social relations in a society that is divided into two emergent social classes, the rulers and the ruled'. They list seven main characteristics to aid recognition: 1) sufficient number of people; 2) citizenship determined by birth in a territory; 3) centralized government; 4) independent, in that the government can prevent fission; 5) regular surpluses exist; 6) social stratification distinguishes emergent social classes; 7) common ideology. R. Cohen, 'State origins: a re-appraisal', in ibid., p. 69, stresses centrality as follows: 'The state is a specifiable variety of political systems distinguishable by its centralized bureaucracy and dominant control of force by the central authority over subordinate segments of the society'. For K. V. Flannery, 'The cultural evolution of civilisations', in ibid. p. 404, the state 'attempts to maintain a monopoly of force and is characterized by true law; almost any crime may be considered a crime against the state . . .'; while for C. Renfrew, 'Space, time and polity', in Friedman and Rowlands, *The Evolution of Social Systems*, p. 99, 'the term state has always proved almost impossible to define – just as difficult indeed as 'city' and 'civilisation', with which it overlaps.

69 See above n. 63 and Service, *Primitive Social Organization*, p. 163, 'a true state, however undeveloped, is distinguishable from chiefdoms in particular, and all lower levels in general, by the presence of that special form of control, the consistent threat of force by a body of persons legitimately constituted to use it'.

70 Examples are given by Flannery, 'The cultural evolution of civilisations', p. 407: 'The critical contribution of state religions and state art styles is to legitimize that hierarchy, to confirm the divine affiliation of those at the top by inducing religious experience'; and by R. Rappaport, 'The sacred in human evolution', *Annual Review of Ecology and Systematics*, vol. 2, 1971, p. 56, where sanctity 'helps to keep subsystems in their place'.

options were practicable. Its development rests on the continual examination of these choices and their resolution.[71]

From our perspective these early states carry many expectations. We expect that they encouraged or required people to work harder, while their products, benefits and rewards were unequally distributed among the participants. Any fair-play view of the past therefore starts with the major question of why anyone started working for the state. While it is unlikely that exploitation ever needed inventing,[72] the loss of autonomy over many, if not all, local decisions, was a more dramatic shift than that between the affluent hunter and the hard-working farmer. With such a shift went changes in the premises upon which alliance systems were founded and a recasting of the relations of power between political units.

While we may no longer wish to see the appearance of early states as a great divide from either earlier or other types of society,[73] this central question of state origins still exists to confound a neat elision of the process. The loss of autonomy affected units of immense variation in scale and differentiation during the many state formations. While the component variables of complexity might measure the units being subsumed and the unit being formed, they ultimately shed no light on the questions of how and why autonomy was lost. Put another way, I am less interested in how complexity was achieved than in how the loss of autonomy occurred and what bearing, if any, this has on the convergence in state formation. Whether this involved developments in complexity is a separate issue and certainly not a guide to the appearance of new premises upon which alliance systems were based.

Another expectation underlying these changed premises is that once tried the state will never be forgotten. The alternative of descent back to savagery has received ridicule from state organizations at all times and places. Dark ages are never associated with a return to complex hunters. The state is quite simply its own best publicity agent when it comes to considering other ways of organizing society, even though the collapse of state systems is as expected as their formation.

Moreover, the state is expected to act in a negative manner in pursuit of these unpredictable and transient moments of formation. The sanctions involved may be economic, for example where material resources are withheld; social, in the guise of exclusion from participation in the

71 An extreme view is put by E. Leach, 'Men, bishops and apes', *Nature*, vol. 293, 1981, p. 21, where 'the ability to tell lies is perhaps our most striking human characteristic', and consequently human culture 'is designed to make the chaos appear more orderly than it is', presumably by minimizing the power of language for deception on a massive and ever increasing scale.

72 E. Gellner, chapter 3 in this volume.

73 MacGuire, 'Breaking down cultural complexity', p. 115.

roles and institutions of the state; and ideological where access is denied to the important rituals and ceremonies of social reproduction. Such forms of control are not exclusively associated with state organizations. They form the basis for control in many non-state societies and are often applied with force. Methodologies have been developed to link our expectations for this type of negative power to the visible and recoverable remains that constituted the paraphernalia of coercion in the prehistoric past.[74] The importance of symbols in early states provided a focus which, combined with dominant systems of ideology and legitimation, helped to define individuals in the polity.[75] Moreover, within the early state some transference could be made between economic, ideological and military groups that may not always be coterminous with the boundaries or the interests of any single state.[76] However, one of the paradoxes of early states was that while they wielded considerable power and exercised authority through recognised sanctions these methods pointed to institutional weaknesses rather than to the success of such state systems.[77]

In summary, early states were not different because they were more complex. The differences stemmed from their networks of alliances where the rules of competitive interaction were based on fundamentally different premises to other social systems and most markedly to hunters and gatherers. This is encapsulated in the central question conerning the loss of autonomy. The rest of this chapter will focus on two separate aspects concerning the question of state origins and where the loss of autonomy figures prominently. The first asks how this happened, since many societies seem to possess checks and balances to prevent such situations. The second deals with why state formation occurred and

74 R. Bradley, *The Social Foundations of Prehistoric Britain: Themes and Variations in the Archaeology of Power*, London, Longman, 1984; D. L. Clarke, T. Cowie and A. Foxon, *Symbols of Power at the Time of Stonehenge*, Edinburgh, H.M.S.O., 1985.

75 D. Freidel, 'Civilization as a state of mind: the cultural eovlution of the lowland Maya', in Jones and Kautz, eds, *The Transition to Statehood in the New World*.

76 M. Mann, chapter 4 in this volume, for discussion of the distinctions between civil and state society and the distinction drawn between *development* associated with infrastructural powers and *variation* in despotic control that has no evolutionary tendency.

77 An archaeological illustration of these weaknesses is termed 'feather waving' by G. Johnson, 'Organisational structure and scalar stress', in C. Renfrew, M. J. Rowlands and B. Abbott-Seagraves, eds, *Theory and Explanation in Archaeology: the Southampton Conference*, London, Academic Press, 1982, p. 405, and where conflict arising from scalar communication stress among larger human groups is alleviated to some extent by intense display with an increase in the number of symbols. The role of monument building, and in particular their religious/cult associations has been commented upon by J. Cherry, 'Generalization and the archaeology of the state', p. 429, who has suggested 'a general inverse relationship between the degree of investment in ideology and the strength of political authority/coercive power'. The most celebrated examples of this form of feather waving are, of course, the pyramids.

where, as we saw earlier, we must consider the negative evidence as well as the big piles of masonry.

The model that follows attempts to show how institutionalized forms of control emerged by taking a pre-neolithic starting points and returning the hunter-gatherers to their place in the process of change in the structure of alliance systems. Particular attention is paid to subsistence production and regional systems.

The Loss of Autonomy: a Model of Development

Among hunter-gatherers there is continual interplay between the organization and scheduling of work parties to exploit the scattered resources of the environment, and the need to participate in much wider systems of alliance through marriage and exchange. The term affluent hunter is in this case very misleading. The so-called leisure time stressed by some ethnographers is put to good use in servicing kinship systems, friendships, trading obligations and partnerships through a constant round of visiting. Indeed it is likely that subsistence work is made as efficient as possible, in terms of time spent doing it, so that more time can be allocated by individuals to these wider networks which are, of course, a form of regional risk-buffering system. These systems are organized around individuals, as shown for example in the extensive hxaro exchange systems among the !Kung San in the Kalahari.[78]

It is possible to see another option that would have been open to groups, rather than individuals, involved in such competitive alliance systems. This alternative has particular implications for reconstructing how autonomy over some local decisions was surrendered by households and groups. The model still recognizes that increases in demand leading to surplus production were a consequence of competitive principles embedded in the alliance systems. However, in this alternative model individuals produce more in order to 'pay' for a representative to take on the tasks of co-ordinating intergroup associations. Such an option would emerge as higher demands on production led to the intensified use of more abundant, but at the same time more expensive food resources. It is a feature of productive resources such as fish, grass seeds, shellfish, nuts, rabbits, birds and acorns that they are small in size and require more time spent in preparation prior to consumption than for instance large-bodied mammals and fruits. The higher costs as measured by energy expended for energy returned may explain why

78 P. Wiessner, 'Risk, reciprocity and social influences on !Kung San economics', in Leacock and Lee, eds, *Politics and History in Band Societies*.

these very abundant resources were first used comparatively late in the development of human subsistence economies.[79] The timetable of when they were first used implies changes in the intensity of production which finally accepted these higher exploitation costs. In the conceptual framework used here this development depended upon changes in the premises that underpinned the alliance systems. Once instituted, the use of such abundant resources, and eventually their domestic descendants in the form of cereals and small-bodied animals, presented a variety of options for sustainable population growth resulting from increased demands upon the production system.

A further consequence of such a developmental spiral lay in the new choices over mobility. In strategies designed to minimize risk and uncertainty in the subsistence quest, prehistoric hunters and gatherers used mobility as a major tactical device to acquire information and balance personnel to resources. The intricate decisions involved in the exploiatation of small package size, highly productive but costly resources placed stresses on the limited time and labour resources available in such small-scale societies. One organizational solution was for a reduction in both the size of annual foraging areas and in the number of residential moves. In other words, some communities became more sedentary and utilized less space. However, with lower mobility and more investment in a smaller foraging area there would have been problems with servicing the varied mechanisms for risk-buffering and social interaction mentioned above, since these involved larger areas than the ranges concerned with acquiring food. The option to invest authority in a representative for the group who could then discuss and negotiate the timing and protocol associated with large inter-group gatherings would have provided a solution to these conflicting interests. Those in such positions derived their authority to speak for the group from the control and knowledge of those symbols, rituals and ceremonies which sustained individuals, reproduced their social roles and which articulated the initial demands on production within the regional ramifications of the alliance system.

Therefore, according to this model it was the initial move to increased production that set this cycle in motion and produced contradictions needing resolution. One of these was the difficulty of locating people in the wider networks since participation in regional alliance systems required increased production at a local level. Consequently there was less opportunity for individuals to participate in the regional system. The deputizing role of the negotiator provided one solution but represented a loss of autonomy in terms of direct participation.

However, the surplus needed for the negotiator was not a new departure requiring additional effort but a supplement to the work effort involved in the process of intensifying to meet demand. This stimulus to production was maintained as the role acquired a special status, since this negotiator had to deal in terms that legitimated such gatherings and meeetings. Such a role stood apart from the household producer and became associated with a body of knowledge now associated with a small, privileged group in society. Moreover, the system had benefits when viewed from the perspective of those now working harder to produce more so that the negotiator could act on their behalf. For example, time previously committed to risk-buffering activities was now freed for other uses by household producers. Consequently more options were opened to develop alternative production systems through increased efficiency and novel systems of intensification such as irrigation, domestication, terracing or trapping in order to produce goods to improve individual positions within the competitive cycles. The loss of autonomy was outweighed by the competitive advantages opened to individuals and the groups to which they belonged in exploiting the competitive structure of alliance systems. The separation into negotiators and clients saw a fruitful basis for the organization of personnel, symbols and rituals into varied constellations of authority and control. At one level these may have excluded several sectors in society – for example juveniles and women – while providing a format for further differentiation by linking the position of negotiator to a developmental cycle of initiation and an individual's rites of passage. Thus the conditions were established for the reinterpretation of the premises upon which power and authority were based and legitimated.[80]

This does not mean that the negotiators eventually became central persons in central places. The tyranny of centrality, with its control over material and symbolic resources, might be a common feature in early states but is not a direct consequence of earlier negotiations by hunters and gatherers. These negotiators need only be seen as a tactical solution to tensions between the social and ecological systems of production and reproduction. Their existence was only possible with some accompanying loss of local autonomy. The only preconditions in this model of how differentiation came about are for regional networks of varied social links based on systems of alliances. These provided access to resources

80 D. Miller and C. Tilley, 'Ideology, Power and Prehistory: an introduction', in Miller and Tilley, eds, *Ideology, Power and Prehistory*, Cambridge, Cambridge University Press, 1983.

and acted as the means for locating individuals in a variety of social networks. In such cases the forms of control, sanction and authority by which the system was maintained were all entirely embedded in the underlying premises of the social system and where mediation took place between any paradoxes and contradictions.

This simple sketch tackles only the question of how differentiation can be accounted for by placing local behaviour under selection from the wider networks of alliance. It shows how the creation of differentiated roles opened up enormous possibilities for change in any number of directions – none of which can be predicted from our standpoint. Why further changes occurred and converged on the origin of social systems with marked central functions should then be sought amongst these same frameworks. I would suggest that these developments in turn continued to make the trade between further systems of organization requiring differentiation and which then released more aspects of the production economy and spawned the mechanisms of control which they required. The premises upon which such organization was instituted underwent transformation in terms of sanctioned force, the exercise of power and the extent of ownership of material and symbolic resources.

A powerful example of this trade is provided by Johnson's work on scalar-communication stress and the development of organizational hierarchies.[81] His model is based on solid uniformitarian principles which link the increasing size of human groups to corresponding increases in communication stress. This leads to disputes and conflict and consequently to the need for additional systems of organization if they are to achieve any permanence. An essential feature of hunter-gatherer groups is that when faced with conflict they respond by fissioning. Mobility is used as a means of resolving crisis by walking away from the problem while at the same time rapidly reducing the size of the group which started the problem. In order to maintain group size and to keep it in one place, Johnson argues for the development of a simultaneous hierarchy.[82] Here control is vested in a small proportion of the population and the problems of scalar-communication stress are met by providing a mechanism for achieving integration. The integrative function of hierarchies permits the extension of spans of control over commonly constituted organizational units such as kin groups, residence units, work groups, religious cells and military units or even over similar-sized polities integrated into an emerging civilization.[83]

81 Johnson, 'Organisational structure and scalar stress'.
82 Idem, 'Information sources and the development of decision-making organizations', in C. Redman et al., eds, *Social Archaeology: Beyond Subsistence and Dating*, New York, Academic Press, 1978.
83 Johnson, ibid., p. 410, defines span of control as 'the number of individuals or

Hunter-gatherers do, however, have other responses to scalar-communication stress. These take the form of sequential hierarchies, a term which describes the hierarchical organization of a non-hierarchically organized group.[84] The solution modelled from !Kung camp site census data is that the basic organizational unit changes as camp site populations, and hence scalar-communications stress, increase. Thus extended families form the organizational units on camp sites with populations over 40 while at smaller camps the basic units consist instead of nuclear families. The sequential hierarchy therefore reduces the number of units which have to be integrated as population size at camps increases. Simultaneous hierarchies achieve this without either the recurrent fragmentation of larger gatherings or the sequential reorganization of the size and nature of the basic units as population size increases in the short term.

The development of the early state can be understood in these terms of coping with communication stress and conflict since for the state, as Cohen argues, 'break up is impossible or unacceptable'.[85] Even chiefdoms have some option to fragment, and the many segmentary systems of organization depend upon such sequential systems to respond to scalar-stress while conflicts and disputes are ultimately resolved by fissioning, so removing the problem.[86]

The early state, while keen to present the opposite image, was in fact a weak political unit. The origins of this weakness lay in the difficulties inherent in co-ordinating the component parts. I argued at the beginning of this paper that we know a great deal about the varieties of early state. The trajectories of state formation appear equally varied and we have already discounted prime movers such as trade, population and subsistence organization in leading the way.[87] Moreover, the trajectories by which such elements were integrated and combined into early states involved at least the separate and combined solutions provided by military, economic and religious mechanisms.[88] But whatever the

---

organizational units directly subordinate to a given individual or organizational unit within a hierarchical structure'. It appears that a narrow span of control over six units produces higher levels of decision performance than a wider span of control, be it in modern corporate structures, late Imperial China or local communities in Basutoland. Johnson notes that if a relatively high degree of control is to be maintained then the span of control must be kept within narrow limits (p. 413), as members of academic departments will all appreciate since scalar stress and disputes provide the selection pressure.

84 Ibid., p. 403.
85 R. Cohen, 'State origins: a re-appraisal', p. 57.
86 M. Sahlins, *Tribesmen*, Englewood Cliffs, Prentice Hall, 1968.
87 Flannery, 'The cultural evolution of civilisations'.
88 Adams, *The Evolution of Urban Society*, chapter 4.

pathway and the dominant mechanisms involved in the prehistory of any single exercise in state formation, collectively they converge on this issue of instituting control in an inherently weak system and the implications this holds for the loss of autonomy. The spatial scale and sequence associated with early state formation was both a formal expression of this weakness and a translation of the multivarious symbols and stratagems of control into the limited, convergent outcome which solved many of the problems.[89]

Conclusion

I have attempted here to answer the question of state origins by looking at the convergence of state formation rather than the variety of trajectories and cultural forms. This undeniably suits a generalizing approach to the question of why the early state converged on a set of limited outcomes. By contrast, the question of what happened during state origins involves a great many ways and means by which this convergence was achieved. However, for all this variety only a limited number of common problems had to be resolved. It is interesting that these problems were part of hunter-gatherer structure. These included the limitations on residential group size due to the increased frequency of disputes, establishing effective sanctions over spatially dispersed populations in independent units, the integration of a complex political geography within world systems of variable scale and the cultural solution of survival problems through devices such as risk-buffering. In response the varied processes and individual prehistories of state formation produced people in central positions who controlled monopolies and a temporary ability to resolve conflicting interests. A model of negotiators and their clients has been put forward as a possible scenario for coming to grips with the central questions of this negative view of power – the how and why surrounding the loss of local autonomy. This model shows how such changes were linked to the negative aspect of power and although negotiators were not always elites they formed part of the necessary hierarchies that coped with the demands placed upon production. By including the hunter-gatherer in the question of state origins we begin to see what needs explaining. This is essentially the move from the options of fission and fusion to the commitment of centrality and permanence based on control. I have adopted a model of

89 For example, Renfrew's discussion of the early state module in Sabloff and Lamberg-Karlovsky, *Ancient Civilization and Trade*.

alliance systems which can be used to look at these processes and separated the issue from measures of complexity.

It might, however, be argued that since alliance systems were present in all types of society then all that changed was the scale of the systems. If we followed this view then the appearance of the early state was just a high order of probability that increased with time within a certain size of world system. This was not so. The process involved changes to the systems of alliance which redefined the relationships between people and their uses of material and symbolic resources. Developments in scale, whether of numbers of people or size of political area, were dependent upon changes in these premises. The change that opened up such possibilities occurred with the appearance of modern humans 40,000 years ago. The question of why no states or why no agriculture now depends on understanding, as the Australian example has shown, the transformation of these competitive alliance systems which can be very varied. This perspective does not make hunters and gatherers into early states but it does make hunters of states.

2

The Tribe and the State

Patricia Crone

The Concept of Tribe

What is a tribe? To this question there are so many answers that some
would have us abandon the concept of tribe altogether.[1] That would not
be easy; I am not even convinced that it would be desirable. (Ought we
similarly to abandon the concept of civilization on the ground that it
breeds endless attempts at definition?) For though it goes without saying
that there are questions for which the concept is unhelpful, it does not
follow that it is meaningless; and what is more, the current dissatisfaction with it would seem to arise from problems susceptible of resolution.

Few would disagree that a tribe is a species of that genus of societies
which create all or most of their social roles by ascribing social importance to biological characteristics, or in other words societies ordered
with reference to kinship, sex and age.[2] No society which makes extensive use of non-biological principles of organization is a tribal one, for
all that kinship, sex and age may still regulate numerous aspects of it;
conversely, no definition of the tribe which omits reference to the
biological principle of organization can be said to do its job;[3] it is the

---

1 Thus for example, E. Colson, 'Contemporary tribes and the development of nation-
alism', in J. Helm, ed., *Essays on the Problem of Tribe*, Proceedings of the 1967 Annual
Spring Meeting of the American Ethnological Society, Seattle and London, University of
Washington Press, 1968, p. 201.

2 Anthropologists usually identify the genus with reference to kinship alone, and
kinship is of course more important than age or sex in that it can be put to far wider use;
but primitive societies are nonetheless shaped with reference to all three principles, and
there are hunting societies so primitive that the organizational role of sex exceeds that of
kinship.

3 Cf. Royal Anthropological Institute, *Notes and Queries in Anthropology*, 6th edn,
London, 1951, p. 66, where a tribe is defined as 'a politically or socially coherent and

organizational principle itself, not the various factors which underlie, accompany or result from it, which demarcates a tribal from a non-tribal society.[4] This is obviously not to say that tribal societies are character ized by perfect correspondence between biological and social relation-ships: biological facts being innumerable, most have to be ignored for organizational purposes,[5] while others may have to be denied outright,[6] and a great many usually have to be invented.[7] But the overlap between biological and social facts is nonetheless both considerable and signifi-cant; the reason why the discrepancy between the two is subject to manipulation is precisely that no discrepancy is supposed to occur.[8]

A tribe is thus a primitive society. It is primitive in that biologically based organization, however diversely elaborated, is given by nature in respect of its starting point (kinship, sex and age inevitably have *some* organizational importance in *all* human societies[9]); further, in that it costs nothing to set up or maintain (indeed its beauty lies in its capacity for fully automatic operation: ideally people step in and out of their social

---

autonomous group occupying or claiming a particular territory'. How does this distin-guish the tribe from the nation-state? For other examples, see D. P. Biebuyk, 'On the concept of tribe', *Civilisations*, vol. 16, 1966, pp. 501 f.

4 Cf. definitions of the tribe in terms of simple technology, subsistence level, self-sufficiency, illiteracy, absence of classes, absence of state organization and so on. (J. H. Steward, *Theory of Culture Change*, Urbana, Ill., University of Illinois Press, 1955, p. 44n.; A. W. Southall, 'The illusion of tribe', *Journal of Asian and African Studies*, vol. 5, 1970, p. 28).

5 Clearly most are ignored for the simple reason that they are not perceived (a great deal would no doubt have been made of blood groups if they had been visible). Others are perceived, but too erratic in manifestation – many societies attach social significance to epilepsy, but they could scarcely base their organization on its incidence. Still others are both perceived and regular, but ignored because they are not wanted (e.g. descent through mothers/fathers, the most famous example).

6 Cf. the outright denial of the father's/mother's role in procreation for which some societies based on unilateral descent are famed, e.g. the Trobriand Islanders.

7 Cf. the huge realm of fictitious kinship and genealogical manipulation. There is less scope for manipulation in the case of age and sex, though there are societies in which men are allowed to adopt the social role of women on condition of wearing women's clothing.

8 For a decisive refutation of the view that physical and social kinship simply happen to coincide, see E. Gellner, 'The concept of kinship' and 'Nature and society in social anthropology', in his *Cause and Meaning in the Social Sciences*, London, Routledge and Kegan Paul, 1973 (reprinted from *Philosophy of Science*, vols. 27, 1960, and 30, 1963). Nobody seems to have taken the sometimes considerable discrepancy between physical and social age to mean that the two have nothing to do with each other, and the same is true of sex (though female liberationists are well on the way).

9 At least as long as science fiction remains fiction. (And though science fiction writers can envisage a society in which mechanized propagation of the species eliminates the few roles which kinship and sex retain under industrialized conditions, even they have failed to dream up ways of endowing children with the knowledge required for adult roles.) By 'nature', a term with Victorian connotations which may offend the reader, I simply mean what others call 'the human biogram'.

roles by the sheer fact of being born, growing up and dying[10]); and finally in that it works best in the absence of social differentiation (the more similar people are in other respects, the more fully kinship, sex and age can differentiate their roles). Tribal societies are thus typically composed of identical and interchangeable units: everybody engages in the same type of food production, and all enjoy much the same level of material income and political influence, such differentiation as keeps arising in these respects being too unstable for the formation of permanent hierarchies; and all typically share the same language, culture and religion too. Since the building blocks of society are identical, the various combinations in which they engage are typically identical too in all or most respects except for size. Evidently there are variations on the tribal theme: *some* degree of socio-economic and political differentiation can be accommodated. But specialization, interdependence and inequality are features more characteristic of relations between tribes (or between tribes and non-tribesmen) than of those within them. In the absence of social differentiation, or significant degrees thereof, the biologically defined roles both can and must perform all the functions which complex societies assign to special agencies, above all the peace-keeping functions which complex societies assign to the state. Whatever else a tribe may be, it is a stateless society: the resolution of conflict rests on self-help, and one of the prime objectives of the tribal organization (including tribal religion) is to regulate and mitigate the disruptive effects of its use. There is of course such a thing as a tribal state. But a tribal state is a state superimposed on a society which is designed to cope without it and which may accordingly revert to statelessness at any time. It is only when the autonomous and self-sufficient nature of the building blocks has been undermined that we have a state *as opposed to* a tribe.[11]

So much for the genus; it is when we turn to the delineation of the species that the disagreement sets in. Some authors simply equate the species with the genus and refer to all primitive societies as tribal,[12] or to all primitive societies above the level of the band as such.[13] Since a great many primitive societies lack groups identifiable as tribes, this usage is strictly speaking unfortunate, but what is the alternative? A label such as 'societies which organize themselves through ascription of social

10 For a superb illustration of this point, see E. Gellner, *Thought and Change*, London, Weidenfeld & Nicolson, 1964, p. 156.

11 For a brilliant analysis of 'the tribal design', see M. D. Sahlins, *Tribesmen*, Englewood Cliffs, Prentice Hall, 1968.

12 Thus for example I. Schapera, *Government and Politics in Tribal Societies*, London, Watts, 1956.

13 Thus Sahlins, *Tribesmen*, p. viii and passim.

importance to biological facts' is not exactly convenient; 'kinship societies' is not entirely accurate, and in any case no adjective can be derived
from either term. I shall thus defer to current usage and refer to all stateless societies above the level of the band (which is too small to stand in
need of much formal orgnization) as tribal in the wider or generic sense
of the word.[14]

A tribe in the specific sense of the word, however, is best defined as a
descent group which constitutes a political community. It may be sub-
divided into smaller descent groups and form part of larger ones, but it is
distinguished from these by the fact that it amounts to 'the most inclusive aggregate of persons who identify with each other as a group, and
who are prepared to regulate their differences by means of decisions
accepted as binding because they are made in accordance with shared
political norms and structures'.[15] A tribe is thus a society which relies on
descent for political integration. Descent generates groups over and
above the level required for production and the allocation of property
rights;[16] and it is this genealogical formalization of political unity which
distinguishes a tribe in the specific sense of the word from 'tribes' which
consist of little but intermarrying bands with a vague sense of unity on
the one hand,[17] and 'tribes' which rely on age organization rather than
descent for political integration on the other.[18]

14 It is in the nature of spectrums that one can disagree about where they begin and
end. The band could be included in or excluded from the tribal spectrum at one
extremity, just as the chiefdom could be included or excluded at the other (cf. M. H.
Fried, 'On the concepts of "tribe" and "tribal society"', in Helm, *Problem of Tribe*, pp. 12 f.
(repr. from *Transactions of the New York Academy of Science*, vol. 28, 1966); M. Godelier, 'The
concept of tribe: crisis of concept or crisis of the empirical foundations of anthropology?',
Diogenes, vol. 81, 1973, pp. 15ff.). It all depends on the use to which one wishes to put the
spectrum in question. I exclude the band, following Sahlins, for the simple reason that I
wish to test one of Sahlins's theories.

15 D. Easton, 'Political anthropology', in *Biennial Review of Anthropology*, ed. B. Siegel,
Stanford, Stanford University Press, 1959, p. 229.

16 Cf. A. M. Khazanov, *Nomads and the Outside World*, Cambridge, Cambridge University Press, 1984, pp. 148ff. Among nomads rights in grazing land frequently remain unal-
located, but those in livestock, wells and cultivable land (if any) always vest in descent
groups far smaller than the tribe.

17 Cf. Fried, 'On the concepts of "tribe"', pp. 12f., versus M. D. Sahlins, 'The
segmentary lineage: an organization of predatory expansion', *American Anthropologist*,
vol. 63, 1961, p. 343n. – a paper in which Sahlins's definition of the tribe does indeed
invite criticism along Fried's lines.

18 Cf. the Karimojong, Turkana and many other East African tribes. Despite the
objections of Schapera (*Government and Politics*, p. 216), Eisenstadt is surely right that age
organization should be seen as an alternative to the use of descent (S. N. Eisenstadt,
'African Age Groups', *Africa*, vol. 24, 1954). Naturally there are peoples who use both;
but where age organization carries the brunt of political integration, descent is reduced to
a minor role and vice versa (cf. the neat contrast between the otherwise very similar Nuer
and Karimojong in E. E. Evans-Pritchard, *The Nuer*, Oxford, Oxford University Press,

Though well entrenched in the anthropological literature, this concept of the tribe does not, however, reign supreme. Some anthropologists reserve the word for groups (or aggregates) which have sufficient awareness and/or appearance of unity in linguistic, cultural, religious and other terms to have a name for themselves and/or to have been given one by outsiders, but which do *not* amount to political communities.[19] According to them, a tribe is a 'socio-cultural-ethnic entity'[20] within which political unity may be either limited to smaller descent groups (duly labelled subtribes)[21] or else completely context-bound (in which case the tribe is precisely a set of bands united by marriage, ritual and the like).[22] The Nuer, Dinka, Tallensi, Yoruba of Africa, the Kalinga of the Philippines, the Murngin of Australia and countless other peoples scattered over the face of the earth may all be adduced as examples of tribes in this sense of the word.[23] Practically all the problems associated with the concept of tribe arise from this use of the word; in this sense the concept ought indeed to be abandoned, and that for two quite different reasons.

First, if we identify the tribe as a cultural rather than a political unit, what are we doing classifying all stateless societies (with or without the band) as tribal in the generic sense of the word? The reason why the word has come to be used of both a specific group and a general level of political organization is evidently that it stands for a certain type of political organization. This may be thought to be a purely terminological inconsistency, but it drags endless conceptual confusion in its wake. A cultural unit exists for neutral observers to observe and measure

---

1940, pp. 249ff., esp. p. 254; and N. Dyson-Hudson, *Karimojong Politics*, Oxford, Oxford University Press, 1966, pp. 87ff., 104, 155ff.).

19 Cf. the review of current usage by G. E. Dole, 'Tribe as the autonomous unit', in Helm, *Problem of Tribe*.

20 Thus Sahlins, 'Segmentary lineage', p. 325.

21 Cf. A. Southall, 'Stateless societies', in *International Encyclopaedia of the Social Sciences*, n.p., New York and London, Macmillan and Free Press, 1968, vol. XV, p. 159.

22 Cf. Sahlins, 'Segmentary lineage', p. 326. (It is thanks to Sahlins's definition of the tribe in this paper that Fried can object that a tribe is simply an assembly of bands, cf. above, n. 17, for all that this is evidently not true of the tribe in the sense of descent group endowed with political autonomy.)

23 Cf. Southall, 'Illusion of tribe'; idem, 'Stateless societies'. It should be noted, however, that Evans-Pritchard did not identify the Nuer as a single tribe, but rather as a plurality thereof, that Lienhardt similarly identified the Dinka as a plurality of tribes (G. Lienhardt, 'The Western Dinka', in J. Middleton and D. Tait, eds, *Tribes Without Rulers*, London, Routledge & Kegan Paul, 1958, pp. 102ff.), and that Warner's study of the Murngin explicitly stated that 'the tribe is almost non-existent among these people' (W. L. Warner, *A Black Civilization: A Social Study of an Australian Tribe*, New York, Harper, rev. edn 1958, p. 9, cf. pp. 35ff. The contrast between text and title neatly illustrates the need for a distinction between tribes in the generic and the specific sense of the word).

regardless of whether its members are aware of its existence or not: tribesmen may speak related dialects, worship the same deity, and share the same customs without knowing this to be the case. But a political community has to exist in the minds of its members in order to have any external manifestation at all: tribesmen will not engage in joint political action without believing themselves to be related and/or in a state of alliance. It follows that the criteria required for the identification of culture-bearing units are quite different from those required for the delineation of political communities. Tribesmen may be of common origin, and even have memories thereof, without attributing any political significance to this fact;[24] conversely they may attribute much significance to a postulate of common descent entirely devoid of objective truth:[25] objective criteria do not on their own regulate behaviour in either case. Yet there are anthropologists who would have us identify tribes with reference to *both* objective criteria such as the distribution of certain morphemes (of which the tribesmen themselves may be quite unaware), *and* subjective ones such as belief in common descent (which may be quite untrue in the eyes of neutral observers), as if linguistic classification were a clue to political behaviour.[26] Zoologists, who classify animals in large descent groups known as tribes (phyla) for the study of animal evolution, do not mix up these tribes with the troops, herds and bands in which social animals live their social lives. Anthropologists ought similarly to have different terms for classificatory and ethological use; and as it happens, the term 'tribe' in a human context has been pre-empted for the study of behaviour.

Second, if the tribe were to be identified as a socio-cultural-ethnic entity within which political communities are located, a people such as

---

24 Thus the Lwo peoples of the Sudan, Uganda and Kenya preserve memories of their common origin in their migration tales, but these tales are not intended or understood as charters of political unity; cf. P. Curtin, S. Feierman, L. Thompson and J. Vansina, *African History*, London, Longman, 1978, pp. 130ff. Similarly, the tribes of the Arabian ʿAnaza group are of common origin in the sense that ʿAnaza was once a single tribe; but though their genealogies proclaim them to be of common descent, they never act together; cf. *Encyclopaedia of Islam*, 2nd edn, Leiden and London, E. J. Brill, 1960– , s.v. 'ʿAnaza').

25 In the 680s the Quḍāʿa tribes of Syria proclaimed themselves to be no longer sons of Maʿadd, but rather sons of Ḥimyar, viz. Yemenis; and though genealogists remembered their previous affiliation, they sided with Yemeni tribes (both real and spurious) thereafter; cf. P. Crone, *Slaves on Horses, the Evolution of the Islamic Polity*, Cambridge, Cambridge University Press, 1980, pp. 34f. There is nothing unusual about this, apart from the fact that memories of the change were preserved. It is well known that genealogies tend to be more or less correct at the level of family and lineage, but to express purely political relationships at the level of tribe and beyond (they remain plausible because they are true where they matter most in everyday life).

26 Biebuyck, 'Concept of tribe', pp. 509f.

the Israelites would have to be recast as a single tribe divided into twelve subtribes, while a people such as the Arabs (in the sense of bedouin) would have to be recast as a single tribe divided into countless subtribes, among the most famous of which one may mention the Rwala and the Āl Murra.[27] To anyone acquainted with the Middle East this sounds absurd. Plainly, the socio-cultural-ethnic entity which some anthropologists would have us call a tribe simply *is* what others call a people;[28] and this venerable word is highly appropriate in that it is vague: a great deal of current agony over the concept of tribe arises from the fact that peoples *cannot* be precisely demarcated, that such unity as they have is frequently unity as seen through the eyes of outsiders, and that they owe this fluidity to the very absence of overall political structuring which a tribe, properly speaking, possesses. The mislabelling of peoples as tribes is so engrained in Africanist literature that Africanists are sometimes as reluctant to divide the Nuer and the Dinka into a plurality of tribes as are Arabianists to fuse the Arabs in a single one;[29] and it is true that the Nuer, Dinka and other peoples of East Africa look like tribes in simple terms of size. But this goes to illustrate an interesting contrast between East Africa and Arabia. Both areas have long had a sizeable pastoralist, that is mobile, population and thus a potential for cultural unity, but the potential has only been realized in Arabia. There was an Arab people even before the Arab conquests;[30] and had the Nuer, Dinka, Turkana, Karimojong, Samburu, Masai and others been camel pastoralists, they would no doubt have been tribes on a par with the Rwala and Āl Murra too. But camel and cattle pastoralism are adaptations to different environments with different cultural results: East Africa has peoples at the level at which Arabia has tribes, and its political communities are correspondingly smaller and/or less tightly integrated. It would be helpful if Africanists (and others) could be persuaded to change their terminology in recognition of this fact.[31]

27 On these tribes, see A. Musil, *The Manners and Customs of the Rwala Bedouins*, New York, American Geographical Society, 1928; D. P. Cole, *Nomads of the Nomads*, Arlington Heights, Ill. AHM Publishing Corporation, 1975.

28 Cf. Evans-Pritchard, *Nuer*, p. 5; Dole, 'Tribe as the autonomous unit', p. 95.

29 Thus Southall, 'Stateless societies', p. 159; idem, 'Illusion of tribe', pp. 43f.

30 Cf. G. E. von Grunebaum, 'The nature of Arab unity before Islam', *Arabica*, vol. 10, 1963.

31 Gellner rightly notes that Middle Eastern tribes are political units, that their cultural role is not very marked, and that they do not 'fill out' the world, but identify themselves in terms borrowed from a wider civilization (E. Gellner, 'The tribal society and its enemies', in R. Tapper, ed., *The Conflict between Tribe and State in Iran and Afghanistan*, New York, Croom Helm, 1983, p. 436). But the implicit contrast with non-Middle Eastern tribes simply shows that Middle Eastern and non-Middle Eastern anthropologists use the word 'tribe' differently. If tribes are political units, they are unlikely ever to be cultural ones (whether they identify themselves in terms borrowed from a wider civilization or

Generally speaking, it is a pity that Middle Eastern and Central Asian tribes figure so rarely in discussions of the nature of tribalism, for they represent an important variety thereof. It is undoubtedly true that most stateless societies lack an overall group identifiable as the political community (viz. the tribe), because political functions are not necessarily clustered at a single level, and because even when they are, so much of social life is conducted outside the grouping in question that society must be defined as more inclusive than that grouping.[32] But this merely goes to show that most stateless societies are less tightly organized in political terms than the pastoralists of the Middle East and Central Asia.[33] Picking out the tribe among the bedouin, for example, is problematic only when basic information is missing (as for example in the context of pre-Islamic Arabia): the tribe is that descent group within which control of pasture land is vested,[34] within which particular rules regarding blood-money and other aspects of behaviour apply,[35] which is endowed with a chief,[36] and within which most of social life is conducted.[37] It may well be that the tribe in the specific sense of the word is an overwhelmingly or exlusively pastoral phenomenon (or so at least if we add the criterion of segmentary organization[38]), but this would scarcely be an objection to the definition proposed: it was after all pastoralists whom God himself singled out as paradigmatic tribesmen in the Bible.

---

shared by a local people); conversely, if they are cultural units, they are unlikely ever to be political ones (whether political communities within them are large, small or occasionalist).

32 Southall, 'Stateless societies'.

33 It is of course true that the tribe may be a relative concept in a segmentary context (cf. Evans-Pritchard, *Nuer*, p. 148), but this is not what Southall appears to be arguing.

34 Cf. Khazanov, *Nomads*, p. 150, and the references cited there, to which many others could be added; Cole, *Nomads of the Nomads*, p. 94.

35 Among the Nuer only fellow-tribesmen recognize the obligation to pay blood-money in compensation for homicide (Evans-Pritchard, *Nuer*, p. 121), but among the bedouin everyone does so; the sum payable for a fellow-tribesman is, however, considerably higher than that for an outsider (Musil, *Rwala*, p. 47; similarly in pre-Islamic Arabia, cf. P. Crone, *Roman, Provincial and Islamic Law*, forthcoming, chapter 4). For other rules, cf. Musil, loc. cit.

36 Exceptions to this rule are few indeed, as Khazanov rightly notes (*Nomads*, p. 150).

37 See, for example, Cole, *Nomads of the Nomads*, p. 93.

38 Khazanov subscribes to the view that there are no characteristics of socio-political organization which are to be found exclusively among nomads (*Nomads*, p. 192); but this depends on how narrowly we define our terms, and to my knowledge nobody has made a systematic study of the question.

The Tribe and the Origin of the State

What then is the evolutionary relationship between the tribe and the state? There is a widespread belief to the effect that the tribe constitutes an indispensable stage in the evolution of mankind from primitivity to statehood. Evidently, if we take the tribe to mean primitive society in general, we are left with a tautology; and if conversely we equate it with the tribe in the specific sense of the word, we are left with a most implausible claim.[39] But did the state evolve from the tribe generically speaking, or in other words from the systematic use of sex, age and/or descent for purposes of social organization? The belief that the tribe in this sense of the word constitutes a halfway house to civilization was perhaps first formulated by Morgan.[40] More recently, it has been taken up by Sahlins and Service, both of whom have argued that the tribal level should be seen as the second stage in the political evolution of mankind: bands in their view have evolved into tribes which have evolved via tribal chiefdoms into states.[41] And though Service has since modified his position,[42] a fair number of historians (including Soviet ones) seem to operate with the same evolutionary scheme.[43] It undeni-

39 Given that the tribe in the specific sense of the word is strongly associated with nomads, it would be plausible only if mankind had passed from hunting to agriculture via a pastoralist stage. But pastoral nomadism emerged after the invention of agriculture (cf. the discussion in Khazanov, *Nomads*, pp. 85ff.).

40 L. H. Morgan, *Ancient Society*, Cambridge, The Belknap Press of Harvard University Press, 1964 (first published 1877), esp. pp. 12, 62f.

41 Sahlins, 'Segmentary lineage', p. 324; idem, *Tribesmen*; E. R. Service, *Primitive Social Organization; an Evolutionary Perspective*, New York, Random House, 1962, rev. edn 1971.

42 When Fried queried the extent to which tribes can be distinguished from bands, Service responded by abolishing the concepts of *both* band *and* tribe, merging them for evolutionary purposes in the Egalitarian Society; at the same time he merged the chiefdom and the primitive state in the Hierarchical Society, which supposedly developed via the Empire-State into Archaic Civilization or Classical Empire (E. R. Service, *Cultural Evolutionism, Theory in Practice*, New York, Holt, Rinehart & Winston, 1971, p. 157). Despite his later work in the same vein (idem, *Origins of the State and Civilization: the Process of Cultural Evolution*, New York, W. W. Norton, 1975), this scarcely represents an improvement: the evolutionary phases are now so broad as to be virtually meaningless.

43 Thus for example R. McC. Adams, *The Evolution of Urban Society*, Chicago, University of Chicago Press, 1966 (where the evolutionary assumptions are derived primarily from Morgan, secondarily from Kirchhoff rather than Sahlins and Service); the Soviet scholars (ultimately inspired by Morgan too) in I. M. Diakonoff, ed., *Ancient Mesopotamia, A Collection of Studies by Soviet Scholars*, Moscow, Sändig Reprint Verlag, 1969; and I. J. Gelb (see, for example, his evolutionary scheme in his 'From freedom to slavery', in D. O. Edzard, ed., *Gesellschaftsklassen im alten Zweistromland und in den angrenzenden Gebieten*, Verlag der Bayerischen Akademie der Wissenschaften, Munich, 1972, p. 81). The assumption that states must have emerged from a tribal organization gives a curiously

ably has an almost instinctive appeal. As formulated by Sahlins and Service, its most sophisticated exponents, it rests on two assumptions: first, material developments generate more complex forms of socio-political organization (whatever its palaeolithic antecedents, the tribe gained dominance on the transition to the neolithic when food production made for more stable and unique resources, denser populations, and thus more scope for conflict[44]); and second, the essential difference between band, tribe and state lies in their level of complexity – a tribe may start as a loose cluster of bands, but the more tribal, that is complex and integrated, it becomes, the more closely it will approximate a chiefdom, which in its turn only requires further complexity to develop into a primitive state.[45] If both assumptions were correct, history should confirm Sahlins and Service's thesis, but in fact it does not. The historical record is against it for the obvious reason that the second assumption is wrong.

Let us start with the historical record: can it be claimed that the first states in history developed out of tribal chiefdoms? In the absence of written evidence it is hard to say much about Olmec America,[46] and the case of Egypt is complicated by the fact that state formation here took place against a background of Mesopotamian influence (though in tune with the anti-diffusionist mood of the time, the formative role of this influence is nowadays denied[47]). But the thesis ought at the very least to

---

cyclical character to Mesopotamian history: since the publication of R. A. Fernea's *Shaykh and Effendi: Changing Patterns of Authority among the El Shabana of Southern Iraq*, Cambridge, Mass., Harvard University, 1970, it has had a distinct tendency to begin and end with the same El Shabana tribes (thus most notably M. Gibson, 'Violation of fallow and engineered disaster in Mesopotamian civilization', in T. E. Downing and M. Gibson, eds, *Irrigation's Impact on Society*, Tucson, University of Arizona Press, 1974; idem, 'By stage and cycle to Sumer', in D. Schmandt-Besserat, ed., *The Legacy of Sumer*, Malibu, Udena Publications, 1976, p. 54).

44 Sahlins, 'Segmentary lineage', p. 324; idem, *Tribesmen*, p. 3; Service, *Primitive Social Organization*, rev. edn, p. 99.

45 Unlike the first assumption, the second is implicit. Had Sahlins and Service made it explicit, they would presumably have modified their evolutionary scheme, for they cannot in general be accused of misunderstanding the nature of either tribes or states.

46 The much later Aztecs are obviously irrelevant to this question (*pace* Adams, *Evolution of Urban Society*).

47 For a convenient survey of Mesopotamian influence on Egypt, see W. A. Ward, 'Relations between Egypt and Mesopotamia from prehistoric times to the end of the Middle Kingdom', *Journal of the Economic and Social History of the Orient*, vol. 7, 1964, which goes so far as to have the (here Syrian) bearers of this influence invade Egypt and set up the First Dynasty all while denying that Mesopotamian influence played a formative role in Egyptian state-formation. Its (once widely accepted) role as a catalyst is also brushed aside by J. J. Jansen, 'The early state in Ancient Egypt', in H. J. M. Claessen and P. Skalník, eds, *The Early State*, The Hague, Paris and New York, Mouton, 1978, pp. 217f.

be applicable to Sumeria, where states emerged before anywhere else in the world; and it is precisely here that it fails.

It fails, that is, if we choose to forget our scholarly qualms; it might well be argued that so little evidence is extant that no verdict is possible. But if we venture to argue with reference to such evidence as survives, it is clear that we can only endow the Sumerians with a tribal past by making it axiomatic that they *must* have had such a past. Obviously, if the so-called conical clan is a *sine qua non* for the growth of states, then the growth of the state in Sumeria *ipso facto* proves that the conical clan had been prevalent there; and if so, it makes good sense to attribute a maximal sense of 'lineage' or 'clan' to the Sumerian word for 'family', to see 'incomplete' kin groups as residues of larger and more inclusive kin organizations, and to suppose that 'kin affiliation played an important role even in many cases where it is not attested.'[48] But if we use the evidence to test the axiom rather than the axiom to make sense of the evidence, then the conical clan disappears together with practically all other evidence for inclusive kinship structures.[49] What remains is evidence for extended families with joint rights in family property,[50] but not for descent groups of any great size or depth[51] or for kinship groups

48 Adams, *Evolution of Urban Society*, chapter 3, with reference to P. Kirchhoff, 'The principles of clanship in human society', in M. H. Fried, ed., *Readings in Anthropology*, New York, Thomas Y. Crowell, 1959, vol. II, p. 268, as far as the conical clan (viz. a clan stratified on the basis of seniority) is concerned.

49 This is not meant as a criticism of Adams's approach which is, as he says, contextual rather than textual. It is extremely interesting to see scrappy evidence ordered in the light of a conjectural context, and Adams is remarkably good at indicating just how conjectural his reconstruction is. But the evidence cannot be said to vindicate, or even to suggest, the context proposed.

50 Cf. I. M. Diakonoff, 'Sale of land in Pre-Sargonic Sumer', in *Papers Presented by the Soviet Delegation at the XXIII International Congress of Orientalists*, Moscow, Publishing House of USSR Academy of Sciences, 1954 (followed by Adams, *Evolution of Urban Society*, pp. 83f.), and other publications by the same author, practically all listed in the editorial note to idem, 'Socio-economic classes in Babylonia and the Babylonian concept of social stratification', in Edzard, *Gesellschaftsklassen*, p. 41; I. Gelb, 'Household and family in Early Mesopotamia', in E. Lipiński, ed., *State and Temple Economy in the Ancient Near East*, Leuven, Department oriëntalistiek Katholieke Universiteit Leuven, 1979, vol. I, pp. 68ff.

51 The evidence comes mainly in the form of contracts of sale in which relatives appear as co-sellers: Gelb counts the kin group as large when the co-sellers number five or more ('Household and family', p. 69). According to Diakonoff, we hear of up to 600 co-sellers ('Sale of land', p. 28; repeated by Adams, *Evolution of Urban Society*, p. 84), but this rests on a tendentious interpretation of the so-called Maništušu obelisk, in which small clusters of related co-sellers do indeed appear, but in which the 600 men referred to by Diakonoff are not among them (cf. the very different interpretation of this text by L. W. King, *A History of Sumer and Akkad*, London, Chatto & Windus, 1910, pp. 206ff.; followed by C. J. Gadd, 'The cities of Babylonia', in *Cambridge Ancient History*, vol. I, part 2, Cambridge, Cambridge University Press, 3rd. edn, 1970, pp. 448ff.; for an attempt to reconstruct the kinship structure of what was by then Akkadian rather than Sumerian society on the basis of this text, see Gelb, 'Household and family', pp. 73f., 81ff.).

of any kind endowed with political functions.[52] There is in fact no sense in Sumerian history that kinship structures of one kind or another had to be broken in order for a specialized political agency to emerge, or that modified versions thereof retained political influence thereafter. No descent groups comparable with the *phylai* of the Athenians served to divide the populations of Uruk, Nippur or Kish into citizens and metics;[53] no vestigial age organization comparable with that of the Spartans can be shown to have survived. There was no use of genealogy to express political relationships,[54] no ranking on the basis of descent, no pride in pure, high or freeborn birth, no stress on honour or the sacred duty to assist one's kinsfolk.[55] There is no trace of a concept of homicide as a loss to a group,[56] nor is there any literature, be it mythological, epical or other, on the theme of feuds and private vengeance.[57] In short the Sumerians come across as singularly *lacking* in a tribal past.

52 A more cautious formulation would be that the philological foundations for an opinion either way scarcely exist, and that non-specialists are particularly badly placed to decide whether a certain term is a kinship term or otherwise. But some of the arguments adduced by anthropologically-minded Akkadianists have a well-worn quality to them: animal names of early rulers and animal emblems of early cities are supposed to be evidence of past totemism, etc. (cf. Gelb, 'Household and family', p. 94). Animal names of Arab tribes were likewise once supposed to be evidence of a totemistic past, but who believes that now?

53 When Gelb compared the semi-free *gurus* class with Roman glebae adscripti, English serfs *and* Greek metics, he had simply misunderstood the nature of metics (I. J. Gelb, 'Social stratification in the Old Akkadian Period', in *Proceedings of the XXV International Congress of Orientalists*, Moscow, 1962–3, vol. I, p. 226. It is clear from the Akkadianization of lower Iraq that Semitic newcomers to Sumerian cities were not relegated to a special status; indeed, their integration seems to have been accomplished with minimal friction; cf. T. Jacobsen, 'The assumed conflict between Sumerians and Semites in Early Mesopotamian history', *Journal of the American Oriental Society*, vol. 59, 1939, reprinted in his *Towards the Image of Tammuz and Other Essays on Mesopotamian History and Culture*, Cambridge, Mass., Harvard University Press, 1970; cf. also the more recent discussion in *IX. Rencontre Assyriologique Internationale*: 'Aspects du contact suméro-akkadien', Geneva, Musée d'art et d'histoire, 1960.

54 For example vis-à-vis the tent-dwelling Martu (Amorites), who are not perceived as a descent group at all (G. Bucellati, *The Amorites of the Ur III Period*, Naples, Istituto Orientale di Napoli, 1966, pp. 330ff.). In general, the Sumerians do not provide much evidence of awareness of ethnicity (cf. H. Limet, 'L'étranger dans la société sumérienne', in Edzard, *Gesellschaftsklassen*).

55 Cf. the myth in which Inanna induces Enki to give her all the fundamental institutions of Sumerian civilization: the long list of her acquisitions includes basic aspects of human society such as sexual intercourse, speech, adornment, rectitude and eldership, but not knowledge of ancestry, genealogical purity, kinship solidarity or the like. (S. N. Kramer, 'Aspects of Mesopotamian society. Evidence from the Sumerian literary sources', in H. Klengel, ed., *Beiträge zur sozialen Struktur des alten Vorderasiens*, Berlin, Akademie-Verlag, 1971, p. 9).

56 Cf. Jacobsen, 'An Ancient Mesopotamian Trial for Homicide', in his *Tammuz*, p. 209; compare idem, 'The myth of Inanna and Bilulu', ibid., p. 55.

[*See page 60 for n. 57*]

Even if we postulate that the Sumerians originated as tribesmen, the evidence is incompatible with the view that tribal chiefs played a crucial role in their transition to statehood. Whichever type of chief we propose as the starting point, chiefdoms develop into states through the gradual accumulation of power in the hands of the chief and his entourage on the one hand, and gradual differentiation of society in socio-economic and political terms on the other. But in Sumeria it was the *gods* who accumulated power, and it was their demands, not those of a chief, priest or other human being, which caused society to be reorganized and differentiated. Sumerian mythology repeatedly states that the gods created man in order to escape the hard work of looking after themselves;[58] and because all human beings were equal in their bondage to the gods, human society was remarkably egalitarian. Political decision-making rested in an assembly composed of all male adult members of the city-state.[59] The gods at any rate reached all decisions of a public nature in such assemblies, and since the myths describe a mode of decision-making well attested for other peoples at a comparable stage of political evolution, it makes sense to assume with Jacobsen that the divine assemblies mirror those of the Sumerians themselves in Pre-Dynastic times.[60] By Early Dynastic times the assembly had come to be subdivided into one of elders and another of townsmen, while at the same time its role had been reduced to that of ratifying or vetoing royal decisions;[61] and though it survived as a judicial and municipal institution, it would appear soon to have lost all control of royal politics.[62] In

---

57 In this respect the Gilgamesh epic is strikingly different from other heroic literature, be it Greek, Germanic or Icelandic.

58 C. J. Gadd, *Ideas of Divine Rule in the Ancient East*, London, Oxford University Press, 1948, pp. 5f.; idem, 'Cities of Babylonia', p. 101.

59 T. Jacobsen, 'Primitive democracy in Ancient Mesopotamia', *Journal of Near Eastern Studies*, vol. 2, 1943; idem, 'Early political development in Mesopotamia', *Zeitschrift für Assyriologie*, vol. 52, 1957 (both reprinted in his *Tammuz*); cf. also G. Evans, 'Ancient Mesopotamian assemblies', *Journal of the American Oriental Society*, vol. 78, 1958.

60 Jacobsen wonders whether women were once members of the assemblies too with reference to Inanna's participation in divine deliberations, but this seems unlikely. Being a goddess, Inanna was powerful, viz. endowed with male prerogatives, and there is no general sense of female participation in the myths.

61 This statement is based on a single source, viz. the story of 'Gilgamesh and Agga' in which Gilgamesh seeks the consent of the elders for warfare against Kish; the elders withhold their consent, whereupon Gilgamesh convenes the men of the city, who overrule the elders (cf. Jacobsen, 'Primitive democracy', pp. 165f.; there is a full translation by Kramer in J. B. Pritchard, ed., *Ancient Near Eastern Texts Relating to the Old Testament*, Princeton, Princeton University Press, 2nd edn, 1955, pp. 44ff.). It is of course impossible to make any firm statements about the division of power between king and assembly on the basis of so limited material, but that there was a division is clear.

62 Cf. Jacobsen, 'Ancient Mesopotamian trial for homicide', p. 204; I. M. Diakonoff, 'On the structure of Old Babylonian society', in Klengel, *Beiträge*, pp. 20, 22f.

other words, it was *after* the creation of city-states that power began to accumulate in the hands of kings and retainers to the exclusion of the masses: chiefs were the outcome of the transition to statehood, not its initiators.

Economically, too, society was egalitarian, Just as it was the gods rather than their slaves who had power, so it was the gods rather than their slaves who owned land. Each city was the personal estate of the god to which it had been assigned on the creation of man,[63] or in other words all city land was owned by the temple. This is admittedly an unfashionable thesis these days, but though it cannot be defended in terms of the evidence originally adduced in its favour, it can scarcely be said to have been refuted.[64] It is generally agreed that the temple had become a large-scale enterprise already before 3,000 BC and that by the third millenium BC its functions included the co-ordination of major projects such as irrigation work, the organization of corvées in general, the production of metal and textile goods, the conduct of long-distance trade, the exchange of commodities within the city itself, as well as the maintenance of widows, orphans, cripples and others unable to look after themselves.[65] It is also agreed that it was a substantial, but not the only landowner at the end of the Early Dynastic period, about 2,400 BC. The question is thus what starting point we postulate: had temple holdings expanded in the period from the emergence of the temple to the end of the Pre-Dynastic Period, or had they contracted? Most scholars now hold them to have expanded: temple and state supposedly developed in tandem at the cost of tribes, clans, lineages and/or self-governing peasant communities to the point that they were in joint political and economic control of the city by about 2,400 BC; temple and state, in short, were different manifestations of the same oppressive powers which appropriate land from peasants or collectivize it at their expense.[66] But temple and state did not develop in tandem. Theoretically, the

---

63 Gadd, 'Cities of Babylonia', p. 101.

64 For a helpful introduction to the controversy, see B. Foster, 'A new look at the Sumerian temple state', *Journal of the Economic and Social History of the Orient*, vol. 24, 1981, which drives a few more nails into the coffin of the temple-state theory as originally proposed; for the alternative (but no less controversial) views which are now being debated, see G. Komoróczy, 'Zu den Eigentumsverhältnissen in der altbabylonischen Zeit: das Problem der Privatwirtschaft', in Lipiński, *State and Temple Economy*, vol. II.

65 Cf. the convenient summary by C. C. Lamberg-Karlovsky, 'The economic world of Sumer', in Schmandt-Besserat, *Legacy of Sumer*, p. 63.

66 Thus the writings of Gelb and Diakonoff (Diakonoff and other Soviet scholars being adherents of the *obščina*); see for example Gelb's evolutionary scheme referred to above, n. 43, and I. M. Diakonoff, 'Socio-economic classes in Babylonia and the Babylonian concept of social stratification', in Edzard, *Gesellschaftsklassen* (with comments by Gelb and others).

city belonged to the god, not to the king, and the temple became a large-scale enterprise at a time when kings barely existed. It is legitimate to assume that divine ownership was originally taken as literally as was the divine need for food, drink, clothing and housing; and the temple can scarcely have acquired its predominant administrative position without owning so much of the land that we may as well postulate that they began by owning all of it. In short, non-temple land arguably only appeared on the development of royal power, perhaps coupled with expansion into new areas.[67] Now Soviet scholars see very well that just as kings were eating away at an egalitarian political structure, so they were eating away at an egalitarian economic organization, but what they do not see is that the *temple* was the institution on which this egalitarianism rested.[68] Yet it was precisely because all were slaves of the god that all were equal;[69] and egalitarianism survived as long as the *en* or *ensi* remained a mere steward on behalf of the divine overlord while at the same time the *lugal* remained a temporary warleader.[70] But inevitably the temple organization, once set up, created that differential access to strategic resouces which spelled the end of socio-economic equality while at the same time the escalating warfare between the cities created a

67 The crucial problem here is accounting for a number of early contracts of land sale to which both Diakonoff and Gelb have called attention (cf. above, n. 51). Practically all involve kings and their associates; indeed the only information we have about one early king is that he sold land (D. O. Edzard, 'Problèmes de la royauté dans la période présargonique', in P. Garelli, ed., *Le Palais et la royauté*, Paris, Paul Geuthner, 1974, p. 143). But though one could easily account for kings using their position to sell off temple land (which was supposed to be inalienable), kings and others do not just sell, but also buy land, and it is on this basis that Diakonoff has constructed his picture of a beleaguered village community. The contracts raise two fundamental questions, viz. where in relation to the city-state were these lands located, and to what extent were the sales genuine sales as opposed to labour and service agreements in (what to us appears as) disguise? After all, a Sumerian contract of sale is not necessarily endowed with the same meaning as a Roman one. To the best of my knowledge, the excitement of seeing land being sold has been such that neither question has been even raised.

68 'If nothing but royal (or temple) land and royal (or temple) servants existed in the south of Mesopotamia until the establishment of Semitic domination, then any mention of self-government organs there becomes enigmatic', as Diakonoff remarks ('On the Structure of Old Babylonian society', pp. 19f.). Note the interchangeability of 'temple' and 'royal'. It does of course become enigmatic if we envisage temple and palace as twins, but this is precisely what we should not do.

69 Service does not see this point either: the political egalitarianism of the early city-states appears to him as a puzzling *departure* from pure theocracy (*Origins of the State*, p. 209).

70 Here we are getting into contentious matters. For an attractive account based on Jacobsen, see H. W. F. Saggs, *The Greatness that was Babylon*, London, Sidgwick & Jackson, 1962, pp. 37ff. (it is gratifying to see that Saggs sticks to the unfashionable theory of temple economy); for a more recent discussion, which is not incompatible with it, see Edzard, 'Royauté'.

need for more permanent and powerful kings. In the last resort the outcome of the venture was indeed a division of power and privilege between temple and state to the exclusion of the rest of the community after the fashion familiar from other pre-industrial societies, but what we are concerned with here is how it began. Clearly, it must have begun with slaves of the gods pooling their resources in order to perform the onerous task of providing their masters with the massive housing and regular quantities of food, drink and clothing required by the latter. The pooling may have created a society characterized by division of labour, but it was the temple which enabled it to diversify to the extraordinary degree characteristic of it already in myths.[71] In other words, socio-economic differentiation was achieved through the creation of a co-operative: of oppression there was plenty, but the oppression was divine. It is for this reason that even privileged persons such as merchants, scribes, stewards and priests were liable to corvée in historical times;[72] indeed, even the much later Assyrian king went through the formal act of carrying a basket of soil on his head.[73]

The first civilization in history was thus the product of religion, or in other words of imagination endowed with supreme authority. One suspects the same is true of the first civilization in America, for here too it begins with the erection of gigantic buildings totally devoid of use to man or beast from a purely material point of view.[74] Why the Sumerians should have conceived of their gods as they did may well be beyond explanation. Certainly, the need for co-operation in matters of irrigation explains nothing, as is now generally agreed.[75] It is not even obvious that it was developments among *agriculturalists* which were of decisive importance. For temple-building in Mesopotamia starts at Eridu, a city built on virgin soil;[76] and whether or not the inhabitants of Eridu were Sumerians, this is where Sumerian history has its roots, as the Sumerians themselves may be said to have conceded by identifying

---

71 When Inanna made off with the basic institutions of Sumerian civilization, her acquisitions included the crafts of the woodworker, metalworker, leatherworker, smith, mason, basket-weaver and scribe (Kramer, 'Aspects of Mesopotamian society', p. 9). Sumerian has hundreds of terms for crafts and professions, as Gelb notes ('Approaches to the study of ancient society', *Journal of the American Oriental Society*, vol. 87, 1967, p. 7).

72 Gelb, *loc. cit.* (Gelb finds this strange in view of the degree of division of labour).

73 Saggs, *Babylon*, p. 169.

74 M. D. Coe, 'San Lorenzo and Olmec civilization' in E. P. Benson, ed., *Dumbarton Oaks Conference on the Olmecs*, Washington, Dumbarton Oaks Research Library and Collections, 1968.

75 See for example Lamberg-Karlovsky, 'Economic world of Sumer', p. 62.

76 M. E. L. Mallowan, 'The development of cities from al-ᶜUbaid to the end of Uruk 5', in *Cambridge Ancient History*, Cambridge, Cambridge University Press, 3rd edn, 1970, vol. I, part 1, p. 330.

Eridu as one of the five anti-diluvian cities, the first city in the world to which kingship descended from heaven, and the city from which Inanna made off with all the appurtenances of civilization for the benefit of Uruk.[77] Now at Eridu, where one temple after another was built on the same site, the remains of the food offered to the local god take the form of massive quantities of fishbones; Adapa, the Sumerian Adam who forfeited the chance of gaining immortality for humanity, was a fisherman doing 'the prescribed fishing for Eridu'; no less than 100 fishermen regularly delivered fish to a temple of secondary importance at Lagash; and a late chronicle explains the rise and fall of dynasties in terms of the punctuality or otherwise of kings with respect to the supply of fish to the supreme god.[78] Clearly there is a clue of some importance here to which practically no attention has been paid so far. Now the interest of fishermen lies in the fact that they are *hunters*, or in other words they are exactly the kind of people whom Sahlins and Service condemn to insignificance on the rise of the neolithic; but they are hunters of a peculiar kind in that they flourish as well under industrial conditions as they did in the palaeolithic: whereas the systematic breeding of plants began about 10,000 BC, the systematic breeding of fish has only begun to acquire importance today, after a hiatus of some 12,000 years. Fishermen are thus exceedingly archaic people capable of adapting to modern conditions, and one suspects that their role in the creation of Sumerian civilization is connected with this fact.

So much for the historical record. We may now turn to the reasons why Sahlins and Service's theory is wrong.[79] It is wrong partly because it has not been formulated with reference to the historical record, but more particularly because, as mentioned already, it rests on a mistaken assumption: tribe and state are not similar types or organization distinguished by their level of complexity, but on the contrary *alternative* forms of organization evolved in response to similar problems. The tribe does indeed represent a natural progression from the band. It differs from the band only in that it is larger, tighter and more complex, as Sahlins and Service say, or in other words in that more systematic use is being made of the embryonic differentiation which is given by nature.

77 T. Jacobsen, ed. and tr., *The Sumerian King-List*, Chicago, Chicago University Press, 1939, p. 71, cf. pp. 58ff.; and the reference given above, n. 55 (this myth is extremely well told by Saggs, *Babylon*, p. 36).

78 Mallowan, 'Development of cities', pp. 333ff.; Pritchard, *Ancient Near Eastern Texts*, p. 101; Gadd, 'Cities of Babylonia', p. 127, cf. p. 126; H.-G. Güterbock, 'Die historische Tradition und ihre literarische Gestaltung bei Babyloniern und Hethitern bis 1200', *Zeitschrift für Assyriologie*, vol. 42, 1934, pp. 54f., 56f.

79 It is worth stressing that Service's theory is no more correct in its revised version than in its original form (cf. above, n. 42).

But spinning highly elaborate social systems out of elementary differences in respect of sex, age and kinship does not amount to a shot at state structures for the simple reason that state structures do not rest on these differences at all. On the contrary, in opting for more systematic use of biologically based differences tribal societies acquire a vested interest in minimizing social differentiation. They may not of course be able to prevent material developments and/or external stimuli from generating such differentiation; but on the one hand they have in-built mechanisms for counteracting such developments,[80] and on the other hand they will respond to such differentiation as cannot be avoided by further elaboration of the biologically based roles.[81] Naturally differentiation may proceed so far that the tribal organization simply bursts, but what matters is precisely that it has to *burst*: the tribal organization does not itself have any dynamic potential.[82] Bands do not have to be destroyed in order for tribes to emerge, but tribes do have to be destroyed in order to make way for states. Behind Sahlins and Service's theory lie the Polynesian chiefdoms of Hawaii and Tahiti, and here socio-economic and political differentiation did indeed proceed so far that states could *almost* be said to have existed.[83] Sahlins and Service clearly assume that proper states would sooner or later have emerged of their own accord if the Polynesians had been left alone, and maybe they would have; but in historical fact it took exposure to the Europeans to wrench these chiefdoms off their tribal moorings, as Sahlins himself concedes.[84] Whether states would or would not have developed on their own, however, the dynamic potential of the Polynesian chiefdoms did not lie in the local version of tribal organization (the famous conical clan), but on the contrary in religion. Had the Polynesian gods been more demanding, temple-building might well have generated new social and political roles here as it did in Sumeria;[85] but for one reason or another they were too complacent. One suspects that they were too complacent precisely *because* a perfectly satisfactory tribal system existed; differently put, one suspects that state structures emerged

---

80 Such as periodic redistribution of land, generosity, potlatches or simply exclusion (after the fashion of smiths in bedouin and other societies).

81 E.g. by ranking in accordance with descent and/or seniority.

82 A point seen by Fried, 'On the concepts', p. 17.

83 See for example H. J. M. Claessen, 'Early state in Tahiti' in Claessen and Skalník, *The Early State*.

84 Sahlins, *Tribesmen*, p. 92; cf. I. Goldman, 'The evolution of Polynesian societies', in A. Howard, ed., *Polynesia, Readings in a Culture Area*, Scranton, London and Toronto, Chandler, 1971 (repr. from S. Diamond, ed., *Culture in History: Essays in Honor of Paul Radin*, New York, Columbia University Press, 1960).

85 Cf. Claessen, 'Tahiti', p. 446.

among the Sumerians all the more easily in that no tribal organization had been developed.

Sahlins and Service's theory raises a fundamental question about the manner in which human society has evolved. It should be clear from what has been said that the tribe (still generically speaking) is a far more obvious solution to the problem of social organization above the familial level than is the state. Human beings easily learn to regulate their behaviour with reference to features which are inherent in themselves, plainly visible or partly so[86] and seemingly given by nature, as may be inferred not only from the constant use which has been made of such features throughout human history, but also from the difficulty with which they are abandoned when they cease to be required: even under industrial conditions people take that plainly visible assembly of features which used to be subsumed under the label of 'race' as a social signal unless they have been specifically trained to ignore it. By contrast the state is an organization based on concepts which are external to people, devoid of visibility and highly unnatural except insofar as sex differences, heredity and the like are allowed to overlay them: a great deal of cultural brainwashing is required in order for *polis*, class or bureaucracy to appear as if given by nature. The discovery that people could be organized with reference to external concepts (viz. the gods and their impersonal successors) was a breakthrough of the same magnitude and the same fatefulness as the neolithic revolution which preceded it and the industrial revolution which was to follow; and the fundamental question which it raises is whether or in what sense one breakthrough can be said necessarily to have led to the next. The fact that plants were domesticated in both Asia and America, at different times but nonetheless at times for which the possibility of diffusion is ruled out, and that in both cases the sequel was the emergence of state structures, evidently suggests a certain inevitability about human history, and this inevitability is built into most evolutionary theories.[87] But it is surely a no less striking fact that the vast majority of hunters did not invent agriculture, that the vast majority of those who borrowed agriculture did not proceed to invent the state, and that the vast majority of those who adopted state structures did not develop in a direction from which industrialization was likely to ensue. In all three cases the *mainstream* development was one towards stability at the new level, and this is as might be expected: after all, the whole of human history may be

---

86 Kinship is not very visible, and it is precisely for this reason that it is more open to cultural development than either sex or age. Still, it is observable that a woman has children and accordingly that her sons are brothers.

87 The fact that industrialism was only invented once is no objection given that its very invention made the process of diffusion almost instantaneous.

summarized as a futile attempt to devise a perfect adaptation to whatever material and cultural environment has existed at any given time. In other words, the breakthroughs were made by people who had somehow *not* participated in the mainstream development:[88] in the case of the Sumerians, by people who had apparently not developed the tribal structures which the neolithic had made so important. Every breakthrough was a precondition for the next, but the next was not its natural outcome, or it was its natural outcome only in the sense that every possibility will be realized given infinite time. The parallel developments in Asia and America show that human beings were statistically more likely to invent agriculture and states than are monkeys of inadvertently typing out Shakespearean plays; but there is nonetheless a freakish quality to all the great advances, as has been noted before.[89] It is because the great advances do *not* represent natural outcomes of earlier developments that band, tribe, chiefdom, state and the numerous variations thereof cannot be ordered along a single evolutionary line, or in other words that mainstream solutions have time and again turned out to be evolutionary dead ends. By the same token, it may be noted, there is something woodenheaded about the current distrust of diffusionism; for if breakthroughs are freakish, they are *ipso facto* unlikely to have been made independently time and again.[90] Would Egypt have developed into a state (as opposed, say, to a tribal chiefdom) if it had not been exposed to Mesopotamian influence?[91] Have states actually been *invented* in any

88 This is not of course to say that those who did not participate in mainstream developments invariably proceeded to make breakthroughs. The majority must have lost out then as later.

89 See for example Service, *Cultural Evolutionism*, chapter 3, for an eloquent account of the discontinuous nature of evolution.

90 Anti-diffusionism began its career as a healthy reaction against the assumption that tracing the cultural origins of a phenomenon amounted to explaining it, but we are surely past having to argue against this assumption by now. What is more, the reaction soon became an over-reaction. Steward, for example, wondered whether diffusion could seriously distort the 'natural' regularity of change: 'one may fairly ask whether each time a society accepts diffused culture, it is not an independent recurrence of cause and effect' (*Culture Change*, p. 182). This is an odd suggestion: are we really to take it that the arrival of factories in Somalia or Tibet constitutes an independent recurrence of industrialization in Britain? Given that we live in a time at which diffusion is rapidly changing the face of the earth, it might be wiser to give some thought to the phenomenon than to persist in belittling its significance.

91 'It is perhaps because we can ascribe a Mesopotamian origin to the most startling and sudden development – massive monuments with niched façades – that Mesopotamia appears to be the motivating force behind the seemingly abrupt appearance of the historic age in Egypt', as Ward puts it ('Relations between Egypt and Mesopotamia', p. 134). So indeed. For if massive monuments with niched façades were instrumental in the emergence of civilization in Sumeria, it is hard not to infer that it was a Sumerian idea which chiefs of one kind or another put to their own use in Egypt.

part of the world apart from Mesopotamia and Meso-America? It is hard to believe that pristine state formation in the true sense of the word has taken place more than twice.[92]

The reason why Sahlins and Service's theory has such instinctive appeal is that *secondary* state formation has more often than not involved a transition from tribe to state: we are all familiar with the reality behind the model. Given that the tribe represents the mainstream solution, whereas the state represents an isolated one which turned out to be infinitely more powerful, it is not surprising that the majority of mankind has been forced sooner or later to make a transition from the one to the other; and this process has indeed in many cases (though by no means always) involved the emergence of chiefs and kinglets, who have hammered away at the autarkic societies underneath them in an attempt to destroy the autonomy and self-sufficiency of the building blocks, and who have been forced to shed blood on a lavish scale by the very fact that tribes and states are diametrically opposed types of organization.[93] But it would of course be a fatal mistake to argue that the manner in which state structures have spread after their invention reduplicates that in which they originated.[94]

Tribes and States: the Nomadic Exception

Turning now to the relationship between tribes and states after their emergence, there can hardly be much dispute about the fact that the superiority of state structures over tribal ones has caused tribal societies to retreat to the point where they have practically disappeared today. It is accordingly difficult to accept Fried's proposition that tribes should

92 The useful distinction between pristine and secondary state formation was introduced by M. H. Fried, 'On the evolution of social stratification and the state', in Diamond, *Culture in History*, p. 713: pristine states are those which developed out of local conditions and not in response to pressures emanating from an already highly organized but separate political entity, whereas secondary states are those which developed in response to pressures, direct or indirect, from existing states. Differently put, pristine states are those for which state structures actually had to be invented, whereas secondary states are those for which they merely had to be adopted. Fried discusses the number of pristine states and considers (but does not favour) the possibility that there were only two, one in the Old World and one in the New, in his *The Evolution of Political Society*, New York, Random House, 1967, pp. 231ff.

93 Cf. A. I. Gurevich, 'The early state in Norway', and L. A. Sedov, 'Angkor: society and state', both in Claessen and Skalník, *The Early State*, for two examples from very different parts of the world.

94 Similarly the evolution of industrialism in its area of birth is quite different from its propagation in new lands, as Service lucidly explains (*Cultural Evolutionism*, p. 44). But the sheer fact that states emerged so long ago makes us apt to ignore this fact in practice.

be seen as the *result* of state formation.[95] Fried is of course right that states have frequently triggered the formation of new political communities among stateless societies by their appointment and/or recognition of chiefs, by their threat to engulf the societies in question, and by their provision of new resources of both a material and an ideological kind; and there is a case to be made for the view that tribes in the specific sense of the word are the outcome, at least in part, of prolonged exposure to superior powers.[96] But even if this is accepted, it is obvious that the response presupposes a starting point which must be labelled tribal in the wider sense of the word,[97] and that moreover it often heralds the end of tribalism altogether.[98] If tribal organization as such were an outcome of exposure to states, tribal groups should have been a transitory phenomenon everywhere except where the environment inhibits the transition to state structures. This is plainly not the case: how would Fried account for the tribal organization of Polynesia?[99] Generally speaking, it is plain that the state has undermined tribal organizations rather than created them.

Beyond this self-evident point, however, the historical relationship between tribes and states is not amenable to easy summary, and the discussion which follows will accordingly be restricted to two particular subjects, the nomadic exception to the general rule on the one hand and the fate of tribal egalitarianism under conditions of statehood on the other.

Generally speaking, the superiority of state structures over tribal ones has caused tribes to disappear wherever the two have confronted each other. Nomads are an exception to this rule in that they have stuck to their tribal organization until recent times and in that every now and again they have proved tribes to be vastly superior.

The reasons why nomads have stuck to their tribal organization are not far too seek. In fact the reader will find them in Khazanov's *Nomads*

95 Fried, 'On the concepts', pp. 15ff. Apparently he has developed this idea in idem, *The Notion of Tribe*, Menlo Park, Cal., Cummings Publ. Co., 1975, but this book does not seem to be available in Britain.

96 Cf. below, n. 103.

97 Fried would scarcely deny this; but since his paper is out to demolish the concept of tribe, it is far from clear what he means by the term when he starts to work with it.

98 Thus obviously in the case of all the modern examples adduced by Fried; similarly in that adduced by Southall, 'Illusion of tribe', pp. 33f.

99 One assumes that there is an answer to this question in the inaccessible book, but it is difficult to guess what it might be. It would hardly be possible to deny that the Polynesians had tribal organization given that their organization (unlike that of the Melanesians) could even be qualified as tribal in the specific sense of the word. Nor would it be possible to claim that this organization was a response to the arrival of the very Europeans who first described it: description was instantaneous whereas a response of the order in question would require considerable time.

and the Outside World, a magisterial work from which it emerges that nomads are doomed to tribalism by the very environment to which they have adapted.[100] They exploit land which is marginal or wholly useless to agriculturalists and which is suitable for stock-breeding only on condition of seasonal migration; the carrying capacity of such land is limited, while at the same time the proceeds of stock-breeding fluctuate wildly under nomadic conditions, so that nomadic populations are necessarily small, widely dispersed, poor and incapable of accumulating the stable surpluses required for the maintenance of states.[101] Since their poverty, mobility and forbidding territories also make them unattractive to external powers, they have generally avoided forcible absorption into foreign states and indeed retained their tribal organization even when their pastures happened to be located within state domains. However, many nomads have found themselves in areas too far away from states and/or bred animals too devoid of military potential to play a major role in history; but as ecology would have it, the nomads who exploited the pastures in the vicinity of the great empires of the pre-industrial world were also the nomads who bred (among other things) swift riding animals which gave them military striking power.[102] Whether in response to their neighbourhood with states and/or to the type of animal they bred, these were also the nomads who were tribally organized in the specific sense of the word, or in' other words nomads with well-developed political communities.[103] We thus have a situation in which two highly developed societies, but highly developed in diametrically opposed directions, coexist and interact; im short, we have the situation in which a contest between the two is likely to occur.

100　Khazanov, *Nomads*, pp. 69ff, 152ff. (for the full reference, see above, n. 16).

101　But Khazanov, *Nomads*, p. 152, nonetheless explains both the periodic emergence of nomad polities *and* their instability with reference to the contradiction between the political need for unity and the economic need for freedom of action. It is hard to believe that this contradiction (which is not explored) was of decisive importance.

102　History would have been very different if Central Asia had happened to be suitable for the herding of reindeer rather than horses, Arabia for the herding of cattle rather than camels.

103　According to Khazanov, the political integration of nomads is related above all to their relations with the outside world (*Nomads*, pp. 148ff, 169ff.). But the large territories required for the herding of camels and horses and the intensity of raiding and warfare which they entail must have been factors of comparable importance, and Khazanov's analysis of the low degree of political integration among reindeer pastoralists (esp. p. 172) does not suggest that internal factors mostly played 'a secondary and attendant role' (pp. 151f). The factors behind the 'upper levels of socio-political organization', viz. the nature of the tribal organization itself, are surely not identical with those behind the periodic emergence of nomadic chiefdoms and states. (Both seem to be subsumed under the label of 'political tribalism'.) Nomad relations with the outside world no doubt played a role in both, but it is only with regard to the second that Khazanov's insistence on their overriding importance convinces.

It is by no means obvious that the nomads should at times have been able to win this contest. It is true that, being mobile, they could avail themselves of settled wealth from time to time, and that their tribal organization gave them a healthy contempt for 'slaves' (a 'slave' being anyone unable to defend himself, be he a slave, a civilian subject of a state or a weak member of tribal society). But their raids notwithstanding, they were frequently pitiful creatures dependent on their imperial neighbours for subsidies, food distributions and the like, not to mention trade.[104] Here as elsewhere, however, imperial governments were apt to trigger the formation of higher political units, including embryonic states, by their very interference in tribal affairs; and since the empires had wealth which the tribesmen both coveted as individuals and needed as members of a novel polity dependent on stable resources, the outcome of state formation among nomads, as among other tribesmen, was usually an attempt at conquest of imperial lands. This is not surprising. What is surprising is the sudden conversion of pitiful creatures into conquerors on a sometimes gigantic scale:[105] the Arabs conquered the civilized world from Spain to India, destroying one empire in the process and severely mutilating another, in some 50 years, while the Mongols destroyed states of every kind from eastern Europe to Burma, narrowly missing the conquest of Egypt in the west and Japan in the east, in less than a century. What was the key to their strength?

The answer to this question takes us to the fundamental difference between tribes and states. As Cohen notes, the superiority of the state over other forms of organization lies in its ability to co-ordinate human activity for a common goal and to expand without constant liability to fission;[106] but it acquires this ability at a cost. The common goal which the state pursues is a public one which, given the differentiated nature of the society it rules, is unlikely to coincide with the private aims of every one or even the majority of its subjects; some, usually the majority, of its subjects must accordingly be coerced, and under pre-industrial conditions most are completely excluded from participation in decision-making. A state, especially a pre-modern state, is thus incapable of swift and efficient translation of policy into action. Action is impeded by the very size of its coercive apparatus, by the sheer amount of coercion it has

104 For the various ways in which nomads have been dependent on settled societies, see Khazanov, *Nomads*, pp. 212ff.

105 They have not of course always invaded societies as members of a state, and even state formation did not always, or even usually, lead to conquest on a gigantic scale. For a historical survey of nomadic state formation and its consequences, see Khazanov, *Nomads*, chapter 5.

106 R. Cohen, 'Introduction', in R. Cohen and E. R. Service, eds, *Origins of the State*, Philadelphia, Institute for the Study of Human Issues, 1978, p. 4.

to do, and by the proliferation of private interests of all kinds in and around it. By contrast a tribe has no coercive apparatus and everybody participates in decision-making; as a result disunity prevails: human activity cannot be coordinated on a large scale, and fission is a normal part of the political process. But if an entire tribal society were to acquire a sense of common purpose, it is obvious that it would be able to co-operate without coercion *and* without liability to fission, or in other words that its very primitivity would give it a huge advantage over the state. This sounds like a utopian thought, and usually it has been; but it is precisely what has happened on a greater or lesser scale from time to time, notably in the cases of the Arabs and the Mongols.

How and why it has happened is a historical question which cannot be answered here, if at all, but it is clear that both nomadic mobility and tribal lack of differentiation were necessary conditions: for it is only when members of a society are in easy contact with each other and structurally identical, or nearly so, that they can have a truly common purpose, or in other words one in which private and public aims coincide. It stands to reason that no society is so undifferentiated or homogeneous as to be devoid of divergent interests, and the creation of a sense of common purpose required coercion and bloodshed in the case of Arabs and Mongols alike.[107] But it did not require *continuous* coercion. Utterly disunited peoples were suddenly transformed as if by a magic wand into utterly united ones under a single leader whose embryonic state provided the overall co-ordination, but who relied on his followers to do the rest of their own accord. No coercive machinery had to be set in motion to raise troops, no politically abject populations had to be battered in order to pay for them, no interest groups of diverse kinds had to be overcome. Practically everyone participated, and practically everyone did so because his wishes were those of everyone else: the Arab tribesman who fought for himself fought for God because God represented the interests of the Arabs as individuals and as a collectivity alike.[108] In other words, nomadic conquerors can make optimum use of their human resources and translate policy into action without delay. It has often been noted that nomadic conquerors are physically unencumbered: they can travel through terrain in which regular armies are likely to perish, live off the land and their animals, and they have no need to defend their homeland. But they are socially unencumbered too,

107 Much more so in the case of the Mongols than in that of the Arabs, who had a greater sense of cultural unity and for whom the common purpose was presented in religious form (two factors likely to be related).

108 Cf. P. Crone, *Meccan Trade and the Rise of Islam* (forthcoming), Princeton, Princeton University Press, chapter 10. Since God told the Arabs to go and enrich themselves, the old question whether they fought for God or for booty is meaningless.

and it was this *social* ability to move fast and in unison which turned their physical mobility into so deadly an instrument.

Clearly, however, their strength was ephemeral. If they succeeded in acquiring imperial resources the character of their state would change,[109] and if they did not it would disintegrate. Either way they would lose the capacity to govern their tribal homeland, so that sooner or later two societies organized along diametrically opposed lines would once more coexist and interact with all the potential for conflict that this implies. It was only when state structures were finally established in the tribal homelands that this cycle was broken. In the *long* run tribes always proved inferior to states, the intense and highly destructive outbursts of energy on the part of nomads notwithstanding.

The Fate of Tribal Egalitarianism

Given that the tribe is an evolutionary dead end, what legacy has it left? More precisely (since this is too large a question), has the political egalitarianism, for which we today have the same esteem as did the tribesmen themselves, been able to survive under conditions of fully developed statehood? The answer to this question is basically no. The extent to which the tribal past of the Greeks contributed to the formation of the Greek city-state is highly disputed, but current scholarship does not favour Morgan's view (enthusiastically adopted by Engels) that Greek democracy should be seen as the child of tribal society.[110] It is not easy to ascertain whether tribal values played a

109 Both the Arabs and the Mongols continued to conquer after they had transferred their capitals from their tribal homelands to imperial centres; but they increasingly did so as wielders of coercive state machinery rather than as leaders of self-firing nomads, and in due course even this residual energy was lost.

110 Morgan, *Ancient Society*, chapters 8–10; F. Engels, *The Origin of the Family, Private Property and the State in the Light of the Researches of Lewis H. Morgan*, ed. E. B. Leacock, London, Lawrence and Wishart, 1972, chapters 4–5. Both make a comparable argument for Rome. That the emergence of republics characterized by greater or lesser degrees of mass participation in politics should be explained with reference to the tribal legacy of the peoples among whom they emerged is an attractive idea which makes good sense in the light of most conventional accounts of the formation of the city state; but it fails to survive exposure to D. Roussel, *Tribu et cité*, Paris, Les Belles Lettres, 1976 (cf. also F. Bourriot, *Recherches sur la nature du génos*, thesis, Lille and Paris 1976). There seems to be no way of disputing Roussel's conclusion that the tribal organization of the Greeks had disintegrated long before the emergence of the city-state. He does not deny that there are residues of such organization or that the Greeks were prone to think in kinship terms; but he decisively refutes the conventional view, crucial for Morgan's interpretation, that the descent groups known as *phylai* into which all city states were divided originated as genuine tribal groups. Snodgrass's objection that there is archaeological evidence of cultural units best identified as tribal ones in archaic Greece rests on the confusion

greater role in the emergence of the northern Indian republics in which
'everybody was a king', as hostile observers put it, and which
bequeathed their decision-making procedures to the Buddhist *sangha*.[111]
But the vast majority of tribal peoples have certainly lost their egalitarianism on their transition to statehood. Still, one people succeeded in
retaining it, with consequences of considerable interest today.

The Arabs are the only tribal conquerors to have caused the cultural
traditions of highly civilized peoples to be reshaped around their tribal
heritage, with the result that their tribal values were restated in a form
far transcending the narrow context in which they were born. They are
alive today in Islam. This is not to say that Arab egalitarianism survived
in political *practice*. On the contrary, as far as practice was concerned it
was doomed by the very enormity of the Arab conquests. No sooner was
the first wave of conquests over than the former convergence between
private and public aims gave way to quarrels over the division and
organization of the spoils. The upshot of these quarrels was a civil war
(656-61) in which the Arab state might well have disintegrated, but from
which it emerged instead in strengthened form, to assume an increasingly imperial appearance thereafter: within 100 years of the conquests
the bulk of the former conquerors had been as thoroughly excluded from
participation in decision-making as were their predecessors in the
Middle East. But the process of exclusion was accompanied by massive
protest.[112] The Umayyad dynasty which, after the end of the civil war,
transferred the capital from the tribal homeland to Syria, was accused of
having unlawfully monopolized power by making succession dynastic,
by refraining from equitable distribution of the proceeds of the
conquests, by failing to show respect for ancient norms and customs, by
turning communal leadership into autocracy where it should have been
theocracy,[113] thus making it tyranny on a par with that of the Byzantines
and Persians against whom the Arabs had fought in the name of God,
and in general by behaving as if of the opinion that 'the land is our land,
the property is our property, and the people are our slaves.'[114] In effect,

---

between cultural and political groupings which which the reader is by now familiar
(A. Snodgrass, *Archaic Greece*, London, Melbourne and Toronto, Dent, 1980, p. 26).

111 Cf. B. Law, *Some Kṣatriya Tribes of Ancient India*, Calcutta and Simla, Thacker,
Spink and Co., 1923.

112 What follows is based on P. Crone and M. Hinds, *God's Caliph: Religious Authority
in the First Centuries of Islam*, Cambridge, Cambridge University Press, 1986, chapter 6 and
passim.

113 Viz. *mulk* (literally 'kingship') rather than *khilāfa* (deputyship on behalf of God or,
classically, succession to the Prophet). I owe the felicitous rendering of this dichotomy as
autocracy versus theocracy to Dr F. W. Zimmermann.

114 Thus Abū Ḥamza al-Khārijī (Crone and Hinds, *God's Caliph*, appendix 3).

the Muslims were clamouring for a government which was both consultative and constitutional; and since another tribal legacy was activism, they fought hard enough for their ideal. Indeed, under different conditions they might well have succeeded.[115] But on the one hand nobody, not even the tribal aristocracy, had much leverage against a caliph endowed with resources so massive that his subjects were dependent on him for their income rather than the other way round;[116] and on the other hand it is unlikely that the caliphs could have preserved the political unity of their huge domains if they had agreed to the demands of their subjects.[117] (And had the political unity been lost at this early stage, the chances are that the Arabs would have been culturally absorbed and/or expelled.) In practical terms, then, the Muslims soon had to concede that autocracy had come to stay.

One might then have expected them to forget their egalitarian tradition. But the Muslims were not just heirs to a tribal past, they were also monotheists, namely adherents of an intrinsically egalitarian faith; and since their monotheist prophet had worked among tribes, their tribal and religious values reinforced and validated each other: there was no question of quietly forgetting either. Having lost the battle against what they perceived to be repressive government, they proceeded to reject their caliphs as illegitimate and to elaborate a charter of communal organization reflecting their own view of things; and eventually even the caliphs, in an effort to regain their moral standing, had to acknowledge this charter as the corner-stone of Islam. The charter in question is Islamic law, and it endorses and perpetuates the egalitarian tradition of the early Muslims in three major ways. First, the elaboration, transmission and interpretation of the charter all vest in the community, not in the head of state (the latter having no say in these matters except in his capacity of ordinary believer). Second, all free male (and to a large extent even female) adult members of the community are given practically the

---

115 The sense that the caliphate and, according to some, even governorships should be elective was so strong that under conditions of civil war one caliph (Yazīd III) and one governor (Naṣr b. Sayyār) endorsed it, the former undertaking to step down if he failed to execute the policies sketched out in his accession speech and the latter agreeing to participate in the nomination of electors charged both with the election of governors for a particular locality and with the formulation of the rules they were to follow (Crone and Hinds, *God's Caliph*, chapter 6).

116 Practically all taxes were paid by non-Muslims, not by Muslims, the ex-conquerors receiving a share of them in the form of stipends. The Umayyad caliphs are constantly being accused of iniquitous distribution of the revenues, not of iniquitous distribution of tax burdens.

117 It is hard to see how a political community of that size could have agreed on procedures for the election of caliphs and governors, organized such procedures, and survived the constant disruption which elective offices would have entailed.

same rights and duties.[118] And third, the head of state is given a minimal sphere of competence while at the same time his subjects are empowered to elect and, under specified conditions, to depose him.[119] In short, communal leadership ('right guidance') vests in an egalitarian community, and government is constitutional in the sense that the head of state is bound by rules (as Khomeini rightly observes[120]). Since, however, no machinery exists for the enforcement of these rules, it is constitutional in a purely nominal sense; but this is not to say that the charter was devoid of effect. On the one hand it rendered Islam incapable of validating the caliphal attempt to shape an Islamic empire, with the result that political unity was lost; and on the other hand it consolidated the moral link between Islam and the many tribes inside its domains, so that tribes were drawn into non-tribal politics on a scale unknown to the pre-Islamic Middle East.[121] In short, the preservation of the tribal tradition stood in the way of full moral acceptance of the state in its premodern form.[122] But in modern times the charter has paid off. Contrary to the claims of modern apologetes, Islam is not a democratic religion but it certainly is a *populist* religion;[123] and it is this, coupled with the fact

118 A few privileges in favour of Arabs survive, but they are of minor importance.

119 This is only true of Sunnī, not Shīʿite Islam. (The Shīʿites chose to beautify dynastic succession and absolutism by vesting the caliphate in descendants of the Prophet endowed with superhuman knowledge, an idea which proved as difficult to translate into practice as constitutionalism.) For one view of the rules of the game, see Y. Ibish, *The Political Doctrine of Al-Baqillani*, Beirut, American University of Beirut, Publication of the Faculty of Arts and Sciences, Oriental Series 44, 1966, chapter 4.

120 Rūḥ Allāh Khumaynī, *Islam and Revolution, Writings and Declarations of Imam Khomeini*, trans. H. Algar, Berkeley, Mizan Press, 1981, p. 55.

121 Gellner explains the importance of tribesmen in Muslim politics with reference to the relative weight of pastoralism and agriculture in the arid region (E. Gellner, *Muslim Society*, Cambridge, Cambridge University Press, 1981, p. 20); but where in the Middle East did tribesmen play a major role in non-tribal politics before the arrival of Islam? Certainly not in the Achaemenid and Sasanid empires, or in the eastern Mediterranean under Greek and Roman rule; they did not even do so in North Africa (on which Gellner's observations are based), though the North African adoption of Christianity led to some suggestive stirrings (the Donatist *circumcelliones*). Islam made a crucial difference, not only in that it gave townsmen and tribesmen a common idiom (cf. Gellner, ibid., p. 24; Christianity had done the same), but also in that this idiom originated in a tribal context and remained highly suitable for tribal use.

122 This argument is developed in Crone, *Slaves on Horses*.

123 *Vox populi* is *vox dei* to the extent that God's will is incarnate in a law elaborated and preserved by representatives of the community, but this does not give the *populus* a share in government, only in the definition of what it ought to be. If the Muslims had developed a machinery for the enforcement of the law vis-à-vis the sovereign, they would indeed have developed a form of government which could loosely be described as representative democracy, but this they did not. In legal theory the caliphate remained an elective office, but in legal theory too the election can be performed by one man: having made their statement of principle, the lawyers chose to draw its political teeth in order to prevent further dissension and bloodshed (the concern for the welfare and unity of the

that it is a *political* religion with a strong activist tradition, which explains why Islam, unlike other world religions, can be used to mobilize the masses for the creation of a modern state today.[124]

Islam thus highlights an affinity between the tribe and the modern state: both are avowedly egalitarian, both espouse mass participation. But it should be obvious that the one cannot be a short-cut to the other. The egalitarianism of tribes rests on the absence of social differentiation whereas that under conditions of statehood must be directly based thereupon; differently put, tribal egalitarianism rests on an even diffusion of power throughout the community, not on its concentration in a single agency, or in other words it rests on the very absence of a state. Their affinity notwithstanding, the tribe and the modern state represent two opposite ends of an organizational spectrum, and the transtition from the one to the other requires a development so complex that one end of the spectrum is likely to have been forgotten long before the other is even in sight. The pious hope of some political scientists that the presence of tribes in the Middle East may assist the cause of democracy in that region is not likely to be fulfilled. Generally speaking, the political values of tribesmen do not long outlive their tribal organization: those of the Arab conquerors would similarly have vanished if they had not fused with monotheism to become tenets of supreme and universal validity. But the fact that they did survive in a world religion is certainly of major historical and contemporary importance.

---

community being very strong indeed). They did not seek to place institutional checks on the exercise of power, but rather to withdraw as much of communal life as they could from its domains.

124 Cf. Gellner, *Muslim Society*, pp. 4f, 65, 67f. There is of course also a strong quietist tradition in Islam: from the ninth century onwards scholars increasingly exhorted the believers to live by the law and to endure such rulers as they had; and Imāmī Shīᶜism has more of a quietist baggage than any other version of Islam. But political activism represents the original pattern and is thus there for anyone to rediscover. What Khomeini rails against in his speeches on Islamic government is precisely the pattern whereby rulers rule as they see fit while religious scholars discuss ordinances 'of menstruation and parturition' and recite Qur'ānic verses which are never applied. Were religion and politics separate in the days of the Prophet? Did not the Prophet apply the law? Did not ᶜAlī make use of the sword? Islam came to establish order in society; it is the religion of militant individuals committed to truth and justice; no-one should passively await the imam of the age (Khumaynī, *Islam and Revolution*, section I). In terms of both style, temperament and ideas he has extraordinary affinities with the Khārijite preachers of the Umayyad period.

3

Soviets against Wittfogel: or, the Anthropological Preconditions of Mature Marxism

Ernest Gellner

V. N. Nikiforov, author of *Vostok i vsemirnaia istoria* (*The Orient and World History*, Moscow, Nanka, 1975), is a distinguished, erudite, scholarly, pugnacious, fair-minded and committed *Pyatchik*. I have coined the term Pyatchik, which is not good or acceptable Russian, to designate adherents of the view that the number five is crucial for the under-standing of human society and history, because there are five and only five stages of social evolution and hence five basic types of human society. The English word Fiver already has another colloquial meaning and sounds vaguely ironic. Quintist is possible but does not sound quite right either. Yet we do need the concept, so as to designate a theory that is important thrice over – on merit, for its historic significance, and for its current political role – and to identify those who uphold it. Among them Nikiforov clearly deserves a place of honour.

A number of intertwined yet separable issues are involved. Perhaps the most general among them is the opposition of Pyatism to Trinitar-ianism. I am myself a convinced Trinitarian and hold that thinkers such as Comte or Frazer or Polanyi were right when they claimed that mankind passes through three and only three fundamental stages in its development. Whether or not they correctly identified the stages is another matter. Three versus five is a crucial issue, within Marxism and outside it, and within and outside the Soviet Union. I strongly suspect

The first version of this chapter appeared in *Différences, valeurs, hiérarchie: Textes offerts à Louis Dumont*, ed. Jean-Claude Galey (Paris, Éditions de l'École des Hautes Études en Sciences Sociales, 1984). This version first appeared in *Theory and Society*, 14, 1985. We are grateful for permission to reprint.

Trinitarianism is the pervasive, tacit, but quite uncodified philosophy of history in the West at present; and it is also a very important, partly codified, and self-conscious strand within contemporary Russian thought, whether overt, implicit or covert. Ironically, it is just because Soviet Trinitarianism needs to define and defend itself vis-à-vis the orthodoxy of Pyatism that it is perhaps better, more clearly, and more consciously argued.[1]

In the West, substantive (as opposed to merely epistemological) philosophy of history, in other words the attempt to specify overall historical patterns, is highly unfashionable and suspect, and this may discourage attempts at defending one specific historical vision against others. The Trinitarianism that is nonetheless pervasive consequently remains implicit in the questions asked, rather than being overtly formulated. Such an under-the-carpet status is probably not conducive to lucid critical examination. One must wonder whether Trinitarianism is better off in the USSR, where it is lucid but politically suspect, or in the West, where it conflicts with an orthodoxy and remains nebulous in its formulations. Moreover, Western and Eastern Trinitarianism are not quite identical in what they uphold. If a Western Trinitarian sees world history as punctuated above all by the neolithic and industrial revolutions, Soviet scholars agree with this only as regards the latter break: in practice, they do indeed classify capitalist and socialist societies together, thus recognizing at least implicitly the genus 'industrial society'. But they diverge concerning the first great *coupure*, for they are still inclined to think in terms of a primordial communalism that is not necessarily or generally pre-agrarian. Ironically, it is the West that is more materialist in making the material mode of production, rather than the form of social organization, primary in determining historic periodization.

Pyatism is the doctrine that mankind or individual societies (all, most or some, indifferent formulations), or both, pass through five stages: the primitive-communal, slave-owning, feudal, capitalist, and finally socialist and communist. Pyatism can be attacked from a diversity of viewpoints, substantive and methodological. For instance, it is possible to deny the relevance of the idea of stages on the grounds that the self-perpetuation of every social structure has to be explained on its own terms, whereas its location within a wider evolutionary scheme – the

1 Western Trinitarianism has the form of pre-agrarian/agrarian/industrial. From a Marxist point of view, this is of course offensive insofar as capitalist and socialist societies are lumped together in a single stage. This can be avoided by means of a *quaternary* scheme, as for instance in G. A. Cohen, *Karl Marx's Theory of History: A Defence*, Oxford, Oxford University Press, 1978, esp. p. 198. But this quaternary scheme becomes a Trinitarian one if its final, quite hypothetical stage is subtracted.

identification of its predecessors and successors – adds *nothing* whatever to the explanation; or, alternatively, it is possible to deny unilinealism, the view that societies (most or all) pass through the same sequence of stages or social types, irrespective of what these may be.

The distinguished Soviet scholar Yuri Semenov, who has worked out a version of contemporary Russian Marxism that is significantly different from Nikiforov's, and who is one of the thinkers with whom Nikiforov polemicizes, has stressed with vigour and lucidity that the issues of Pyatism and unilinealism are independent. Pyatchiks must be unilinealists, but unilinealists need not be Pyatchiks. It is for instance possible to hold, as Semenov does, that a pan-global unilinealism, applicable to mankind as a totality rather than to single societies, is both essential for Marxism and valid, though the precise number of stages along that single line as well as their correct characterization remains open and can be debated within Marxism without affecting its essence.[2]

It is possible to accept both the idea of stages as such *and* unilinealism, but to deny the claim that the five-term scheme within Marxism correctly identifies the stages and the line of development. Trinitarians such as myself are, I suppose, both historicists and unilinealists, at a very abstract level, in that we hold the three stages to be inevitable and universal, but we part company with Pyatchiks on the matter of both identification and enumeration of the stages of the global line of development.

A Spectre is Haunting Marxism

Nikiforov's book is a passionate and richly orchestrated defence of orthodox Pyatism in general and against all comers; but it concentrates on one particular attack, namely that based on the alleged existence of one further stage, which a truly inspired typing error once specified as the Asiatic Motor Production. The view that there is a distinct Asiatic Mode of Production (henceforth AMP) can of course be used to undermine Pyatism in a number of different ways, among which the mere

2 Cf. Yu. I. Semenov, 'The theory of socio-economic formations and world history', in *Soviet and Western Anthropology*, ed. Ernest Gellner, London, Duckworth, 1980, 29–58, and Ernest Gellner, 'A Russian Marxist philosophy of history', ibid., 59–82. In a more recent work, Semenov reformulates the Asiatic Mode of Production thesis, but deliberately gives it a new and non-geographic name, and a very suggestive one – *politocracy*. In contrast to Nikiforov, he affirms that Marx never abandoned the idea, even in the least degree, but merely refrained from using the *term* when he realized that the social form it designated was also to be found outside Asia. See Semenov's chapter in *Gosudarstvo i agrarnaia evolutsia* (*Government and Agrarian Evolution*), ed. V. G. Rastrianikov et al., Moscow, Nauka, 1980.

addition of a sixth stage to the existing five is perhaps by far the most innocuous.

The idea of the AMP, if pushed further, as can be done most naturally, breaks up the unity of mankind and of human history; it suggests that the East or some parts of it are prone to a quite distinctive mode of social organization, one absent from the West and one that is particularly tyrannical and inimical to human dignity, liberty and progress, and that is specially prone to indefinite self-perpetuation and stagnation. As Perry Anderson puts it:

Marx's . . . refusal to generalize the feudal mode of production beyond Europe had its counterpart in his . . . conviction . . . that there was a specific 'Asiatic mode of production' characteristic of the Orient, which separated it historically and sociologically from the Occident. . . . The political history of the Orient was thus essentially cyclical: it contained no dynamic or cumulative development.[3]

East is East and West is West. The AMP fuses Marx and Kipling – and there was indeed a distinct streak of Kipling in Marx, with his firmly stated view of the beneficial effect of the British drill sergeant on India. It is as if there were one sociological law for the West and another for the East. On one hand, such a view is uncomfortably close to racism, or at best to Western ethnocentric self-congratulation; and at another level, such a view undermines the faith in progress as a universal expectation as of right – as a salvation that may at worst be delayed, but that is present at least as a germ in *every* society.

Nikiforov's book contains two principal theses, which must be sharply distinguished: the negative claim that there is no such thing as a distinctive Asiatic type of society, comparable to and coordinate with slave-owning society, feudalism and capitalism, as a valid explanatory idea and as a stage of human society and history; and the positive thesis that Pyatism in its classical form is valid and tenable. I do not anticipate seeing many converts to his positive view (I openly avow my own anti-Pyatism and Trinitarianism); but his negative view, his critique of the notion of an Asiatic Mode, seems to me stronger. This argument, to the effect that the Asiatic Mode is incompatible with a coherent Marxism, seems to me entirely cogent. His attempt to demonstrate that the *magistralnaia doroga*, the unique historical highway, does apply, and that slave and feudal societies are regular stages of social development generally, is admirably concrete and empirical (whether or not it is cogent), though it does inspire scepticism about a typology so pliable that it can absorb Indian caste and Chinese bureaucracy in one and the

3 Perry Anderson, *Lineages of the Absolutist State*, London, New Left Books, 1974, 482–3.

same form, and do the same for Greco-Roman and ancient Near Eastern 'slave' societies. Nikiforov is fully aware of this diversity and indeed comments on it, yet continues to find the five categories useful. His uni-linealist determination to see the development of diverse societies as parallel leads him to see *too few* differences between societies, and *too many* between successive stages of the same society. As a Soviet reviewer, L. B. Alaev, says of Nikiforov's book: '. . . one must conclude: the author has not succeeded in establishing a qualitative difference between the ancient and the medieval Orient.'[4] In other words, the canonical stages do seem to be missing in the East.

Nikiforov *contra* Wittfogel

The most celebrated and influential book on the AMP is of course Karl Wittfogel's *Oriental Despotism*, and Wittfogel is indeed a prime object of Nikiforov's criticism. Nikiforov generally goes out of his way to maintain a high level of courtesy, insisting that disagreement should not preclude mutual respect, that scholarship progresses above all through debate, and that political interference is to be deplored. Wittfogel is one of the very few about whom he speaks harshly, describing him as a renegade from communism, a reactionary, and one eager to use the hypothesis of the Asiatic Mode for anti-communist ends. Leaving aside the emotive associations of the words used, there is nothing here that Wittfogel him-self would wish to deny. Wittfogel's central point is summed up with admirable clarity and fairness: 'The point is that the Asiatic Mode of Production characterized by the absence of private ownership of the means of production – land – provided a basis for despotism in the East, and this cannot fail to suggest the idea of the inevitability of despotism under the socialist mode.'[5] Nikiforov goes on to stress, derisively, that Wittfogel 'failed to produce even a single quotation or fact that would confirm that K. Marx and F. Engels ever perceived implications of the hypothesis of the Asiatic Mode of Production that would prove appalling for socialism'.[6] This is one of the points Nikiforov does score against Wittfogel. The Wittfogelian idea that Marx and Engels were, so to speak, Stalinists-by-anticipation, that they foresaw what was to come, and (before the event) went out of their way to spare Stalin

4 L. B. Alaev, review of *Vostok i vsemirnaia istoria*, by Nikiforov, *Nauchnye doklady Vysshei Shkoly Filosofskie Nauky*, 1977, no. 4, 169–75.
5 Nikiforov, *Vostok i vsemirnaia istoria*, p. 131. All translations from the Russian are mine.
6 Ibid.

embarrassment, is speculative, implausible and not altogether consistent internally. Yet there is more to be said.

Consider the points on which Nikiforov seems justified. Wittfogel argues that, given Marx's premises and the data at his disposal, he *had* to endorse the idea of the Asiatic Mode; hence if he failed to do so, some extraneous considerations must have inhibited him.[7] Now the world is absolutely full of people who have eyes but see not, who on the evidence clearly before them ought to reach some sensible conclusions, but who mysteriously and perversely fail to do so. I see no reason to make an exception of Marx, and to insist that if he failed to draw a conclusion that is obvious to Wittfogel, and perhaps obvious in fact, he must therefore have been deliberately hiding or distorting something. It seems unlikely that Marx had a gift of such perspicacious and detailed prophetic vision, or that, mysteriously, he went out of his way to protect those who were, much later, to distort his aspirations. Wittfogel is much more plausible, though questionably consistent, when he accuses Marx and Engels of harbouring 'fanatical superstitions' – precisely as they had criticized the early Utopians.[8] But if, as is eminently plausible, they did have such 'superstitions', could they have attained *at the same time* such incredibly prescient but negative and pessimistic anticipations, and could they also have been fiendish and perverse enough then to take steps to protect those guilty of perpetuating the unwelcome distortions of their own utopian ideals? Could they *both* be utopian *and* anticipate, with dreadful and brutal realism, the coming of Stalinism? And what motives has a man for protecting those who would distort and tarnish his ideal? I do not believe Marx was so clever, or that he had any motive to be so devilish.

But it seems significant to me that while Nikiforov plausibly stresses that there is no evidence that Marx and Engels really were concerned with, or troubled by, the Asiatic or despotic potential of socialism,[9] Nikiforov's interesting list of people who are unjustly credited by Wittfogel with this anticipatory cover and cover-up does *not* stretch to include Lenin. Lenin's name is missing from the list when Nikiforov argues the 'baseless misinterpretation' accusation against Wittfogel. Yet, in fact, Wittfogel cites Lenin in the same context as Marx and Engels. And indeed, when we come to Lenin, Wittfogel's 'fiendish foresight' ascription ceases to be speculative, unbased on facts, or in collision with them. On the contrary, it acquires very interesting factual support.

---

7 Karl A. Wittfogel, *Oriental Despotism: A Comparative Study of Total Power*, New Haven, Yale University Press, 1957, p. 381.

8 Ibid., p. 388.

9 Nikiforov, *Vostok i vsemirnaia istoria*, p. 131.

Wittfogel quotes a 1921 speech of Lenin's in which Lenin singles out dangerous contemporary developments in the USSR and, without actually using the expression 'Asiatic', characterizes these undesirable and then current trends in terms that correspond exactly to the earlier characterization of Oriental despotism: 'small production, and a bureaucracy connected with the dispersed character of the small producers'.[10] Of course, for Lenin in 1921, a sense of this kind of danger no longer presupposed any unusual prophetic powers, with which the *ex ante* cover-up theory would have to credit Marx and Engels.

Even more significant than Nikiforov's failure to mention Lenin here is that while he quite plausibly contends that, contrary to Wittfogel, there is no adequate evidence to establish that Marx and Engels saw the danger to Marxist socialism lurking in the idea of the Asiatic Mode of Production, he does not deny that the notion *in fact* contains such dangerous implications. On the contrary, although he does not say so in this passage, evidence from other parts of the book suggests that the AMP idea does indeed have such an undesirable potential. The general trend of Nikiforov's argument seems to be that the AMP idea is invalid *and* incompatible with Marxism, and that though Marx and Engels commendably saw this, they only perceived it rather late. It is not clear whether they ever saw the full extent of the danger.

Here we come to a paradoxical but interesting and significant point: in many ways, Nikiforov's position is very close to Wittfogel's. Leaving aside their politics and values, they agree on points that are by no means trivial in the history of ideas: that the idea of the AMP is incompatible with Marxism; that nevertheless, Marx and Engels initially endorsed it; and that they repudiated it only later (wrongly or rightly, according to Wittfogel and Nikiforov's respective viewpoints). This leaves Wittfogel and Nikiforov firmly united against those who say that Marx and Engels never held the AMP idea at all, or that they always persisted in holding it, and that it is an integral part of Marxism. Wittfogel and Nikiforov are at one in seeing Marx's abandonment of the idea of the AMP as a very important development on this issue, though one of them sees it as a (very mysteriously motivated) betrayal, while the other sees it as a laudable advance and victory of truth and reason, without which (though Nikiforov does not say this in so many words) Marxism would have remained sadly defective. They also differ, less significantly, on the precise timing of this development: Wittfogel places what he sees as a betrayal earlier than Nikiforov dates the full self-realization of Marxism through the elimination of the AMP. They also differ, of course, in their speculation about Marx's motivation, and here plausibility would seem

10 Wittfogel, *Oriental Despotism*, pp. 399–400.

to be on Nikiforov's side. They diverge, finally, on the substantial question of whether the AMP actually exists in the real world. This disagreement cuts right across both the East/West and Marxist/non-Marxist oppositions. On this point, Nikiforov has radical opponents in the USSR, just as Wittfogel has radical critics in the West.[11]

From Hegel to Morgan: or, the Exorcism of the AMP

It is interesting to follow Nikiforov's account of Marx's development. In the West, there have been diverse studies attempting to locate the precise instant of the incarnation of Marxism. These studies combine the fascination of literary, historical and hermeneutic detective work with a deep moral significance: tell me just when you think Marxism sprang from the head of Zeus – when the *coupure* took place – and I will tell you what your values are. There is for instance Professor Robert Tucker's intriguing demonstration of how Marx, in the spring or early summer of 1844, invented Marxism 'in an outburst of Hegelizing', when he saw in a flash of illumination that Hegelianism was the encoded economic history of mankind.[12] If Nikiforov is right, however, Marxism proper was only completed in an outburst of anthropologizing or Morganizing around 1881.

Nikiforov does not of course say that Marxism did not exist before 1881, but argues that until then, in a profoundly important way, it had been incomplete and seriously flawed. And the flaw was, precisely, the inclusion, before the final completion or purification of the system, of the idea of the AMP. This is not a question of the addition to, or subtraction from, a system of one notion or category more or less; it is a question of the excision of something whose logical implications pervade, infect and devalue all the rest. If this is so, then in an important sense Marxism was not fully formed until 1881, and its complete elaboration is as indebted to Morgan and Kovalevsky (and through him indirectly even to the Russian populists), just as its earlier elements were indebted to German idealism and British economics. The slogan of this interpretation could well be: from Hegel to Morgan.

11 See, for instance, Edmund R. Leach, 'Hydraulic society in Ceylon', *Past and Present*, no. 15, 1959; Robert E. Fernea, *Shaykh and Effendi: Changing Patterns of Authority among the El Shabana of Southern Iraq*, Cambridge, Harvard University Press, 1970; and Mark Elvin, 'On water control and management during the Ming and Ch'ing periods', *Ch'ing-shih wen-t'i*, vol. 3, 1975.

12 Robert C. Tucker, *Philosophy and Myth in Karl Marx*, Cambridge, Cambridge University Press, 1961.

In what way is the AMP so noxious for the Marxist system? In a number of ways. It impairs, perhaps destroys, the unity of human history by postulating a sideline of historical development that perhaps leads nowhere and ends in stagnation. This comes dangerously close to having two kinds of humanity, one turbulent and progressive, the other stagnant and despotism-prone. More subtly and significantly, it undermines the univocal economic theory of evil, which makes political domination a consequence of exploitation and class antagonism. Thirdly, it affects our vision of the starting point of man's calvary. Is it specifically the East, or is it anywhere in the universal primitive community? Does human history begin in the East, as text-obsessed, old-fashioned historiography made us suppose, or does it begin much more symmetrically with primitive bands, as a vision focused on nature rather than on written history would suppose? Hegel or Darwin? These concerns are not unknown in the West:

Perhaps the most puzzling section of *Pre-Capitalist Modes of Production* is its argument that the Asiatic mode of production does not exist – not, mind you, because nothing in Asian social history ... corresponds [to it]. . . . [T]he Asiatic mode of production cannot exist because its 'concept' entails the self-contradictory notion of a state ruling over a classless society of peasant producers. This is, of course, a contradiction only because Hindess and Hirst hold ... [that] states ... exist simply to preserve a pre-existing class society. . . .[13]

This same reviewer quotes some terrible remarks from Hindess and Hirst to the effect that history only exists in terms of the present, and that 'the current situation does not exist independently of the political practices which constitute it as an object.'[14] In other words, current politics roll their own past. . . .

It should be stressed that Nikiforov's book nowhere sinks to the level of such Western private-world Marxism. He sees and stresses with clarity that the AMP is incompatible with a coherent Marxism, but his arguments against the existence of the AMP are properly historical and empirical, and hinge on whether, *in fact*, the syndrome of the AMP really materialized in history. He may or may not convince one, but the argument is clear, concrete, and devoid of mumbo jumbo.

Something should be said about the distinctive, morally saturated quality of Soviet Russian discussions of modes of production or social typologies. (This applies equally to 'conservative' versions and to more daringly revisionist or dissident ones.) A Western social scientist who tries to handle the problem of classification of societies is dealing with a

13 Rod Aya, in an admirable review of *Pre-Capitalist Modes of Production*, by Barry Hindess and Paul Q. Hirst, *Theory and Society*, vol. 3, 1976 p. 626.

14 Ibid., p. 628.

theoretical or technical issue, which may of course be in one way or another distantly connected with his moral commitments, his general vision of the human condition. But these connections will tend to be indirect, complex, contentious and, above all, not something to be pursued in office hours.

The situation is quite different in Soviet and Russian *nauka*, a term closer to the German *Wissenschaft* than to the English 'science'. One has the same feeling that one may well have while looking at some medieval church mosaic, which is only incidentally and unselfconsciously *art*, but whose prime and manifest motive was to convey to those who saw it the pathos, the options, the dangers and the final aim of human life. *This* is how the sinners will be punished, and see how the torments fit their transgressions; and *that* is how the saints will be blessed; *this* is how they suffered, and behold how they will be rewarded. Yet the sufferings were necessary. If Asia would not budge on her own (an important theoretical question, as we shall see), then, Marx observed, we must approve of what the English did to India, whatever our personal feelings about it.[15] Marx went on to quote Goethe, as Nikiforov reminds us:

> Sollte diese Qual uns quälen,
> Da sie unsre Lust vermehrt,
> Hat nicht Myriaden Seelen
> Timurs Herrschaft aufgezehrt?

Loosely translated: Should we torment ourselves with the thought that we have benefited (from history) – that Tamerlane's domination devoured myriads of souls? Both Tamerlane and the English, whatever their sins, are necessary agents in a global morality play.

And so it is with modes of production. These are not, or not merely, cold categories, justified simply by the contribution they make to our classification and understanding of social structures. They are far, far more than that: these are the great stages in man's calvary. To get them wrong is not merely to commit a scholarly error: like a mistake in an inscription on a martyrs' memorial, it verges on mockery of those who have suffered and died. Nikiforov quotes with warm approval Engels's remarks in *The Origin of the Family, Private Property and the State* – the true vision had prevailed by the time Engels wrote it: 'Slavery is the first form of exploitation, appropriate to the ancient world, and after it follows serfdom in the Middle Ages and wage labour in modern times.' The main message of Nikiforov's book is the exhaustiveness of these three stages or modes of exploitation and, to a lesser and qualified extent, their universality. Specifically, what matters is the exclusion of that

15 Nikiforov, *Vostok i vsemirnaia istoria*, p. 116.

extra, Asiatic stage. A fourth form of exploitation, distinct from alienation of the person, of the land, and then of tools under 'wage slavery', has
never been found by the partisans of the 'Asiatic' hypothesis. That is the
essence of Nikiforov's case.[16]

So there is no room for a fourth panel on the triptych of our calvary.
The point is repeated where Engels is praised for the significant title of a
work he never completed: 'Three basic Forms of Enslavement'.[17] These
three forms, and three only, first noted by Saint-Simon and incorporated into the *Communist Manifesto*, cannot be complemented by a
distinctive Asiatic Mode of Production.

Who's Afraid of the AMP?

So Pyatism is fundamental. Why so? Not, evidently, through any mystical attachment to the number five. On the contrary, Nikiforov objects to
the Asiatic Mode, not because it increases the number of historic stages
by one, but because of its particular properties. The Asiatic Mode of
Production, as Nikiforov stresses, is defined by 'the formula well-known
to us: primitive community plus government'.[18] This is the heart of the
matter. The other traits associated with the notion – despotism, absence
of private ownership in land, irrigation, etc. – are indeed connected with
these two central features, as either their precondition or their consequence.[19] Another feature that is significantly invoked, the combination of crafts and agriculture within the closed community, is
theoretically *necessary* because there is no other place where crafts *could*
be located. As Marx observed, there were no real cities – only spin-offs
of the royal camp. There is no supra- or extra-communal urban
bourgeoisie that could supply craft products to state and peasant. The
initial formula excludes it.

The model defined by the formula seems to describe something
perfectly conceivable, though I will not pursue the question of whether
that something ever existed in historical fact. But Nikiforov seems
entirely reasonable to insist that it is incompatible with Marxism – or at
any rate with a coherent Marxism that upholds certain tenets. The
crucial point is simple: Where are the classes and the antagonisms that,
according to one of these tenets, are supposed to generate political

16 Ibid., p. 30.
17 Ibid., p. 142.
18 Ibid., p. 146.
19 There is an admirably succinct acount of the interrelation and intellectual origins
of these various traits in Anderson, *Lineages of the Absolutist State*, p. 472.

domination, and alone are capable of doing so? Not within the individual closed communities, since they are as yet undifferentiated. Perhaps between them and the despotic, hydraulic bureaucracy that dominates them? That would seem realistic enough; but just whose interests does this oppressive state machinery represent? Its own? Or that of the peasants who compose the dominated communities? Or both? One of these three answers *has* to be the right one – for *there simply is no one else* in the list of available dramatis personae, with which the formula for this mode has provided us, whose interests could conceivably be considered. No one else is present.

On a commonsensical or 'functionalist' view, the state might indeed be impelled or bound at least in part by concern with the peasants' interest. This is indeed the point at which stress on irrigation agriculture normally enters the argument. In arid lands, no agriculture without complex irrigation works; but no edification or maintenance of complex agriculture without central direction and supervision; hence the state is necessary, and without it, those communities of peasants could not exist at all, or (at best) their number would have to be drastically reduced. So the state, however despotic, is also functional: without it, most of its oppressed subjects would not survive at all. Better alive under a hydraulic bureaucracy than dead from famine. So the state can afford to be despotic, knowing itself to be indispensable. Perhaps it even needs to be despotic. That is the 'hydraulic' argument.

Alternatively, the state can be explained, not by invoking express or tacit calculation on the part of its subjects about the relative merits of starvation and oppression, but simply by the self-interest of the soldiers and officials who man it. They do very nicely out of it, thank you, and given that they control the necessary means of coercion and persuasion – which may or may not include rational calculation on the part of their subjects – they will keep the system going.

The two explanations – the functionalist and the despotic – can of course be combined. There is no incompatibility between them. In practice, most societies that look like candidates for the AMP also possess additional ideological legitimation, which may or may not be of significant help in securing compliance from their subjects. But above all, the despotic organization serves either the peasants or itself, or both. *There is no one else.*

But either of these explanations (and *a fortiori* their conjunction) is quite incompatible with the theoretical requirement that the state can only emerge as the consequence or reflection of *pre-existing* class antagonism and exploitation. There is of course an old theory of such an independently existing state, whether conceived as malevolently self-serving, or as above-the-battle-and-neutral and beneficial, or as some combination of these. Peter Nikitich Tkachev, for instance, maintained in the nineteenth century that the Tsarist autocracy did not emanate from Russian society, but 'hung in thin air'. Much to Nikiforov's delight, Friedrich Engels let Tkachev have it straight from the shoulder: 'It is not Russian government, but rather Gospodin Tkachev himself, who hangs in thin air.'[20] Whatever the fate of the levitating Gospodin Tkachev, whom Engels also accused of generating pure hot air, it is most essential for Marxist theory that *governments* at least should not hang in thin air. Their inability to do so would seem to be an essential part of the materialist conception of history. That materialist conception is violated equally, whether these levitating governments are impelled by brutal self-interest, or whether they float benevolently, like a Madonna on a mural, in the interests of reconciling and furthering the needs and wishes of their subjects, or both. For present purposes, the distinction is immaterial.

Nikiforov's insistence here is, ironically, the same as Wittfogel's: the possibility that government should be either functional (and constitute the genuinely essential precondition of satisfying a shared social need), or evil but self-sufficient and self-serving (propelled into existence by the availability of means of coercion, and not rooted in any prior social malady) is indeed incompatible with an eschatology and theodicy that see domination as the price or consequence of an economic ill – of *prior* exploitation, appropriation, property and class antagonism. When these go, the derivative evil of domination will also go. This vision is clearly contradicted by either a functional or a self-serving despotism. If such despotism is possible, it also follows that it cannot be exorcised by the canonical methods that orthodoxy specifies.

Apart from the manifest head-on collision of the AMP with Marxist orthodoxy, there is also a set of minor contradictions between them. The stability of Asian despotism, whether in the model or in the real societies that are held to exemplify it, would also seem to undermine the eschatological hope, inspired by ever-present change and conflict; for it is the pervasive and fermenting internal 'contradictions' of societies that would guarantee instability and thus justify hope for progress. Marx himself tended to think of the Orient as stagnant, as when he remarked that the English brought India its only *social* revolution (as opposed to, presumably, mere gyrations of tribes or dynastic merry-go-rounds); and Nikiforov does not hesitate at this point to correct Marx for saying what, in Nikiforov's view, he could not possibly have meant literally.[21]

20 Nikiforov, *Vostok i vsemirnaia istoria*, p. 136.
21 Ibid., p. 117. By contrast, Yuri Semenov willingly invokes Marx's remarks about Oriental stagnation and takes them at full and face value ('Theory of socio-economic formations', pp. 55–6).

The notion of the Asiatic Mode thus destroys the crucial Marxist diagnosis of the general ills of mankind (the indentification of *the* original sin) by allowing the existence of another and independent sin (namely functional or self-serving political domination), and thereby also undermines the hope of a guaranteed salvation tied to the eradication of that one original sin. Perdition then becomes, so to speak, uncontrollable, *freischwebend*, ineliminable. The unity of human history and of the human race itself is thus also impaired: mankind falls apart into two halves, one dynamic and destined for salvation, the other static and either doomed to perpetual damnation or at best only available for salvation through the efforts of others. For this other half, revolutionary salvation will have to be imported. It will be its passive beneficiary, receiving it gratefully, as once it was supposed to receive *civilization*. Once again, it is instructive to compare Nikiforov's version of Marxism with Semenov's. Semenov evidently has no such strong aversion to a vision of Orientals open only to a grant-aided, exogenous salvation. If Nikiforov and Semenov were to be used as charters of alternative Soviet policies toward China, then clearly Nikiforov would suit the doves and Semenov the hard-liners.

The difference between these two versions of Soviet Marxism has a curious resemblance to the erstwhile dispute in the West between Lévi-Strauss and Sartre, in which Lévi-Strauss reproached Sartre for ethnocentrically making much of mankind available for salvation only by incorporation in the 'dialectic' of the West.[22] Nikiforov, like Lévi-Strauss, repudiates such unsymmetrical and Western-ethnocentric theories.

In Nikiforov's version, man's calvary does not begin on the Nile or between the Tigris and the Euphrates; it does not begin at any one place or time at all. It begins all over the place in the primitive community, the *p'ervobytnaia obshchina*, which is basically the same everywhere: no property, no classes, no antagonism, no state. It is not only much the same everywhere, at least to the extent of everywhere exemplifying the same social form; it is also much the same at all times: specimens of it even survive into the modern period, as elements within more complex and class-endowed societies. Our beginning remains ever with us, virtually till the present day. Nikiforov comments on how very many class-endowed societies were once but islands in a sea of primitive communities.

22 Claude Lévi-Strauss, *La pensée sauvage*, Paris, Plon, 1962, chapter 9.

How Morgan Saved Marxism

For Nikiforov, the discovery or rediscovery of the 'community' was crucial to that final crystallization or coming to full self-awareness of Marxism, which on his view came so strangely late, in 1881. And one particular anthropologist is the hero of this story, namely, Lewis Henry Morgan. In Nikiforov's version of Marxism, Morgan acquires the status of a key contributor to its theoretical wealth, alongside the more obvious and much earlier names, notwithstanding the late hour at which Marx encountered his work: 'The new achievement of science, which radically changed the conceptions of primitive society, and enabled K. Marx and F. Engels to make a new approach to the problem of pre-capitalist formations, was L. H. Morgan's discovery of tribal social structure [*otkrytie L. G. Morganom rodovogo stroia*]'.[23] Engels is quoted as saying that only this provided a solid basis for primitive history, and Nikiforov significantly observes that only thus was it possible to complete the 'harmonious structure' of the Marxist theory of (social) formations, which concludes with 'prevalence – in the distant past and the more or less distant future – of the communal ownership of the means of production'.[24] What is essential is that this line separating the presence and absence of communal ownership should *not* cut across the line between non-oppressive and oppressive (state-endowed) societies, while the idea of the AMP does precisely this, by postulating a social order devoid of private property yet highly oppressive. It provides an example of political oppression *without* an economic root.

Morgan's discovery of the principles of tribal organization links us to our true tribal past. Nikiforov points out that this shift of vision led Engels to add an important new phrase to the 1888 English edition of the *Communist Manifesto*, qualifying the famous statement that all history is the history of class struggles by adding the remark: 'That is, all *written* history.' So, it appears, it was the *un*written sources of archaeology and ethnography that modified this generalization. They were, Engels noted, 'all but unknown' in 1847. Yet without them, Nikiforov argues, Marxism could not be correctly formulated.

So the prehistory of societies and communal organization was almost wholly unknown in the 1840s, and the real context of propertylessness could not then be understood. But more than that, this discovery seemed to replace the linear philosophy of history, characteristic of Hegelianism, which leads from slavery to freedom, by a new, so to speak,

23 Nikiforov, *Vostok i vsemirnaia istoria*, p. 144.
24 Ibid., pp. 146, 148.

'detour' soteriology that is distinctively Marxist: from freedom to free-dom via alienation – since communal ownership is apparently estab-lished by Morgan's findings for *both* the distant past *and* the future.

In our end is our beginning. This semicircular pattern of history, interestingly enough, is linked (as stated) to a more naturalistic and less historicist vision. The semicircular naturalistic picture is this: history begins with any or every internally undifferentiated primordial com-munity; through internal differentiations, it takes a bitter detour through three modes of alienation, and finally returns to an undifferentiated, classless, and stateless condition. By contrast, the earlier, more Hegelian, linear-historicist pattern was: history begins in the despotic East and culminates in the free West. Nikiforov gives the impression that the Founders of Marxism moved from the latter vision to the former, thanks to the empirical discovery of the 'community' in the 1870s.

Morgan was crucial for this development. Engels is quoted as observ-ing that: 'Within the limits of this subject, Morgan independently redis-covered Marx's materialist conception of history.' Government could not occur in primitive society; hence the Asiatic Mode is impossible, for government in it would have to *create itself*, there being no classes within society that could engender it. This then enabled Marx to sneer at the outmoded fantasy of despotism in primitive society, a fable that was 'John Bull's main and favoured doctrine, as he becomes intoxicated with primitive "despotism" '.[25]

As Perry Anderson points out, the first person to blame John Bull for concocting this fable was one Anquetil-Duperron, in 1778, whose senti-ments have earned him accolades as an early anti-colonialist. Anderson maliciously shows that Anquetil-Duperron was merely a disappointed rival colonialist, regretting the French defeat in the carve-up of India and campaigning for a French return to the subcontinent.[26] Anquetil-Duperron earned Marx's approval as the first man to deny the Great Mogul's exclusive possession of land under his control. So it was, Nikiforov observes, that Marx finally overcame two centuries of error concerning the socio-economic structure of the East. But Morgan was essential for this final demystification.

From Russia with Love

Morgan did not, however, achieve this alone or without a mediator. Russian developments in the 1870s, Russian thought, and one Russian

25 Ibid., pp. 146, 145.
26 Anderson, *Lineages of the Absolutist State*, pp. 465–6n.

in particular, M. M. Kovalevsky, played a crucial part. Morgan was not the only person to discover the community in the 1870s, and the Iroquois were not the only people to have maintained *the* community into modern or near-modern times. Besides the Iroquois there were the Russian *muzhiks*; besides Morgan there were the Russian populists.

The closeness, in space and time and moral relevance, of the very beginnings of human society to *us*, for anyone thinking and living within this conceptual framework, is something that ought to be noted here. As indicated, the taxonomy of social forms contained in Pyatism is not just an analytic classification; it is the graphic portrait of man's struggle and suffering, of the successive forms of human bondage. But the first step on this path still remained so close that we could, at any rate in the nineteenth century, literally touch it.

Human history and the social forms it exhibits are not only morally significant, they are also intimate and close; they are part of world history, which is foreshortened, not just chronologically, but also through the paucity in number, the ready intelligibility, the easily available exemplification, and the moral saturation and political relevance of the social forms found in it. Just as love is different in a cold climate, so anthropology is rather special in a populist country. Once again, one feels as if one were seeing some mosaics that graphically sum up the human situation, but their dramatic impact and intelligibility are heightened because there are so *few* of them. Our destiny is dramatic, but its options and stages are few. The story has drama and pathos, but also great simplicity.

It was indeed the moral and political significance of the primitive community that led the Founders of Marxism to it:

In our view, it is particularly in the study by Marx and Engels of Russian materials in the 1870s, that we must search for the point of departure, which prepared the ground for the change of view by the founders of Marxism concerning the historical development of the East. What is at issue is their investigation of problems concerned with rural communities. In effect, the periodic redistribution of land – that significant survival of communal ownership – was incomparably more common [in Russia] than in India. Russia, like Oriental countries, had a despotic government. On the other hand, Russia in the 1870s was an unambiguously European country, with bourgeois and prebourgeois forms of private ownership of land. . . .

Russian populists, disregarding one aspect, the growth of capitalism, absolutized and idealized the other, the communal organization.[27]

27 Nikiforov, *Vostok i vsemirnaia istoria*, p. 135.

The tendency of populism to idealize the peasant was the obverse of its tendency to put the blame on governmental oppression and violence, without seeking its class roots. The two errors and their connection are both highly relevant.

Nikiforov stresses that after the failure of the Paris Commune and the termination of the First International, Marx and Engels gave much attention to revolutionary Russia. This involved taking over ideas about the distinctive role of the rural community, in part from Herzen, Bakunin and Chernyshevsky, and in part directly from the Slavophiles, but without repeating the mistake (which had once been built into the idea of the AMP) of seeing governmental authority as possibly independent of these communities. As Nikiforov rightly observes, by endorsing the class-transcending conception of government and of the creation of social forms by government, the views of the *narodniks* coincided with those of the liberal Westernizers, even if the latter viewed the community with contempt as an artificial offspring of central policy. The supposition that human society can be based on violence is but the general form of an error of which the AMP is the most significant single example. No wonder that Plekhanov was tempted by the AMP and even applied it to Russia: 'As is well known,' Nikiforov reminds us maliciously, Plekhanov reached Marxism from populism. What can you expect from people like that?

But among these Russians, the one who made the greatest contribution, and at various levels, was M. M. Kovalevsky. In him, the two currents whose inclusion of the great river of Marxism was to save it from the previous error of the AMP – the current flowing from the Iroquois and the one flowing from the *muzhiks* – merged into one mighty tributary, ready to enter and enrich the mainstream. Kovalevsky is both a *causa essendi* and a *causa cognoscendi* of the final, crucial self-correction of Marxism. He helped bring it about; but also, thanks to him (or, specifically, to Marx's annotations of his book) we *know* about it, or at any rate Nikiforov does. On the one hand, the notes Marx made on Kovalevsky's book about communal land tenure are crucial for Nikiforov's case and for his detective work concerning Marx's illumination on this point. Nikiforov claims that it is Marx's notes on Kovalesky that justify the conclusion that Marx saw the presence from early times in India of private ownership of land, coexisting with collective communal land (and hence *not* the alleged 'Asiatic' monopolization of land by the state), and that he saw the progress of 'feudalization' in medieval India, and (like Kovalevsky) considered this process to be uncompleted. A critical reader may find some of Nikiforov's reasoning less than fully cogent. For instance, he stresses that while Kovalevsky's book is very hostile to the thesis of exclusive state ownership of land in the Orient,

Marx's notes contain not a single objection to this tendency of the work. Marx's failure to comment is treated as assent.[28]

Absence of private property, especially in land, is central to the idea of the AMP. The demonstration of the pervasive existence in Oriental polities of private landownership is thus crucial for Nikiforov's demolition of the idea of the AMP. Private ownership *had* been absent, but *only* in the primordial commune, and *not* in any centralized polity. (Perry Anderson also uses Marx's annotation of Kovalevsky to reach a partially different conclusion.[29]) Kovalevsky was also familiar with North African material, and Marx's annotations make clear that he saw this. So one has the feeling that by the late 1870s, tribesmen and peasants from all over the world – Iroquois, Kabyles, *muzhiks*, Indian villagers – were converging on Kentish Town and angrily insisting that the record be put straight. The commune then replaces the Oriental despotism as the one and only place where private landownership really was lacking. The negative fact – the lack of critical comment by Marx in his private notes on Kovalevsky's book – leaps to the eye, Nikiforov says, and it seems to him very weighty, establishing that Marx accepted the presence of private landownership in India, and hence the nonexistence of the AMP.

Against this, Nikiforov has to explain away Marx's comment on a book published in 1880 by an English lawyer, Sir John Budd Phear: 'That ass Phear describes the organization of the [Indian] rural community as feudal.'[30] Nikiforov would have us believe that Phear was an ass only for describing the *internal* organization of the Indian commune in this way. Poor Phear seems rescued from oblivion only by being called an ass by Marx in two languages, German and Latin; Marx even describes him, in that Anglo-German mix he used for his jottings, as a 'respectable *Esel*' (ass). With ironic condescension, Marx also repeatedly refers to Phear as a *Bursch* (lad).[31] Evidently, in Nikiforov's view, Phear could have avoided this fate had he spoken of society *as a whole* as feudal (correct), rather than so describing its constituent communities (wrong). Nikiforov insists that Marx at that time had endorsed the feudalization of Indian society as a whole, even if it was not complete – whatever his view of the quality of Phear's intellectual equipment and maturity.

But, on the other hand, Kovalesky's role in crystallizing the correct

28 Ibid., pp. 138, 137.
29 Anderson, *Lineages of the Absolutist State*, pp. 405–7.
30 Karl Marx, *Ethnological Notebooks*, ed. Lawrence Krader, Assen, Van Gorcum, 1972, p. 256.
31 Ibid., pp. 281, 262, 271.

version of Marxism, purged of the AMP, was not merely the passive one of provoking the evidence found in Marx's notes on him. He was also an active agent. Kovalevsky acquired a copy of Morgan's *Ancient Society* on a visit to the United States. In the late 1870s, he was a frequent visitor to Marx's household in London, and even lent his own copy of Morgan's book to Marx. At the same time, he was of course in a good position to put Marx in touch with Russian material. The impact of Morgan's work on Marx is shown in the drafts of his reply to Vera Zasulich's letter, where he alludes directly to Morgan.[32]

According to Nikiforov, these drafts also prove his repudiation of the notion of the AMP, because the term no longer appears; instead, there is reference to the 'archaic formation'. This would not seem conclusive on its own, Nikiforov admits, for it would be compatible with merely renaming the AMP and treating it as the last stage of primitive communal organization (as indeed some have done). Nikiforov replies that the drafts of Marx's answer to Vera Zasulich do not even once mention government – which had always been present in earlier discussions of the AMP, as indeed it should be – but proceed instead to invoke Morgan's general thesis, in which there is no room for the AMP.[33]

I have the feeling that Nikiforov exaggerates the Hegel-to-Morgan transformation of Marx. Nikiforov's young Marx seems to be a kind of Hegelian for whom history begins in the East with despotism; his old Marx is a man enlightened by the facts of Russian, Indian, and other communities, who is liberated from Anglo-French colonialist slanders about the East, and who is committed to a vision of development more Darwinian than Hegelian, in that it is not blinkered by text-bound history, but places man in the context of prehistory and anthropology – and all this thanks to Morgan and his mediator, Kovalevsky. Nikiforov's late Marx thus deprives the Orient of the glory of *initium*, of starting history, but also of the indignity of stagnation and passivity in the face of despotism. Nikiforov himself may feel he is pressing his case too hard and perhaps rushing in where Engels fears to tread, for he remarks apologetically: 'After all, all these facts are not brought forward by us with the aim of denying the indisputable fact that Engels was the sole

32 Nikiforov, *Vostok i vsemirnaia istoria*, pp. 110, 144, Marx alludes to Morgan in the second draft of his reply to Vera Zasulich, written in late February or early March 1881 (Karl Marx, 'Drafts of a reply [February-March, 1881]: the "first" draft,' in *Late Marx and the Russian Road: Marx and 'the Peripheries of Capitalism'*, ed. Teodor Shanin, London, Routledge & Kegan Paul, 1983, 107). On why the 'first' draft was actually the second, see Haruki Wada, 'Marx and Revolutionary Russia', ibid., pp. 63–9.

33 Actually, Marx's first and second drafts do mention a 'central despotism above the communes' ('Drafts of a reply', pp. 103, 111).

author of *The Origin of the Family, Private Property and the State*, and
responsible for its conception. . . .[34]

Let us leave the question, which each reader must answer for himself,
of whether Nikiforov clinches his case that in or by 1881 Marx firmly
changed his mind and eliminated the AMP from his scheme. Nikiforov
fully persuades me, however, that there is indeed no room for the AMP
in a Marxism that requires the state to be endogenously generated by
class conflict, nor in one that is to give us faith in the state's eventual disappearance under conditions of classlessness. In other words, the very
notion of the AMP contradicts both the story of the Fall *and* the hope of
Salvation. On this, Nikiforov and Wittfogel are agreed; on the question
of Marx's motivation, Nikiforov's theory seems to me more plausible,
though it does questionably assume full consistency in the Marxist
scheme, and in its formulation in Marx's mind.

The Primordial Community and its Political Implications

Needless to say, the reformulated Marxist doctrine is full of practical-
political implications, which indeed played a crucial part in crystallizing
the true picture. Its attainment was a political as much as a scholarly
achievement, for it involved seeing the true role of the rural masses, in
communities, *in our time* as well as in the distant past. They were potential allies, not inert obstacles or opponents. It all affects the interpretation of, on the one hand, backward societies such as
nineteenth-century Russia and, on the other, the erstwhile colonial, now
'Third' World. As Teodor Shanin puts it: '. . . the future of Russia was
seen as dominated by the peasantry . . . the majority of the nation. . . .
Marxism and Populism . . . formed, together with varying degrees of
revolutionary voluntarism, the hard core of Russian revolutionary
ideology.'[35]

For instance, the formula that is rightly held to sum up the essence of
the Asiatic Mode, namely primitive community plus government, is still
admitted by Nikiforov to have application, and he quotes a letter from
Engels to Kautsky of 1884 that makes this perfectly plain: but the AMP
is here seen only to arise as a result of the extraneous imposition of
government on the primitive communities. The case described in
Engels's letter is Java, and the imposition of domination from the
outside was carried out by the Dutch. This handling of the matter faces

34 Nikiforov, *Vostok i vsemirnaia istoria*, p. 147.
35 Teodor Shanin, *The Awkward Class: Political Sociology of Peasantry in a Developing
Society: Russia, 1910–1925*, Oxford, Clarendon, 1972, p. 47.

both empirical and theoretical difficulty. A reading of Javanese history that could treat Javanese society simply as primitive-communal prior to colonialism is somewhat implausible, though perhaps the pre-Western state formations could also be credited to other (e.g., Muslim and Hindu) intruders; and at a more fundamental level, there are difficulties for Nikiforov in the whole notion of diffusion, of the explanation of social forms not by the logic of their internal development, but by the transplantation of ideas, institutions, or personnel. In this 'Javanese' passage, Nikiforov seems to be saying, in effect, that what is not possible as a natural endogenous growth (i.e., the AMP) is nevertheless perfectly possible as the result of the impact of one society on another. But given the frequency with which societies do indeed make an impact on each other, is there not the danger that this qualification might in the end allow too much? So, significantly and interestingly, Nikiforov characterizes diffusionism as an 'idealist' doctrine, which indeed it must be if everything non-materialist is idealist, and if materialism requires the endogenous development of societies.[36] All the same, no one can deny that some diffusion has occurred in history. The question is: How much of it can be allowed without submerging the original endogenous view?

So something resembling the recipe for the AMP has in fact existed, but only as a result of extraneous superimposition of a governmental apparatus on primitive communities. But what about correct political strategy in societies where the community still survives in some measure? It is precisely this question that, on Nikiforov's view, led to the final, correct formulation of Marxism. If the material for the correct assessment of prehistory was lacking until 1877, the year of Morgan's crucial work, as Engels asserted, then the situation that inspired the correct *Fragestellung* in the minds of the Founding Fathers existed as of 1871. The failure of the Paris Commune on the one hand, and the emergence of a revolutionary movement in Russia on the other, led them to reassess the role of the rural community. Marx studied Bakunin, Engels polemized with the levitating Gospodin Tkachev. The outcome, Nikiforov observes, was a fundamental revaluation of the community. In the 1870s, 'they reached the conclusion of the possibility of using the community for a peaceful transition of backward countries to socialism, bypassing developed capitalist society.[37] The transition can never, however, be direct and unaided. It will only be possible if the community does not disintegrate before there has been a victorious proletarian revolution in Western Europe, which alone will provide the Russian peasant with the preconditions for such a transition. Instead of the

36 Nikiforov, *Vostok i vsemirnaia istoria*, p. 247.
37 Ibid., p. 134.

White Man's Burden, there would seem to be a kind of *mission civilisatrice du prolétariat*. Moreover, the community will only prove its capacity if (in Engels's words) it is able 'to develop in a manner such that peasants will no longer till the soil separately, but together'.[38] One wonders whether this text or similar ones were not crucial for the establishment of *kolchozy*.[39]

Nikiforov goes on to observe that the dream of Russian thinkers about a non-capitalist path, which had remained a mere utopia in the hands of Chernyshevsky, only became scientific when Marx and Engels combined it with the idea of a proletarian revolution in the West.[40] Populism is the Pelagian heresy of Marxism. It teaches the possibility of independent, unaided salvation for retarded communities by their own efforts. From a Marxist point of view, it was important to encourage hope and effort, and yet not allow anyone the illusion of the dispensability of Grace – for the proletariat still retained the monopoly of Grace. *Extra plebem nulla salus.*

This reassessment seems to have been due to the interaction of diverse elements – the populist 'discovery' of the community, the geographical displacement of revolutionary zeal, and the desire to find theoretical warrant for some measure of optimism on its behalf. Prior to this period, the community, though known to exist, was sadly deficient in great potential for either good or evil, for salvation or damnation. It was also not clear how, or indeed that, it was capable of initiating the historical process and giving birth to class society, from its own resources, so to speak: Engels seemed willing to consider the possiblity of the state being set up by the conquest of one tribe by another, without pre-existing class antagonism.[41] On the other hand, if the rural community survived as part of complex class society, it was inert and reactionary. The commune, you might say, was an object, not a subject, of history – contributing from its inner resources little that was essential to the expulsion from Eden, and even less to the eventual redemption.

Perry Anderson derides Marx for simultaneously treating the Indian village community as primordial and as stagnant, thus 'squaring the

38 Ibid.

39 On the interaction of ideological and social constraints in establishing and organizing of collective farms, see Caroline Humphrey, *Karl Marx Collective: Economy, Society and Religion in a Siberian Collective Farm*, Cambridge, Cambridge University Press, 1983.

40 Nikiforov, *Vostok i vsemirnaia istoria*, p. 135.

41 ICf. Wittfogel, *Oriental Despotism*, p. 383. It is also hard for Nikiforov's thesis that in 1894–5, Engels returned to a stagnant/cyclical view of the East, though this time echoing the views of Ibn Khaldun – which *also* seem to have been brought to his notice by the universal cross-fertilizer – Kovalevsky. Cf. Ernest Gellner, *Muslim Society*, Cambridge, Cambridge University Press, 1981, pp. 46–7, and the references cited there, as well as Bryan S. Turner, 'Orientalism, Islam and capitalism', *Social Compass*, vol. 25, 1978.

circle'.[42] Nikiforov himself quotes Marx as speculating whether the English conquest was necessary if India was ever to move. But if this were so, how could history get started? One may suppose that Marx was not so much inconsistent as tacitly relying on a non-endogenous (e.g., conquest) initiation to history. But that leads to more trouble still. Nikiforov seems to me right: if force is ever allowed to be a prime mover in history, and not merely an echo of prior class antagonism, the whole Marxist system becomes faulty. If violence came spontaneously and independently, why should it ever leave us – and why should it not return if expelled? Salvation can only be guaranteed if the source of evil is known and eventually controlled, if the jinn can be put back in the bottle, and if in fact there is only one jinn. If not, evil cannot be eliminated. It is curious that Western Marxists such as Perry Anderson and Maurice Godelier, who avoid these difficulties by including political or other 'superstructural' elements in their definition of social forms, are not worried by this problem.[43] Unless it is solved, Marxism has no logical claim whatever to promise social salvation.

The AMP and the China Lobby

To recapitulate Nikiforov's argument: the political exigencies and opportunities of the 1870s (the failure of the Paris Commune, the emergence of a revolutionary movement in Russia, the populist stress on rural communities) led Marx and Engels to reconsider the inadequacy of the community as an agent, ally, or catalyst of the future: perhaps, if purged of the utopianism that pervaded it in the hands of the populists, there might be something to this idea. Then came Morgan, who showed that the community led *directly* to class societies, from an inner compulsion, not necessarily requiring conquest, and that basically the same mechanisms were to be found among the Iroquois and in the ancient Mediterranean. And when Kovalevsky, who had already done well by history in introducing Marx to Russian material, also lent him his copy of Morgan's book, brought from America, all this flowed together. Before, the AMP had been required at the start of history – to set history proper going, history being the history of class struggle. The primordial community, an Eve without sex appeal, had been only questionably capable of triggering it all off. The AMP had also been needed at the end, to explain the stagnant passivity of certain societies. Now it was no

42 Anderson, *Lineages of the Absolutist State*, p. 490.
43 Cf. ibid., pp. 403–4, and Maurice Godelier, 'Infrastructures, society, and history', *Current Anthropology*, vol. 19, 1978.

longer needed either at the beginning or at the end. Eve herself was seen as capable of arousing passion and action. And the AMP was no longer needed to explain the absence of private property in land in the East. This absence of private landownership, in class- and state-endowed societies, was exposed as a myth. Nikiforov insists that this syndrome has always been located by scholars in whatever Oriental society was at their point of time least well studied and understood. The primordial classless and stateless community, which alone really possessed this negative trait, and occasionally preserved features of it even when incorporated into larger wholes, thus led to the crucial mistake. Nikiforov makes clear that European ethnocentrism, which projected stagnant despotism and absence of private landownership onto the East, and used it to justify its own domination and expropriation there when convenient, had also been willing to do this to Russia. Indeed, some Russians were willing to speak of themselves in this manner. The same mistake had also led to a failure to perceive revolutionary potential anywhere in the East. Wogs begin at Calais, and the Asiatic Mode of Production began on the Neman.

Thus the central point of Nikiforov's argument is this: the elimination of the idea of the AMP is the obverse of the correct assessment of the historic role of the primordial community. The AMP had been a kind of theoretical cloud of unknowing, obscuring the crucial and dynamic role of the rural community, whether at the start of history or during its later stages, in our own time. Absence of private ownership of land *does* occur, but not in any of the class-endowed stages of man's historical ordeal. (That disastrous error is the very essence of the AMP.) It occurs only at the start and at the end, before and after the ordeal. The harmony (Nikiforov's own word) of the theoretical structure of Marxism is thus recovered.

It is also interesting to consider the implications of Nikiforov's analysis, as noted by himself, for contemporary political issues.[44] As he observes, 'Some authors try to make use of the materials drawn from the discussion of pre-capitalist formations, to explain the causes of recent changes in China. They consider the temporary domination of Maoism a rebirth of the Asiatic Mode of Production or its survival.'[45] Two authors, Yu. Ostrovityanov and A. Sterbalova, are cited as holding this view. But Nikiforov's polemics become even more interesting when he argues with L. V. Stepanov and A. V. Meliksetov. Stepanov

44 Cf. Samuel H. Baron, 'Marx's *Grundrisse* and the Asiatic Mode of Production', *Survey*, vol. 21, 1975, pp. 94–5, and Marian Sawer, 'The Soviet discussion of the Asiatic Mode of Production', ibid., vol. 24, Summer 1979, p. 108.

45 Nikiforov, *Vostok i vsemirnaia istoria*, p. 268.

apparently coined the term 'statist-peasant' to characterize the Maoist regime in China. Meliksetov seems to have taken the term over and extended it to cover class societies throughout the whole of Chinese history. Meliksetov, as quoted from a symposium on China published in Moscow in 1968, argues as follows: 'Economic, objectified relations, expressed in the circulation of goods, played a big role in the life of traditional Chinese society, but what nevertheless dominated were personal relations, for the general unifying force of small, mutually isolated producers could only be political association, political power, i.e., government'.[46] Nikiforov points out, dismissively, that all this – domination of personal, noneconomic relations, of a government divorced from classes – has already been dealt with. Indeed, this is what the AMP debate is all about. But Meliksetov, as Nikiforov reports, takes the argument further and into the present. China in his view had always, in antiquity and the Middle Ages, been characterized by the dominance of state ownership and the suppression of private property. Sun Yat-sen's teaching combined traditional principles with some Western elements and proposed a non-capitalist line of development for China. Chiang Kai-shek, invoking Sun Yat-sen, also followed this line. Thus only the externals change; the class essence of these various military-bureaucratic dictatorships remains unchanged. But if this were so, Nikiforov asks, how could one explain peasant revolt against landlords under the Guomindang, or the deadly enmity between the Guomindang and the Communist Party?

It is of course perfectly clear what Meliksetov is up to. He is doing unto Maoist China what Wittfogel was endeavouring to do unto Stalinist Russia. Nikiforov, very consistently, rejects such an analysis, and repeats emphatically that the AMP, the ideas of non-economic determining factors, personal relations, etc., are as baseless in contemporary history as they are in the past.[47] If an idea is indefensible in serious analysis, it cannot be used for political denigration either. And though Nikiforov derides political interference with scholarship in Mao's China, including the willingness to treat the Chairman as 'the final court of appeal on issues of ancient history', he does not stoop to attributing such habits to Asian traditions. When he earlier mentions that a mistaken theory was *also* discredited politically, 'compromised . . . by its employment by Trotskyists', he punctiliously separates the scholarly and political issues.[48]

One might put it this way: the obverse of the 'optimistic' discovery of

46 Ibid.
47 Ibid., p. 270.
48 Ibid., pp. 222, 175.

the community in the 1870s, of its progressive potential (though *only* if allied with a proletariat), is the *pessimistic* rediscovery of the AMP. Both concern the consequences of 'progressive' strivings in a backward country. If the formula for the optimistic discovery is the community-proletariat alliance, which saves at least one of the partners from having to pass through the capitalist stage, then the formula for the alternative and pessimistic diagnosis is that the very endeavour to bypass capitalism, in a society whose basic form is the AMP, results in stagnation or even deterioration under a new name and with new equipment of domination. Does this apprehensive view preclude, as Nikiforov suggests by way of refutation, social turbulence or bitter conflict between rivals for control of the new superstructure? If Nikiforov is one kind of Sovietski Wittfogel, in his acute sense of the incompatibility of the AMP with Marxist theodicy, and in his, all in all, similar view of Marx's intellectual development, then Meliksetov resembles Wittfogel in his willingness to extend the consequence of the AMP to the present (even though he applies it to another country) and in his sense of the grave danger of 'noncapitalist paths of development'.

The Importance of Being Materialist

Nikiforov's Marxism has an admirable coherence. It is capable of offering a sociological typology that is consistent with the political eschatology and salvation promise of Marxism. It is also most lucid about the sense in which that theory is 'materialist', which is more than can be said for many Western crypto-idealist neo-Marxisms.

Nikiforov interestingly refers, in so many words, as do other Soviet anthropologists, to the *idealist* theory of violence:

The meaning of the 'theory of violence' [is] the underestimation of the determining role of the economic factor. The protagonists of this viewpoint are naturally attracted by the view that Oriental society consists of stagnant communities, devoid of internal inequalities of wealth; in them, government is unconnected with classes and plays a self-sufficient role; in other words, relationships of pure violence prevail. ... Kautsky ... reached the idealist 'theory of violence'.[49]

And, commenting on Kautsky's *Materialist Conception of History* (1927), Nikiforov observes:

All [his] conclusions are plainly un-Marxist: instead of government being the product of the irreconcilable nature of class relations, it is class contradictions and exploitation that are the result of the emergence of government.[50]

49 Ibid., p. 155.
50 Ibid., p. 154.

There are formulations that make 'materialism' sound obvious: people have to eat and survive before they can think. Nikiforov's formulation, brought into such sharp relief by the AMP issue, shows materialism not to be obvious at all but, on the contrary, to constitute a very strong and interesting thesis. What is excluded by it is not just the priority of *thought*, but also equally the priority of *violence*. The phrase about 'production and reproduction' may allow kinship to enter the 'base' and escape the superstructure; but there is *no way* of extending the same courtesy to violence and the means of coercion. Marxism does not of course deny their existence; but they cannot be primary. On its view, they reflect or express pre-existing conflict; they do not finally engender it.

This materialism has, as we have seen, another most unobvious and interesting trait: its aversion to, or reserve toward, the notion of diffusion. Once again, Nikiforov puts it bluntly: 'The nations of pre-Columbian America ... did everything to prove the generality of global-historical regularities and the viciousness of the idealist theory of "diffusion".'[51] Diffusion is objectionable in much the same way as autonomous violence, with which it overlaps: if societies change radically at the behest of their accidental neighbours, by emulation or osmosis or coercion, this destroys the inner necessity both of social sin and of salvation. Moreover, just *how* do they change at the behest of neighbours? Either by sheer mimesis – the demonstration effect – which, by making fundamental changes hinge on conscious emulation, would seem to be blatantly idealist; or by violence, in which case diffusion is open once again to whatever objections may be raised against making violence crucial to social change. (If they trade voluntarily and are thereby influenced, the objection no longer applies – but then they must be *ready* to trade, so the transformation becomes to an important degree endogenous, and thus acceptable to Marxist theory.)

Yet obviously diffusion cannot be denied altogether. Both the facts of history and the works of the Founders of Marxism testify to its reality eloquently, most markedly perhaps in connection with the expansion of capitalism. Nikiforov has no wish to deny its empirical occurrence. He admits, for instance, that many nations, possibly most, including the Teutonic and Slav ones, passed from primordial communalism directly to feudalism, bypassing slave-owning society.[52] Moreover, the perception of the possibility of bypassing capitalism was a crucial element in the plot that led up to the final and correct formulation of Marxism, as Nikiforov himself insists.

51 Ibid., p. 247.
52 Ibid., p. 264.

Nikiforov allows at least four occasions of diffusion: conquest by one tribe of another, the spread of feudalism to slaveless society, the spread of capitalism, and of course the aid of backward countries by socialist ones. But the condition of diffusion, in each case, is that the diffusing *agent*, so to speak, has *endogenously* attained the higher form – has discovered exploitation or socialism, for example. Diffusion must never be a genuinely innovative agent in history. It may spread both exploitation and liberation when conditions are ripe, but it cannot independently engender either.

Against the conquest/diffusion theory of the origin of the state, Nikiforov observes:

So as to conquer an alien tribe and keep it under their power, the conqueror must have a complete (albeit primitive) government apparatus. The beginnings of an army and officialdom are phenomena unthinkable without the attainment of a definite level of production, a more or less marked accumulation of surplus product; i.e., conquest itself is the fruit of economic development.[53]

In fact, some conquests seem to have been carried out by tribal 'armies' that were virtually coextensive with the adult male population of the tribe. The tribe itself was an army, and its chiefly lineage constituted all the officialdom it needed. Nikiforov's claim here is in conflict with the views of another Soviet scholar, A. M. Khazanov, who suggests that tribal nomads could constitute a state vis-à-vis conquered populations and yet be, so to speak, stateless when at home. Moreover, Khazanov is evidently willing to consider a 'non-Morganatic' origin of the state: 'Conquest followed by the transformation of inter-ethnic into class contradictions appears to be one of the best-known paths of state-formation.'[54]

'But there is more to come,' says Nikiforov. And indeed there is:

The very idea of subjugating an alien tribe with the aim of making it work for the conquerors could not enter the head of a community of equals: the emergence of such ideas testifies to the fact that the members of the community were already familiar with the use of the labour of some for the benefit of others. And that shows that in the given community there already existed exploitation, and thus classes – even if but weakly developed and still masked by primordial forms of social organization.[55]

My intuitions diverge from Nikiforov's on this point. Though the method of imagining what-would-I-do-were-I-primitive-man has been

53 Ibid., p. 154.

54 A. M. Khazanov, *Sotsialnaia istoria Skifov* (*The Social History of the Scythians*), Moscow, Nauka, 1975, p. 237.

55 Nikiforov, *Vostok i vsemirnaia istoria*, p. 154.

much decried, it is quite irresistible here. Had *I* been primitive man, and had I lived a thousand years, then agriculture, domestication, pottery, weaving, not to mention smelting, would have remained uninvented and awaiting their discover. That's a fact. My capacity for *bricolage* does not reach that far. But as for appropriating the fruits of the labour of another, I would have stumbled onto that one, provided only that there had been someone stupid or weak enough to let me get away with it. The idea that exploitation needed *inventing*, which is evidently inherent in Marxist anthropology – Nikiforov is not the only Soviet scholar to express it – is profoundly endearing.

But what is significant for understanding the underlying pattern of Nikiforov's argument is this: the primordial community is a kind of moral baseline, from which both exploitation and domination are absent. But it is also a sociological baseline, indicating what requires *explanation*. Of the two elements, only exploitation emerges spontaneously and initially, as the original sin in the global drama. It, but only it, in turn, engenders domination, which is a kind of derivative sin, incapable of independent existence or of an autonomous role in the great collective passion play of history. No domination without (prior) exploitation.

The discovery of the primordial community, or rather of its real social potential, solved all at once a problem in both prehistory and modern political strategy. At the same time, this discovery dissipated its own evil shadow, the AMP, which had usurped one of its traits – the absence of private property – and which fused it with the idea of self-sustaining, self-serving violence. *Were* it possible for such domination to exist independently, then sin and salvation would no longer be the rational pattern of human history: suffering and oppression could enter at *any* point and, worse still, could not be relied on to depart again. Both the understanding and eventual control of history would escape us.

Dénouement

But the name for such an autonomous, socially congealed, and ineradicable domination by violence is, precisely, the Asiatic Mode of Production. So it *may not* exist if history is to be comprehensible and, eventually, if man is really to make his own history, if he is to become fully the subject, not the object, of history, if prehistory is to end. Happily, says Nikiforov, brushing the sweat of temporary fear from his brow, the facts of history firmly established that indeed it does not exist. Private property was ever present under all *political* systems. Only the primordial community lacked it. But these facts have only been properly available since the 1870s, and entered the final and correct formulation of Marxism thanks to Morgan and Kovalevsky. Both the scholarly *and* the political problem situations of the 1870s and early 1880s allowed *and* impelled the truth to emerge, a mere couple of years before Karl Marx's death. The drama of this revelation is a story Nikiforov tells admirably, and it was a cliffhanger indeed. It was just as well, perhaps, for the nerves of the then participants that they did not fully realize how much, how very much, was at stake.

4

The Autonomous Power of the State: Its Origins, Mechanisms and Results

Michael Mann

Introduction

This chapter tries to specify the origins, mechanisms and results of the autonomous power which the state possesses in relation to the major power groupings of 'civil society'. The argument is couched generally, but it derives from a large, ongoing empirical research project into the development of power in human societies.[1] At the moment, my generalizations are bolder about agrarian societies; concerning industrial societies I will be more tentative. I define the state and then pursue the implications of that definition. Two essential parts of the definition, centrality and territoriality, are discussed in relation to two types of state power, termed here *despotic* and *infrastructural* power. State autonomy, of both despotic and infrastructural forms, flows principally from the state's unique ability to provide a *territorially centralized* form of organization.

Nowadays there is no need to belabour the point that most general theories of the state have been false because they have been reductionist. They have reduced the state to the pre-existing structures of civil society. This is obviously true of the Marxist, the liberal and the

This chapter was first published in the *Archives européennes de sociologie*, vol. 25, 1984, pp. 185–213. We are grateful for permission to reproduce it here.

1 To be published as a three-volume work: *The Sources of Social Power*, vol. I: *A History of Power from the Beginnings to 1760 AD* is published by Cambridge, Cambridge University Press, 1986; vol. II: *A History of Power in Industrial Societies* will appear from the same press in 1987; vol. III: *A Theory of Power* will follow, consisting of a series of essays comparable in scope and style to this one.

functionalist traditions of state theory, each of which has seen the state predominantly as a place, an arena, in which the struggle of classes, interest groups and individuals are expressed and institutionalized, and – in functionalist versions – in which a General Will (or, to use more modern terms, core values or normative consensus) is expressed and implemented. Though such theories disagree about many things, they are united in denying significant autonomous power to the state. But despite the existence of excellent critique of such reductionism[2] and pite the self-criticism implied by the constant use of the term 'relative autonomy' by recent Marxists,[3] there has still been a curious reluctance to analyse this autonomy.

One major obstacle has been itself political. The main alternative theory which *appears* to uphold state autonomy has been associated with rather unpleasant politics. I refer to the militarist tradition of state theory embodied around the beginning of the century in the work of predominantly Germanic writers, like Gumplowicz,[4] Ratzenhofer and Schmitt. They saw the state as physical force, and as this was the prime mover in society, so the militaristic state was supreme over those economic and ideological structure identified by the reductionist theories. But the scientific merits of these societies were quickly submerged by their political associations – with Social Darwinism, racism, glorification of state power and then fascism. The final (deeply ironic) outcome was that militarist theory was defeated on the battlefield by the combined forces of (Marxist) Russia and the (liberal democratic and functionalist) Western allies. We have heard little of it directly since. But its indirect influence has been felt, especially recently, through the work of 'good Germans' like Weber, Hintze, Rüstow and the anarchist Oppenheimer, all influenced to one degree or another by the German militarist tradition, and all of whose major works have now been translated into English.[5]

I am not advocating a return to this alternative tradition, even at its scientific level. For when we look more closely, we see that it is usually also reductionist. The state is still nothing in itself: it is merely the embodiment of physical force in society. The state is not an arena where

2 S. Wolin, *Politics and Vision*, Berkeley, University of California Press, 1961.

3 N. Poulantzas, *Pouvoir politique et classes sociales*, Paris, Maspero, 1972; G. Therborn, *What Does the Ruling Class Do When It Rules?*, London, New Left Books, 1978.

4 L. Gumplowicz, *The Outlines of Sociology*, Philadelphia, American Academy of Political and Social Science, 1899.

5 O. Hintze, *The Historical Essays of Otto Hintze*, ed. F. Gilbert, New York, Oxford University Press, 1975; F. Oppenheimer, *The State*, New York, Free Life Editions, 1975; A. Rustow, *Freedom and Domination: An Historical Critique of Civilisation*, Princeton, Princeton University Press, 1975.

domestic economic/ideological issues are resolved, rather it is an arena in which military force is mobilized domestically and used domestically and, above, all, internationally.

Both types of theory have merit, yet both are partial. So what would happen if we put them together in a single theory? We would assemble an essentially dual theory of the state. It would identify two dimensions: the domestic, economic/ideological aspect of the state and the military, international aspect of states. In the present climate of comparative sociology, dominated by a Marxified Weberianism, domestic analysis would be likely to centre upon class relations. And as states would now be responding to two types of pressure and interest groups, a certain 'space' would be created in which a state elite could manoeuvre, play off classes against war factions and other states, and so stake out an area and degree of power autonomy for itself. To put the two together would give us a rudimentary account of state autonomy.

That is indeed precisely the point at which the best state theory has now arrived. It is exemplified by Theda Skocpol's excellent *States and Social Revolutions*. Skocpol draws upon Marx and Weber in about equal quantities. She quotes enthusiastically Otto Hintze's two-dimensional view of the determinants of state organization: 'first, the structure of social classes, and second, the external ordering of the states – their position relative to each other, and their over-all position in the world', and she then expands the latter in terms of military relations. These two 'basic sets of tasks' are undertaken by 'a set of administrative, policing and military organizations headed, and more or less well co-ordinated by, an executive authority' for whom resoures are extracted from society. These resource-supported administrative and coercive organizations are 'the basis of state power as such'. This power can then be used with a degree of autonomy against either the dominant class, or against domestic war or peace factions and foreign states.[6] A very similar approach underlies Charles Tilly's recent work;[7] and Anthony Giddens has argued in similar vein.[8]

Now I do not wish quite to abandon this 'two-dimensional' model of the state – for I, too, have contributed a detailed analysis of English state finances in the period 1130–1815 starting from such a model.[9] All these

6 T. Skocpol, *States and Social Revoolutions*, Cambridge, Cambridge University Press, 1979, pp. 29–31.

7 C. Tilly, *As Sociology Meets History*, New York, Academic Press, 1981, chapters 5 and 8.

8 A. Giddens, *A Contemporary Critique of Historical Materialism*, London, Macmillan, 1981.

9 M. Mann, 'State and society, 1130–1815: an analysis of English state finances', in M. Zeitlin, ed., *Political Power and Social Theory*, vol. I, Connecticut, J.A.I. Press, 1980.

works advance beyond reductionism. We can develop their insights considerably further, and so penetrate to the heart of state autonomy, its nature, degree and consequences. But to do this we must make a far more radical, yet in a sense peculiar and paradoxical, break with reductionism. I shall argue in this chapter that the state is merely and essentially an arena, a place, and yet this is the very source of its autonomy.

Defining the State

The state is undeniably a messy concept. The main problem is that most definitions contain two different levels of analysis, the 'institutional' and the 'functional'. That is, the state can be defined in terms of what it looks like, institutionally, or what it does, its functions. Predominant is a mixed, but largely institutional, view put forward originally by Weber. In this the state contains four main elements, being:

1 a *differentiated* set of institutions and personnel, embodying
2 *centrality*, in the sense that political relations radiate outwards from a centre to cover a
3 *territorially demarcated area*, over which it exercises
4 a monopoly of *authoritative binding rule-making*, backed up by a monopoly of the means of physical violence.[10]

Apart from the last phrase which tends to equate the state with military force (see below), I will follow this definition. It is still something of a mixed bag. It contains a predominant institutional element: states can be recognized by the central location of their differentiated institutions. Yet it also contains a 'functional' element: the essence of the state's functions is a monopoly of binding rule-making. Nevertheless, my principal interest lies in those centralized institutions generally called 'states', and in the powers of the personnel who staff them, at the higher levels generally termed the 'state elite'. The central question for us here, then, is what is the nature of the power possessed by states and state elites? In answering I shall contrast state elites with power groupings whose base lies outside the state, in 'civil society'. In line with the model of power underlying my work, I divide these into three, ideological, economic and military groups. So what, therefore, is the power of state elites as against the power of ideological movements, economic classes, and military elites?

10 See for examples the definitions of S. Eisenstadt, *The Political Systems of Empires*, New York, The Free Press, 1969, p. 5; R. N. MacIver, *The Modern State*, Oxford, Clarendon, 1926, p. 22; C. Tilly, 'Reflections on the History of European State-making', in

Two Meanings of State Power

What do we mean by 'the power of the state'? As soon as we begin to think about this commonplace phrase, we encounter two quite different senses in which states and their elites might be considered powerful. We must disentangle them. The first sense concerns what we might term the *despotic power* of the state elite, the range of actions which the elite is empowered to undertake without routine, institutionalized negotiation with civil society groups. The historical variations in such powers have been so enormous that we can safely leave on one side the ticklish problem of how we precisely measure them. The despotic powers of many historical states have been virtually unlimited. The Chinese Emperor, as the Son of Heaven, 'owned' the whole of China and could do as he wished with any individual or group within his domain. The Roman Emperor, only a minor god, acquired powers which were also in principle unlimited outside of a restricted area of affairs nominally controlled by the Senate. Some monarchs of early modern Europe also claimed divinely derived, absolute powers (though they were not themselves divine). The members of the contemporary Soviet state/party elite, as 'trustees' of the interests of the masses, also possess considerable despotic (though sometimes strictly unconstitutional) power. Great despotic power can be 'measured' most vividly in the ability of all these Red Queens to shout 'off with his head' and have their whim gratified without further ado – provided the person is at hand. Despotic power is also usually what is meant in the literature by 'autonomy of power'.

But there is a second sense in which people talk of 'the power of the state', especially in today's capitalist democracies. We might term this *infrastructural power*, the capacity of the state actually to penetrate civil society, and to implement logistically political decisions throughout the realm. This was comparatively weak in the historical societies just mentioned; once you were out of sight of the Red Queen, she had difficulty in getting at you. But it is powerfully developed in all industrial societies. When people in the West today complain of the growing power of the state, they cannot be referring sensibly to the despotic powers of the state elite itself, for if anything these are still declining. It is, after all, only 40 years since universal suffrage was fully established in several of the advanced capitalist states, and the basic political rights of

C. Tilly, ed., *The Formation of National States in Western Europe*, Princeton, Princeton University Press, 1975, p. 27; and Max Weber, *Economy and Society*, New York, Bedminster Press, 1968, vol. I, p. 64.

groups such as ethnic minorities and women are still increasing. But the complaint is more justly levelled against the state's infrastructural encroachments. These powers are now immense. The state can assess and tax our income and wealth at source, without our consent or that of our neighbours or kin (which states before about 1850 were never able to do); it stores and can recall immediately a massive amount of information about all of us; it can enforce its will within the day almost anywhere in its domains; its influence on the overall economy is enormous; it even directly provides the subsistence of most of us (in state employment, in pensions, in family allowances, etc.). The state penetrates everyday life more than did any historical state. Its infrastructural power has increased enormously. If there were a Red Queen, we should all quail at her words – from Alaska to Florida, from the Shetlands to Cornwall there is no hiding place from the infrastructural reach of the modern state.

But who controls these states? Without prejudging a complex issue entirely, the answer in the capitalist democracies is less likely to be 'an autonomous state elite' than in most historic societies. In these countries most of the formal political leadership is elected and recallable. Whether one regards the democracy as genuine or not, few would contest that politicians are largely controlled by outside civil society groups (either by their financiers or by the electorate) as well as by the law. President Nixon or M. Chaban-Delmas may have paid no taxes; political leaders may surreptitiously amass wealth, infringe the civil liberties of their opponents, and hold onto power by slying undemocratic means. But they do not brazenly expropriate or kill their enemies or dare to overturn legal traditions enshrining constitutional rule, private property or individual freedoms. On the rare occasions this happens, we refer to it as a *coup* or a revolution, an overturning of the norms. If we turn from elected politicians to permanent bureaucrats we still do not find them exercising significant autonomous power over civil society. Perhaps I should qualify this, for the secret decisions of politicians and bureaucrats penetrate our everyday lives in an often infuriating way, deciding we are not eligible for this or that benefit, including, for some persons, citizenship itself. But their power to change the fundamental rules and overturn the distribution of power within civil society is feeble – without the backing of a formidable social movement.

So, in one sense states in the capitalist democracies are weak, in another they are strong. They are 'despotically weak' but 'infrastructurally strong'. Let us clearly distinguish these two types of state power. The first sense denotes power by the state elite itself *over* civil society. The second denotes the power of the state to penetrate and centrally coordinate the activities of civil society through its own infrastructure. The second type of power still allows the possibility that the state itself is a mere instrument of forces within civil society, i.e. that it has no despotic power at all. The two are analytically autonomous dimensions of power. In practice, of course, there may be a relationship between them. For example, the greater the state's infrastructural power, the greater the volume of binding rule-making, and therefore the greater the likelihood of despotic power over individuals and perhaps also over marginal, minority groups. All infrastructurally powerful states, including the capitalist democracies, are strong in relation to individuals and to the weaker groups in civil society, but the capitalist democratic states are feeble in relation to dominant groups, at least in comparison to most historical states.

From these two independent dimensions of state power we can derive four ideal-types in figure 1 below. The *feudal* state is the weakest, for it

		Infrastructural co-ordination	
		Low	High
Despotic power	Low	Feudal	Bureaucratic
	High	Imperial	Authoritarian

Figure 1 Two dimensions of state power

has both low despotic and low infrastructural power. The medieval European state approximated to this ideal-type, governing largely indirectly, through infrastructure freely and contractually provided and controlled by the principal and independent magnates, clerics and towns. The *imperial* state possesses its own governing agents, but has only limited capacity to penetrate and co-ordinate civil society without the assistance of other power groups. It corresponds to the term 'patrimonial state' used by writers like Weber and Bendix.[11] Ancient states like the Akkadian, Egyptian, Assyrian, Persian and Roman approximated to this type. I hesitated over the term *bureaucratic* state, because of its negative connotations. But a bureaucracy has a high organizational capacity, yet cannot set its own goals; and the bureaucratic state is controlled by others, civil society groups, but their decisions once taken are enforceable through the state's infrastructure. Contemporary capitalist democracies approximate to this type as does the future state hoped for by most radicals and socialists. *Authoritarian* is intended to

11 M. Weber, *Economy and Society*; R. Bendix, *Kings or People*, Berkeley, University of California Press, 1978.

suggest a more institutionalized form of despotism, in which competing power groupings cannot evade the infrastructural reach of the state, nor are they structurally separate from the state (as they are in the bureaucratic type). All significant social power must go through the authoritative command structure of the state. Thus it is high on both dimensions, having high despotic power over civil society groups and being able to enforce this infrastructurally. In their different ways, Nazi Germany and the Soviet Union tend towards this case. But they probably traded off some loss of infrastructural penetration for high despotic powers (thus neither attained as high a level of social mobilization during the Second World War as the 'despotically weak' but participatory Great Britain did). Nor is this to deny that such states contain competing interest groups which may possess different bases in 'civil society'. Rather, in an authoritarian state power is transmitted through its directives and so such groups compete for direct control of the state. It is different in the capitalist democracies where the power of the capitalist class, for example, permeates the whole of society, and states generally accept the rules and rationality of the surrounding capitalist economy.

These are ideal-types. Yet my choice of real historical examples which roughly approximate to them reveals two major tendencies which are obvious enough yet worthy of explanation. First, there has occurred a long-term historical growth in the infrastructural power of the state, apparently given tremendous boosts by industrial societies, but also perceptible within both pre-industrial and industrial societies considered separately. Second, however, within each historical epoch have occurred wide variations in despotic powers. There has been no general developmental tendency in despotic powers – non-despotic states existed in late fourth-millennium BC Mesopotamia (the 'primitive democracy' of the early city-states), in first-millennium BC Phoenicia, Greece and Rome, in medieval republics and city-states, and in the modern world alike. The history of despotism has been one of oscillation, not development. Why such wide divergencies on one dimension, but a developmental trend on the other?

The Development of State Infrastructural Power

The growth of the infrastructural power of the state is one in the logistics of political control. I will not here enumerate its main historical phases. Instead, I cite some logistical techniques which have aided effective state penetration of social life, each of which has had a long historical development.

1   A division of labour between the state's main activities which it co-ordinated centrally. A microcosm of this is to be found on the battle-fields of history where a co-ordinated administrative division between infantry, cavalry and artillery, usually organized by the state, would normally defeat forces in which these activities were mixed up – at least in 'high intensity' warfare.

2   Literacy, enabling stabilized messages to be transmitted through the state's territories by its agents, and enabling legal responsibilities to be codified and stored. Giddens emphasizes this 'storage' aspect of state power.[12]

3   Coinage, and weights and measures, allowing commodities to be exchanged under an ultimate guarantee of value by the state.

4   Rapidity of communication of messages and of transport of people and resources, through improved roads, ships, telegraphy etc.

States able to use relatively highly developed forms of these techniques have possessed greater capacity for infrastructural penetration. This is pretty obvious. So is the fact that history has seen a secular process of infrastructural improvements.

Yet none of these techniques is specific to the state. They are part of general social development, part of the growth of human beings' increasing capacities for collective social mobilization of resources. Societies in general, not just their states, have advanced their powers. Thus none of these techniques necessarily changes the relationship between a state and its civil society; and none is necessarily pioneered by either the state or civil society.

Thus state power (in either sense) does not derive from techniques or means of power that are peculiar to itself. The varied techniques of power are of three main types: military, economic and ideological. They are characteristic of all social relationships. The state uses them all, adding no fourth means peculiar to itself. This has made reductionist theories of the state more plausible because the state seems dependent on resources also found more generally in civil society. If they are all wrong, it is not because the state manipulates means of power denied to other groups. The state is not autonomous in this sense.

Indeed, the fact that the means used are essentially also the means used in all social relationships ensures that states rarely diverge far from their civil societies. Let us examine what happens when a state pioneers an increase in logistic powers. A characteristic, though slow-paced example, is literacy. The first stages of literacy in Mesopotamia, and probably also in the other major independent cases of the emergence of

12   A. Giddens, *Contemporary Critique of Historical Materialism*.

civilization, occurred within the state. In this respect, the state was largely codifying and stabilizing two kinds of emergent norms, 'private' property rights and community rights and duties. The first pictograms and logograms enabled scribes at city-state temple-storehouses to improve their accountancy systems, and denote more permanently who possessed what and who owed what to the community. It solidified relations radiating across the surrounding territory and centred them more on itself. Writing then simplified into syllabic cuneiform script still essentially within the state bureucracy, and performing the same dual functions. Writing was an important part of the growth of the first imperial states, that is of the Akkadian and subsequent empires of the third and second millennia BC. Literacy was restricted to the bureaucracy, stabilized its systems of justice and communications, and so provided infrastructural support to a state despotism, though apparently in some kind of alliance with a property-owning economic class.

Yet the general utility of literacy was now recognized by civil society groups. By the time that the next simplifications, alphabetic script and parchment, became common (around the beginning of the first millennium BC), state domination had ended. The main pioneers were now not despotic states but decentralized groups of peasant-traders, village priests, and trading peoples organized into loose federations of small city- or tribal-states like the Arameans, the Phoenicians and the Greeks. From then on, the power of such groups, usually with non-despotic states, rivalled that of the despotic empires. What had started by bolstering despotism continued by undermining it when the techniques spread beyond state confines. The states could not keep control over their own logistical inventions. And this is generally the case with all such inventions, whatever period of history we consider. In our time we have instances such as 'statistics': originally things which appertain to the state, later a useful method of systematic information-gathering for any power organization, especially large capitalist corporations.

However, converse examples are not difficult to find either, where states appropriate infrastructural techniques pioneered by civil society groups. The course of industrialization has seen several such examples, culminating in the Soviet Union whose state communications, surveillance and accountancy systems are similar to those pioneered by capitalist enterprises (with their states as junior partners) in the West. In this example what started in civil society continued in state despotism. Infrastructural techniques diffuse outwards from the particular power organizations that invented them.

Two conclusions emerge. First, in the whole history of the development of the infrastructure of power there is virtually no technique which belongs necessarily to the state, or conversely to civil society. Second, there is some kind of oscillation between the role of the two in social development. I hope to show later than it is not merely oscillation, but a dialectic.

The obvious question is: if infrastructural powers are a general feature of society, in what circumstances are they appropriated by the state? How does the state acquire in certain situations, but not others, despotic powers? What are the origins of the autonomous power of the state? My answer is in three stages, touching upon the *necessity* of the state, its *multiplicity of functions*, and its *territorialized centrality*. The first two have often been identified in recent theory; the third is, I think, novel.

Origins of State Power

1   *The necessity of the state*

The only stateless societies have been primitive. There are no complex, civilized societies without any centre of binding rule-making authority, however limited its scope. If we consider the weak feudal cases we find that even they tend to arise from a more state-centred history whose norms linger on to reinforce the new weak states. Feudal states tend to emerge either as a check to the further disintegration of a once-unified larger state (as in China and Japan) or as a post-conquest division of the spoils among the victorious, and obviously united, conquerors.[13] Western European feudalism embodies both these histories, though in varying mixtures in different regions. The laws of the feudal states in Europe were reinforced by rules descending from Roman law (especially property law), Christian codes of conduct, and Germanic notions of loyalty and honour. This is a further glimpse of a process to which I will return later: a perpetual dialectic of movement between state and civil society.

Thus societies with states have had superior survival value to those without them. We have no examples of stateless societies long enduring past a primitive level of development, and many examples of state societies absorbing or eliminating stateless ones. Where stateless societies conquer ones with states, they either themselves develop a state or they induce social regress in the conquered society. There are good sociological reasons for this. Only three alternative bases for order exist, force, exchange and custom, and none of these are sufficient in the long run. At some point new exigencies arise for which custom is inadequate; at some point to bargain about everything in exchange

13 O. Lattimore, 'Feudalism in history: a review essay', *Past and Present*, no. 12, 1957.

relations is inefficient and disintegrating; while force alone, as Parsons emphasized, will soon 'deflate'. In the long run normally taken-for-granted, but enforceable, rules are necessary to bind together strangers or semi-strangers. It is not requisite that all these rules are set by a single monopolistic state. Indeed, though the feudal example is extreme, most states exist in a multi-state civilization which also provides certain normative rules of conduct. Nevertheless most societies seem to have required that some rules, particularly those relevant to the protection of life and property, be set monopolistically, and this has been the province of the state.

From this necessity, autonomous state power ultimately derives. The activities of the state personnel are necessary to society as a whole and/or to the various groups that benefit from the existing structure of rules which the state enforces. From this functionality derives the potentiality for exploitation, a lever for the achievement of private state interests. Whether the lever is used depends on other conditions, for – after all – we have not even established the existence of permanent state cadre which might have identifiable interests. But necessity is the mother of state power.

2   *The multiplicity of state functions*

Despite the assertions of reductionists, most states have not in practice devoted themselves to the pursuit of a single function. 'Binding rule-making' is merely an umbrella term. The rules and functions have been extremely varied. As the two-dimensional models recognize, we may distinguish domestic and international, or economic, ideological and military functions. But there are many types of activity and each tends to be functional for differing 'constituencies' in society. I illustrate this with reference to what have been probably the four most persistent types of state activities.

1   *The maintenance of internal order.* This may benefit all, or all law-abiding, subjects of the state. It may also protect the majority from arbitrary usurpations by socially and economically powerful groups, other than those allied to the state. But probably the main benefit is to protect existing property relations from the mass of the propertyless. This function probably best serves a dominant economic class consti-tuency.

2   *Military defence/aggression*, directed against foreign foes. 'War parties' are rarely coterminous with either the whole society or with one particular class within it. Defence may be genuinely collective; aggres-sion usually has more specific interests behind it. Those interests may

be quite widely shared by all 'younger sons' without inheritance rights or all those expansively-minded; or they might comprise only a class fraction of an aristocracy, merchants or capitalists. In multi-state systems war usually involves alliances with other states, some of whom may share the same religion, ethnicity, or political philosophy as some domestic constituency. These are rarely reducible to economic class. Hence war and peace constituencies are usually somewhat idiosyncratic.

3   *The maintenance of communications infrastructures*: roads, rivers, message systems, coinages, weights and measures, marketing arrangements. Though few states have monopolized all of these, all states have provided some, because they have a territorial basis which is often most efficiently organized from a centre. The principal constituencies here are a 'general interest' and more particular trade-centred groups.

4   *Economic redistribution*: the authoritative distribution of scarce material resources between different ecological niches, age-groups, sexes, regions, classes etc. There is a strongly collective element in this function, more so than in the case of the others. Nevertheless, many of the redistributions involve rather particular groups, especially the economically inactive whose subsistence is thus protected by the state. And economic redistribution also has an international dimension, for the state normally regulates trade relations and currency exchanges across its boundaries, sometimes unilaterally, sometimes in alliance with other states. This also gives the state a particular constituency among merchants and other international agents – who, however, are rarely in agreement about desirable trade policy.

These four tasks are necessary, either to society as a whole or to interest groups within it. They are undertaken most efficiently by the personnel of a central state who become indispensable. And they bring the state into functional relations with diverse, sometimes cross-cutting groups between whom there is room to manoeuvre. The room can be exploited. Any state involved in a multiplicity of power relations can play off interest groups against each other.

It is worth noting that one example of this 'divide and rule' strategy has been a staple of sociological analysis. This is the case of a 'transitional state', living amid profound economic transformations from one mode of production to another. No single dominant economic class exists, and the state may play off traditional power groups against emergent ones. Such situations were discussed by both the classic stratification theorists. Marx analysed and satirized Louis Bonaparte's attempts to play off the factions of industrial and finance capital, petite bourgeoisie, peasantry and proletariat to enhance his own independent power. This is the 'Bonapartist balancing act', so stressed by Poulantzas[14] – though Marx (and Poulantzas) rather underestimated Bonaparte's ability to succeed.[15] Weber was struck by the ability of the Prussian state to use a declining economic class, the agrarian landlord Junkers, to hold onto autocratic power in the vacuum created by the political timidity of the rising bourgeois and proletarian classes.[16] All the various groups in both examples needed the state, but none could capture it. Another example is the development of absolutism in early modern Europe. Monarchs played off against each other (or were unable to choose between) feudal and bourgeois, land and urban, groups. In particular, military functions and functions performed in relation to dominant economic classes were different. States used war as a means of attempting to reduce their dependence on classes.[17]

These are familiar examples of the state balancing between predominantly classes or class factions. But the balancing possibilities are much more numerous if the state is involved in a multiplicity of relations with groups which may on some issues be narrower than classes and on others wider. Because most states are pursuing multiple functions, they can perform multiple manoeuvres. The 'Bonapartist balancing act' is skill acquired by most states. This manoeuvring space is the birthplace of state power.

And this is about as far as the insights contained within current two-dimensional theory can be expanded. It is progress, but not enough. It does not really capture the distinctiveness of the state as a social organization. After all, necessity plus multiplicity of function, and the balancing act, are also the power source and stock in trade of any ruthless committee chairperson. Is the state only a chair writ large? No – as we will now see.

3   *The territorial centrality of the state*

The definition of the state concentrates upon its institutional, territorial, centralized nature. This is the third, and most important, precondition of state power. As noted, the state does not possess a distinctive means of power independent of, and analogous to, economic, military and

14 Poulantzas, *Pouvoir politique et classes sociales*.
15 V. Perez-Diaz, *State, Bureaucracy and Civil Society: A Critical Discussion of the Political Theory of Karl Marx*, London, Macmillan, 1979.
16 L. Lachman, *The Legacy of Max Weber*, London, Heinemann Educational Books, 1970.
17 Skocpol, *States and Social Revolutions*; E. Trimberger, *Revolution from Above: Military Bureaucrats and Development in Japan, Turkey, Egypt and Peru*, New Brunswick, Transaction Books, 1978.

ideological power. The means used by states are only a combination of these, which are also the means of power used in all social relationships. However, the power of the state is irreducible in quite a different socio-spatial and organizational sense. Only the state is inherently centralized over a delimited territory over which it has authoritative power. Unlike economic, ideological or military groups in civil society, the state elite's resources radiate authoritatively outwards from a centre but stop at defined territorial boundaries. The state is, indeed, a place – both a central place and a unified territorial reach. As the principal form of state autonomous power will flow from this distinctive attribute of the state, it is important that I first prove that the state does so differ socio-spatially and organizationally from the major power groupings of civil society.

Economic power groupings – classes, corporations, merchant houses, manors, plantations, the *oikos* etc. – normally exist in decentred, competitive or conflictual relations with one another. True, the internal arrangements of some of them (e.g. the modern corporation, or the household and manor of the great feudal lord) might be relatively centralized. But, first, they are oriented outwards to further opportunities for economic advantage which are not territorially confined nor subject to authoritative rules governing expansion (except by states). Economic power expansion is not authoritative, commanded – it is 'diffused', informally. Second, the scope of modern and some historic economic institutions is not territorial. They do not exercise general control of a specific territory, they control a specialized function and seek to extend it 'transnationally' wherever that function is demanded and exploitable. General Motors does not rule the territory around Detroit, it rules the assembly of automobiles and some aspects of the economic life-chances of its employees, stockholders and consumers. Third, in those cases where economic institutions have been authoritative, centralized and territorial (as in the feudal household/manor of historic nobilities) they have either been subject to a higher level of territorial, central control by the (imperial) state, or they have acquired political functions (administering justice, raising military levies etc.) from a weak (feudal) state and so become themselves 'mini-states'. Thus states cannot be the simple instrument of classes, for they have a different territorial scope.

Analogous points can be made about ideological power movements like religions. Ideologies (unless state-led) normally spread even more diffusely than economic relations. They move diffusely and 'interstitially' inside state territories, spreading through communication networks among segments of a state's population (like classes, age-cohorts, genders, urban/rural inhabitants etc.); they often also move transnationally right through state boundaries. Ideologies may develop central, authoritative, church-like institutions, but these are usually functionally, more than territorially, organized: they deal with the sacred rather than the secular, for example. There is a socio-spatial, as well as a spiritual, 'transcendence' about ideological movements, which is really the opposite of the territorial bounds of the state.

It is true, however, that military power overlaps considerably with the state, especially in modern states who usually monopolize the means of organized violence. Nevertheless, it is helpful to treat the two as distinct sources of power. I have not the space here fully to justify this.[18] Let me instead make two simple points. First, not all warfare is most efficiently organized territorially centrally – guerrillas, military feudalism and warrior bands are all examples of relatively decentred military organizations effective at many historical periods. Second, the effective scope of military power does not cover a single, unitary territory. In fact, it has two rather different territorial radii of effective control.

Militaristic control of everyday behaviour requires such a high level of organized coercion, logistical back-up and surplus extraction that it is practical only within close communications to the armed forces in areas of high surplus availability. It does not spread evenly over entire state territories. It remains concentrated in pockets and along communications routes. It is relatively ineffective at penetrating peasant agriculture, for example.

The second radius enables, not everyday control, but the setting of broad limits of outward compliance over far greater areas. In this case, failure to comply with broad parameters such as the handling of tribute, the performance of ritual acts of submission, occasional military support (or at least non-rebellion), could result in a punitive expedition, and so is avoided. This radius of military striking power has normally been far greater than that of state political control, as Owen Lattimore brilliantly argued.[19] This is obviously so in the world today, given the capabilities of modern armaments. It is also true of the Superpowers in a more subtle sense: they can impose 'friendly' regimes and destabilize the unfriendly through client military elites and their own covert paramilitary organizations, but they cannot get those regimes to conform closely to their political dictates. A more traditional example would be Britain's punitive expedition to the Falklands, capable of defeating and so delegitimizing the Argentine regime, and remaining capable of repeating the punishment, but quite incapable of providing a political future for the Islands. The logistics of 'concentrated coercion' – that is, of military

18 For a full justification see Mann, *Sources of Social Power*, vol. I, chapter 1.
19 O. Lattimore, *Studies in Frontier History*, London, Oxford University Press, 1982.

power – differ from those of the territorial centralized state. Thus we should distinguish the two as power organizations. The militarist theory of the state is false, and one reason for this is that the state's organization is not coterminous with military organization.

The organizational autonomy of the state is only partial; indeed, in many particular cases it may be rather small. General Motors and the capitalist class in general, or the Catholic Church, or the feudal lords and knights, or the US military, are or were quite capable of keeping watch on states they have propped up. Yet they could not do the states' jobs themselves unless they changed their own socio-spatial and organizational structure. A state autonomous power ensues from this difference. Even if a particular state is set up or intensified merely to institutionalize the relations between given social groups, this is done by concentrating resources and infrastructures in the hands of an institution that has different socio-spatial and organizational contours to those groups. Flexibility and speed of response entail concentration of decision-making and a tendency towards permanence of personnel. The decentred non-territorial interest-groups that set up the state in the first place are thus less able to control it. Territorial centralization provides the state with a potentially independent basis of power mobilization, being necessary to social development and uniquely in the possession of the state itself.

If we add together the necessity, multiplicity and territorial centrality of the state, we can in principle explain its autonomous power. By these means the state elite possesses an independence from civil society which, though not absolute, is no less absolute in principle than the power of any other major group. Its power cannot be reduced to their power either directly or 'ultimately' or 'in the last instance'. The state is not merely a locus of class struggle, an instrument of class rule, the factor of social cohesion, the expression of core values, the centre of social allocation processes, the institutionalization of military force (as in the various reductionist theories); it is a different socio-spatial organization. As a consequence we can treat states as actors, in the persona of state elites, with a will to power and we can engage in the kind of 'rational action' theory of state interests advocated by Levi.[20]

The Mechanisms for Acquiring Autonomous State Power

Of course, this in itself does not confer a significant degree of actual power upon the state elite, for civil society groups even though slightly

20 M. Levi, 'The Predatory theory of rule', *Politics and Society*, vol. 10, 1981.

differently organized may yet be able to largely control it. But the principles do offer us a pair of hypotheses for explaining variations of power: (1) State infrastructural power derives from the social utility in any particular time and place of forms of territorial centralization which cannot be provided by civil society forces themselves; (2) The extent of state despotic power derives from the inability of civil society forces to control those forms of territorial centralization, once set up. Hence, there are two phases in the development of despotism: the growth of territorial centralization, and the loss of control over it. First function, then exploitation; let us take them in order.

Because states have undertaken such a variety of social activities, there are also numerous ways in which at different times they have acquired a disproportionate part of society's capacity for infrastructural co-ordination. Let me pick out three relatively uncontentious examples: the utility of a redistributive economy, of a co-ordinated military command for conquest or defence, and of a centrally co-ordinated 'late development' response to one's rivals. These are all common conditions favouring the territorial centralization of social resources.

The redistributive state seems to have been particularly appropriate, as anthropologists and archaeologists argue, in the early history of societies before the exchange of commodities was possible. Different ecological niches delivered their surpluses to a central storehouse which eventually became a permanent state. The case is often over-argued,[21] but it has often been archaeologically useful.[22] The military route was, perhaps, the best-known to the nineteenth-century and early twentieth-century theorists like Spencer, Gumplowicz and Oppenheimer.[23] Though they exaggerated its role, there is no doubt that most of the well-known ancient empires had the infrastructural powers of their states considerably boosted by their use of centralized, highly organized, disciplined, and well-equipped military forces for both defence and further conquest; Rome is the example best-known to us.[24] Third, the response of late industrial developers in the nineteenth and twentieth centuries to the interference of their early-industrializing rivals is well known: a cumulative development through countries like France, Prussia, Japan and Russia of more and more centralized and territorially confined mobilization of economic resources with state financing and

21 E. Service, *Origins of the State and Civilization*, New York, W. W. Norton, 1975.
22 C. Renfrew, *The Emergence of Civilisation: the cyclades and the Aegean in the Third Millennium B.C.*, London, Methuen, 1972.
23 H. Spencer, *Principles of Sociology*, 1-vol. abridgement, London, Macmillan, 1969; Gumplowicz, *Outlines of Sociology*; Oppenheimer, *The State*.
24 K. Hopkins, *Conquerors and Slaves*, Cambridge, Cambridge University Press, 1978.

state enterprises sheltering behind tariff walls.[25] But it also has earlier parallels – for example, in the history of Assyria or the early Roman Republic, imitating earlier civilizations, but in a more centralized fashion.

Note that in all cases it is not economic or military necessity *per se* that increases the role of the state, for this might merely place it into the hands of classes or military groups in civil society. It is rather the more particular utility of economic or military *territorial centralization* in a given situation. There are other types of economy (e.g. market exchange) and of military organization (e.g. 'feudal' cavalry or chariotry, castle defence) which encourage decentralization and so reduce state power. In all these above examples the principal power groupings of civil society freely conferred infrastructural powers upon their states. My explanation thus starts in a functionalist vein. But functions are then exploited and despotism results. The hypothesis is that civil society freely gives resources but then loses control and becomes oppressed by the state. How does this happen?

Let us consider first that old war-horse, the origins of the state. In some theories of state origins, the loss of control by 'civilians' is virtually automatic. For example, in the militarist tradition of theory, the leading warriors are seen as automatically converting temporary, legitimate authority in wartime to permanent, coercive power in peacetime. Yet as Clastres has pointed out, primitive societies take great precautions to ensure that their military leaders do not become permanent oppressors.[26] Similarly, the redistributive state of the anthropologists seems to have contained a number of checks against chiefly usurpation which makes its further development problematic. In fact, it seems that permanent, coercive states did *not* generally evolve in later prehistory. Only in a few unusual cases (connected with the regional effects of alluvial agriculture) did 'pristine' states evolve endogenously, and they influenced all other cases.[27] The problem seems to be that for centralized functions to be converted into exploitation, organizational resources are necessary that only actually appeared with the emergence of civilized, stratified, state societies – a circular process.

However, the process is somewhat clearer with respect to the intensification of state power in already established, stratified, civilized societies with states. It is clearest of all in relation to military conquest states. We know enough about early Rome and other, earlier cases to

25 This strategy was classically described by A. Gerschenkron, *Economic Backwardness in Historical Perspective*, Cambridge, Mass., Belknap Press, 1962.

26 P. Clastres, *Society against the State*, Oxford, Blackwell, 1977.

27 I make this argument at greater length in my *Sources of Social Power*, vol. I, chapters 2–4.

extend Spencer's notion of 'compulsory co-operation'.[28] Spencer saw that conquest may put new resources into the hands of the conquering centralized command such that it was able to attain a degree of autonomy from the groups who had set it in motion. But Spencer's argument can be widened into the sphere of agricultural production. In pre-industrial conditions increasing the productivity of labour usually involved increasing the intensity of effort. This was most easily obtained by coercion. A militarized economy could increase output and be of benefit to civil society at large, or at least to its dominant groups. Obviously, in most agricultural conditions, coercion could not be routinely applied. But where labour was concentrated – say, in irrigation agriculture, in plantations, mines and in construction works – it could. But this required the maintenance of centalized militarism, because a centralized regime was more efficient at using a minimum of military resources for maximum effect.

This would really require considerable elaboration. In my work I call it 'military Keynesianism' because of the multiplier effects which are generated by military force.[29] These effects boost the despotic power of the state vis-à-vis civil society because they make useful the maintenance of centralized compulsory co-operation, which civil society cannot at first provide itself. It is an example of how centralization increases general social resources – and thus no powerful civil society group wishes to dispense with the state – yet also increases the private power resources of the state elite. These can now be used despotically against civil society.

Provided the state's activities generate extra resources, then it has a particular logistical advantage. Territorial centralization gives effective mobilizing potentialities, able to concentrate these resources against any particular civil society group, even though it may be inferior in overall resources. Civil society groups may actually endorse state power. If the state upholds given relations of production, then the dominant economic class will have an interest in efficient state centralization. If the state defends society from outside aggressors, or represses crime, then its centrality will be supported quite widely in society. Naturally, the degree of centralization useful to these civil society interests will vary according to the system of production or method of warfare in question. Centrality can also be seen in the sphere of ideology, as Eisenstadt argues.[30] The state and the interests it serves have always sought to

28 I outline this process in 'States, ancient and modern', *Archives européennes de sociologie*, vol. 18, 1977.

29 *Sources of Social Power*, vol. I, chapter 9.

30 Eisenstadt, *Political Systems of Empires*.

uphold its authority by a claim to 'universalism' over its territories, a detachment from all particularistic, specialized ties to kin, locality, class, church etc. Naturally in practice states tend to represent the interests of particular kinship groupings, localities, classes etc., but if they appeared merely to do this they would lose all claim to distinctiveness and to legitimacy. States thus appropriate what Eisenstadt calls 'free-floating resources', not tied to any particular interest group, able to float throughout the territorially defined society.

This might seem a formidable catalogue of state powers. And yet the autonomous power achievements of historical states before the twentieth century were generally limited and precarious. Here we encounter the fundamental logistical, infrastructural constraints operating against centralized regimes in extensive agrarian societies. We return to the greater effective range of punitive military action compared to effective political rule. Without going into detailed logistical calculations here, but drawing on the seminal work of Engel and van Creveld, we can estimate that in Near Eastern imperial societies up to Alexander the Great the maximum unsupported march possible for an army was about 60 to 75 miles.[31] Alexander and the Romans may have extended it to nearly 100 miles, and this remained the maximum until the eighteenth century in Europe when a massive rise in agricultural productivity provided the logistical basis for far wider operations. Before then further distances required more than one campaigning phase, or – far more common if some degree of political control was sought – it required elaborate negotiations with local allies regarding supplies. This is enhanced if routine political control is desired without the presence of the main army. So even the most pretentious of despotic rulers actually rules through local notables. All extensive societies were in reality 'territorially federal'. Their imperial rule was always far feebler than traditional images of them allows for.[32]

So we have in this example two contrary tendencies: militaristic centralization followed by fragmenting federalism. Combining them we get a dialectic. If compulsory co-operation is successful, it increases both the infrastructural and the despotic power of the state. But it also increases social infrastructural resources in general. The logistical constraints mean that the new infrastructures cannot be kept within the

31 D. W. Engel, *Alexander the Great and the Logistics of the Macedonian Army*, Berkeley, University of California Press, 1978; M. van Creveld, *Supplying War: Logistics from Wallenstein to Patton*, Cambridge, Cambridge University Press, 1977.

32 This is now well recognized by many writers, for example J. H. Kautsky, *the Politics of Aristocratic Empires*, Chapel Hill, University of North Carolina Press, 1982; E. Gellner, *Nations and Nationalism*, Oxford, Basil Blackwell, 1983; and A. Giddens, *Contemporary Critique of Historical Materialism*, pp. 103–4.

body politic of the state. Its agents continually 'disappear' into civil society, bearing the state's resources with them. This happens continually to such regimes. The booty of conquest, land grants to military lieutenants, the fruits of office, taxes, literacy, coinage all go through a two-phase cycle, being first the property of the state then private (in the sense of 'hidden') property. And though there are cases where the fragmentation phase induces social collapse, there are others where civil society can use the resources which the despotic state has institutionalized, without needing such a strong state. The Arameans, Phoenicians and Greeks appropriated, and further developed, the techniques pioneered by the despotic states of the Near East. Christian Europe appropriated the Roman heritage.

My examples are relatively militaristic only because the process is easiest to describe there. It was a general dialectic in agrarian societies. In other words, imperial and feudal regimes do not merely oscillate (as Weber, Kautsky and many others have argued), they are entwined in a dialectical process. A range of infrastructural techniques are pioneered by despotic states, then appropriated by civil societies (or vice versa); then further opportunities for centralized co-ordination present themselves, and the process begins anew. Such trends are as visible in early modern societies as in the ancient ones from which I have drawn my examples.

Such a view rejects a simple antithesis, common to ideologies of our own time, between the state and civil society, between public and private property. It sees the two as continuously, temporally entwined. More specifically it sees large private property concentrations – and, therefore, the power of dominant classes – as normally boosted by the fragmentation of successful, despotic states, not as the product of civil society forces alone. So the power autonomy of both states and classes has essentially fluctuated, dialectically. There can be no general formula concerning some 'timeless' degree of autonomous state power (in the despotic sense).

But the contemporary situation is relatively unclear. Power infrastructures leaped forward with the Industrial Revolution. Industrial capitalism destroyed 'territorially federal' societies, replacing them with nation states across whose territories unitary control and surveillance structures could penetrate.[33] Logistical penetration of territory has increased exponentially over the last century and a half.

What happens if a state acquires control of all those institutions of control divided historically and elsewhere between states, capitalist enterprises, churches, charitable associations etc.? Is that the end of the

33 Giddens has argued this recently in his *Contemporary Critique of Historical Materialism*.

dialectic, because the state can now keep what it acquires? Obviously, in macro-historical terms the Soviet Union can control its provincial agents, and hence its provinces, in a way that was flatly impossible for any previous state. Moreover, though its degree of effective authoritarianism can be easily exaggerated (as in 'totalitarian' theories, for example), its centralization tendencies are novel in form as well as extent. Group struggles are not decentralized, as they are substantially in the capitalist democracies, nor do they fragment as they did in agrarian societies. Struggle is itself centralized: there is something pulling the major contending forces – the 'liberals', 'technocrats', 'military/ heavy industry complex' etc. – towards the Praesidium. They cannot evade the state, as agrarian dissenters did; they cannot struggle outside the state, as capitalists and workers often do. Does this authoritarian state exist despotically 'above' society, coercing it with its own autonomous power resources? Or does its authoritarian despotism exist in milder terms, firstly as a place in which the most powerful social forces struggle and compromise, and secondly as a set of coercive apparatuses for enforcing the compromise on everyone else? This has long been debated among theorists of the Soviet Union. I do not pretend to know the answer.

The bureaucratic states of the West also present problems. They are much as they were in relative power terms before the exponential growth in logistical powers began. Whatever the increases in their infrastructural capacities, these have not curbed the decentred powers of the capitalist class, its major power rival. Today agencies like multi-national corporations and international banking institutions still impose similar parameters of capitalist rationality as their predecessors did over a century ago. State elites have not acquired greater power autonomy despite their infrastructural capacities. Again, however, I am touching upon some of the central unsolved theoretical issues concerning contemporary societies. And, again, I offer no solution. Indeed, it may require a longer-run historical perspective than that of our generation to solve them, and so to decide whether the industrial revolution did finish off the agrarian dialectic I described.

Thus the impact of state autonomy on despotic power has been ambiguous. In terms of traditional theory results might seem disappointing: the state has not consistently possessed great powers – or indeed any fixed level of power. But I have discussed interesting power processes of a different kind. In agrarian societies states were able to exploit their territorial centrality, but generally only precariously and temporarily because despotic power also generated its own antithesis in civil society. In industrial societies the emergence of authoritarian states indicates much greater potential despotism, but this is still somewhat controversial and ambiguous. In the capitalist democracies there are few signs of state autonomous state power – of a despotic type.

But, perhaps, all along, and along with most traditional theory, we have been looking for state power in the wrong place. By further examining infrastructural power we can see that this is the case.

Results: Infrastructural Power

Any state which acquires or exploits social utility will be provided with infrastructural supports. These enable it to regulate, normatively and by force, a given set of social and territorial relations, and to erect boundaries against the outside. New boundaries momentarily reached by previous social interactions are stabilized, regulated, and heightened by the state's universalistic, monopolistic rules. In this sense the state gives territorial bounds to social relations whose dynamic lies outside of itself. The state is an arena, the condensation, the crystallization, the summation of social relations within its territories – a point often made by Poulantzas.[34] Yet, despite appearances, this does not support Poulantzas' reductionist view of the state, for this is an active role. The state may promote great social change by consolidating territoriality which would not have occurred without it. The importance of this role is in proportion to its infrastructural powers: the greater they are or become, the greater the territorializing of social life. Thus even if the state's every move towards despotism is successfully resisted by civil society groups, massive state-led infrastructural reorganization may result. Every dispute between the state elite and elements of civil society, and every dispute among the latter which is routinely regulated through the state's institutions, tends to focus the relations and the struggles of civil society onto the territorial plane of the state, consolidating social interaction over that terrain, creating territorialized mechanisms for repressing or compromising the struggle, and breaking both smaller local and also wider transnational social relationships.

Let me give an example.[35] From the thirteenth century onwards, two principal social processes favoured a greater degree of territorial centralization in Europe. First, warfare gradually encouraged army command structures capable of routine, complex co-ordination of specialized infantry, cavalry and artillery. Gradually, the looser feudal levy of knights, retainers and few mercenaries became obsolete. In turn this presupposed a routine 'extraction-coercion cycle' to deliver men,

---

34 Poulantzas, *Pouvoir politique et classes sociales.*
35 This is elaborated in much greater detail in my 'State and society, 1130–1815'.

monies and supplies to the forces.[36] Eventually, only territorially centred states were able to provide such resources and the grand duchies, the prince-bishops, and the leagues of towns lost power to the emerging 'national' states. Second, European expansion, especially economic expansion taking an increasingly capitalistic form, required increased military protection abroad, more complex legal regulation of property and market transactions, and domestic property forms (like rights to common lands). Capitalistic property-owners sought out territorial states for help in these matters. Thus European states gradually acquired far greater infrastructural powers: regular taxation, a monopoly over military mobilization, permanent bureaucratic administration, a monopoly of law-making and enforcement. In the long run, despite attempts at absolutism, states failed to acquire despotic powers through this because it also enhanced the infrastructural capacities of civil society groups, especially of capitalist property-holders. This was most marked in Western Europe and as the balance of geopolitical power tilted westwards – and especially to Britain – the despotically weak state proved the general model for the modern era. States governed with, and usually in the interests of, the capitalist class.

But the process and the alliance facilitated the rise of a quite different type of state power, infrastructural in nature. When capitalism emerged as dominant, it took the form of a series of territorial segments – many systems of production and exchange, each to a large (though not total) extent bounded by a state and its overseas sphere of influence. The nation-state system of our own era was not a product of capitalism (nor, indeed, of feudalism) considered as pure modes of production. It is in that sense 'autonomous'. But it resulted from the way expansive, emergent, capitalist relations were given regulative boundaries by pre-existing states. The states were the initially weak (in both despotism and in infrastructure) states of feudal Europe. In the twelfth century even the strongest of them absorbed less than 2 per cent of GNP (if we could measure it); they called out highly decentralized military levies of at most 10–20,000 men sometimes only for 30 days in the campaigning system; they could not tax in any regular way; they regulated only a small proportion of total social disputes – they were, in fact, marginal to the social lives of most Europeans. And yet these puny states became of decisive importance in structuring the world we live in today. The need for territorial centralization led to the restructuring of first European, then world society. The balance of nuclear terror lies between the successor states of these puny Europeans.

36 See the brilliant treatment of this matter by S. Finer, 'State and nation building in Europe: the role of the military', in Tilly, *Formation of National States*.

In the international economic system today, nation-states appear as collective economic actors. Across the pages of most works of political economy today stride actors like 'The United States', 'Japan', or 'The United Kingdom'. This does not necessarily mean that there is a common 'national interest', merely that on the international plane there are a series of collectively organized power actors, nation-states. There is no doubting the economic role of the nation-state: the existence of a domestic market segregated to a degree from the international market, the value of the state's currency, the level of its tariffs and import quotas, its support for its indigenous capital and labour, indeed, its whole political economy is permeated with the notion that 'civil society' is its territorial domains. The territoriality of the state has created social forces with a life of their own.

In this example, increasing territoriality has not increased despotic power. Western states were despotically weak in the twelfth century, and they remain so today. Yet the increase in infrastructural penetration has dramatically increased territorial boundedness. This seems a general characteristic of social development; increases in state infrastructural powers also increase the territorial boundedness of social interaction. We may also postulate the same tendency for despotic power, though it is far weaker. A despotic state without strong infrastructural supports will only claim territoriality. Like Rome and China it may build walls, as much to keep its subjects in as to keep 'barbarians' out. But its success is limited and precarious. So, again we might elaborate a historical dialectic. Increases in state infrastructural power will territorialize social relations. If the state then loses control of its resources they diffuse into civil society, decentring and de-territorializing it. Whether this is, indeed, beginning to happen in the contemporary capitalist world, with the rise of multinational corporations outliving the decline of two successively hegemonic states, Great Britain and the United States, is one of the most hotly-debated issues in contemporary political economy, but one which must here be left as an open issue.

Conclusion

In this chapter I have argued that the state is essentially an arena, a place – just as reductionist thories have argued – and yet this is precisely the origin and mechanism of its autonomous powers. The state, unlike the principal power actors of civil society, is territorially bounded and centralized. Societies need some of their activities to be regulated over a centralized territory. So do dominant economic classes, churches and other ideological power movements, and military elites. They, therefore, entrust power resources to state elites which they are incapable of fully recovering, precisely because their own socio-spatial basis of organization is not centralized and territorial. Such state power resources, and the autonomy to which they lead, may not amount to much. If, however, the state's use of the conferred resources generates further power resources – as was, indeed, intended by the civil society groups themselves – these will normally flow through the state's hands, and thus lead to a significant degree of power autonomy. Therefore, *autonomous state power is the product of the usefulness of enhanced territorial-centralization to social life in general.* This has varied considerably through the history of societies, and so consequently has the power of states.

I distinguished two types of state power, despotic and infrastructural. The former, the power of the state elite over civil society classes and elites, is what has normally been meant by state power in the literature. I gave examples of how territorial-centralization of economic, ideological and military resources have enhanced the despotic powers of states. But states have rarely been able to hold on to such power for long. Despotic achievements have usually been precarious in historic states because they have lacked effective logistical infrastructures for penetrating and co-ordinating social life. Thus when states did increase their 'private' resources, these were soon carried off into civil society by their own agents. Hence resulted the oscillation between imperial/patrimonial and feudal regimes first analysed by Max Weber.

By concentrating on infrastructural power, however, we can see that the oscillation was, in fact, a dialectic of social development. A variety of power infrastructures have been pioneered by despotic states. As they 'disappear' into civil society, general social powers increase. In volume I of my *The Sources of Social Power*, I suggest that a core part of social development in agrarian societies has been a dialectic between centralized, authoritative power structures, exemplified best by 'Militaristic Empires', and decentralized, diffused power structures, exemplified by 'Multi-Power Actor Civilizations'. Thus the developmental role of the powerful state has essentially fluctuated, sometimes promoting it, sometimes retarding it.

But I also emphasized a second result of state infrastrutural powers. Where these have increased, so has the territoriality of social life itself. This has usually gone unnoticed within sociology because of the unchallenged status of sociology's master-concept: 'society'. Most sociologists – indeed, most people anywhere who use this term – mean by 'society' the territory of a state. Thus 'American society', 'British society', 'Roman society' etc. The same is true of synonyms like 'social formation' and (to a lesser extent) 'social system'. Yet the relevance of state boundaries to what we mean by societies is always partial and has varied enormously. Medievalists do not generally characterize 'society' in their time period as state-defined; much more likely is a broader, transnational designation like 'Christendom' or 'European society'. Yet this change between medieval and modern times is one of the most decisive aspects of the great modernizing transformations, just as the current relationships between nation-states and 'the world system' is crucial to our understanding of late twentieth-century society. How territorialized and centralized are societies? This is the most significant theoretical issue on which we find states exercising a massive force over social life, *not* the more traditional terrain of disute, the despotic power of state elites over classes or other elites. States are central to our understanding of what society is. Where states are strong, societies are relatively territorialized and centralized. That is the most general statement we can make about the autonomous power of the state.

5

City-States

Peter Burke

A symposium on the state would be incomplete without some discussion of the city-state, examining its essential characteristics: identifying the times when and the places where it has existed on the earth's surface in human history, and the geographical, economic, social and political conditions for its existence; and describing how it worked. These are laughably ambitious questions for a brief essay to attempt to answer, especially so given the patchy nature of the secondary work in this field. What follows should be taken as no more than an outline sketch or series of notes on a few main problems, pending a more thorough comparative study of this form of political organization – assuming, as one should not, that it has a single essential form.

Most of us think we know what a city-state is, but base our impressions on a very small number of famous examples, notably ancient Greece and northern Italy c.1100–1500 (not to say 'Athens and Florence'). These examples present a misleadingly clear picture of the city-state as a small but autonomous political unit, the home of liberty and democracy, at least for the citizens (as opposed to slaves or to the peasants in the surrounding countryside under the city's domination). Described in this way, the city-state seems to offer the best possible illustration of Max Weber's famous thesis that it is their autonomy which has been the most distinctive feature of Western cities, with important consequences for the history of Western 'civilization' (the very term reveals the cultural hegemony of the city).[1]

I should like to thank the audiences who commented on earlier drafts of this chapter at seminars at the London School of Economics and the Institute of Historical Research, 1980–1.

1 Max Weber, *Die Stadt*, written c.1911–13, posthumously published 1921; English trans. Glencoe, Free Press, 1958.

If I did not think that Weber's thesis contains a nugget of great value, I would not be writing this chapter. However, – as in the case of Weber's still more famous thesis, about the relationship between the 'Protestant Ethic' and the 'Spirit of Capitalism' – the nugget needs to be washed clean of the dubious assertions and assumptions surrounding it, whether these are Weber's own, or the contribution of his followers, or part of the historiographical tradition which he inherited.

It would be interesting to study how and why this favourable image of the city-state became established, the extent to which it was the result of good public relations work in Periclean Athens and early Renaissance Florence, and the extent to which it was an example of the nineteenth century 'invention of tradition'. The cult of the Renaissance city-state, for example, owes much to two nineteenth-century historians who had strong personal reasons for identification with the phenomenon they were studying. J. C. L. Simonde de Sismondi's 16 volumes on the *Histoire des républiques italiennes* appeared between 1807 and 1818. Sismondi came of a patrician family from Pisa and spent his early life in Switzerland. What attracted him to his subject was the theme of liberty. He set out to do for the Italian republics what had already been done for ancient Greece and medieval Switzerland, and he ended his history in 1530, when the Medici returned to Florence.[2]

Sismondi's work was eclipsed by the still more famous study by Jacob Burckhardt, *Die Kultur der Renaissance in Italien* (1860). Burckhardt had a good deal to say about Renaissance despots, but his sympathy was reserved for the independent republics of Florence and Venice. This was hardly surprising, in the case of a Swiss patrician whose own city, Basel, had still been administered in the traditional manner at the time of his birth in 1818. Burckhardt's historical essay expresses not only the fascination felt by a Protestant northerner for the Catholic south, but also a certain nostalgia for the Basel he had known, and which he so much preferred to what he called 'the modern centralised state ... worshipped as a god and ruling like a sultan'.[3]

In our own day, an example of strong identification with the Florentine city-state of the Renaissance is provided by Hans Baron, the historian of 'civic humanism'. Baron grew up in the Weimar Republic and after its destruction he went to live in another republic, the USA. Like a second Sismondi, he has concentrated on the theme of republican liberty.[4]

2 On him, G. Gargallo, 'Sismondi e la storia delle repubbliche italiane', *Clio*, vol. 20, 1984.

3 On him, Werner Kaegi, *Jacob Burckhardt*, vol. I, Basel, Schwabe, 1947.

4 Hans Baron, *The Crisis of the Early Italian Renaissance: Civic Humanism and Republican Liberty in an Age of Classicism and Tyranny*, Princeton, Princeton University Press, 1955.

These remarks on the cultural background of some famous historical studies of city-states are not presented as a refutation of their authors' arguments (though they may serve to encourage criticism of some of these arguments). The point I want to make is that the 'classical' image of the city-state is in need of qualification for two complementary reasons. In the first place, research on non-Western cities, especially the cities of the Middle and Far East, in the last 30 years or so has suggested that their autonomy, however unofficial, was often greater than Weber and others used to think. On the other hand, recent research on Athens, Florence and other classical and Renaissance city-states has tended to emphasize the limitations on their famous liberty. The differences between the two groups of cities and regimes, the 'free' and the 'unfree', therefore turn out to be differences in degree rather than differences in kind.

Similar conclusions are suggested by the difficulties inherent in the very concept of 'city-state' and the problems which arise whenever the attempt is made to put it to practical use in historical analysis. The Greeks did not have a word for it. There was *polis*, of course, a term which reminds us that Aristotle's famous definition of man as a 'political animal' (*zōon politikon*) might be better translated 'a being whose nature is to live in a *polis*'. However, the term was often used 'in a loose sense, of places which were not true cities, but simply large villages or market-towns'.[5] As for modern historians, Sismondi used the term *république*, while Burckhardt wrote of 'the free Polis' in the case of Greece, and 'the republics' in the case of Italy. His phrase about the power 'which made the city into a state' ('welche die Stadt zum Staate macht') did not congeal into a technical term.[6] Such a term seems to have made its first appearance in print in English in 1893 in the work of the classicist Ward Fowler. Writing about Greece and Rome, Fowler referred to this 'unique form of the state' in which 'it was in the city that the heart and life was centred, and the territory was only an adjunct'.[7] The term has passed into general currency among classical, medieval and Renaissance historians in the English-speaking world. However, it is very much less popular elsewhere, although the terms *état-ville*, *stato-città*, and *Stadt-Staat* occur from time to time.

It may be useful to ask at this point how much weight the term will

5 Aristotle, *Politics*, Book 1; G. E. M. de Ste Croix, *The Class Struggle in the Ancient Greek World*, London, Duckworth, 1981, p. 428; cf. W. Gawantka, *Die Sogennante Polis*, Stuttgart, Kröner, 1985, esp. chapter 3.

6 Jacob Burckhardt, *Weltgeschichtliche Betrachtungen*, Stuttgart, Kröner, 1935, pp. 88f.

7 William Warde Fowler, *The City-State of the Greeks and Romans*, London, Macmillan, 1893, p. 8. E. A. Freeman referred to 'city-commonwealths' in the 1860s, while George Grote, in the early nineteenth century, wrote of 'the autonomous city-community'.

bear; whether it is merely a label or a useful model as well. By 'model' I mean a simplified description presented in the form of a set of inter-dependent elements, a description with some general applicability, at least within a culture and often cross-culturally. If 'city-state' is a model, then it is worth discussing its strengths and weaknesses and the limits of its applicability.

To answer these questions the obvious thing to do is to attempt to construct a model of the city-state, working in the first instance from one of the two 'classic' examples (ancient Greece and Renaissance Italy), and widening out from there. I shall choose the Italian example, because I know the region and the period better.[8]

In the year 1200 there were between 200 and 300 cities in north and central Italy which could be described as autonomous. Some of them were very small, but they were still independent.[9] In the course of the next 300 years or so, the number rapidly diminished as the bigger fish devoured the smaller, but the sheer number of Italian city-states puts the historian in a relatively good position for generalizing or model-building. The model to be described here includes ten elements.

1   The city is autonomous. It is free from control by any prince, bishop, lord or any other city. It has its own laws and it issues its own coins (Florentine florins, Venetian ducats and so on), this being a common sign of sovereignty. It is highly conscious – indeed extremely proud – of this autonomy.

2   The city is not economically self-sufficient but it does control a *contado*, in other words a piece of rural territory ranging from a small strip of land outside the walls to a substantial empire. The city buys food from its *contado*, on its own terms (fixing quotas and prices) and it taxes this subject population (often at a higher rate than it taxes its own citizens). It needs this *contado*, which in the economic sense at least is no mere 'adjunct' as Fowler put it.

3   The city is in competition with its neighbours. It needs troops (whether to conquer others or merely to defend its autonomy), and it can raise these troops in one of two ways. The first is to raise a militia of amateur soldiers from the citizens, and the second is to hire professional mercenaries. Machiavelli has provided the classic statement of the dis-

8 Cf. Sergio Bertelli, *Il potere oligarchico nello stato-città medievale*, Florence, La Nuova Italia, 1978, pp. 12f., an 8-point model.

9 Daniel Waley, *The Italian City-Republics*, London, Weidenfeld & Nicolson, 1969, p. 11. More recent research is summarized in Lauro Martines, *Power and Imagination*, 1979; Harmondsworth, Penguin Books, 1983.

advantages of mercenaries.[10] But militias also had their disadvantages, as Machiavelli discovered when the one he had recruited from the *contado* to defend Florence ran away from the Spanish army.

4   To pay mercenaries, taxes and loans are necessary. The pressures of war led to the creation of a fundamental institution of the Italian city-state, its public debt. The richer citizens financed the government through loans. To repay the loans the state had to raise taxes. Direct taxation made it necessary to number the people and estimate the value of the property of each family, a was done for some 60,000 families in the famous Florentine *catasto* of 1427. Whether or not we think that 'small is beautiful', we should recognize in the case of the census and the publc debt that small is precocious.

5   Taxes are socially divisive, the rich preferring indirect taxes and the rest some form of property tax. It should be clear that the historian cannot talk about the actions of 'Florence' or 'Venice' without asking 'whose city?'[11] However, social divisions within the city differed from those which obtained elsewhere in Europe. At a time when European society was generally divided into three 'estates' (clergy, nobles and 'third estate'), the inhabitants of Italian city-states divided themselves into three income groups, rich, middling and poor (*popolo grasso, popolo minuto, plebe*).

6   The overlap between these social distinctions and the main political divisions within the city is significant if incomplete. Politically the city was divided into (1) the governing body, generally recruited from a patricide of old and wealthy families; (2) a larger group of citizens, who could at least cast votes on occasion; and (3) those without political rights. This homology between social and political structures allowed social conflict to take political forms, as in the famous case of the revolt of the *plebe* in Florence in 1378. Most of the time, however, the patricians were able to 'manage' the city. The way in which they did this may be summed up in two maxims (whether these were consciously followed or not).

7   The first maxim is *panem et circenses*. The urban poor were kept quiet by a policy of cheap bread. Public granaries were set up and in time of dearth grain would be sold below the market price. This was generosity at the expense of the peasants of the *contado*, who may not have received a fair price for their grain in the first place. However, the

10 In chapter 12 of his *Prince*. For a contrary view, see W. H. McNeill, *The Pursuit of Power*, Oxford, Oxford University Press, 1982, chapter 3.
11 Ray Pahl, *Whose City?*, Harmondsworth, Penguin Books, 1975.

peasants, who were scattered and relatively distant, were less of a threat to the patricians than the plebs were. As for 'circuses', they included Carnival (when meat was distributed free) and the feast of the city patron, a ritual reaffirmation of the solidarity of the commune. I would not wish to reduce the famous civic patriotism of the Italian city-states, which found expression in so many forms, from town halls to town chronicles, into the status of a 'trick' played by patricians on citizens and plebs. Patricians too participated in this *campanilismo*; however, the solidarity thus created was to their advantage.

8   The second maxim is *Divide et impera.* The conflicts already mentioned were to a large extent neutralized by others. Each city was divided into quarters, wards and parishes, which in turn divided loyalties. Each city was full of voluntary associations such as guilds, religious fraternities and political factions. All these associations (factions in particular) cut across the 'horizontal' solidarities of *popolo grasso, popolo minuto* and *plebe.*

9   Factions (in other words, patron-client groupings) not only reduced conflicts based on horizontal solidarity but generated conflicts of their own, leading to street fighting, the siege of towers and palaces, and other forms of violence. One common solution to the problem of faction was to choose office-holders by drawing lots. Another solution was to bring an outsider into the city to act as umpire: the *podestà.*

10   If there is a state of equilibrium it is highly unstable and any model of the Italian city-state must be dynamic, as Machiavelli suggests by his adoption of the polybian cycle of constitutions from monarchy to monarchy via aristocracy and democracy. Curiously enough, the most obvious cycle in the Italian city-state system does not fit the polybian model but goes monarchy-democracy-aristocracy-monarchy instead. Another major change over time was of course the decline in the numbers of city-states from hundreds in 1200 until the last survivors, such as Venice and Genoa, disappeared at the end of the eighteenth century.

The model outlined above does seem (to me, at least) to have its uses in understanding the course of Italian history over several centuries. Yet the model (and, as suggested above, the very term 'city-state') does raise some awkward problems, which the example of Florence may serve to illustrate. When did Florence cease to be a city-state (which controlled a substantial amount of territory in Tuscany), and become a territorial state (in which the metropolis remained dominant in many respects)? The conventional answer, that this happened with the rise of the

Medici, reveals some confusion between the notion of city-state and that of 'republic'. The question of the constitution of the city (the rule of one, few or many) needs to be separated, analytically speaking, from that of the relationship between city and territory (dominant, dominated or autonomous).

It may make confusion less confounded to introduce a third term at this point, that of the 'small state'. This is another traditional term, at least in the German-speaking world (Burckhardt for one used to refer to *Kleinstaaterei*).[12] Not all small states are republics; not all republics are small. However, traditional republics needed to be small in order to work efficiently (Aristotle and Montesquieu, among others, have explained why this should be the case), and small states containing large cities are likely to be dominated by them.[13] Size is of course a relative matter – but so is autonomy. Was Verona a city-state or was it not after its incorporation into the Venetian empire in 1405?[14]

Professor Teodor Shanin has described peasants as 'a class of low classness'.[15] Some city-states, we might suggest, have less stateness or cityness than others. They form a political spectrum or continuum. So we should not be searching for an exact fit between a particular example and the glass slipper or ideal type: we should simply be observing family resemblances between situataions. The wider the net of historical comparison is thrown, the more important it will be to bear this warning in mind. But let us first see whether or not the ten-point model has its uses for what Marc Bloch called 'neighbourly' comparisons; in this case, comparisons with other parts of Europe in the late Middle Ages and the early modern period.[16]

The cities of Dalmatia (more especially the republic of Ragusa, now Dubrovnik) were so close to Italy as to be a virtual extension of the Italian city-state system.[17] A more difficult case is that of the South of France. Geographical, economic and social conditions in Provence and Languedoc were not so different from those of north and central Italy, and there was in fact a 'rise of the communes' there as in northern Italy

12 Burckhardt, *Weltgeschichtliche Betrachtungen*, 34f. Cf. Werner Kaegi, 'Der Kleinstaat im europäischen Denken', in his *Historische Meditationen*, vol. I, Basel, Schwabe, 1942, 251–314.

13 Aristotle, *Politics*, Book 7, chapter 4; Montesquieu, *Esprit des Loix*, Book 8, chapters 15–19.

14 Angelo Ventura, *Nobiltà e popolo nella società veneta del '400 e '500*, Bari, Laterza, 1964, pp. 92f.

15 Teodor Shanin, *The Awkward Class*, Oxford, Oxford University Press, 1972, p. 213.

16 M. Bloch, 'Pour une histoire comparée des sociétés européennes', 1928; English trans. in his *Land and Work in Medieval Europe*, *Selected Papers of Marc Bloch*, New York, Harper and Row, 1969.

17 B. Krekić, *Dubrovnik in the 14th and 15th Centuries*, Norman, University of Oklahoma Press, 1972.

in the twelfth century. Avignon, Marseilles, Nîmes, Toulouse and other cities freed themselves from their local lords (at a time when these lords were minors or absentees), and ruled themselves through their consuls, a patriciate which was, as in Italy, a hybrid group of nobles and merchants. Civic militias were raised and some cities undertook the conquest of the surrounding countryside. It was not, however, easy for these communes to retain their independence, which was at its height in the late twelfth century and the first years of the thirteenth. After this, counts and kings were able to reassert control.[18]

All the same, the French city-states were to enjoy a brief revival when the centralizing state began to disintegrate in the second half of the sixteenth century. Royal minorities (from 1559 on) and civil wars (from 1562 on) provided a golden opportunity for the reassertion of civic autonomy in the south. Catholic Marseilles was virtually independent in the 1590s, when Henri IV was campaigning for recognition, and issued its own currency. However, the principal examples of the revived city-state were the towns of the Protestant south-west (La Rochelle, Nîmes, Montauban, Castres and so on), which established a federal organization in 1572–3, a kind of 'United Provinces of the South' under the protection of the prince of Condé, who challenged the sovereignty of the King of France by striking coins with his own head on them. The cities, however, did not.[19]

Turning now to the north of Europe, we find more or less autonomous cities in the Netherlands and in central Europe, with outposts as far north as Bergen and as far east as Novgorod. The most obvious parallel with Italy is that other highly urbanized region of late medieval Europe, the Netherlands. Here too urban militias were important. The pitched battles between knights and craftsmen, notably at Courtrai in 1302 – when the craftsmen won – are reminiscent of the heroic age of the Italian city-states 100 years or so earlier. The high point of urban autonomy was the 11-year period 1338–49 in the *drie steden*, the 'three towns' (Ghent, Bruges and Ypres). As in the case of Italy, historians used to stress the rise of urban 'democracies', but have come to recognize that in practice a group of patricians ruled the free cities. There were, however, at least two important differences between the two situations. In the first place, the cities of the Netherlands lacked a *contado*. Perhaps they did not need one, because they could more easily import grain from abroad by sea than (say) Florence could. Insofar as they did want to

18 J. H. Mundy, *Liberty and Political Power in Toulouse 1050–1230*, New York, Columbia University Press, 1954; E. Baratier, ed., *Histoire de Provence*, Toulouse, Privat, 1969.

19 Janine Garrisson-Estèbe, *Protestants du Midi 1559–98*, Toulouse, Privat, 1980, pp. 181f.; David Parker, *La Rochelle and the French Monarchy*, London, Royal Historical Society, 1980, pp. 33f.

control the countryside it was to prevent industrial competition (Ypres forebade the weaving of woollen cloth within three miles of the city walls). In the second place, the lack of mountains in the Netherlands made the three cities vulnerable to attack – and they did in fact surrender to the count of Flanders in 1349.[20]

As in the case of France, however, it would be a mistake to end the story in the Middle Ages, especially since city-stateness has been defined as a matter of degree. The Revolt of the Netherlands, which broke out at the same time as the French religious wars in the 1560s, was to a large extent a defence of municipal privileges against a centralizing monarch who happened to be an absentee, Philip of Spain. Although the leader was a member of the upper nobility, William of Orange, the revolt was essentially urban, and the citizen militias played an important part in defending the cities against Spanish troops. Like Ghent, Bruges and Ypres in the fourteenth century, the towns united for defence, and although the Union of Arras, comprising the southern Netherlands, was unable to resist reconquest, the northern Union of Utrecht became the United Provinces of the Dutch Republic. In this federal state, the towns were dominant. They had little *contado* in the literal sense, although Rotterdam, Leiden and other cities owned a few villages in their vicinity. There might be a case for calling the whole Dutch Republic the *contado* of the city-state of Amsterdam, given its size (200,000 people in the seventeenth century), and its wealth (it paid 30 per cent of the costs of government). Even if this point is somewhat exaggerated and ignores the fact that the Amsterdammers did not always get their own way in the conflicts of interest among Dutch cities, it is worth remembering that Amsterdam was the last city in European history to have her own 'empire of trade and credit . . . unsustained by the forces of a modern unified state'.[21]

The Swiss, like the Italians, had the advantage of mountains to protect their autonomy, and like the Netherlanders, they united for defence. The qualities of Swiss pikemen were well known throughout Europe. The cities which most obviously fit our city-state model are Bern, Zürich and Basel. Bern had the most territory; in the sixteenth century it contained only 4–5,000 people but ruled over an *Oberland* with more than 70,000 inhabitants. Zürich extended its territory until it became second only to Bern, a city of fewer than 6,000 inhabitants dominating a

20 Henri Pirenne, *Les anciennes démocraties des Pays-Bas*, 1910; English trans., Manchester, Manchester University Press, 1915; J. Lestocquoy, *Les villes de Flandre et d'Italie sous le gouvernement des patriciens*, Paris, Presses Universitaires de France, 1952; David M. Nicholas, *Town and Countryside*, Bruges, Ghent University Press, 1971.

21 Violet Barbour, *Capitalism in Amsterdam in the Seventeenth Century*, Baltimore, Johns Hopkins University Press, 1950, p. 13.

rural population of about 60,000. Other autonomous Swiss cities include Fribourg, Lucerne, Schaffhausen, Solothurn and Geneva from the age of Calvin to that of Rousseau. The *Contrat social* describes a system which works in city-states if it works anywhere and the parallel between the situations of eighteenth-century Geneva and sixteenth-century Florence gives extra significance to Rousseau's interest in the *Discourses* of Machiavelli.[22]

Some German towns were also relatively close to the Italian model, in particular the imperial cities or *Reichstädte* of the late Middle Ages, about 65 of them, subject only to the emperor. They were not quite as autonomous as the Swiss cities, but the emperor's weakness was their freedom. Some of them, notably Nuremberg and Ulm, came to dominate the countryside around them; Nuremberg, a city of about 20,000 people in 1500, had a *Territorium* of 25 square miles. Still less autonomous, but retaining significant freedom of action, were the so-called 'free cities' (*Freistädte*), such as Erfurt; this was legally subject to the archbishop of Mainz, but he was an absentee and could not exert close control. Erfurt was a little smaller than Nuremberg but controlled rather more territory, a rural hinterland of some 24,000 people, regarded by the citizens as their subjects and supplying them with food. It had a reasonable degree of stateness.

Like the Italian cities, these German ones were ruled by a hybrid patriciate involved in both trade and land. They too had their civic militias and their civic patriotism expressed in town chronicles, town halls and so on. They were much smaller than the major Italian city-states (the 20,000 inhabitants apiece of Nuremberg and Strasbourg contrasts with 70,000 for Florence and Milan, 160,000 for Venice, and over 200,000 for Naples, all in the early to middle sixteenth century). However, they had more freedom of action in some ways than their Italian counterparts, for it was the town councils of the imperial cities which decided whether or not to accept the Protestant Reformation. Most of them did so, and to some extent on civic grounds; there was for example hostility to the Catholic clergy because they were not citizens and failed to pay their share of taxes.[23]

There were also a number of more or less autonomous cities on the

---

22 Richard Feller, *Geschichte Berns*, 4 vols, Bern, Lang, 1946–60; Anton Largiader, *Geschichte von Stadt und Landschaft Zürich*, 2 vols, Zurich, Rentsch, 1945; E. William Monter, *Calvin's Geneva*, New York, Wiley, 1967.

23 Christopher R. Friedrichs, 'The Swiss and German city-states', in Robert Griffeth and Carol G. Thomas, eds, *The City-State in Five Cultures*, Santa Barbara and Oxford, ABC-Clio, 1981, 109–42; Berndt Moeller, *Reichstadt und Reformation*, 1962; English trans., Philadelphia, Fortress Press, 1972; Gerald Strauss, *Nuremberg in the 16th Century*, New York, Wiley, 1966.

German model on the northern and eastern periphery of Europe. Bergen, for example, was a member of the North German trading league, the Hansa, and so were Gdańsk, Riga, Reval and Novgorod. Gdańsk, which owned more than 70 villages, was one of the most fully autonomous cities in central Europe in the sixteenth century, with its own currency as well as courts and taxes. In 1575, it was independent enough to refuse to recognize Stefan Bathory as King of Poland until he guaranteed its privileges. Further east, Pskov was more or less autonomous till 1510, Novgorod till 1478 (and to a lesser degree till Ivan the Terrible destroyed the city in 1570). On the other hand, the German imperial cities retained their privileges till the abolition of the Holy Roman Empire in 1806, or in some cases, such as those of Hamburg and Lübeck, still longer.[24]

This brief European survey has no space to consider a few more marginal cases – Catalonia, for example, where Barcelona was a power to be reckoned with in the late Middle Ages even if civic autonomy was below that of neighbouring Languedoc. So far as England is concerned, precocious centralization should not allow us to forget that her cities enjoyed a certain degree of autonomy, whether in the late Middle Ages (York, say), or even the nineteenth century (Chamberlain's Birmingham). It is clear all the same that relatively autonomous cities could be found in Europe clustering most thickly in what has been called the 'trade-route belt' and in the later Middle Ages.[25] In the early modern period, the privileges of many of these cities were suppressed by centralizing monarchs (Ghent's by Charles V, Florence's by the Grand Duke Cosimo de'Medici, Novgorod's by Ivan IV, La Rochelle's by Louis - XIII and so on). Only a few survived, like Venice and Hamburg, to the end of the old regime.

It is time to throw the net of comparison still wider and to consider the city-states of the ancient world and those outside Europe. These cases deserve more attention than space permits, but even the briefest of surveys should help place Europe in perspective.

The ancient Mediterranean is of course the classic country of the city-state. It is hard to discuss the subject in English without using Greek and Latin words: autarchy, autonomy, civic democracy, patrician, plebeian, even 'political'. Ancient Greek and medieval Italian city-states are so often considered in parallel that it may be worth emphasizing the

24 Philippe Dollinger, *La Hanse*, 1964; English trans., London, Macmillan, 1970; Richard Pipes, *Russia under the Old Regime*, London, Weidenfeld & Nicolson, 1974, pp. 198f.; Maria Bogucka, *Zycie codzienne Gdańska w xvi—xvii w.*, Warsaw, PWN, 1967.

25 Stein Rokkan, 'Dimensions of state formation and nation-building', in C. Tilly, ed. *The Formation of National States in Western Europe*, Princeton, Princeton University Press, 1975, p. 576.

differences between the two systems. Slaves, for example, were rare in Italy, but they performed a crucial role in the Greek *polis*, giving ordinary citizens leisure to engage in politics. Italian cities were (as Weber noted), centres of production, while Greek cities were centres of consumption. Another major difference concerns law. Although the Greek city-state was an example of the rule of law, it lacked professional lawyers, while medieval Italy swarmed with lawyers and notaries. It was harder to become a citizen in ancient Greece than in medieval Italy, for descent from a citizen was required. Greek cities literally had their own gods, rather than simply claiming a special relationship to patron saints to whom others could also pray. The relation between city and country-side was not the same. The Greek city did not rule the countryside. It was (*pace* Fowler) no 'adjunct'. Athenians, it has been said, lived all over Attika, and so the *hora* was not a *contado* in the Italian sense, although it supplied food to the city. There was no true Italian parallel (even in Venice), to the Athenian *ekklesia*, a weekly open-air general assembly. Despite these differences, the similarities between the two city-state systems remain striking; the councils, the choice of office-holders by lot, the rivalry between cities, the festivals, the factions, the civic militia.[26]

The ancient city-state was not of course confined to Greece. Since we are concerned with degrees of autonomy, it is worth considering the Hellenistic cities of Asia Minor, which had a fair amount of practical independence under the emperor. Ancient Rome has some claim to be regarded as the most successful city-state in history, posing on a grander scale the problem already discussed with respect to Florence – the dating of the end of its city-state phase. Before Rome, there had already been seven important city-states in Etruria: Tarquinii, Caere, Vulci, Vetulonia, Volaterrae, Clusium and Veii (which was sacked by Rome in the fifth century BC). Rome's great enemy Carthage was also a city-state, complete with senate and general assembly; indeed, 'Each Phoenician city', we are told, 'constituted an autonomous political entity, ruling over the inhabited area and the surrounding country-side.'[27]

Earlier still, from about 2,800 BC, there had been a city-state system

26 Moses Finley, *The Ancient Greeks*, London, Chatto & Windus, 1963, chapter 4; idem, 'The ancient city: from Fustel de Coulanges to Max Weber and beyond', *Comparative Studies in Society and History*, vol. 19, 1977; Carol G. Thomas, 'The Greek polis', in Griffeth and Thomas, *The City-State in Five Cultures*; Robin Osborne, *Demos: the Discovery of Classical Attika*, Cambridge, Cambridge University Press, 1985.

27 A. H. M. Jones, *The Cities of the East Roman Provinces*, Oxford, Oxford University Press, 1937; Michael Crawford, *The Roman Republic*, London, Fontana, 1978; Michael Grant, *The Etruscans*, London, Weidenfeld & Nicolson, 1980; Sergio Moscati, *the World of the Phoenicians*, 1965; English trans., London, Weidenfeld & Nicolson, 1968, p. 27.

in Mesopotamia; a number of small autonomous units, each consisting of a city and the surrounding countryside, much of which was owned by the townsmen; Kish, Ur, Uruk, Lagash, Umma, Eridu and others. Each had a general assembly as well as a council of elders, although in theory the city was owned and ruled by a god, and in practice the temple of that god was usually the largest landowner. The rivalry between cities and the threat of invasion from outside led to the rise of individual rulers, notably Hammurabi of Babylon and Sargon the Great, whose conquest of Sumer brought the city-state system to an end, replacing it by the Assyrian Empire. Lack of evidence makes it difficult to say how much power the general assemblies enjoyed (this is a problem even in the case of Athens) and to assess the importance in practice of the rule of written law, but at all events the general parallel between this system and that of ancient Greece should be clear.[28]

The example of Mesopotamia should be a warning against regarding the city-state as a uniquely western phenomenon. Are there other counter-examples? This is an important question, but it needs to be formulated more precisely. It would, I think, be a serious mistake to take a complex model (of the kind which has already been elaborated for Italy and might have been for ancient Greece), and ask whether or not it can be 'applied' elsewhere. To take western political arrangements as the norm from which deviations may be measured is an obviously ethnocentric procedure, and at a more practical level we can learn from the mistakes made by historians of 'feudalism' in the days when they tried to impose a Western European paradigm on the more or less recalcitrant social political and military arrangements of Byzantium, Rajasthan, Japan and China.[29]

It may be more useful to begin by posing a more open-ended question about the degree of urban autonomy and the forms it has taken in different parts of the world, leaving comparisons – and contrasts – with the west to a final section. An obvious place to start – not far from Mesopotamia – is the Muslim Middle East, with its long tradition of urban civilization in centres such as Baghdad, Damascus, Cairo, Istanbul, and so on. From a formal point of view the cities of Islam were not autonomous. As one specialist has put it, 'The town as such is unknown in Muslim law.'[30] This is of course one of a number of examples of the lack

28 Henri Frankfort, *The Birth of Civilisation in the Near East*, Bloomington, Indiana University Press, 1950, chapter 3; Mogens Trolle Larsen, *The Old Assyrian City State and its Colonies*, Copenhagen, Akademisk Forlag, 1976, pp. 116f.; Song Nai Rhee, 'Sumerian city states', in Griffeth and Thomas, *The City-State in Five Cultures*.

29 On Rajasthan, Daniel Thorner, 'Feudalism in India', in Rushton Coulborn, ed., *Feudalism in History*, Princeton, Princeton University Press, 1956, chapter 7.

30 S. M. Stern, 'The constitution of the Islamic city', in Albert Hourani and S. M.

of institutions intermediate between the ruler and the people, a significant absence which allowed the rulers of the Ottoman Empire, Iran and Mughal India (to take only three famous examples) power of a kind almost inconceivable to the so-called 'absolute monarchs' of early modern Europe.

On the other hand, there is considerable evidence of some degree of practical or unofficial independence in some cities at certain periods, when the central government for some reason relaxed its hold (a hold which in an age without modern communication technology, could never have been what we would call 'strong' anyway). Thus the cities of Syria and Mesopotamia, for example, enjoyed some degree of unofficial autonomy between the eighth and tenth centuries AD. There was a similar situation in Nishapur, in Persia, between the tenth and the twelfth centuries, where the 'patriciate' (to use one scholar's deliberately provocative translation of *ulema*), 'was capable of acting as if it governed the city'. Similar points might be made about Muslim cities and medieval Spain; about Algiers in the fourteenth and fifteenth centuries (before its incorporation in the Ottoman Empire); in the Ottoman Empire itself in the seventeenth century, when a group of urban notables or *ayan* (patricians?) emerged with unofficial power; and in Morocco as late as the nineteenth century, when the city of Salé, for example, was under the official rule of the sultan but was controlled in practice by a local elite.[31]

A similar distinction between official and unofficial autonomy needs to be made in the case of Japan. Most of the leading cities of modern Japan developed from the castle-towns of the Edō period (1600–1868), and they lacked formal autonomy from the first. Edō (Tokyo) itself is the most spectacular example; a mere village before the Tokugawa shoguns made it their capital. However, there are older cities with a rather different history. The most famous for independence is the so-called 'Venice of Japan', the seaport of Sakai, more especially during the Muromachi era of civil war (the fifteenth and sixteenth centuries), when the Ashikaga shoguns were losing their grip on the country. Sakai was a substantial

Stern, eds, *The Islamic City*, Oxford, Cassirer, 1970, quoting Claude Cahen. There were exceptions to this rule in the Ottoman Empire, e.g. Sarajevo: M. Hadžijhaić, 'Die privilegierten Städte zur Zeit des osmanischen Feudalismus', *Süd-Ost Forschungen*, vol. 20, 1961, 130–58.

31 Richard W. Bulliet, *The Patricians of Nishapur*, Cambridge, Harvard University Press, 1972; R. I. Burns, *Islam under the Crusaders*, Princeton, Princeton University Press, 1973, chapter 16; W. Spencer, *Algiers in the Days of the Corsairs*, Norman, University of Oklahoma Press, 1976; Halil Inalcik, *The Ottoman Empire*, London, Weidenfeld & Nicolson, 1973, pp. 161f.; Keith Brown, *The People of Salé*, Manchester, Manchester University Press, 1976.

city; in 1530 it had about 30,000 inhabitants. Unlike most Japanese towns, it was fortified, surrounded by a moat and a bamboo palisade. Its inhabitants were armed. It was not officially self-governing and it had no legal privileges. In practice, however, it was independent of the central government till the beginning of the seventeenth century, when the shogun Toyotomi Hideyoshi disarmed the inhabitants and weakened the city economically by favouring its more obedient neighbour Osaka.[32]

Japan and the Muslim world are not the only regions where examples of unofficially autonomous cities may be found. In China, historians have tended to stress the dependence on the central government of even important cities such as Kaifeng during the Sung dynasty – but it would be good to know more about the periods of transition from one dynasty to another.[33] Something might be said about the Muslim cities of South-East Asia; about the cities of Java, for example.[34] Something has been said about Muslim cities in Africa south of the Sahara; a recent study of Timbuktu betwen 1400 and 1900 emphasizes its autonomy and the role of its 'patriciate'.[35] A recent essay on Kano, Katsina, Daura, Gobir and Zauzau from about 1450 to 1804 describes them as 'The Hausa City-States'. These were not republics but subject to hereditary rulers; in other words they resembled Renaissance Mantua or Ferrara rather than Florence or Venice. However, they were small states (up to 13,000 square miles in extent) in which the capital city was of great importance.[36]

This whirlwind tour of non-western examples may at least help to place ancient Greece, medieval Italy and central Europe in some sort of perspective. The concept 'city-state' has its difficulties, as we have seen. It does not lend itself to precise use, and so it leaves historians in something of a dilemma. The choice is between giving the concept up or resigning oneself to using it imprecisely. I have chosen the second alternative and have discussed degrees of autonomy rather than its

32 John W. Hall, 'The castle town and Japan's modern urbanisation', *Far Eastern Quarterly*, vol. 15, 1955; V. Dixon Morris, 'Sakai', in John W. Hall and Toyoda Takeshi, eds, *Japan in the Muromachi Age*, Berkeley and Los Angeles, University of California Press, 1977, chapter 10.

33 Lack of autonomy is underlined by Etienne Balazs, *Chinese Civilisation and Bureaucracy*, New Haven, Yale University Press, 1964, chapter 6. Cf. Jaques Gernet, 'Note sur les villes chinoises au moment de l'apogée islamique', in Hourani and Stern, *The Islamic City*.

34 Clifford Geertz, *The Social History of an Indonesian Town*, Cambridge, Harvard University Press, 1965.

35 E. N. Saad, *Social History of Timbuktu*, Cambridge, Cambridge University Press, 1983.

36 Robert Griffeth, 'The Hausa City-States from 1450 to 1804', in Griffeth and Thomas, *The City-State in Five Cultures*.

presence or absence. Ancient Greece and medieval Italy have not been presented as unique but they remain spectacular examples at the autonomous end of a broad spectrum. Why states of this type should have been concentrated on particular portions of the earth's surface (notably western Europe) at particular periods remains an intriguing question, no less intriguing if we put it the other way and ask why centralization was successful in (say) China or in the Ottoman Empire, but not, until recently, in Italy.

I am not sure that there are any universal necessary conditions for a successful city-state, let alone sufficient ones, but a few favourable conditions may be listed. Mountains are the terrain of liberty, making a division into small political units a natural one. But the Greek and Italian mountains have outlasted the city-states which grew up among them, and the association of flatness with freedom in the Low Countries is an obvious counter-example. Braudel's suggestion that there are times propitious to small states and times propitious to large ones only takes us one step further towards an explanation.[37] Given that history is not always on the side of great empires (any more than of the big battalions), what made the times propitious?

This is the place to introduce what might be called the 'vacuum theory' of the city-state: that they and other small autonomous units – think of feudalism – grow up when central authority is weak (a royal minority, for example, or a disputed succession), and flourish in the interstices between major powers, as the small Italian states did in the no-man's-land between empire and papacy.[38] However, some small states are easily swallowed up by their neighbours, while others offer more resistance, whether because of their natural defences (the Venetian lagoons being even more effective than mountains in this respect) or their man-made ones, such as a civic militia, a mercenary army or an alliance (the Achaian League, the Lombard league of the twelfth century, the Swiss Confederation, and so on). Economic factors also help explain the survival of particular city-states, whch need to supply themselves with imported food, either by land from a source close at hand (transport costs overland being high in the pre-industrial world), or from more distant parts by sea.

Finally, the legal factor must not be neglected. There is a powerful tradition in Western social thought, from Montesquieu to Max Weber (via Alexis de Tocqueville), which would explain the unique destiny of

37 Fernand Braudel, *La Méditerranée*, 1949; English trans., London, Fontana, 1975, pp. 660f., 701f.

38 A point made with reference to Italy by Jacob Burckhardt, *Kultur der Renaissance in Italien*, 1860; English trans., London, Phaidon, 1944, chapter 1, and by Bertelli, *Il potere oligarchico*, pp. 14f.

the West in terms of liberties, privileges, autonomies and semi-autonomies of various kinds, of which free cities are an outstanding example. This essay, which began from Weber's contrast between the autonomous cities of the West and dependent cities elsewhere, has tended to blur, if not to obliterate, the distinction on the basis of research on Islam and Japan since his day. Once this distinction breaks down. It is necessary to take a new look at conventional explanations for urban autonomy, to place less stress on legal privilege and more on informal or unofficial factors. Looking back at Weber, two generations later, he now looks in some respects like a product of a German legal (or even legalistic) tradition. However, he had a point which needs to be taken seriously and incorporated in any account of the survival of more or less autonomous cities. Where (as in the case of Nishapur, say, or in that of Sakai), urban autonomy lacked an institutional basis, this may well have made it more precarious, more of a temporary makeshift – even if makeshifts of this kind endured on occasion for centuries. Conversely, the community spirit of a city such as Venice, an ethos nourished by awareness of its liberties and privileges, was an important factor in the long survival of that great city-republic.

6

States and Economic Development: Reflections on Adam Smith

John A. Hall

Adam Smith apparently believed that 'little else is required to carry a state to the highest degree of opulence from the lowest barbarism, but peace, easy taxes, and a tolerable administration of justice.'[1] This chapter does not analyse the specific relationships between states and the provision of justice, but seeks to cast light on the larger claim that economic development is achieved under aegis of a 'tolerable' state, i.e. a minimal liberal state, operating according to classical *laissez-faire* principles. The issue can be addressed in two ways. Firstly, we can seek an explanation, in comparative perspective, of the relationship between the state and the economy in the rise of the dynamic of North-West Europe. Secondly, we must ask how states affect economic development in the modern era.

All this requires us first to appreciate Smith's own view, so that we may then improve upon it. Smith did *not* believe that commerce was simply the result of *laissez-faire* politics, but rather that commerce itself accounted for the creation of a particular type of state in Europe which respected the rule of law. The crucial factor in the emergence of the rule of law is held to be the relative weakness of the medieval monarch who, in order to gain revenue and to balance baronial power, allowed towns to purchase their independence. This small change was held to have had an enormous impact upon the feudal nobility. The king could not tame

---

1 Dugald Stewart reported this as the view of his friend Smith in his 'Account of the life and writings of Adam Smith, Ll.D', in vol. III of *The Glasgow Edition of the Works and Correspondence of Adam Smith*, that is, *Essays on Philosophical Subjects*, Oxford, Oxford University Press, 1980, p. 322. D. Winch, *Adam Smith's Politics*, Cambridge, Cambridge University Press, 1978, is a brilliant exposition of Smith's general social theory.

the nobles, and so install a respect for law: but what the king could not achieve was managed by the taste for luxuries provided by the productive and autonomous city. The feudal lords suddenly had something on which to spend their money. Instead of simply buying retainers, the lords, selfish to a degree, could buy *things* and so live ostentatiously, gratifying their pride. But as lords lost their retainers, the rule of law – and their own demise – became a possibility. The causal chain here is exceptionally interesting. Commerce results from the rule of law, and that in turn is created by the productive and autonomous city; but the prime mover responsible for this type of city is the political factor of the parcellization of sovereignty into weak monarchies after the fall of Rome. We shall see that there is truth to Smith's general view, but we will need to complement it and reinterpret it in order to understand the relationship between forms of the state and economic development. Once this is done we can turn, in the light of Smith's social theory as a whole, to the relationships between states and economic development in the industrial era.

State Forms and the Emergence of Capitalism

The general argument of the first half of this chapter can be couched as a commentary on Michael Mann's observation that state power has despotic and infrastructural aspects.[2] I consider first two types of state which are high in despotism and low in infrastructure; by means of diagrams I am able to distinguish, as Mann cannot, between the general character of the Chinese empire and the states of classical Islam. This then allows me to introduce a measure of dynamism into his four-fold table when considering the West. If high despotism/low infrastructure states were a dead end, the same was not true, in North-West Europe at least, of the feudal state. Its despotic and weak infrastructural powers necessitated it becoming an organic state, low in despotism but increasingly strong in the provision of services for the society. The character of that transition and its impact upon economic development need to be described.

The Chinese empire

One very important question that we can ask of pre-industrial conditions is that of the manner in which large geographical spaces were held together.[3] In the Chinese case, as in that of Rome, there can be no doubt

2 M. Mann, 'The Autonomous Power of the State', chapter 4 in this volume.
3 This question is asked by O. Lattimore, *Studies in Frontier History*, Oxford, Oxford University Press, 1962, p. 548.

but that political/military means created and maintained imperial unity, and that cultural unification 'reflected' the primacy of the political.[4] This is graphically represented in figure 1.

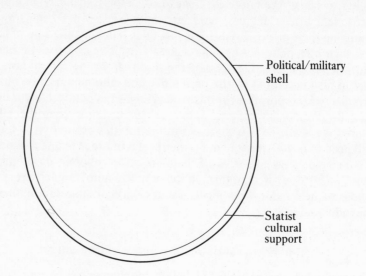

Political/military shell

Statist cultural support

Figure 1   Culture and politics in Imperial China

How did the economy fare in this situation? Medieval China witnessed considerable economic advance. The state itself sought to encourage agricultural advance and technical productivity. Interestingly, however, the great expansion which took place under the Sung occurred during a period of disunity. The Northern Sung did rule all China from 960–1127, but even they were faced with the militant nomadic Jurchen. Disunity encouraged the Southern Sung to build a navy in order to man all waterways which stood between them and their Northern competitors. More generally, the market and cities gained autonomy during this period of disunity in Chinese history, as happened in other periods of disunity. The quality of coinage provided by states tended to improve during disunity because traders would not return to or trust governments which manipulated the coinage.[5]

How did the empire, when it was reunited, react to the capitalist

4 This was the argument of Max Weber in his *Religion of China*, New York, Free Press, 1964, and it is also that of my *Powers and Liberties*, Oxford, Basil Blackwell, 1985, chapter 2.

5 M. Elvin, *The Pattern of the Chinese Past*, California, Stanford University Press, 1973, chapter 14.

forces that had flourished previously? The state controlled the autonomy of cities. Little is known about the collapse of the iron and steel industries in Sung China. However, we can explain the collapse of Sung naval strength. The foundation of a native dynasty which improved the Grand Canal (so no longer necessitating ocean-going transport from south to north) undermined the navy; most obviously, between 1371 and 1567, all foreign trade was banned. *The* most spectacular way in which politics could affect the economy concerned the fate of the explorations undertaken by the eunuch admiral Cheng-Ho in the 1430s. The mandarins were always extremely jealous of the emergence of sources of power alternative to their own; they were naturally opposed to Cheng-Ho precisely because he was a eunuch whose cause was promoted by the eunuchs at court. As a result they were able to block further explorations by saying that funds were more urgently needed to combat nomad invasion. The centralization of political life mattered: although the bureaucracy was not in fact able to penetrate far into society, it could and did prevent other forces from gaining much autonomy. Another classic instance of this was that of the suppression of Buddhist monasteries.

Chinese imperial government deserves the appellation *capstone*. The Chinese elite shared a culture, and sat atop a series of separate 'societies' which it did not wish to penetrate or mobilize; it feared that horizontal linkages it could not see would get out of control. This capstone government blocked the emergence of capitalist relationships. The concern of the mandarinate was less with intensifying social relationships than in seeking to prevent any linkages which might diminish its power. This can be seen particularly clearly in an analysis of Ming taxation.

As the Ming adminstrators saw it, to promote those advanced sectors of the economy would only widen the economic imbalance, which in turn would threaten the empire's political unity. It was far more desirable to keep all the provinces on the same footing, albeit at the level of the more backward sectors of the economy.[6]

This is not, it must be said immediately, to say that the impact of the state upon capitalism must always be negative. A different type of state, the European organic state, provided, once capitalist relationships were established, crucial services for capitalism. The Chinese state was incapable of providing such infrastructural services. Its negative rule gave it a low tax yield, and consequently it could not pay for such key

6 R. Huang, *Taxation and Governmental Finance in Sixteenth Century Ming China*, Cambridge, Cambridge University Press, 1974, p. 2.

services as decent credit arrangements for the peasantry. Huang's comment sums up the situation forcefully:

> It must be pointed out that in the late Ming most of the service facilities indispensable to the development of capitalism were clearly lacking. There was no legal protection for the businessman, money was scarce, interest rates high and banking undeveloped. . . At the same time merchants and entrepreneurs were hindered by the frequent road-blocks on the trade routes, government purchase orders and forced contributions, the government's near monopoly of the use of the Grand Canal and active involvement in manufacturing. On the other hand, the security and status of land ownership, the tax-exemption enjoyed by those who purchased official rank, and the non-progressive nature of the land tax increased the attractions of farming to the detriment of business investment.[7]

States inside Islam

It is relatively easy for us to understand the Chinese situation, for our notion of society depends upon social rules being created and maintained by a state. But cultural identities can be larger than any single state, and this was certainly true of classical Islam. The large area that comprised Islam was held together by a culture rather than by a polity. Perhaps the fundamental reason for this was that the leadership of the Arab community was split after the conquest. Intellectuals in China were integrated into the state, and   provided it with a service ethic. In contrast, the Ulama who codified Islamic doctrine by about 750 did so outside the old imperial heartlands and away from Caliphal Syria in the demilitarized cities of Iraq.[8] Their vision looked back to a tribal past of simplicity and egalitarianism, and their message struck chords amongst the Arabs themselves, unused to taxation and loath to accept it. The Ulama came to control the sacred norms of society, and these norms showed a deep distrust for the mundane, rather than the sacral, workings of political power.

One further point needs to be added before we can graphically represent states inside Islam. The Ulama were not in a position to rule society completely by themselves. The Arid Zone that comprises the heartland of classical Islam is populated by nomads whose high military participation ratio makes them capable of great military surges which can disrupt urban life. Importantly, as the great Muslim philosopher of history Ibn Khaldun realized as early as the fourteenth century, Arab nomadic tribesmen are not completely independent: they themselves require

7 Ibid., pp. 318–19.
8 P. Crone, *Slaves on Horses*, Cambridge, Cambridge University Press, 1980, pp. 62–3 and passim.

urban life for trade and exchange.[9] But urban markets require government to function, and such government in Islam has been the gift of the tribe or of slave soldiers. However, such government has tended to be rather short-lived. The rulers are imported from the outside and do not possess deep roots in society. Their capacity to act as professionals depends upon the possession of social solidarity. Solidarity, however, is a resource of tribal life which the ease of urban living slowly destroys. So although citizens support the tribal rulers at first, they eventually become restive-often by the third generation of the ruling dynasty. The Ulama begin by serving the ruling house as administrators and judges; yet they possess the sacred norms of Islam which, because of their precise codification, are not nearly as much at the mercy of secular power as was the relatively spiritual doctrine of Christianity. Some Ulama become discontented with the ruling house as it becomes 'corrupt'. In time, they declare the ruling house to be impious, and invite in one of the tribes from the area of dissidence outside the city walls. It is here that the presence of an ideology shared with the tribesmen matters. This manner of accession to power probably explains why Islamic culture, more extensive than any state, was maintained: a ruling house coming to power as the result of a religious spasm was unlikely to turn against Islam and in any case never had the time to do so effectively. This Ibn Khaldunian circulation of elites sugests the term *cyclical* polity for the states of classical Islam. The Islamic situation as a whole is graphically represented in figure 2, showing a large cultural shell within which states, of variable size and variable duration come and go.

How did Islamic states affect economic life? The political fragmentation of the Islamic world meant that the bureaucratic interference of a single imperial centre was not possible, and this helps account for the capacity of merchants to move freely throughout the larger culture. However, fragmentation by itself is not enough to ensure economic advance. The states of the Islamic world, being the short-lived creations of military professionals, had, if anything, even more deleterious affects on economic life than did the Chinese imperial state. The latter was often long-lasting, and at times sought positively to encourage agricultural productivity. Rulers in Islam paid virtually no attention to the needs of the economy. The state was purely predatory. We can see this in two ways. Firstly, the state interfered with the workings of the market, as Ira Lapidus has strikingly shown in the case of the cities of Mamluk Egypt.[10] These cities lacked autonomy, and merchants either had to

9 Ibn Khaldun, *Muqaddimah*, London, Routledge & Kegan Paul, 1978. See also E. Gellner, *Muslim Society*, Cambridge, Cambridge University Press, 1981.

10 I. M. Lapidus, *Muslim Cities in the Later Middle Ages*, Cambridge, Harvard University Press, 1967.

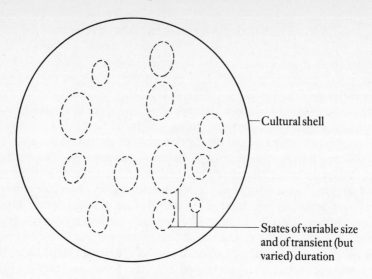

Figure 2 States inside Islam

bribe to stay in business or were in constant danger of despoliation. Secondly, however, it is worth noting that the state was much too weak to provide any of the services that capitalist, commercial society needed, as can be seen by examining the two classic forms of Islamic landholding, the *iqta* and the *waqf*.[11] The former of these were land grants given to the supporters of a ruling dynasty. Crucially, as dynasties changed, so did landholders. This partly explains the character of the *waqf*, formally a religious endowment and therefore not typically touched by a new ruling house, but often in fact a means whereby a family could draw a certain income from the land in covert form. This dual type of landholding proved inimical to economic advance. The fact that the state was not long-lasting enough to provide security of tenure placed a premium upon speedy extraction, and there was little genuine investment in land. Equally importantly, *waqf* donations constantly lowered the tax base on which the cyclical state could rely; there was that much less money to pay the state servants who might have provided services, whether adminsitrative, judicial or intellectual, to the larger society. Capitalism could not flourish in such a climate.

11 C. Cahen, 'Economy, society, institutions', in *The Cambridge History of Islam.* vol. II, *The Farther Islamic Lands, Islam, Society and Civilisation*, Cambridge, Cambridge University Press, 1970.

The multipolar system of north-west Europe

Economic historians of the European Middle Ages agree that there was very considerable economic advance quite early on, roughly during the period from 800 to 1100.[12] In this period the church served, in the words of Thomas Hobbes, as the 'ghost of the Holy Empire'. It held together the extensive area formerly joined by the legions, and thereby made economic interaction possible. Importantly, however, this 'governmental' service did not mean that the church was a government in the full sense of the word. It provided an umbrella of social identity in which an acephalous but intensive agrarian civlization with an increasingly strong trading element could flourish; it did not, however, have the political/ military muscle to interfere and despoil these developments.

The intensive nature of the early medieval economy is not unique; similar bursts of development took place in other civilizations. What concerns us is the relation between commercial capitalism and state organization in Europe. The earliest economic advance had been made, by and large, without the real presence of states, for monarchies and chiefdoms were short-lived and feeble. But from about 1100, and slightly earlier in the case of England, it became clear that a number of states were likely to remain part of the political scene. The situation is graphically presented in figure 3. How did this multipolar system affect capitalism?

The first and most obvious consideration takes the form of a counterfactual. Imagine what European history might have been like had the Roman empire somehow been reconstituted, or had any empire taken its place! Pre-industrial empires are too centralized for their logistical capacity, and thus have produced capstone government based on their sensible appreciation that secondary organizations are dangerous. Such empires sought to encourage the economy, but this form of government never ultimately allowed sufficient leeway to the economy for it to gather self-sustaining momentum. Why should an imperial Europe have been any different?

This can be put in a rather different manner. A decentralized market system came into place during those years in which there was no government which could interefere with its workings, but an organization which nevertheless made medieval men realize they belonged to a single civilization. An imperial form would very probably have sought to control such 'natural' processes. Consider the European city. All historians agree

12 Two accessible general accounts are: C. Cipolla, *Before the Industrial Revolution*, London, Methuen, 1976, and M. M. Postan, *Medieval Economy and Society*, London, Penguin, 1975.

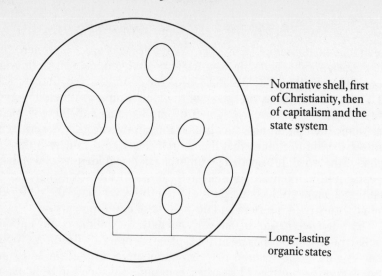

Normative shell, first
of Christianity, then
of capitalism and the
state system

Long-lasting
organic states

Figure 3 States in Europe

that Max Weber *was* correct in the more materialist part of his theory
concerning the rise of the West, namely in his contention that only in
Europe did the city gain full autonomy. This autonomy provided a space
in which the merchant was king, and in which bourgeois values could gell
and solidify. We live in the world created by this civilization. With a
matter of such import, it is essential to seek to *explain* this autonomy. The
most satisfying explanation is that the autonomy of north Italian cities
resulted from the absence of a single centre of power in Europe. Specifically, they gained their autonomy as the result of a power vacuum
between pope and emperor, such that they were able, as is often the case
in Third World countries today, to get the best for themselves by
opportunistically chopping and changing their allegiance.[13] How much
they owed to their freedom from interference and ability to experiment
is simply seen: once they became part of the Spanish mini-empire they
contributed virtually nothing new to European civilization. And much
the same point could be made by indulging in a 'thought-experiment':
had Philip II created a long-lasting empire based on his new Spanish
possessions, what would have happened to the social experiments taking
place in Holland and Great Britain? Had an empire been established at
any time it seems likely that social experiments at the peripheries would
have been ruled out.

13 P. Burke, 'City-States', chapter 5 in this volume.

This first point amounts to reiterating that political fragmentation was a necessary condition for the autonomy of the market. But the Islamic case has demonstrated that such fragmentation is not sufficient by itself to encourage economic dynamism. What else was involved? It might at first sight seem contradictory to say that the organic state helped economic development after the largely negative comments made to this point about state 'interference'. But there are different types of state in different historical and social circumstances. Two general principles about the relations of government to the economy can be maintained. Firstly, the absence of all government is disastrous since it encourages disorder and localism, and thus prevents trade; the emphasis on Europe's 'normative shell' shows that no anarchistic vision is entertained here. Secondly, bureaucratic and predatory governments were indeed hostile to economic development. As noted, it is mistaken to consider such government strong since it was based on weak infrastructural penetration of the society; indeed, arbitrariness in part results from weakness. This gives us the clue to the distinctiveness of the European state: a limit to arbitrariness combined with and in part caused considerable and ever-increasing infrastructural penetration. Two such limits are important.

The first limit is straightforward. The European state evolved slowly and doggedly in the midst of pre-existent social relationships. One uniqueness of the West is the role that parliaments played in its history: indeed so unique has this role been that German historians have considered the *Standestaat*, the representation of the three functional estates, Church, Noble and Burgher, a distinctive stage in world history.[14] It is quite clear that the prominence of such assemblies owes a great deal to the church, which owned so much land that it was as jealous as any noble of the powers of the crown to tax. Hence it generalized two tags of canon law – 'no taxation without representation' and 'what touches all must be approved by all' – and these became crucial to these estates. But 'liberties' were widely diffused throughout society, and churchmen had allies amongst nobles, burghers and yeomen. European pluralism, in other words, has an extremely long history. In these circumstances, there was a movement, in terms of Mann's argument, between a feudal state, week despotically and infrastructurally, to a more *organic* state, still low in despotism but with ever-increasing infrastructural penetration. The monarch's only way of gaining money was to co-operate with this pre-existing civil society.

The paradox of this situation is that restraint on government in the

14 A. R. Myers, *Parliaments and Estates in Europe to 1789*, London, Thames & Hudson, 1975.

end generated a larger sum of power in society. Perhaps the most important mechanism in this process was the making of money via the provision of a certain infrastructure to the society. This is most clearly seen in the provision of justice. Fees were charged for every legal transaction, and these came to provide an important part of the revenue of most monarchs after about 1200. This is not to say that the law was equally open for all to use; but it was available. European states provided other sorts of infrastructural help. They became good at managing disasters of various sorts; by the eighteenth century, for example, considerable help was available to the victims of earthquakes, whilst disease was quite rigidly controlled by quarantine laws.[15] Furthermore, the internal colonialism whereby Scots, Irish and Welsh were integrated into a single community – a process repeated elsewhere in Europe – created a single market. In the more advanced European states (i.e. not France until post-1789) this process went hand in hand with the removal of internal tariff barriers, and this was an incentive to trade. These policies were not designed with the improvement of the economy in view, but rulers *had* consciously encouraged trade for a long time. They did so because a disproportionate bulk of their revenues came from customs and excise; hence they sought to attract traders – a typical piece of legislation being Edward I's *Carta Mercatoria* of 1297. What is apparent as a whole is that large sections of the powerful were prepared to give quite high taxation revenues to the crown because they realized that their own interests were usually being served. Tocqueville was right to note that the English aristocracy and gentry manned local government and taxed itself. The level of infrastructural support and penetration was correspondingly high. A Confucian bureaucrat moved every three years simply could not know enough about local conditions to serve a particular area well. Representation to a central assembly by local aristocrats created a different result.

The second general restraint on the arbitrariness is also the third general point to be made about the European polity. The complete 'formula' of the European dynamic is that competition between 'long-lasting' states inside a larger culture encouraged the triumph of capitalism. Individual states did not exist in a vacuum. They were rather part of a competing state system, and it was that system, particularly the military organization it engendered, that played a considerable part in determining the character of individual states. Why was this?

A state system leads to a high degree of emulation. This emulation can be very clearly seen in artistic matters, but it extended to the establishment of various scientific clubs in eighteenth-century France in

15 E. L. Jones, *The European Miracle*, Cambridge, Cambridge University Press, 1981.

conscious imitation of their English rivals. Such emulation is ultimately only possible between states which recognize each other as of more or less similar standing; empires do not tend to copy the culture of their small neighbours – mere barbarians! And the reference to empires brings out other factors about the state system that proved beneficial for economic growth. A state system always had an inbuilt escape system. This is most obviously true in human matters. The expulsion of the Jews from Spain and the Huguenots from France benefited, and was seen to benefit, other countries and this served in the long run as a limitation on arbitrary government. Very importantly, capital was equally mobile. Thus Philip II's abuse of Antwerp led within a matter of years rather than decades to the rise of Amsterdam. In a brilliant passage making this point, McNeill has shown that time and again Philip II wanted to behave like an autocrat but the mobility of capital defeated him.[16] This was particularly true of his relationship with Liège, the foremost cannon producer of late sixteenth century Europe. When Philip squeezed them too hard, artisans and capitalists simply went elsewhere. A certain measure of decent and regularized behaviour was ensured by these means. However, perhaps the fundamental mechanism at work was that of military competiton. The positive impact of competition on European society can most dramatically be seen in the modern world. The revelation of German industry applied to war in 1870, for example, sent a ripple of anxiety and counter-measures throughout European capitals; states were forced to rationalize their societies to survive. Yet state competition was responsible for rationalizing European societies prior to the age of industry. Consider again the German case. Dramatic defeat by Napoleon was not ascribed to greater industrial development, but to the impact of an ideologically motivated citizen army. The reform group around Hardenburg (including Scharnhorst and Gneisenau, and with Clausewitz as their greatest intellectual figure) realized that serfs could not provide such an army; the reforms of 1807, 1811 and 1818 changed the Prussian social structure at a stroke. The purpose of such changes was military but the commercialization of agriculture that resulted was economically beneficial. This mechanism was at work in Europe roughly from 1100 when the multi-state character of Europe finally crystallised. Throughout the Middle Ages there was a breeding race to provide heavier, more effective cavalry, and other great changes were associated with the rise of bowmen and pikemen, the adoption of gunpowder and the consequent need for new Italian defences, the vast increase in army size in the seventeenth century, and the creation of a citizen army during the French Revolution. Each of these changes

16 W. McNeill, *The Pursuit of Power*, Oxford, Blackwell, 1982, chapter 1.

required money, and it was the search for funds that necessitated the king calling his estates, and raising funds by providing the infrastructures mentioned.

As noted, the European state became able to generate far more power than its imperial rivals: thus the France of Louis XIV probably had as large an effective army as Ming China even though her population was only 20, not about 150, million. This raises an important and interesting question. The organic quality of the European state arose from its having to accept and co-operate with other elements in civil society. Why was it, however, that the more powerful European state did not turn inwards in order to establish something more like an imperial system? Roughly speaking, European absolutism represents just such a move, and it is important to stress how unsuccessful it was. It is conventional to compare absolutist France with England in order to give the impression of greater strength in the former case. This is mistaken, since English society generated more power without an absolutist façade; it proved this in defeating France in war on every occasion bar one in which they met in the eighteenth century. This returns us to the question of competition. No state could afford to go it alone without risking defeat. It is hugely significant that by the middle of the eighteenth century France was sending its intellectuals to England, and was in other ways trying to copy her secrets. All this suggests that there must be a prime mover amongst the states in order to get competition to work in the first place. In fact there were several prime movers in European history, the torch of progress being passed from Italy to Holland and to England. The latter played a highly significant part as such a torch bearer, and it seems no accident that this state possessed a powerful and, crucially, *centralized* estates system which insisted on the state remaining organic during the absolutist period.[17] It is important to stress this since the reaction to the discovery that imperial strength hides feet of clay has been to say that the European state was always more powerful. Put like this the statement is misleading. Power operates, as Mann stresses, in two dimensions and the real contrast is between arbitrary government generating little power and the organic government of a civil society generating a great deal.

Reflections

The argument to this point can be summarized. For market relationships to gain autonomy, extensive social interaction networks are

17 There are interesting comments on England in A. MacFarlane, 'The cradle of capitalism', in *Europe and the Rise of Capitalism*, J. Baechler, J. A. Hall and J. M. Mann, eds, Oxford, Blackwell, 1987.

needed. In China, such extensive networks were provided by the polity. However, imperial rule was, perhaps could only be, based upon the negative tactic of preventing horizontal linkages that it could not control, and it was because of this that bureaucratic interference eventually proved deleterious for the economy. In the non-imperial civilizations, extensive networks were guaranteed by ideological organizations without the presence of a central polity. But in Islam states were weak, and had no more capacity to penetrate and organize social relationships than had the Chinese imperial state. In addition, states in Islam were short-lived, thereby predatory, and this accounts for its negative effect on economic relationships. Only when long-lasting states were forced by military competition to interact strongly with their civil societies was economic progress possible.

How does this argument square with Adam Smith's theory of society? Smith's argument is exceptionally suggestive, and it does indeed seem to me correct to argue that the key breakthrough in economic development could only occur in a capitalist form. Beyond this, we need to add to and complement his theory since it is half right and half wrong. Let us consider international society to begin with, before turning to the internal workings of particular nation states.

Internationally we have seen that there is a great deal to Smith's notion that freedom from interference helps account for the triumph of capitalism. If capitalists were persecuted in one state, they had the possibility of fleeing to another; military competition required, as capitalists increasingly proved their capacity to create intensive economies, that states did not act precipitately in this manner, and a certain respect for the rule of law thereby followed. Smith was not particularly aware of the importance of multipolarity (although his contemporary Gibbon was[18]), and he had no inkling at all of a much larger point. The revival of trade after the collapse of Rome was only possible because a reversion to localism was avoided by the sense of extensive identity provided by Latin Christendom. Contracts, in the lapidary Durkheimian formulation, were obeyed because of a hidden consensus.[19] This consensus was maintained after the Reformation, remarkably and without benefit of particular institutional regulation, as the culture of international diplomacy and of international capitalism.

Internally, it is very important to stress that the role of the state in the

18 E. Gibbon, *The Decline and Fall of the Roman Empire*, vol. I, London, Everyman, 1905, p. 93.

19 I am indebted for this Durkheimian understanding of ideology to Michael Mann, *The Sources of Social Power*, vol. I, *From the Beginning to 1760 AD*, Cambridge, Cambridge University Press, 1986. See also my 'Religion and the rise of Capitalism', *European Journal of Sociology*, vol. 26, 1985.

triumph was by no means negative. The organic state was long-lasting, penetrated into its society and generated a great deal of power. A tolerable administration meant a great deal – not least, as Smith himself stressed, the protection of property. If one asks about the nature of, say, the eighteenth-century English state, there is at first glance much to be said for calling this state a 'capitalist state' since parliament was comprised of the commercial aristocracy of the time, and of their clients; enclosures and colonial expansion were definitely in their interest. This is not to say, however, that class interests completely determined all activities of states; real autonomy existed in much of foreign policy-making and, as noted, developments in this realm often set the pace for economic advance. However, within the boundaries created by this sort of state help, *laissez-faire* internally certainly played its part in the success of economic relations.

But if Smith's general account needs to be amended by saying, for international and national society, that there was an element of organization to capitalism as well as an element of competition, it is possible to accept one striking claim of his social theory as a whole without demur. Smith was not a neo-classical thinker, but an Enlightenment figure who valued capitalism for the pragmatic reason that it brought in its train a decent political system. For Smith capitalism allowed liberty quite as much as *laissez-faire* allowed capitalism. He *was* right to note an elective affinity between capitalism and liberty in North-West Europe, albeit we must remember that this 'liberty' comprised the rule of law rather than the rule of democracy. This link between commerce and liberty deserves to be called 'the European Miracle'.[20] Was this link merely fortuitous and accidental, or was it based upon a necessary conjunction of these factors? These are huge issues, but an examination of more modern conditions can allow some light to be cast on them.

Commerce *and* Liberty in the Industrial Epoch?

Forced industrialization as a baseline

One reason that Smith so praised *laissez-faire* was because he felt that economic energies were present which, once 'uncorked', would naturally flow forth. He had some inklings that these energies might be uniquely European.[21] This can be put in an alternative way. Capitalism

20 See Jones, *The European Miracle*, and Baechler, Hall and Mann, *Europe and the Rise of Capitalism*.
21 Stewart, 'Life and Writings of Adam Smith', p. 313.

may be blocked in two ways. Actual economic enterprise, as in the case of Cheng-Ho, can be blocked by interference, but equally – as was the case to some extent in China and in Islam, and as would have been very clear had India, where this was especially true, been discussed[22] – a social order can prevent 'the economic' from having much significance in the first place. This distinction has great importance when we turn to modern conditions. Once European capitalism became *industrial* capitalism – something which Smith and his contemporaries felt could not happen, and a process which is still mysterious[23] – the rules of state competition meant that imitation remained the price of survival. In the European sphere itself, imitation by Germany, possessed of a similar social order, looked relatively 'natural'. But imitation elsewhere has been an entirely different matter; it has involved creating the human material suited to the modern period *ab initio*. As the nature of modernizing social engineering needs, even if only cursorily, to be at the forefront of our attention, let us consider two 'functional prerequisites' of the modern industrial era.

1 *Nation-building.* The most dramatic task is that facing countries which are entirely new. The citizens of industrialism must have the capacity to communicate with each other at an abstract level, preferably in a single language. This involves all states, including those of the old heartland of North-Western Europe, in the creation of schooling systems which both mobilize the people and give them the skills to operate in a literate and technical society. New states, however, must do more than simply establish educational systems. In addition they have such tasks as the removal of tribal linkages, the destruction of rival cultures and the creation of some new lingua franca, the establishment of national bureaucracies and so on. *The Wealth of Nations* simply had no conception that it would be necessary to create nations out of nothing in large parts of the world.[24]

2 *Sectoral change.* Most agrarian societies require something like 90 per cent of the work force to act as agricultural producers in order that a very small elite may be supported. In contrast, most advanced Western societies now have a primary sector of something like 5 per cent of the workforce. Whilst it was never the case that a majority of the workforce in industrial societies was engaged in the secondary industrial sector, this is not to downplay the fundamental insight of Barrington Moore's great *Social Origins of Dictatorship and Democracy* that modernization,

22 See my *Powers and Liberties*, chapter 3.
23 A. M. Wrigley, 'Rethinking the industrial revolution', Conference Paper, 1985.
24 E. Gellner, *Nations and Nationalism*, Oxford, Blackwell, 1983.

under whatever aegis, involves at the least disciplining the peasantry, and at the most forcibly removing it from the land.[25]

These are both obvious points, and others could be added to them.[26] Two sets of conclusions about the relationship between state and economic development follow; they concern *laissez-faire* and the commerce *and* liberty equation so dear to Smith's heart.

Forced and speedy industrialization has no place for *laissez-faire* on the part of the state. Such development is absolutely necessarily based upon the centralization of political power, and the creation of a new form of society by means of bureaucratic central planning. The transition to the modern world is such a vast matter, involving the creation of a new type of person, that the notion of *laissez-faire* simply has no sense. We can see this in the most obvious of ways. The Soviet Union pioneered a form of industrialization based on central planning by a monopolistic elite armed with a salvationist ideology. The efficacy of this model has been clearly recognized by many regimes the world over, perhaps especially those which are involved in nation-building.

State socialism is, however, but one system in the world, and its ideology anyway militates against *laissez-faire*. But there is a sense in which all economically successful modern societies are socialist, that is, are necessarily involved with the provision of infrastructural services, and we can see this particularly clearly by looking at the Newly Industrializing and advanced countries inside the larger capitalist arena. It would be a very grave mistake to believe that such Newly Industrializing Countries as Taiwan, Hong Kong and South Korea, simply because they are capitalist and despite their own self-advertisement, pay any real obeisance to *laissez-faire* ideology. The state plays a considerable and vital role in this type of society as investor and planner, and it regulates the market: indeed these societies as a whole deserve the appellation 'state capitalist'.[27] One suspects that an important part of the secret of the Confucian capitalist miracle is precisely that these societies inherited a strong bureaucratic and literate tradition which sees governmental interference as normal and desirable.

When one turns to the liberal and economically advanced societies of the West it is impossible not to note a decided artificiality to the notion of *laissez-faire* given the structural tasks that states have to undertake if the economy is to function. The role of government has increased, is expanding and seems very likely to grow. A modern workforce needs not

25 London, Penguin, 1969, passim.   26 See my *Powers and Liberties*, pp. 147–57.
27 See all the papers in G. White and R. Wade, eds, *Developmental States in East Asia*, Brighton, Institute for Development Studies, Rr 16, 1984; A. Amsden, 'Taiwan's economic history', *Modern China*, vol. 5, 1979.

just to be literate but 'computer literate' as well, and it is the provision of this sort of infrastructural service on the part of the state that keeps children in education for such a long time; this helps account for the incredibly high proportion of GDP that is funnelled through the modern state. None of this is to say that there are not areas in such societies in which the market is allowed to rule, and more is said about the boundaries of such areas below. But those areas are smaller than they were, and tend to be delimited by the state itself. The states in question try and produce cohesive societies capable of competing in the international capitalist arena; to do so rules out internal *laissez-faire* in most crucial areas. What else is the Japanese state but a research and marketing body for the large business organizations of its national capitalism?

The second conclusion is a consequence of 'forcing' modernization, particularly nation-building and sectoral change, so that a state may continue to compete geopolitically. Quite simply, forced industrialization tends to go hand in hand with dictatorship. The Soviet Model necessitates keeping consumption low and investment high, and it typically involves collectivization; the pressures that this involves effectively entails centralizing power, and it is hard to imagine how things could be otherwise.[28] All this is to say that certain societies have broken Smith's equation by rejecting capitalism altogether, and in the process embracing a centralizing regime. Perhaps more worrying than this is the disruption of the liberty *with* commerce equation by combining authority *with* capitalism, a linkage first pioneered by Imperial Germany and Imperial Japan. Geopolitical defeat means that we are simply not in a position to judge the long-term efficacy of the authority with capitalism combination since the Allies imposed a different social order as the result of their victory. But the attractions of this route have by no means disappeared, and it is one that has been much in favour in those 'NICs' that have already been mentioned. South Korea is an exceptionally authoritarian state, and it is by no means the only one of its type. One reason for this authoritarianism is the necessity for creating citizens suitable to an industrial milieu, that is, the accomplishment of those functional prerequisites that also dominate the very being of state socialism. But there is a second general reason. To say the least, the capitalist middle classes in these societies are no friends to liberal democracy. Capitalists may not have destroyed the Weimar Republic, but they were conspicuously reluctant allies in its defence. Beyond this, there are certain societies in the Third World where it is true – for very often this statement is not justified[29] – that involvement an international capitalist

---

28 Hall, *Powers and Liberties*, chapter 7.   29 Ibid, chapter 8.

society actually prevents economic development; and international corporations themselves have certainly often opposed democracy in such countries. Capitalism and liberty do not always go hand in hand.

This makes the combination of commerce and liberty in European history all the more remarkable. That combination remains, but it is worth noting that it now looks somewhat more shaky. The organic state had depended upon various sources of power in society co-operating together, as the result of trusting the state in which they participated to manage properly commercial society; there were, in other words, strong and autonomous plural groups, i.e. a real civil society, and the possession of their 'liberties' went hand in hand with economic development. The late nineteenth and early twentieth century has seen the emergence of labour movements with their own 'liberties', and there is now a great deal of discussion as to whether this new power source will oppose various other groups with a corresponding loss of total social energy. One call made in such circumstances is for trade union 'liberties' to be removed. If that were to happen it would of course signal the end of the commerce and liberty equation.

Second thoughts

This baseline argument made so far about Adam Smith's political hopes in modern circumstances seems unrelievedly gloomy. But second thoughts suggest that any surrender to pessimism would be mistaken. The most obvious reason for this is that economic development, even under dictatorial regimes, is better than poverty. But deeper reflections about the relations between economic development and political forms in the societies discussed need to be aired.

The equation of dictatorship with development is too crude. Mere dictatorship does not guarantee development, and it has become generally obvious that central planning is much better at creating an industrial society than it is at running it once it is in place. As a result, a relatively optimistic scenario has an air of plausibility. If late industrial society depends upon a large technical and scientific stratum, whose work depends upon a measure of genuine autonomy, then liberalization of societies that have industrialized according to the Soviet Model may well be on the cards. Such societies could yet gain legitimacy via affluence rather than ideology.[30] The Hungarian case interestingly suggests that a measure of *laissez-faire* attitudes to the economy, that is, a reintroduction of market mechanisms in selected areas, may be involved as a

30 E. Gellner, 'Plaidoyer pour une libéralisation manquée', *Government and Opposition*, vol. 14, 1979.

part of this process. It may be impossible to create speedy industrial growth by *laissez-faire* means, but a measure of regulated market activity may help in the liberalization of such societies once they have made the transition to industrialism. But it would be a great mistake to believe, as the theorists of 'convergence' between East and West once supposed, that either capitalism or liberal democracy is likely to be reintroduced in such circumstances. One may merely hope that late industrialism in socialist societies may bring with it softer political rule.

A similar hope may be entertained about the advance of industrialism inside Newly Industrializing Countries. It is important to note that the combination of authority with capitalism may well not be particularly stable. It is impossible, as noted, to tell whether Imperial Japan and Germany would have cemented this union, but it is noticeable that some other countries failed to do so. The combination seemed assured in Francoist Spain, but the more that economy advanced, and thereby crucially came to depend on educated labour, the more the pressures mounted for liberalization. Very interestingly, Spanish capitalists by and large welcomed liberalization since they had come to realize that accommodation is cheaper than repression.[31] Special circumstances pollute the Spanish evidence, but it is again very striking to note that Newly Industrializing Countries like Brazil and Argentina are involved in processes of liberalization that seem to be aided by the stage of economic development they have now reached; the supporters of liberalization in Brazil, for example, include the newer middle-class elements of educated labour whose position in the economy is coming to outweigh the influence of old plantation capitalists.[32] There may yet, in other words, be something in some societies – most obviously those with a history of parliamentary rule – to Adam Smith's equation of commerce and liberty, at least in the long run, as the result of such social pressures. Similarly, those societies are likely to pay some allegiance to the market principle internally, if only to remove the power of large, traditional monopolists, even if the dominant drive of their development remains that of a state creating a strong national society so as to be able to compete in the international market.

Let us finally consider the position of the economically advanced liberal democracies of capitalist society. As noted, the key question of politics in such societies is that of combining pluralism with co-operation. Three 'recipes' seem to be on offer at the moment. The first is

31 S. Giner and E. Sevilla, 'From despotism to parliamentism: class domination and political order in the Spanish state', in R. Scase, ed., *The State in Western Europe*, London, Croom Helm, 1978.
32 J. G. Merquior, 'Power and identity: politics and ideology in Latin America', *Government and Opposition*, vol. 19, 1984.

that of 'micro-corporatism', pioneered by Japan and currently being extended in West Germany, in which highly trained labour, guaranteed employment in large corporations for life, coexists with a notably Social Darwinist labour market for the rest. A second solution seems to be that favoured by Sweden, in which an extension of citizenship rights is designed to go hand in hand with an acceptance of the logic of the international marketplace by the working class as a whole.[33] Both these strategies have current success, but it is probably too soon to say whether this will continue. It is, however, possible to be definite about the likelihood of failure of the solution currently being tried in Great Britain. This strategy suggests that *laissez-faire* should rule internally in very many areas, perhaps including education as a whole, and that the key to industrial competitiveness depends on lowering wages so that our products again price themselves into the international market; it seeks to discipline a workforce rather than to co-operate with it. It is ironic to note that this strategy is often profferred in the name of Adam Smith, given that the great thinker preferred a high wage/high productivity labour force so that rich nations could retain prosperity. In modern conditions British wages would have to fall exceptionally far to make it possible to compete with the Third World in this way. One cannot resist the conclusion that a country like Denmark, with a huge social infrastructure and notably high levels of education, will be in a better position to adapt to the late twentieth century than Great Britain, possessed of an uneducated, if servile, working class. None of this is to say that the market has *no* place inside the advanced societies. In West Germany and in France, policy has characteristically been more state-oriented in the provision of infrastructure and more market-oriented in particular areas of the economy. In France, industrial policy for much of the post-war period centred upon investing in new and advancing companies so that old industries could be killed off quicker. In West Germany, the state invested in a series of computer companies and then left the market to find out which one was best. The British state, in contrast, propped up ailing industries, and chose to invest massively in a single computer company. The argument as to the diminished role of *laissez-faire* inside capitalist nations can be summed up by saying that a part of the infrastructural service of the modern nation-state is that of making the internal market work effectively. The British state has not yet learnt how to do this.[34]

---

33 See the papers in J. H. Goldthorpe, ed., *Order and Conflict in Western European Capitalism*, Oxford, Oxford University Press, 1984.

34 G. Ingham, *Capitalism Divided?*, London, Macmillan, 1984, argues that this can be explained in terms of the British state's involvement with finance rather than with industry. This factor is important, but it is only an element in a larger situation. For a com-

My argument has been that *laissez-faire* never had complete sway inside nation-states, and that its sway is now considerably diminished. But there is no doubt that the market 'rules' in one way. Capitalism fundamentally escapes political interference because its culture remains larger than that of any single state. This larger realm had needed initial organization by the creation of a consensual Christian arena within which contracts were obeyed, and this whole matter needs to be considered once again. It is quite remarkable that the larger capitalist culture did not have much regulation for long periods, but the increase of world trade, first under British hegemony and really effectively under American hegemony since 1945, has meant that a single leading power has had the capacity to manage the larger system. This leads us to a final reflection of very great importance. American handling of the modern world political economy is becoming destabilizing in line with the ever continuing increase in the size of the state budget deficit. This has meant high interest rates as the American state has borrowed from the rest of the world, and it is likely to lead, now that America's net debtor status makes this policy less attractive, to a bout of protectionism in the world economic system. Both these policies cause great problems for Third World countries; if continued over time, they could rule out any possibility of liberalization in the NICs of the capitalist arena. This is not something that the advanced nations of the capitalist world can regard with any tranquillity, and it is fair to say that a main task confronting those who would wish to cement the commerce and liberty equation is that of changing American policy. To do so involves changing those American military commitments which have led to her becoming overextended, and thereby abusing the rules of international economics she imposes on all other states inside the capitalist arena.

Conclusion

The argument of this chapter can usefully be concluded by making explicit a disagreement with the general ethic of the previous chapter. Michael Mann's position has a certain symmetry in allowing for different – in particular, development by means of acephalous capitalism or by means of state despotism – political economies of economic advance in agrarian and in industrial conditions. My argument is asymmetrical, largely because of a relatively negative assessment of imperial rule. I do not doubt the benefits that imperial peace and consolidation could and

parison, see my 'The state', in G. A. Causer, ed., *Inside British Society*, Brighton, Wheatsheaf, 1987.

did bring, and am well aware that many groups welcomed inclusion in pre-industrial empires precisely for these reasons. But the crucial transition in the agrarian world seems to me to be that which created an autonomous economic dynamic of broadly capitalist hue which eventually bred industrialism, and that transition *was created* and, I suspect, *could only have been created* by curtailing the despotic powers of the state. Once that happened, however, economic advance tended to be achieved under the aegis of state despotic forms, albeit the 'logic' of late industrialism may allow for a certain 'softening' of political rule.

7

Sharing Public Space: States and Organized Interests in Western Europe

Colin Crouch

Without doing too much violence to individual cases it is possible to speak of a 'parliamentary parenthesis' as a universal phase in Western European societies, starting some time in the eighteenth or nineteenth centuries and lasting until the final quarter of the nineteenth. The phrase is C.S. Maier's.[1] He uses it to draw attention to the fact that before the high-water period of liberal parliamentarianism politics was mainly a matter of organized functional interests (land-owners, guilds etc.), and that over the past century there has been a new rise of organized economic interests, mainly those of capital and labour. Between came the era of parliamentary politics, of bourgeois individual representation, when organized functional groups were treated with extreme suspicion. He points to both the commonality of both the overall experience and the common crisis point in the wake of the economic collapse of 1873.

However, the variety of experience in the ways in which different nation-states moved into and out of the liberal period deserves separate examination. It is my contention that the extent to which modes of behaviour based on the pre-parliamentary phase survived during the high period of parliamentary liberalism had a significant impact on the

The final version of this paper has benefited greatly from discussions of earlier drafts at the sociology seminar at Nuffield College, Oxford, and at the London 'Wednesday group', the latter having also been more generally important in sustaining the spirits of those of us venturing down the difficult path of comparative historical macro-sociology.

1 C. S. Maier, '"Fictitious bonds . . . of wealth and law": on the theory and practice of interest representation', in S. D. Berger, ed., *Organizing Interests in Western Europe*, Cambridge, Cambridge University Press, 1981.

shaping of modern interest politics. In particular, this earlier experience helps us explain the differential extent to which different societies have adopted neo-corporatist institutions in the period since the Second World War. This is a dimension which has been neglected by most recent research into neo-corporatism, which has tended to concentrate on far more recent events in explaining variations among contemporary states; the power of social-democratic parties,[2] consociationism,[3] the size of the welfare state,[4] being the three, rather closely related, favourite variables.

In seeking to take the explanation further back into history I in no way wish to decry the significance of these factors, nor to pretend that the experiences of the twentieth century – two world wars, fascism and communism, universal suffrage, a period of unparalleled full employment – have not been critically important to the shaping of patterns of relations between states, organized capital and organized labour. My task is far more modest; I wish merely to offer a reminder that complex societies very rarely present *tabulae rasae*, even after events as shattering as the two world wars, and that recent institutions and behaviour have deep historical roots. Indeed, as we shall see, the two nation states whose identities were most disrupted by those wars, Germany and Austria, are two of the most telling examples of the power of historical continuity.

The changes that have occurred in the twentieth century in the politics of organized interests mainly concern the balance of power among the different social forces. It is in the means by which, the style in which, various groups have grappled with these changes that the deeper historical continuities may be seen. 'Style' may seem a trivial variable compared with the balance of power; an ephiphenomenon if ever there was one. But it is not to be written off in this way. When the active groups in a particular society tackle the latest conflict that has occurred in relations between them, they do not work out how, in some abstract way, a problem of that kind should ideally be resolved. No-one has the

2 W. Korpi and M. Shalev, 'Strikes, industrial relations and class conflict in capitalist societies', *British Journal of Sociology*, vol. 30, 1979; P. Lange and G. Garrett, 'The politics of growth: strategic interaction and economic performance in the advanced industrial democracies, 1974–1980', *Journal of Politics*, vol. 46, 3, 1985; L. N. Johansen and O. P. Kristensen, 1982, 'Corporatist traits in Denmark', in G. Lehmbruch and P. C. Schmitter, eds, *Patterns of Corporatist Policy-Making*, London, Sage, 1982.

3 G. Lehmbruch, 'Consociational democracy, class conflict and the new corporatism', in P. C. Schmitter and G. Lehmbruch, eds, *Trends toward Corporatist Intermediation*, London, Sage, 1979.

4 C. J. Crouch, 'Corporative industrial relations and the welfare state', in R. J. B. Jones, ed., *Perspectives on Political Economy*, London, Frances Pinter, 1983; H. Wilensky, *The New Corporatism, Centralization and the Welfare State*, Beverley Hills, Cal., Sage. 1976.

kind of knowledge needed to answer such questions in complex matters, and in any case only a few component variables are loosened from the historical package for manipulation at any one time. Usually therefore a solution will be sought that involves as little disturbance as possible to known and understood principles of organization, that enables most use to be made of predictabilities from past experience. This does not mean that striking innovation never happens. To move from having trade union leaders put in prison to inviting them to ministerial talks, or *vice versa*, to cite a particularly common case of policy shift, is dramatically innovative. But perhaps precisely because such moves involve a step into the unknown, there will usually be attempts to carry them out in a manner that is in as many respects as possible tried and familiar.

The two decades after the crash of 1873 were such a period of institutional innovation. Everywhere industrialism was moving out of its purely competitive phase into the epoch of 'organized capitalism',[5] a development, impelled principally by conditions of international competition, which struck different societies at very different stages of their individual economic progress. At the same time the organization of labour became an issue that all states needed to take seriously. What clues did an earlier age of functional-interest politics bequeath to these industrial or industrializing states? In turn, what relevance did the solutions found in the final quarter of the nineteenth century have for the new organizational politics of the second half of the twentieth? The main task of this chapter is to examine the first of these questions, concluding with a forward glance at the second.

The analysis is concentrated on Western Europe, though the eastern boundary of that entity is rather flexible, being dependent on the varying extents of the Hapsburg and Hohenzollern states. Since my ultimate interest is in relating historical patterns to the current state of affairs in liberal democratic regimes, there is little point in extending the account further eastwards. To move beyond Europe to consider Japan, the USA, the British Commonwealth or other industrialized parts of the world would involve adding many extra variables. While Western Europe embodies a wide range of historical experiences, they are all broadly embraced by the key experiences of feudalism and absolutism, Christianity and the Reformation, capitalist industrialization and working-class protest.

The central concept for this discussion is political space. By that I

5 The phrase was originated in the early twentieth century by Rudolf Hilferding – inevitably an Austrian (see T. Bottomore and P. Goode, *Austro-Marxism*, Oxford, Oxford University Press, 1978, and H. A. Winkler, ed., *Organisierter Kapitalismus*, Göttingen, Vandenhoeck and Ruprecht, 1974).

mean that range of issues over which general, universal decisions are made within a given political unit, particularly decisions which are seen by political actors to affect overall social order. The territory so designated is variable, and to that extent its definition may well be a matter of conflict within societies. The articulation of such definitional conflicts is ultimately relevant to the current thesis, but to introduce it as a variable here would make the analysis too complex.

It is a crucial feature of the classic liberal political economy that political space is monopolized by specialized political institutions: legislature, executive and judiciary. Civil society enters these institutions only through its members adopting formal, specialized political roles, whether as a member of one of these institutions or as individual citizen-electors. Functional and other specifically denominated social interests may approach the political institutions as external lobbies and pressure groups, but their entry *within* them is regarded as a form of corruption or (as in the British House of Lords) an odd compromise between liberal and earlier forms of government.

That a form of political monopoly lies at the heart of liberalism may seem paradoxical, but it is part of the important truth that *laissez-faire* is not anarchism. The state has vital functions within liberal market capitalism; if they are not performed by the state, they will be taken over by groups within civil society, which will therefore cease to be the non-political actors that participants in the market system are required to be. On the other hand, if the state steps beyond its vital functions, it will begin to intervene in civil society in a manner that more obviously disturbs market relations. Theoretically, therefore, a pure liberal market economy requires a state that is not only limited and restrained but which is, within its proper sphere, sovereign. It is the clarity of state-society boundaries that distinguishes this kind of political economy rather than state restraint as such.

The theory is reflected in history. In most capitalist states a period of absolutism preceded the development of capitalism as the dominant economic system.[6] In feudalism political authority is too parcellized and mixed with land-holding to enable civil society to function in proper market fashion. The typical urban associations, the guilds, differed from pure associations of interests by carrying out delegated political functions of maintaining order within their craft. By concentrating and distilling political sovereignty into itself, the absolutist state

---

6 For a good guide to the relationship between feudalism, the *Ständestaat*, absolutism and the modern state, see G. Poggi, *The Development of the Modern State*, London, Hutchinson, 1978; and for a discussion of variations in absolutism, see P. Anderson, *Lineages of the Absolutist State*, London, New Left Books, 1974.

depoliticized civil society in a manner useful to the development of market relations, though in many cases it 'went too far' and began to use its accretion of power to interfere in civil society itself.

It is important to distinguish these questions from that of 'strong' versus 'weak' states, which refers to the capacity of a state to carry out effectively those functions which it claims to be able to perform; a strong state does not have to be a highly interventionist one. While a state that occupies only a fragment of potential political space is likely to be a weak one, a restricted state which nevertheless carries out all the functions needed to secure basic order may well rate as a very strong state precisely because it concentrates its power and does not try to achieve 'too much'. Indeed, a need to restrict the state in order to make its strength effective was part of the new right's critique of the arguably over-extended states of the 1970s.[7] Similarly, while it takes a very strong state to act effectively as a highly interventionist one, it is quite possible to envisage states that intervene beyond their means and end by consequently being ineffective.

To return to Maier's idea of the parliamentary parenthesis, the period before it can be envisaged as one in which political space was shared. The state typically both left several aspects of social regulation to guilds, *Stände* and similar corporate bodies, and interfered in economic affairs. During the parliamentary parenthesis these essentially organizational forms of regulation were dismantled. Order was typically secured through a combination of direct but external state regulation and market forces, with the state guaranteeing the private property rights necessary for market relations and contract to operate. After the period of the parliamentary parenthesis, essentially from the 1870s onwards, organized economic interests became increasingly important. Could the state continue to cope with them through the mixture of market forces and external regulation, or would it interpenetrate them in order to co-opt their organizational resources for the task of securing order, as envisaged in corporatist theory and ideology? Almost everywhere there were moves in the latter direction, but, just as parliamentarism penetrated different societies to very different degrees, these varied widely in extent, with ramifications in differences between polities that are still with us.

Prior to consideration of the relationship between the two eras of organized interests itself, it is first necessary to consider the effect on different societies of settlement of the relationship between state and

7 For example, R. Rose and G. Peters, *Can Governments Go Bankrupt?* New Haven, Yale University Press, 1977; M. Crozier, S. P. Huntingdon and J. Watanaki, *The Crisis of Democracy*, Trilateral Commission, 1978.

church. This was the key question affecting state sovereignty and the occupation of political space before the emeregence of issues of the market and civil society, and in several societies it remained an issue throughout the subsequent period too. To the extent that the liberal state had to struggle to assert its autonomy from and superiority over an established religion, it became exceptionally 'jealous' of political space, reluctant to share it, and thus exclusive in its claims to sovereignty; while pro-church forces tended to inherit traditions of space-sharing. This led to profound divisions over access to political space. Other religious patterns have been less determinative or have inclined towards greater consensus over space-sharing.

Having examined this it will be possible to confront more squarely the central thesis: the longer the interval, or the sharper the breach, between the destruction of ancient guild and *Ständestaat* institutions and the construction of typically 'modern' interest organizations, the more committed did the state become to liberal modes of interest representation, and the less likely to tolerate sharing political space; the less likely were modern organizations to target their ambitions on participation of that kind; and the less likely were neo-corporatist institutions to become established.

Religion and the State

We can distinguish here between four basic patterns: (1) one in which secular liberalism and Catholicism confronted each other in a fundamental and continuing way; (2) a similar pattern but where Catholicism was able to achieve a degree of hegemony that eventually ensured a more general acceptance of elements of its concept of the state; (3) one in which an established Protestant church provided few political challenges; and (4) one where a mixture of religious and secular forces achieved an elaborate *modus vivendi* through consociationism.

Secular liberalism versus Catholic corporatism

The paradigm case of the exclusive claims of the secular state is of course the French Republic. In their drive to integrate the nation around republican symbols as opposed to the Catholic church, the various French republics asserted the sovereignty and inaccessibility of the state, which clearly stood above and outside society and its many claims.[8] The issue is seen at perhaps its sharpest and most permanent in the struggle over church schools. A major outcome is a long-term

8 J. E. S. Hayward, *Governing France: the One and Indivisible Republic*, London, Weidenfeld & Nicolson, 2nd ed, 1983, pp. 55ff.

confrontation between a jealous secular state and a determinedly active church.[9] At least in the immediate post-1789 period it is rather difficult to separate this drive by the state from the second theme of the state's autonomy from ancient corporate forms, as so many of these were combined with church power.

At a later stage there was a secondary development: the state rendering itself both inaccessible and dominant, the newly developing labour movement found little chance of influencing it and therefore became highly oppositional, much of it embracing first syndicalism and then communism.[10] This reinforced the existing tendency of the state, because labour now rendered itself increasingly unattractive as a potential 'social partner' by both the state and capital; a process of cumulative mutual hostility was thus set in train.

The fact that much corporatist ideology originated within French Catholicism does not refute this analysis. When the Vatican finally marked its reconciliation with pluralism and industrial society with the publication of the encyclical *Rerum Novarum* in 1891, its doctrine of accepting the organization of labour but rejecting class conflict led, in the context of the period, automatically to a corporatist approach to industrial relations among Catholics. This assisted in both the elaboration of doctrines of corporatist politics and the development of a Catholic minority wing of the labour movement. In fact, in France and elsewhere, corporatism proved a troublesome asset for Catholics, as it could be interpreted to mean a variety of relationships between labour and capital, ranging from employer-controlled syndicates to forms of antagonistic co-operation.

But so long as the republican tradition of suspicion of religion remained central to French state practice, as it did throughout the Third Republic, there was no scope for corporatism becoming a national model. It remained a minority stream to which both the state and its main opponent, the increasingly socialist majority wing of labour, remained impervious. In that context, even if Catholicism had been more influential among French employers, it is unlikely that that would alone have changed politics. A corporatist *Staatslehre* was a highly contentious issue in France as it raised fundamental issues of the autonomy of the republic. Consequently it could find expression only following a victory of Catholic conservatism over liberal republicanism. This eventually happened only with the partial and temporary triumph

9 S. M. Lipset and S. Rokkan, 'Cleavage structures, party systems and voter alignments', in Lipset and Rokkan, eds, *Party Systems and Voter Alignments*, New York, Free Press,1967, pp. 15, 38–40; D. A. Martin, *A General Theory of Secularization*, Oxford, Blackwell, 1978, pp. 40, 118–20.

10 J.-D. Reynaud, *Les Syndicats en France*, vol. 1, Paris, Seuil, 1975, chapter 3.

of the Vichy regime, which suppressed both the republican tradition and its labour antagonists; but then, with labour reduced to shadow front organizations, that state had little need for anything other than a façade of corporatism.

Despite striking differences, a not dissimilar story applies to the other southern European countries where modernizing forces found it necessary to take an anti-Catholic, militantly liberal-secular form: Spain, Portugal and, above all, Italy.[11] While in each case both the economies and the forces of liberalism were far weaker than in France (in Portugal exceptionally so), what liberal regimes there were had still found it necessary to assert their monopoly claim to political space against the Church.[12] There was, as in France, a pattern of labour-movement oppositionalism and Catholic reactionary corporatism; and in all three cases the dependence of a corporatist outcome on a fascist authoritarian form was more sharply demonstrated than in France, with prolonged fascist regimes making use of façades of corporatism within dictatorship. That they were only façades is made clear by several authors[13] and again results from the fact that, once labour opposition had been completely destroyed, there was little need even for its incorporated representation.

Italy was perhaps the sharpest case of the state's search for autonomy, as for many years the Vatican opposed even the existence of a secular state governing the peninsula.[14] But it is perhaps more difficult to understand subsequent Italian history. Of all the four southern European states it has seen Christian Democracy installed as the dominant political force since 1945. If the state no longer faces its mission of secularizing sovereignty, why has there been no sharp reversal of practice? First, the religious question is but one force being considered, and we have yet to examine the others; but second, there are large time-lags in these historical processes. If organizations and state practices have developed in a certain way over many years, they will not easily make rapid adaptations to a changed situaton. The pre-fascist legacy of Italian labour was one of opposition and of disaggregated, decentralized action. These structures could not suddenly change in the expectation that things might now be different. And third, a later factor

11 Martin, *General Theory of Secularization*, pp. 36–41.

12 For a good account of this process as it affected Spain, see J. Linz, 'A century of interest and politics in Spain', in Berger, *Organizing Interests in Western Europe*.

13 G. Giner and E. Sevilla, 'Spain: from corporatism to corporatism', in A. Williams, ed., *Southern Europe Transformed*, London, Harper & Row, 1984, pp. 119–20; P. J. Williamson, *Varieties of Corporatism*, Cambridge, Cambridge University Press, 1985, chapter 7.

14 Lipset and Rokkan, 'Cleavage structures' p. 40; Martin, *General Theory of Secularization*, pp. 124–6.

outside the scope of this thesis, the fact that communism became the main driving force of the labour movement and that capitalists after 1945 reverted to labour repression, further lessened the changes of change.

The fascist interlude in these societies did not clear away organizational realities and learned modes of behaviour; in some respects the opposite was the case. The labour movement had been forged within an inaccessible liberal state that wished to develop no relations with it; the movement had adopted its various *modi vivendi* in response to that. The underground movement's experience of fascism only confirmed and reinforced that response. For any of the major actors to change historical track would have required strong evidence disconfirming their experience of the past. This began to occur, in France as well as Italy, from 1944 to 1947, but the international politics of the Cold War intervened and returned relations to their familiar path before major changes could be implanted. This demonstrates why early nineteenth-century patterns of state-society relations have been of such enduring importance. The emergence of Spain and Portugal from fascism is still too recent to permit easy generalization about their subsequent development.

Hegemonic Catholic corporatism

Liberal traditions in Portugal, and to a certain extent Spain, were pitifully weak, but they did establish a resistance to corporatist hegemony that was not amenable to compromise. The Hapsburg Empire is therefore left as the only case where dominant corporatist traditions gradually suffused the responses even of oppositional groups. The brief liberal episode of the 1860s took place within imperial hegemony. Also, backward though many of the Hapsburg lands were, they contained more sectors of modern industry than Spain or Portugal, and there was therefore greater scope for synthesis between *ancien régime* and industrialization. The only other partial case, Belgium, is better discussed as an example of consociationism.

For reasons that go beyond our present scope, the legacy of liberalism in the Hapsburg lands was one of the weakest in the whole of Europe: the short reign of Joseph II; a few months in 1848; and the 1860s which, being followed by the great crash of 1873 (which indeed started in Vienna), led to a setback rather than a beach-head for subsequent liberal progress. Beyond that, the assorted lands that were ruled by the Vienna-based state, leader of the counter-reformation, remained a stronghold of Catholicism until the challenges from socialism and pan-Germanism at the end of the century. State and church reached their *modus vivendi* with little need for the state to assert its rights. The state therefore remained unmodernized and essentially organic; it experienced no difficulty in the idea of sharing space with suitable approved interests; outside the liberal interlude of the 1860s, it had indeed an historical disposition to base its practice precisely on such arrangements, fashioning them in a highly conservative form.[15]

However, as in the Latin Catholic states, a *displaced* social Catholicism was likely to generate an authoritarian corporatism of a fascist kind, as it did in the 1930s. It is important to distinguish this organic, Catholic fascism from the secular Nazism of Germany. This was made dramatically clear by Austrian history following the *Anschluß*, when the whole edifice of *Austrofaschismus* and its corporatism was abolished and replaced by the Nazi system, based on the *Führerprinzip* rather than corporatism.[16] But the abiding, specifically Austrian tradition remained corporatist and space-sharing. Therefore, while Austria shares the southern European experience of authoritarian, fascist corporatism, it is distinguished from those countries by its more generalized corporatist legacy.

Protestant neutrality

Lutheran churches have historically been obedient national institutions, accepting something approaching civil service status within the state and asserting no superior political loyalty as did the Vatican-based Catholic church.[17] Lutheran states have therefore suffered no major inhibitions on these grounds concerning sharing political space, though this implies a noncommittal neutralism towards organized interests, not the positive organism of the unreformed Hapsburg state. This lack of 'jealousy' reduced the extent to which these states subsequently provoked the formation of highly oppositional labour movements; the spiral of mutual rejection seen so clearly in the French case does not apply here.

This pattern is most clearly seen in the Scandinavian countries (Denmark, Norway, Sweden). Finland was a Grand Duchy of Russia throughout the nineteenth century, and therefore, like Ireland, was strictly speaking not a polity for our purposes, but governed by a state with a different religious base. However, the Russians left almost intact the religious organization of Finland and its governmental structures. These were derived from the preceding five centuries of Swedish rule. Both Finland and Norway lack any native central state tradition –

---

15 E. Talos, *Staatliche Sozialpolitik in Österreich*, Vienna, Verlag für Gesellschaftskritik, 1981, chapters 1, 2.
16 Ibid., chapter 6.
17 Martin, *General Theory of Secularization*, p. 23.

Norway being under first Danish and then, in the nineteenth century, Swedish rule until 1905;[18] but given the consonance of Lutheranism throughout the Nordic cultures, this does not present any problems for the variable under discussion.

The situation in Bismarckian Germany was somewhat different in that the south German Catholic minority was large and, left to produce its own nation-states, would probably have developed similarly to Austria. But the Prussian-German state did not encounter the same problems as Republican France or Italy in relations with the church; it was after all a Catholic minority and could not threaten to impose a political form on all Germany. The state was therefore unencumbered by a need to guard jealously its hold on political space, giving a legacy in this regard similar to the Scandinavian.

For purposes of the present discussion the Anglican Church behaved like a Lutheran one. It never subordinated itself to the state in the same way through state bureaucracy, but relied on essentially informal, 'gentlemanly' arrangements in order to keep its peace with the English ruling class – a fact relevant to the structure of British interest organizations, as we shall see in due course. But, during the period under discussion, the British state had little cause for jealousy over political space on religious grounds. While discussing Britain it is also opportune to mention that Ireland was at that time completely subsumed under British authority. Unlike the Finns under the Russians, the Irish did not have an opportunity to develop a polity consistent with their religious preference.

Consociationism

There remain the divided religious cultures, where a Catholic-Calvinist division was eventually supplemented by a religious versus secular split. There are only two clear cases in Europe – the Netherlands and Switzerland – but they are particularly interesting. The Swiss case is made more complex by the virtual absence of a state in the commonly accepted form, and this is a variable to which we shall return. Common to both cases was that, attempts by one community to dominate having failed, these polities established the form now known as consociationism: the major public activities of both state and civil society are compartmentalized and run separately by and for the different groups.[19]

---

18 S. Kuhnle, *Patterns of Social and Political Mobilization: a Historical Analysis of the Nordic Countries*, London, Sage, 1975, pp. 7–10.

19 A. Lijphart, *The Politics of Accommodation*, Berkeley, University of California Press, 1968; Martin, *General Theory of Secularization*, pp. 113–15; Lipset and Rokkan, 'Cleavage stuctures' pp. 15–18, 39.

Where state functions are concerned, this means in effect parcelling out state power among the communities and delegating state functions to their representative organizations. This form of political organization goes beyond the 'permissive' approach to political space implicit in the Lutheran and Anglican states, positively *embodying* the sharing of political space as a rule of procedure. These thus form examples of the state needing to co-opt groups in civil society because it cannot itself effectively monopolize political space as a result of the inter-cultural conflicts.

There was a secondary consequence in that, Catholicism being established as part of the modern state, its doctrines of corporatism were able to enter industrial and class relations without a need to resort to authoritarian forms. This was strengthened by the easy compatibility of consociational and corporatist principles of organization.[20] In particular, in the Netherlands employers, familiar with consociational structures, developed strong, centralized organizations by the end of the nineteenth century.[21] Among Calvinists and Catholics these were in turn relatively easily able to establish good relations with the labour movements within their respective pillars. In particular, Catholic doctrines of *Rerum Novarum* were able to diffuse a far more realistic version of corporatism than in either southern Europe or in Austria where relations with secular liberalism were so antagonistic. It is partly for this reason that the *Hoge Raad van Arbeid*, established in 1917, had much greater longevity than similar Great War creations designed to integrate labour in other societies, lasting until it formed the basis for similar structures after the Second World War.[22]

More recently, important elements of consociationism have found their way into the Second Austrian Republic as a means of resolving the Catholic/socialist division; and there are minor traces of it in Federal Germany and Italy. In terms of a longer historical trajectory, however, there is only one other likely case: Belgium. In part Belgium follows the southern European pattern of a liberal state in conflict with Catholicism. However, a major complicating factor was the early Catholic/ Liberal alliance against Dutch Calvinist rule that founded the independent Belgian kingdom. The conflicts were therefore never as strong, and important elements of consociationism, while not quite as clear as the Dutch, developed. Again, as a secondary development, Catholic corporatist doctrines were able to combine with this.

20 Lehmbruch, 'Consociational democracy'.
21 J. P. Windmuller, *Labor Relations in the Netherlands*, Ithaca, Cornell University Press, 1969, p. 46.
22 Ibid., pp. 60–5, 83.

In the twentieth century this factor has been intensified by the particular strength of the Catholic wing of the Belgian labour movement.[23] This has enabled Catholic corporatist doctrines of industrial relations to occupy a place similar to that found in the Netherlands. The Belgian experience is thus perched uncomfortably between the Latin and the consociational pattern. Matters have been complicated by the fact that Catholicism and secularism in part follow the contours of Flemish–Walloon relations, an element in Belgian life which has never been effectively subjected to consociational agreements.

From *Ständestaat* to Interest Organizations

There has in several countries been an extensive debate over the extent to which modern trade union organization is built on guild traditions. The issue here is slightly different. We are interested, not so much in whether workers from guild backgrounds began to construct unions, but in the extent to which modern interest organizations were able to occupy a *political* role similar to that of their pre-modern corporate predecessors. While they did represent interests, late medieval corporate structures also helped secure order and discipline. They acted under state licence and not as purely self-standing autonomous bodies. And our interest is not limited to unions; guild members were also precursors of modern employers, and often the continuities in their organizations are stronger, *laissez-faire* states rarely being even-handed in their treatment of capital and labour and therefore opposing combinations of workers far more ruthlessly. Furthermore, guilds as such are not the relevant institutions. The crucial point about the *Ständestaat* was its centralized use of functionally arranged collective representation for the achievement of social order.

The issue is not legal form or ideology, but differing national traditions of how interests are to be dealt with. Is the use of functional organizations as co-opted agents of order something that contradicts fundamental assumptions about the occupation of political space, of legitimate boundaries between public and private, state and society? Or is it something which political elites and dominant groups find familiar and unchallenging? It is important here to avoid treating either extreme as somehow more 'natural' than the other. Strictly theoretically, one could start with a Hayekian model of a pure liberal market society and treat all cases of functional representation as particularistic anachron-

---

23 G. Spitaels, *Le Mouvement Syndical en Belgique*, Brussels, Université Libre de Bruxelles, 1967, pp. 46–75.

isms. Alternatively one might treat liberalism as some kind of oddity, brought in by particular religious clashes or unusual rises to prominence of wool merchants and other bourgeios groups. But if we are treating the matter historically we have to recognize that *all* social arrangements stem from specific circumstances. Indeed, the social is by definition not natural; everything needs to be explained, and we cannot treat any particular form of society as the norm against which others rank as special cases.

Seen in that light, we can best distinguish between societies in the following terms:

1   Those societies in which a deliberate and successful attack by forces antagonistic to *Ständestaat* institutions long preceded the late nineteenth century and effectively destroyed legacies of shared political space. This category is sub-divided into: (1) those where the attack took the form of the confrontation between Catholic and secular forces described above; and (2) those where it came from a rising urban bourgeoisie seeking to liberate the market. Individual countries might fall into both these sub-categories, as their defining criteria are not mutually exclusive.

2   Those societies in which either or both the preceding clashes were muted or compromised, including (1) those in which the state's dominance of political space was restricted, leaving room for organized interests; and (2) those having a legacy that made possible a continuity of space-sharing traditions from the early to the modern period. Some cases of the latter phenomenon have been less passive, with powerful social groups having a positive continuing interest in *maintaining* various corporate institutions, and making deliberate use of them to structure the institutions of industrial society.

3   Finally, separate attention has to be paid to those countries that were not autonomous nation-states in the late nineteenth century, and whose institutional legacy was therefore heavily determined by other states.

Corporate-liberal conflict via church – state conflict

The starting point is the same as that for the discussion of religion. In those societies that saw a struggle between the secular state and the Catholic church, guilds were among the medieval corporations that were thoroughly absorbed within the institutions of the *ancien régime*. Their abolition was therefore central to the state's thrust for autonomy and for the construction of a liberal economic order. Again France serves as the paradigm case. The well known Le Chapelier laws of 1791 started the process of placing *syndicats* of workmen and, to a lesser extent, capitalists beyond the pale of the law. Such legislation was later reinforced by the Code Napoléon, which imposed a distinctively French state-guided liberalism wherever France exercised authority.[24] Even though the law was often only haphazardly applied, especially in the case of employers, there could be no question of such organizations sharing authority with the state.

By the 1870s there had been some change: the *bourses de travail* were established as odd but imaginative combinations of labour exchange, club and embryonic trade unions.[25] But these were kept at arm's length where any wider functions were concerned. By the time they formed a national federation they had become fiercely anarcho-syndicalist.[26] It is indicative of French liberalism that, although the right to strike was recognized in 1864, unions as such remained illegal until 1884; organized interests were even more difficult for the French Republic to accept than overt protest.[27] Even employers organized only locally and for *ad hoc* purposes, such as opposition to a tax,[28] and formed no national organization until they did so under government prompting in the wake of the First World War.[29] Until the exigencies of that war, French governments had little need for capitalist organizations. France settled down into her long period of relative economic stagnation, a combination of financier liberalism, peasant agriculture and family businesses. Few forces had much use for organized capitalism.

Some forms for such organizations had long existed. The original Napoleonic system had installed compulsory chambers of commerce in France and Italy.[30] But whereas in Austria and Germany such bodies came to play a considerable part in the organization of capital and as interlocuteurs between state and business, the French state had little use for them, and capitalists did not use them for much beyond local

24 A. S. Milward and S. B. Saul, *The Economic Development of Continental Europe 1780–1870*, London, Allen & Unwin, 1973, chapter 4.

25 Ibid., p. 265; E. Shorter and C. Tilly, *Strikes in France*, Cambridge, Cambridge University Press, 1974, chapter 2.

26 Reynaud, *Les Syndicats en France*, chapter 3; Shorter and Tilly, *Strikes in France*, pp. 166–7.

27 V. Lorwin, 'France', in W. Galenson, ed., *Comparative Labor Movements*, New York, Russell & Russell, 1952, p. 318.

28 Reynaud, *Les Syndicats in France*, p. 33; M. Gillet, 'The coal age and the rise of coalfields in the Nord and Pas de Calais'; English trans. 1966, in F. Crouzet, W. H., Chaloner and W. M. Stern, eds, *Essays in European Economic History 1789–1914*, London, Edward Arnold, 1969, p. 200.

29 Shorter and Tilly, *Strikes in France*, pp. 33–6.

30 Maier, 'Fictitious bonds' pp. 40–1.

activities. Just as the Crédit Mobilier had been invented in France but was used far more extensively in countries engaged in a more determined industrialization,[31] so French interest representation structures remained undeveloped.

All the time, of course, nostalgia for effective corporate organization remained in the restorationist and Catholic right; Williamson's survey of nineteenth-century European corporatist thought includes many French writers.[32] But so long as such groups remained ineffective, as they did in the Third Republic, their ideas remained little more than nostalgia: impractical and not developing alongside the changes of the period, unable to come to the fore before the illusions of Vichy.

In Italy the guilds were not finally abolished until 1864,[33] but their legacy was of little use to the architects of the new nation, being organized not only around Catholic institutions but also within the fragmented policy of pre-unification Italy. The secular state had little interest in or connection with such organizations, a fact reinforced by the discontinuity between this modernization of the Italian polity and the continued backwardness of the economy. By the 1890s the Italian state, unlike the French, was engaged in a determined attempt to induce rapid industrialization with the help of groups of capitalists in the north.[34] By then, too, Catholicism and the state had effected something of a reconciliation. But it is remarkable how ineffective this was in establishing a model at all resembling the German case discussed below, especially when it is recalled that at this period Germany and Italy, as the two recently unified large European states, had much in common. Partly the explanation lies in the extreme regional differences between the north and the very backward south. But also relevant, and contrasting with Germany, is the absence of continuity with the past produced by the abrupt break of Risorgimento liberalism. A turn to corporatism had to await the rise of the undemocratic right in the 1920s.

Economic backwardness also helps explain Spanish and Portuguese developments. The brief liberal episodes saw a discontinuity between the modern state and old corporate forms at a period before the representational needs of an industrial economy had made themselves felt.[35] Medieval forms of interest organization were eventually inter-

---

31 D. Landes, 'The old banks and the new: the financial revolution of the 19th century', *Revue d'Histoire Moderne et Contemporaine*, 3, 1956.

32 Williamson, *Varieties of Corporatism*, chapters 2–5.

33 J. C. Adams, 'Italy', in Galenson, *Comparative Labor Movements*.

34 A. S. Milward and S. B. Saul, *The Development of the Economies of Continental Europe 1850–1914*, London, Allen & Unwin, 1977, pp. 255ff.; V. Sellin, 'Kapitalismus und Organisation in Italien', in Winkler, *Organisierter Kapitalismus*.

35 I. T. Berend and G. Ránki, *The European Periphery and Industrialisation 1780–1914*, Cambridge, Cambridge University Press, 1982, pp. 35–9.

preted by authoritarian forces of the right, and the stage was set for the fascist-corporatist period. It is necessary here to distinguish between the Italian and Iberian cases. Mussolini's fascism was in several respects a genuinely modernizing force, and although the fascist corporations were largely bogus, they were aimed at reconciling economic modernization and hierarchical social forms. Salazar and Franco were more concerned with ensuring that any modernization that did take place would be contained within traditional hierarchical forms; but they were in no hurry to assist the modernization.[36] When advanced industrialism finally began to affect the Spanish economy in the 1960s, the corporatist structures proved to be irrelevant.

There were elements of the French model in Belgium. As we saw above, Catholic doctrines were able to climb to prominence through far more peaceful means here than elsewhere, though it is doubtful whether this provided a genuine continuity of organizational form. Unlike much of Catholic Europe, Belgium was not a backward area. Its economic history more closely resembles that of Britain, and though its liberalism was of the aggressive secular variety, the most important force in eroding its corporate traditions was the great lapse in time between the onset of industrialization and the arrival of organized capitalism. Despite the economic stagnation of much of the nineteenth century, this latter point also applies to France. These two countries therefore appear in the category under discussion as well as in the next section.

Free-market liberalism

The paradigm case in this category is the United Kingdom. That there was a strong continuity between guild and union organization in Britain is, *pace* the Webbs, now well established,[37] though links with modern organizations of employers remain relatively unexplored. But our main interest here is in any legacy of the guilds as delegated polities. The situation is not straightforward. On the one hand, much of this role was entirely lost. First, British unions (and, to a far lesser extent, combinations of employers) experienced their equivalent of the Le Chapelier laws in the form of the Combination Acts. Although the full force of this exclusion lasted only 20 years, the concept of organized interests being essentially outside the Common Law endured, in effect, until the 1970s. The most sigificant moment for this development was the Trade Union Act of 1871, which made the historically important decision to embody

36 Linz, 'Interests and politics in Spain'; Williamson, *Varieties of Corporatism*, pp. 105–6.

37 A. Fox, *History and Heritage: the Social Origins of the British Industrial Relations System*, London, Allen & Unwin, 1985, esp. chapter 1.

trade union rights in the negative form of immunities rather than positive rights, on the grounds that to grant rights to organizations would impugn the essential individualism of the Common Law. This is significant, not only in itself, but in demonstrating how alien to English liberalism was the idea of co-opting organizations as components of public order. It is the equivalent of the French acceptance of strikes 20 years before the legality of trade unions.

In addition to this essentially ideological component in the birthplace of *laissez-faire* and liberal individualism, a discontinuity between guilds and both modern employer association and union practice was ensured by the exceptionally drawn-out character of English industrialization. The period of organized capitalism after the 1870s was widely separated in time from the high period of guild organizaton. Therefore, while English unions as local bodies of craftsmen, or employers associations as local groupings of price fixers, were able to build on guild traditions and establish an impressive level of organization, these groupings lacked any political role and hence any centripetal tendency. This set the pattern for what has become the most prominent characteristic of British interest organization: decentralization and reluctance to become involved with the state.

On the other hand, these organizations were not pure pressure-groups in the style of American lobbies, nor did they possess the extreme oppositionalism of many French interest groups, confronted as the latter were by a powerful and inaccessible state. For most of the nineteenth century the British state retained its oddly informal character, reflected in such institutions as the voluntary magistrature and the rule of the elite London clubs as private places where public business was transacted. This provided a certain mixing of state and society, a phenomenon achieved in many societies through various forms of corporatism, but attained here through informal, personal, 'gentlemanly' arrangements, very different from the formal organizational relationships developed under organized capitalism proper. This gentlemanly code, which enjoined a certain restraint on the maximization of immediate self-interest for the sake of maintaining a wider unity, was eventually opened, at the margins, to the representatives of organized labour. In this way it has been a mild functional equivalent of corporatism, and in the longer term probably served by its very strength to inhibit the development of corporatism of a more formally organizational kind. This constitutes another chapter in the paradoxical story of the emergence of industrial Britain: the nation that invented industrialism but underwent the process more slowly and reluctantly than most of its imitators; the society that first developed contractual, individualistic liberalism but ringed it around with quasi-aristocratic norms and gentlemanly restraints.[38]

Britain is the only case where assertive free-market liberalism appeared unalloyed as the force dissolving pre-modern corporate forms; it is the country where the 'parliamentary parenthesis' was both more early installed and more enduring than anywhere else in Europe. In France and Belgium, as has been noted, this force was *supplemented* by the church–state split. In some other countries it was *offset* by corporatist continuities. Most of these other societies were influenced by British developments, hence their participation in the parliamentary parenthesis for at least a few years and in some institutions – just as Britain and France bear some traces of corporatism and organized capitalism. But it is the strength of the offsetting factors that demands attention. In the consociational countries – Switzerland, Netherlands and, yet again, in part Belgium – liberalism was particularly strong, but they will here be considered as a separatate category.

States failing to fill political space

The most extreme case is Switzerland. There is ostensibly much here that resembles Britain. But the characteristic which in Britain provides a weak functional equivalent for corporatism existed, and still exists, in a strong form in Switzerland: an indefinite boundary between state and society, leading to many apparently public functions being borne by private groups. This happens in Switzerland because the extreme weakness of the state renders the burden to be borne by 'gentlemen's agreements' among private-sphere elites peculiarly high. It thus provides a clear demonstration of that paradox of the liberal state, which must be both confined but clearly sovereign within its curtailed sphere. In the Swiss case much administration of what would elsewhere be state functions is carried out by representative *Selbstverwaltung* groups.

Combined with the effects of consociationalism already discussed, all this provided Switzerland with heavily shared political space, though of a rather distinctive kind. It can hardly be said to constitute straightforward corporatism, lacking the level of centralization this requires. But neither is it straightforward liberalism. While in some respects Switzerland might seem to possess the ideal bourgeois liberal capitalist state, its state is in fact so weak that it invites an organizational sharing of state functions otherwise characteristic of interventionist states.

The Dutch state has been more orthodox than the Swiss, but only partly so, having been similarly dominated for centuries by bourgeois

38 M.J. Wiener, *English Culture and the Decline of the Industrial Spirit 1850–1980*, Cambridge, Cambridge University Press, 1981.

rather than aristocratic groups and therefore experiencing no absolutist phase. Belgium, partly sharing the Dutch legacy and being originally an artificial buffer state, also lacked a clear state heritage. Both have therefore shared something of the Swiss dependence of the state on private groups for the management of public space. And, as noted, the institutions of consociationism reinforce this. In all three cases liberalism, however important and early, could never make the strong claims for clearly defined state sovereignty found in Britain and France.

Continuing *Ständestaat* legacies

An example of a mixed liberal and corporatist legacy is Denmark. In contrast to neighbouring Sweden, the Danish monarchy had an extensive suffrage and bore many of the hallmarks of liberalism. But this had not implied the same attack on old corporate forms as had occurred in Britain or France. There had been no large factory development; the basic modernizing thrust was in agriculture and related industries.[39] The rural liberal groups that represented this development did not want an aggressive *laissez-faire* to prosecute their interests. In fact, from the 1840s onwards the crucial unit of Danish agriculture was the co-operative.[40] And from this base developed the distinctive Danish network of state-subsidized but autonomously organized local institutions, incuding schools and cultural life; neither market nor state, but organization, a non-state public arena, or shared political space.

In this context, guild structures remained relatively intact.[41] Right into the 1890s there were major attempts to revive them.[42] As in Britain the union movement developed on a former guild basis, imparting a craft-based character to Danish unionism that continues to differentiate it from its Scandinavian neighbours. But unlike Britain, this structure had not been uprooted from its political role by a prolonged period of anti-combination liberalism. When industrial conflict threatened industrial order at the end of the century, Danish employers were easily able to resort to centralized, co-ordinated action at national level – admittedly a far easier thing to do in an economy as small as the Danish, but also evidence of the older historical continuity. Their strategy was to engage the unions in centralized action, regulating the labour market between them, a move to which the Danish unions, also close to their

39 Milward and Saul, *Economic Development of Continental Europe*, p. 514.

40 Ibid., pp. 506–9; N. F. Christiansen, 'Denmark: end of the idyll', *New Left Review*, no. 144, 1984.

41 N. Elvander, 'The role of the state in the settlement of labor disputes in the Nordic countries: a comparative analysis', *European Journal of Political Research*, vol. 2, 1974, p. 366.

42 Milward and Saul, *Economic Development of Continental Europe*, p. 515.

guild origins, responded.[43] Since that period centralized organizations of capital and labour have organized the labour market between them, with very few signs of state jealously at this invasion of political space.[44]

This was a development very different from the more coercive forms of involvement that first drew Austrian, German and Swedish organized capital and labour together, but the Danish Basic Agreement of 1899 that stimulated it was in many ways a precursor of the kind of peaceful neo-corporatism that would develop in those countries once the balance of power and the character of the political régime had changed in labour's favour. As such, Danish neo-corporatism, beginning extremely early, remained in a relatively under-developed form, with craft and general unions rather than industrial unions surviving until the present day.

The Scandinavian countries are usually bracketed together in discussions of neo-corporatism, and there is some evidence of mutual imitation behind their similarities, first Denmark and more recently Sweden being the exemplars. But the institutional bases from which their systems originated differed considerably. Whereas Denmark became a liberal state relatively early, the Swedish state remained a rather rigid, authoritarian one until the end of the nineteenth century.[45] Some authors, implicitly contrasting Sweden with Prussia and concentrating on certain aspects of Swedish society, have argued that it was a relatively liberal state.[46] But this neglects the non-liberal character of the system of interest representation. Not only was universal suffrage long delayed, but the state showed a marked preference for collective representation. The guilds were abolished in 1846, but until 1864 they were replaced by trade associations with legal powers.[47] Indeed, formal functional *Ständestaat* representation lasted until 1865. As Lipset[48] has pointed out, late nineteenth-century Sweden rivalled Germany in the rigidity of its class structure and perpetuation of late medieval organic political forms.

Though the later 1860s saw a more wholehearted liberalism with the abolition of both legal trade associations and the estates, this was less

43 W. Galenson, *The Danish System of Labor Relations: a Study in Industrial Peace*, Cambridge, Harvard University Press, 1952, pp. 58, 59 and chapter 5.

44 Ibid., pp. 97ff.

45 Kuhne, *Patterns of Social and Political Mobilization: a Historical Analysis of the Nordic Countries*, pp. 14–19.

46 Berend and Ránki, *The European Periphery*, pp. 30–2; P. Jackson and K. Sisson, 'Employers confederations in Sweden and the United Kingdom and the significance of industrial infrastructure', *British Journal of Industrial Relations*, vol. 14, 1976.

47 W. Galenson, 'Scandinavia', in idem, *Comparative Labor Movements*, p. 108.

48 S. M. Lipset, 'Radicalism or reformism: the sources of working-class politics', *The American Political Science Review*, vol. 77, 1983, p. 4.

than a decade before the era of organized capitalism, which in fact coincided with Sweden's rapid if late industrialization. Both institutional legacy and the international economic environment of the industrial economy's *Gründerjahre* therefore favoured organized capitalism. Capitalists began to form associations in the 1880s, and by the early years of the twentieth century had established a highly centralized organizational system.[49] The combination of a tough state and organized capital had also stimulated labour's centralized organization, and the two sides of industry embarked on a mutually reinforcing spiral of organization and centralization.[50]

If Denmark and Sweden embodied complex and contrasting mixes of liberal and old-corporate institutions, a much simpler case is presented by the Hapsburg territories. The backward, ramshackle nature of the empire had itself inhibited any thorough-going rationalization of absolutism, and old-corporatist structures therefore played an even greater part here than in other *anciens régimes*. As a result they exercised an extraordinary influence. An important outcome of the liberal uprising of 1848 had been, not the abolition of such structures, but the addition of the new middle classes to them.[51] Where other bourgeoisies sought *laissez-faire*, the Austrian and Czech middle classes sought representation in compulsory *Kammer*, and secured it. Organized labour in its turn therefore made the achievement of *Kammer* representation (albeit alongside orthodox trde unions) a key demand. It secured this in republican *Restösterreich* after 1918; retained it (though with radically 'rearranged' political forces) during the brief period of *Austrofaschismus*; lost it under the Nazis; and promptly reconstructed it in the Second Republic after 1945.[52] Austrian business also remained wedded to *Kammer* representation, to this day retaining it as more important than its voluntary employer associations.

After the crash of 1873 the reversal of liberalism meant that industrialism was viewed with suspicion by the returning conservative elite. Whereas in Prussia the state used corporate structures to engineer industrial society, in Austria they were used to control and impede it. Just as in Britain old paternalistic Tory ideas generated a concern for social welfare as a reaction against industrialism, so similar measures

49 G. K. Ingham, *Strikes and Industrial Conflict: Britain and Scandinavia*, London, Macmillan, 1974, pp. 50–2; Jackson and Sisson, 'Employers confederations in Sweden and the United Kingom'.

50 J. D. Stephens, *The Transition from Capitalism to Socialism*, London, Macmillan, 1979, pp. 129–40.

51 F. Traxlar, *Evolution Gewerkschaftlicher Interessenvertretung* Vienna, Braumüller, 1982, p. 2.

52 Talos, *Staatliche Sozialpolitik in Österreich*, passim.

were taken in the Hapsburg lands. But while in Britain this occurred in a country irrevocably immersed in a liberal market economy, in Austria much remained of a corporate legacy in which the new measures could be embodied. Compulsory trade associations were introduced in 1879;[53] and several *Selbstverwaltung* institutions were established to run early welfare policies, in which it was possible for trade unions to participate,[54] including the state social insurance institutions set up in imitation of similar German bodies.[55]

All this was happening in a non-democratic, authoritarian *Obrigkeits-staat*. While autonomous protest action or campaigns for suffrage were seen as major threats to authority, the incorporation of labour as well as capitalist interests within corporate forms could be accommodated to a long and familiar tradition. Unlike its Danish counterpart, modern Austrian trade unionism has transcended guild organization and established more or less an industrial pattern of organization, but it has always retained from the guild period the concept of organizational representation as an aspect of public regulation. Even while confronting the late nineteenth-century Hapsburg state or the increasingly catas-trophic First Republic, organized labour's claim remained funda-mentally a bid for a share in the management of the state.[56] This helps to explain the long recognized paradox of Austrian socialism, which has seemed to be at once the most Marxist and the most reformist of the continental labour movements. The anti-liberal authoritarianism of the old régime predisposed labour towards a revolutionary strategy; but the curious way in which that same régime provided some space for limited and state-regulated organized interest representation, gave something to aim for of a kind very different from revolutionary transformation.

One can contrast this with France, where the state remained highly involved in economic affairs, indirectly and unwillingly encouraging a politicized labourism, but resisted formal incorporation, leading to a more thoroughgoing Marxist rejectionism within the majority wing of labour. One can also conrast it with Britain, where a non-interventionist state tolerated union growth of a non-formal, non-participative kind, making possible a unionism that rarely had to make explicit any real choice between opposition to the system and participation within it. If French labour became the main western representative of orthodox Marxism, and British labour of its own form of liberal socialism, the distinctive innovation of *Austromarxismus* in the inter-war years was the

---

53 Ibid., chapter 2.
54 Ibid., chapter 3; Traxler, *Evolution Gewerkschaftlicher Interessenvertretung*, chapter 1.
55 Ibid., pp. 55, 56.
56 Talos, *Staatliche Sozialpolitik in Österreich*, chapters 3, 7.

model of the participatory economy, with proposals for workers' councils governing industry from the plant level to the national economy.[57] Acceptance of the need to develop such institutions in a *Junktim* with existing capitalist and managerial forces may have been seen in theory as a temporary pragmatic necessity given the prevailing balance of power, but over the years that changed imperceptibly into a more permanent acceptance.

The state based on Berlin eventually proved far more successful than its older Viennese counterpart in securing domination of Germany, largely because of its own more modernized, rationalized bureaucracy. However, although it was Prussian rationalism that had excited the admiration of French *philosophes* dispirited by the structure of their own *ancien régime*, the Prussian state ironically incorporated apparent anachronisms that disappeared from post-revolutionary France. Initially a state in search of a society, Prussia absorbed existing forms of political order into itself in order to provide a structure and legitimacy; at least within its Protestant lands it had no fear of incorporating older institutions. Thus the aristocracy was incorporated into the bureaucracy in an almost Russian manner, and guild and corporate structures were absorbed rather similarly to the Hapsburg pattern.[58]

But if Austrian conservatism sought to restrict industrialization, the Prussians sought, successfully, to unify Germany through it. As is well known, the country developed a new model of state-sponsored industrialism, using tariffs, cartels and bank finance to produce it.[59] A coalition of manufacturers in heavy industry, especially armaments, and bankers gathered around Bismarck's government, making industrial politics central to German public life in a manner not previously known anywhere. This was especially important after the 1873 recession and the onset of a new defensiveness and avoidance of risk. It is important to recognize that this was not a system of pure state direction; much detailed work was left to the cartels of associations of interests.[60] The German state was authoritarian, but it shared political space with approved organized interests.

While liberalism was a slightly stronger force in Prussia than in the Austrian empire, it was far weaker than in France or Britain and, again as in Austria, was state-dependent. Guild and corporate structures were

57 T. Bottomore, 'Introduction', in Bottomore and Goode, *Austro-Marxism*, pp. 23–30, 38–41.

58 H. Rosenberg, *Bureaucracy, Aristocracy and Autocracy: Prussia 1660–1815*, Cambridge, Mass., Harvard University Press, 1958.

59 Milward and Saul, *Development of the Economies of Continental Europe*, pp. 28 ff.

60 E. Maschke, 'Outline of the history of the German cartels from 1873–1914', 1964; English trans. (in Crouzet et al., *Essays in European Economic History 1789–1914*).

never fully abolished, and the régime, lacking both a bourgeois conquest of power and a need for assertive secularism, never found it necessary to establish a clear state-society distinction. Here too we therefore find *Kammer* of the new middle classes that eventually became *Kammer* of modern industry and commerce, and a willingness to incorporate functional interest representation provided it was separated from liberal democratic forces.

Of course, labour was marginalized within this structure, but even at this early stage one gets some glipses of how the fact of an organized capitalism encourged a tightly organized bureaucratic labour movement. The motive for developing in this way was oppositional; if capital and the state expressed their strength in this way, labour must too. But once such organizations were developed they were in a position to take advantage of the chinks of representational opportunities presented by the German state. For example, the local sickness funds, established under the Bismarckian welfare policy, were run by elected boards. From 1889 the Social Democratic trade unions began to run slates of candidates for these, and – thanks to their organizational resources – soon came to dominate them, affording the unions a new and important base within the official structures.[61] This provided a model of formal, organizational incorporation that, similar to and indeed developing mutually alongside the Austrian case, stimulated later Weimer plans for a council-governed economy among German Social Democrats and eventually the *Mitbestimmung* model of the contemporary German economy. It is not surprising that the German labour movement was second only to the Austrian in the ambiguity of being concurrently Marxist and incorporationist. It is also remarkable that, while somewhat similar institutions were much later initiated in France,[62] they developed nothing like the same importance. French labour lacked the resources to exploit them in the same way, and a major reason why they lacked resources was that the institutions of the Third Republic had given them little incentive to acquire them.

European new nations

Three countries – Ireland, Norway and Finland – were neither autonomous nation states nor at all industrial during the crucial decades. Ireland and Finland did not achieve independence until 1921, from Britain and Russia respectively; both had to undergo violent struggle to

---

61 A.J. Heidenheimer, 'Unions and welfare state development in Britain and Germany: an interpretation of metamorphoses in the period 1910–1950', Berlin: Internationales Institut für Vergleichende Gesellschaftsforschung, mimeo., 1980, pp. 8, 9.
62 Lorwin, 'France', p. 337.

achieve autonomy, and both subsequently endured civil wars. Norway's path was much easier. Although the country had been a Danish and then a Swedish colony, it enjoyed considerable autonomy in domestic affairs during its final century of Swedish rule, little struggle was needed to secure independence, and the transition was achieved without domestic conflict. How did the institutions eventually established by these states relate to the issues of shared political space discussed here? As new-born states did they provide real examples of institutional *tabulae rasae*?

When Ireland eventually secured independence it did so under a régime that resembled Spain and Portugal in its commitment to maintaining a Catholic, rural society[63] – though in this case within a democratic polity. But Ireland's political, legal and associational institutions were deeply coloured by the British past, and despite autonomy from Britain being one of the main motivations of Irish political life, very little has been done to disturb that legacy over the years. The crucial Trade Union Act of 1871 remains the origins of Irish trade union law, supplemented by the other English Acts of 1906 and 1913.[64] Also, many Irish unions are autonomous local branches of British unions.

Given Catholicism's virtually unchallenged position, one might have expected some development of Catholic corporatism, and there have been attempts at that. During the 1930s the quasi-fascist blueshirt movement developed the classic corporatist policies and rhetoric, but this had little resonance in the Irish context.[65] The prevailing reality of British procedures and ways of treating political space proved a far more substantial guide to everyday practice than any idealized but unrehearsed Catholic models.

The institutional inheritance of independent Finland was neither Finnish nor Russian, but Swedish. Apart from some late attempts at russification, the Tsarist state had allowed the Grand Duchy to retain the administrative system of its previous centuries of Swedish rule. As in Sweden, this included a *Ständestaat* structure that lasted down to1906, though guilds had been abolished earlier. There was therefore nothing in the Finnish legacy to encourage state jealousy towards political space; and neither the country's extreme economic backwardness nor the need for unity in the independence struggle encouraged any liberal challenge. Not being present on the historical stage during the crucial late nineteenth century, the Finnish state was not endowed with a particularly powerful legacy for dealing with organized capitalism, but one can

---

63 T. Brown, *Ireland: a Social and Cultural History 1922–79*, London, Fontana, 1981, chapter 5.
64 A. Boyd, *The Rise of the Irish Trade Unions*, Tralee, Anvil, 1972, p. 68.
65 Brown, *Ireland*, pp. 160 ff.

descry an incipient corporatism waiting in the wings. This has come into its own in far more recent times, beyond the scope of this paper.[66]

Norway was not dominated by Swedish institutions, but was able to develop autonomously to the extent that it had a far more liberal and participative political system than the dominant power. With no local aristocracy and no *Ständestaat*, it had many of the elements of a liberal system. However, as in Denmark, this was the liberalism of small farmers. They were not concerned to develop the *laissez-faire* state; indeed, the partly autonomous local Norwegian state was a symbol of the country's identity. The small firms that developed in the 1880s prior to Norway's later full industrialization easily formed trade associations, and the guilds had not been abolished until 1866.[67] However, it was not until the extraordinary period of industrial conflict in the 1920s that these institutions were called upon to cope with major problems of organized labour. When they did, Norwegian organizations quickly established a centralized system for regulating the labour market, with few problems of jealousy over political space on the part of the state.

Norway is perhaps the nearest we come to a society free from historical constraint: neither a French nor an English model of aggressive anti-corporate liberalism existed in this former dependent territory on the European periphery; nor was there any strong pressure to tight organizational incorporation on Swedish lines. There was a slight corporate bias in the easy access to past guild traditions, but the eventual establishment of the Norwegian Basic Agreement in industrial relations in 1935 appears more as a result of organized groups in a small economy taking the shortest available means of overcoming extreme conflict, rather than any powerful historical determinacy.

Pathways to Late Twentieth-Century Industrial Politics

It is possible to summarize the previous discussion by treating the different patterns discovered as constituting different pathways: developments and events having pushed a particular society down one path, its subsequent development will tend to proceed further down the same way unless something happens to divert it. In constructing such a model we must of course indulge in some over-generalization, but it will help

---

66 V. Helander, 'A liberal corporatist sub-system in action: the incomes policy system in Finland', in Lehmbruch and Schmitter, *Patterns of Corporatist Policy-Making*; V. Helander and D. Anckar, *Consultation and Political Culture: Essays on the Case of Finland*, Helsinki, Societas Scientiarum Fennica, 1983.

67 W. Galenson, *Labor in Norway*, Cambridge, Harvard University Press, 1949, chapter 4.

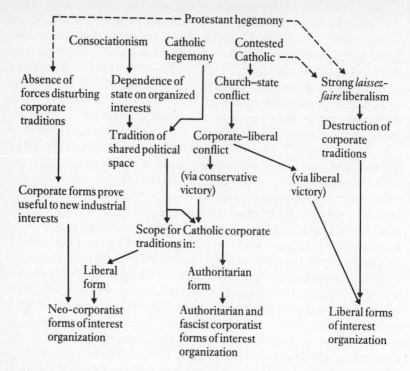

Continuous arrows indicate direct causal links; broken arrows indicate possible associations.

Figure 1 Historical preconditions of organizational politics

clarify what has been happening. Figure 1 provides the overall mapping, using the main historical processes we have discussed.

This both helps us to show why countries have differed in their overall degree of corporatism or liberalism, and also suggests why the characters of their respective degrees of corporatism or liberalism vary so much. Both these tasks are important. Although some scholars object to the unidimensional nature of studies of the extent to which organized interests play an intermediary role, it is a valuable issue in its own right. But the differences in the manner in which that one variable operates are equally important. Analysis should capture both aspects.

So far the discussion has been focused on processes and variables, countries being used as examples. But we are also interested in countries as particular combinations of variables, and in the extent to which countries' present institutional balances were influenced by past legacies. The following discussion will try briefly to address these questions. For a guide to the present degree of neo-corporatism or liberalism in a society's institutions, I use the two commonly cited rankings listed in table 1. That by Schmitter uses certain purely quantitative indicators; that by Lehmbruch is based on descriptive, qualitative material. Unfortunately Lehmbruch's list deals with only seven countries; Schmitter excludes only Spain and Portugal, which can easily be remedied.

Table 1: Rankings of neo-corporation in contemporary societies

Schmitter's quantitative ranking in descending order of degree degree of corporatism	*Lehmbruch's qualitative assessment of strength of neo-corporatism*	
1 Austria	Austria	Strong
2 Norway	Netherlands	Strong
3 Denmark	Sweden	Strong
4 Finland		
5 Sweden	Denmark	Medium
6 Netherlands	United Kingdom	Medium
7 Belgium	West Germany	Medium
8 West Germany		
9 Switzerland	France	Weak
10 Ireland		
11 France		
12 United Kingdom		
13 Italy		

Source: P. C. Schmitter, 'Interest intermediation and regime governability in contemporary western Europe and North America', in S. D. Berger, ed., *Organizing Interests in Western Europe*, Cambridge, Cambridge University Press, 1981, p. 294; G. Lehmbruch, 'Neo-corporatism in comparative perspective', in Lehmbruch and Schmitter, eds, *Patterns of Corporatist Policy-Making*, London, Sage, 1982, pp. 16–23. Schmitter's list also included Canada and the USA, on the same level as Ireland.

In nearly everybody's rankings of societies on a scale of corporatism versus liberalism, the Austrian Second Republic stands near the corporatist pole. Despite the enormous upheavals and complete reshaping of the old Hapsburg lands that intervened, it is easy to discern why. Nowhere was the continuity of functional interest representation and organized capitalism less broken; nowhere was representation of that kind so clearly a possible route to acceptance and influence for the young labour movement. When, after both world wars, the rival camps of

Austrian politics tried to come to terms with each other, this form of representation provided a promising model and one of which they had experience. After 1918 the balance of social forces did not permit a successful adjustment, but the model lived on to shape the strategy of both the fascist victors of the civil war and the socialist and Catholic forces that emerged from the Second World War, albeit on radically different terms. The balance of forces changed dramatically, but the model survived. To complete the link between my historical account and contemporary structures it is necessary to take account of the forces that engineered this change and imparted a strong degree of consociationism.

Schmitter's listing of Norway ahead of the other Nordic societies is not well anticipated by my account, because of the immaturity of the society's institutions during the relevant period. Possibly this very indeterminacy made it easier for a country which already had a shared administrative history with Denmark and Sweden to respond with unique prescience to the labour-movement pressures of the 1930s. About Finland too our model was necessarily non-committal, though an incipient corporatism was detected. As already noted, the development of a neo-corporatism of any strength has been a very recent development, and the events that first retarded and then assisted this recent emergence of earlier incipient tendencies have all occurred beyond the period under consideration here.

However, that the Nordic countries all stand towards the corporatist pole is well anticipated by the model. Most observers would probably agree with Lehmbruch's reasoned decision to place Sweden clearly above Denmark, though that is not caught in Schmitter's quantitative study. The main feature of Nordic societies, especially Norway and Sweden, to develop after the period discussed here was of course the unique strength of the labour movement, which made it highly advisable for capital to come to terms with it through bipartite and tripartite national instituions. But this was itself partly a secondary development of the Lutheran legacy. Through its social passivity, Lutheranism imposed few blocks to the formation of a unified working class, thereby indirectly creating unparalleled labour-movement power and making it possible for the polity, already encumbered by any problems of the secular state, to embrace the organizational politics that is implied by non-revolutionary labour-movement strength. Thus, while Austria and Scandinavia can both be seen as highly corporatist polities, the differences between them are marked, the latter group being more dependent on labour-movement strength.

The other country that is usually bracketed alongside Austria and Scandinavia as highly corporatist is the Netherlands. This is also well anticipated, even though there were important elements of liberalism in Dutch history. My thesis depends here, not unreasonably, on the fundamental importance of the very direct legacy of political space-sharing imparted by consociationism and by the absence of absolutism. The other consociational cases do not refute this, as will be discussed below. While these structures have begun to fall apart somewhat in recent years,[68] for most of the post-war period they were even stronger than we might predict. The new element here was the determination of the country's elites, including the labour leadership, to construct a strong industrial economy in the wake of occupation and disaster during the Second World War. Shared experiences in the war-time Resistance strengthened existing consociational ties, and the commitment to a strong economy in place of the rather sleepy backwardness of pre-war Holland provided new tasks for tripartite agencies.[69] However, it should again be noted that, while elements of consociationism in contemporary Austria should not be ignored, a consociationally rooted neo-corporatism is qualitatively very different from the previous cases discussed here.

Germany's location as only medium in Lehmbruch's account and its similar placing between Belgium and Switzerland in Schmitter's scale is surprising. (That the other two countries should occupy median positions is not surprising, as will be discussed below.) Imperial and Weimar Germany were as rich in corporatist potentialities as any other cases discussed here, except Austria. Here too we need more recent events in order to complete the story.

The particularly strong authoritarianism of German capital made it difficult for proper access to corporatist institutions to be extended to labour until this characteristic had changed. This did not happen until after 1945. Unlike Austria, where this change took the form of *returning* to 'Austrian' forms after the *Anschluß*, in the Bonn Republic it was achieved through the adoption of the 'social market' and through the imposition of certain British and American liberal political forms on the defeated country. This, coupled with the inherent difficulties of managing simple neo-corporatism in a large country, weakened the strength of corporatist elements in the contemporary German polity. However, given how strenuous were the efforts to impose Anglo–American liberalism, the really remarkable feature is now fundamentally corporatist institutions were rapidly reconstructed and combined with

68 T. Akkermans and P. Grootings, 'From corporatism to polarisation: elements of the development of Dutch industrial relations', in C. J. Crouch and A. Pizzorno, eds, *The Resurgence of Class Conflict in Western Europe since 1968*, vol. I, *National Studies*, London, Macmillan, 1978.

69 Windmuller, *Labor Relations in the Netherlands*, chapter 3.

the new liberal components.[70] Indeed, several observers describe German industrial relations today as being essentially neo-corporatist,[71] and one suspects that quantitative indicators often fail to capture this.

Of Belgium and Switzerland the former is more straightforward. Its place in the centre of a scale of corporatism is where our analysis would put it, as it draws on so many different legacies: Catholic/liberal confict but consociationism; early liberal industrialization but dependence of the state on organized interests interests to unite its fractured polity; unique in the strength of its Catholic labour movement but also in its regional divisions. Subsequent history has merely ramified these cross-cutting pressures as the rise of Flanders and decline of Wallonia have both strengthened the Catholic labour movement and hence the corporatist legacy, *and* exacerbated Flemish–Walloon conflict and hence reduced cohesion.[72]

Switzerland is very different, since we are here dealing with what should be a classic liberal, non-corporatist society but which has experienced both consociationism and the peculiar responsibilities that fall on organized interests in the absence of a proper state. Partly because all this remains very decentralized except in the most informal ways, we should properly speak here of a functional equivalent of corporatism.[73]

In the remaining countries corporatism has developed only weakly. Britain stands out rather oddly here in Catholic company – though this would not apply were the analysis to be extended beyond Europe to embrace North America. Lehmbruch ranks Britain much higher, but this is because he concentrates on the 1970s, one of the UK's occasional corporatist moments. Schmitter, on the other hand, ranks Britain below France, though this is probably because a purely quantitative account cannot pick up the subtleties of Britain's 'gentlemanly' legacy.

Lacking the history of the church–state conflict, Britain developed, despite its liberalism, characteristically more 'relaxed' politics than divided Catholic states. This helps explain the odd character of

70 C. Crouch, 'Conditions for trade union wage restraint', in L. N. Lindberg and C. S. Maier, eds, *The Politics of Inflation and Economic Stagnation*, Washington D.C., Brookings Institution, 1985.

71 W. Müller-Jentsch, 'Vom gewerkschaftlichen Doppelcharakter und seiner theoretischen Auflösung in Neokorporatismus', *Gesellschaftliche Arbeit und Rationalisierung*, Leviathan Sonderheft vol. 4, 1981; W. Streeck, 'Gewerkschaftsorganisation und industrielle Beziehungen', in J. Matthes, ed., *Sozialer Wandel in Westeuropa*, Frankfurt am Main, Campus, 1979; W. Streeck, 'Organizational consequences of neo-corporatist co-operation in West German labour unions', in Lehmbruch and Schmitter, *Patterns of Corporatist Policy-Making*.

72 M. Molitor, 'Social conflicts in Belgium', in Crouch and Pizzorno, *The Resurgence of Class Conflicts in Western Europe since 1968*.

73 H. Kriesi, 1982: 'The structure of the Swiss political system', in Lehmbruch and Schmitter, *Patterns of Corporatist Policy-Making*.

corporatism and its relative absence in Britain, as captured in Middle-mas's[74] description: 'corporate bias' rather than corporatism. There have been persistent tendencies towards corporatist experiments, which have been cut short, partly by the strength of the liberal tradition, and partly by the very fact that the 'gentleman's agreements' that constitute much of the corporate bias themselves inhibit any more thoroughgoing institutional arrangements. Sometimes, therefore, Britain climbs further up the corporatism scale; but its fundamental liberalism is soon reasserted. To update the description of Britain implied in my model is to trace this development through the world wars and their aftermath: a story of continuing oscillation.

Ireland is ranked slightly above Britain by Schmitter. It is ranked in my model as overwhelmingly dependent on the British inheritance. In the 1970s a centralized bipartite system of incomes restraint was erected, and for some years it seemed that Ireland had finally moved into a corporatist path.[75] However, by 1981 Irish employers opposed renewal of such agreements, and the edifice collapsed easily. It had outlived similar British experiments had had shown more success and continuity than them, but in retrospect it seems that once again Irish policy has moved broadly parallel with that in the UK.

France and Italy normally come at the foot of any European corporatist ranking, and this is well anticipated in our analysis, provided one accepts that the incipient corporatism in northern Italy was destined to be too weak. Throughout the late nineteenth and early twentieth centuries everything combined to prevent the sharing of political space – except perhaps through clientilistic and personal relations between politicians and individual businessmen, but that is corruption rather than corporatism.

If one were to continue the themes of the analysis through to the present period, one might predict even less corporatism in France than in Italy, though Schmitter reverses this. The French state has its own well-tried regulatory alternatives to corporatism when it wishes, for example, to mobilize the economy. Modern Italy, on the other hand, possesses certain elements of consociationism in the 'windows' that the rival political blocs have upon each other through the complex structure of parties and unions.[76] Efforts are repeatedly made to co-opt these for

74 K. Middlemass, *Politics in Industrial Society*, London, André Deutsch, 1979.

75 N. Hardiman, 'Centralized collective bargaining: trade unions, employers and government in the Republic of Ireland, 1970–1980; University of Oxford, unpublished DPhil thesis, 1985.

76 P. Lange, G. Ross and M. Vannicelli, *Unions, Change and Crisis: French and Italian Union Strategy and the Political Economy 1945—1980*, London, Allen & Unwin, 1982, chapter 2.

wider political order functions – a distinct sharing of political space – although to date the long-term anti-corporatism of the political legacy continues to debilitate these strategies. Indeed, since the late 1860s Italy has rather resembled the UK in its variability, though for rather different reasons, and during the 1980s it has stood above the UK in any corporatist ranking. This leaves France as having been over the past few decades unequivocally the least corporatist established state within western Europe.

Spain and Portugal are usually excluded from analyses of neo-corporatism in the post-war period because of the length of their fascist periods, rendering them difficult to compare with other cases. They certainly cannot be placed on a neo-corporatism/liberalism continuum for most of the past half century, as they remain examples of countries that could develop corporatism only under authoritarian conditions. But this is a past that they partly share with France, Italy and Austria. The most important issues now in those countries is how the fascist legacy will effect their current policy experiments, which are un-doubtedly of a neo-corporatist kind; but it remains early to assess.

This paper has stressed continuities. Once certain patterns of state/society relations have become established, they can be very enduring indeed, surviving dramatic regime changes and major shifts in the balance of power between interests. These continuities are perhaps seen most clearly in the states based on London, Paris and Vienna, but they apply generally. However, as the discussion of Finland has suggested, and as may be made clear by a further analysis of contemporary Spain, change does sometimes take place. One must also consider the important current attempts by political forces associated with some business interests in Denmark, Sweden, the Netherlands, Germany and Belgium to reduce the neo-corporatist component in their polities. To discover the circumstances in which change can occur and those in which it seems doomed to fail is an important task, but one which lies beyond the scope of the present chapter.

8

State and Politics in Developed Socialism: Recent Developments in Soviet Theory

Karen Dawisha

Analysis in the West of the general direction and nature of Soviet politics has always been split into various camps, with thinking about the role of the state in Soviet society no exception. In the broadest of terms, it is possible to discern several major strands in the debate on this subject in the West. There are those who would posit the existence of an exceedingly strong state in the USSR, but who would deny that any theorizing within the Soviet Union about the working and dynamics of this state bears any relationship to the real world. Thus, the far right continues to view the Soviet state as a basically totalitarian entity whose inner workings, they contend, is far better explained by Hannah Arendt than Vladimir Ilyich Lenin. Arendt viewed the similarities between fascism and Stalinism as significant and saw them both as examples of a political system dominated by a single party in which all political, economic and social activities are controlled by the state exercising control through terror and total monopoly of information.[1]

Neo-Marxists of the Frankfurt School, Eurocommunists associated with both Gramsci and Carrillo, and even dissident Soviet and East European writers have de-emphasized the materialist and dogmatic aspects of Marxism–Leninism, many of them going back instead to the more humanistic and Hegelian interpretations of early Marxism. As a

I would like to thank members of the Political Theory Seminar at the University of Maryland, College Park, for extremely useful comments on an earlier draft of this paper. Portions of this paper are taken from my forthcoming book on Eastern Europe, to be published by the US Council on Foreign Relations in 1986.

1 Hannah Arendt, *Origins of Totalitarianism*, London, Allen & Unwin, 1958.

result, writers as diverse in other respects as Lukács, Althusser, Sakharov, Marcuse and Bahro are united in their willingness to view the Soviet state as more than a mere reflection of dominant economic interests. All of them see the Soviet state as exercising an existence independent of material forces, and many of them view the state in both socialist and capitalist societies as potential vehicles for reification, alienation and hegeomonial relations with both the society and other socialists and non-socialist states.[2]

Many of them also draw a distinction between the strong and oppressive state in the USSR and the states in Eastern Europe where efforts to construct a strong state remain more a desire than a fact. In these countries popular alienation results not so much from the state's opppressive nature as from its lack of legitimacy and its failure to reflect and represent indigenous culture.

A further school of thought is a reaction to the Weberian notion of bureaucracy as a rational form of state organization characterized by legal rules, a salaried administrative staff, the authority of the office rather than the person and the keeping of written documents. Most of the writing on the role of bureaucracy has focused not on its rational and desirable nature, but on its essentially irrational and repressive form. Novelists like Dickens, Balzac, Gogol, Kafka, Orwell and Solzhenitsyn, each in their turn, have seen the modern state as synonymous with an independent bureaucracy dominating and terrorizing the lives of citizens. And liberal theorists like Mill, presaging Mosca, saw bureaucracy as a threat to both representative government and to liberty.[3]

Political analyses of the Soviet state have focused great attention on the role of the bureaucracy. The far left search for explanations in theories of state capitalism or notions of a degenerate workers' state, popularized first by Leon Trotsky and kept alive by writers of the Fourth International like Tony Cliff.[4] Although Marx paid little attention to this aspect of political life, it has become a central issue in contemporary analyses of the Soviet state, beginning with Milovan Djilas's work on *The New Class* and continuing with Mikhail Voslensky's analysis of the

2 Antonio Gramsci, *The Modern Prince and Other Writings*, London, Lawrence & Wishart, 1957; Santiago Carrillo, *Eurocommunism and the State*, London, Lawrence & Wishart, 1977; Gyorg Lukács, *History and Class Consciousness*, Cambridge, M.I.T. Press, 1971; André Sakharov, *Progress, Coexistence and Intellectual Freedom*, London, André Deutsch, 1968; Herbert Marcuse, *One-Dimensional Man*, London, Routledge & Kegan Paul, 1964; Rudolf Bahro, *The Alternative in Eastern Europe*, London, NLB, 1978.

3 John Stuart Mill, *On Liberty*, Chicago, The Great Books Foundation, 1955; Gaetano Mosca, *The Ruling Class*, London, McGraw-Hill, 1939.

4 Leon Trostsky, *The Revolution Betrayed*, New York, Pathfinder Press, 1972; Tony Cliff, *State Capitalism in Russia*, London, Pluto Press, 1974.

nomenklatura in the USSR as a homogenous, self-generating and class-conscious ruling group.[5]

With the advent of the 'behavioural revolution' and systems analysis in political science, Soviet specialists tended more and more to de-emphasize totalitarianism as a model with continuing relevance to the analysis of a Soviet system which they believed had undergone substantial change after Stalin's death. Rivalries for leadership, factionalism and the emergence of interest groups and hierarchies parallel to, and in competition with, the Party gave the Soviet system a greater semblance of pluralism than had previously been observed. And whether one adopted a 'Kremlinological' explanation (in which policies are seen as the irrational outcomes of rivalries over power between top leaders whose tenure is never assured in advance and whose position can be undermined at any time by the constantly shifting and unstable pattern of alliance-building which characterize Kremlin politics) such as that forwarded by Michel Tatu, or an 'interest group' approach (in which policies are determined more rationally by competition between groups functionally interested in promoting their own sectors) such as that prompted by Skilling and 'Griffith or by Jerry Hough, both models severely curtailed the applicability of the totalitarian model.[6]

These are the main schools of thought in the West about the role of the state in the Soviet society. It is readily apparent that many of these strands of thought may not qualify *per se* as theories of the state, insofar as they do not see the state as a distinct force theoretically separate from the bureaucracy, the ruling Party, the leadership, or the class. In this sense they share common aspects with the official Soviet view of the role of the state in a socialist society.

Relationship between Theory and Politics

In the USSR, the official view of the role of the state and the development of that view is intrinsically bound up with politics. Thus, the boundaries of political action are accepted by political leaders to be those imposed by Marxism–Leninism. Conversely, it is the dominant political leaders in any given period who preroge to themselves the rights both to exclusive interpretation of that doctrine and to the formulation of all policies that derive from it. Far from seeing any

5 Milovan Djilas, *The New Class*, London, Thames & Hudson, 1957; Mikhail Voslensky, *Nomenklatura*, New York, Doubleday, 1984.

6 Michel Tatu, *Power in the Kremlin*, New York, Viking Press, 1969; Gordon Skilling and Franklyn Griffith, *Interest Groups in the USSR*, Princeton, Princeton University Press, 1971; Jerry Hough, *How the Soviet Union is Governed*, Cambridge, Harvard University Press, 1979.

inconsistency in such a potentially contradictory relationship, Soviet leaders justify the interconnection and promote it on the basis of Marx's own views that belief and actions are inseparable. Through their acceptance of *praxis*, Soviet leaders see the unity between actions, on the one hand, which should be in harmony with the world represented through them, and theories, on the other, which are constantly being subjected to creative development in the light of experience.

The state in socialist society is seen, therefore, as deriving its *raison d'être* not through the assent of a population or any other relationship of governance or jurisdiction but rather by virtue of its role both as a reflection of, and as a vehicle for, the historical process. The problem immediately arises that as every student of Soviet politics or political theory will know, both Marx and Lenin forecast the withering away of the state under socialism. As expressed most clearly by Marx in *The German Ideology*, the state is viewed as an organization of the political interests of the dominant economic class required primarily to sustain the oppressive production relations of capitalism. Gradually, after the overthrow of capitalism, as the benefits of a social order without private property are realized, neither law nor coercion would be required, and men would enter the stage of full communism in which society exists and flourishes without a controlling state. Then the 'government of people' would give way, according to Marx, to the 'administration of things'.

Marxist notions of the state as an instrument of coercion and consequently an object of revolutionary wrath quickly gave way after 1917 to the development of a theory of the state which while reflecting Marxist principles also took into account the need for political consolidation. The state having been attacked as the major previous impediment to proletarian rule would now have to the justified both as an expression of the dictatorship of the proletariat (under Lenin) and a vehicle for the historical process transforming the USSR to socialism and aiding in similar transformation elsewhere. The need to unify theory and practice was, therefore, established early in the Leninist period as a direct result of the competing demands to use and strengthen state power in the defence of the revolution while actively preparing for the decline and disappearance of such power. The extent to which the Soviets have addressed this tension between theory and practice, viewing it dialectically at times and distorting it at others, becomes clear through a discussion of the Soviet view of the role of the socialist state in three crucial areas – the state in international relations, the state and society, and the state as a central agent of historical change.

The Soviet State in International Relations

There are three major strands in Soviet foreign policy which require theoretical backing: support for non-ruling communist parties and national liberation movements, relations with bourgeois-democratic states, and ties with other socialist states. Each relationship is buttressed by doctrines developed sometimes at great political expense since the revolution. The Bolsheviks were faced from the onset by competing demands of support, on the one hand, for non-ruling communist parties in their efforts to overthrow the bourgeois order; and requirements, on the other, to provide a breathing space from Western pressure. This situation produced a series of classic political and theoretical debates in the 1920s between those who saw class as the major and only legitimate actor in international affairs and those who argued that until the correlation of forces shifts more decisively in favour of socialism it will be necessary to conduct relations with capitalist states in the basis of the accepted norms of (bourgeois) international law.

Just as these two tendencies co-existed uncomfortably in the 1920s, with the Comintern under Zinoviev and the Narkomindel (Peoples' Commissariat for Foreign Affairs) under Chicherin often working at cross purposes, so too does that contradiction continue to exist today. While rejecting the notion of exporting revolution, nevertheless the Soviet leadership by virtue of its proclaimed self-definition as the vanguard of the world's proletariat, recognizes that class as a major and growing force in international relations and abrogates to itself the right to support appeals for assistance from any group whose success would further shift the correlation forces in favour of socialism. In this respect, liberal notions of the sanctity of state sovereignty, the right of self-determination and self-defence are over-ridden in the Soviet context by emphasis on challenges to the Western status quo and a clear legitimization of actions across, and in violation of, state boundaries which express solidarity with forces seeking to undermine Western interests.

This tension between the revolutionary mission of the new Soviet leadership as vanguard of the international workers movement and their clear desire to function successfully as a member of the system of states created immeasurable and obvious problems with both the West and non-ruling parties. The German Social Democrats charged that the regularization of relations with the German authorities, as indicated by both the Brest-Litovsk and the Rapallo Treaties, would sound the death knell for the chances of a revolution in Germany. These were echoed by the charges made in the early 1970s by Third World movements that Soviet support for detente with the United States was at the expense of revolutionary goals. Those charges also appeared in the Soviet Union with advocates of detente ultimately gaining the upper ground. Nevertheless, this is an ongoing debate which has become inbuilt into the Soviet system as a result of this contradictory early self-image.

While one would expect this contradiction to exist in Soviet relations with non-ruling parties and bourgeois states, it is more difficult to understand how and why similar theoretical tensions have arisen in intra-socialist relations. If theory were the driving force of politics, one would expect to see integration far advanced with a commonwealth of socialist societies working together to break down bourgeois state relations. At the core of almost all the disputes between Moscow and other ruling communist parties is Moscow's claim that Marxism–Leninism is a universal and scientific doctrine applicable in all socialist countries without exception *and* that the Soviet Union as the longest established, most developed, and most powerful socialist state has the right to determine the appropriate interpretation of that doctrine in any given circumstances. To be sure there have been occasions when the Soviet Politburu as a whole or individual Soviet leaders recognized this interpretation as too intolerant of national differences. The 1955 Belgrade Declaration recognized 'differences of concrete forms' of socialist development. In Khrushcev's speech to the Twentieth Party Congress in 1956, the Soviet Union recognized the legitimacy of 'separate roads to socialism', but as was evident in the continuing polemics with the Yugoslavs, the invasion of Hungary, and the rifts with China, Albania and Romania, even Khruschev found intolerable any efforts to assert the primacy of 'state sovereignty' over Soviet-defined 'universal class laws'.

This debate became more acute under Brezhnev, with clearer ramifications both in the political arena (with the invasion of Czechoslovakia) and the theoretical arena (with the promulgation of the doctrine of limited sovereignty, or the so-called Brezhnev doctrine). Czechoslovak attempts to formulate 'socialism with human face' led to an inevitable clash of political wills and principles. The Czechs not only exposed the dominant strands of Soviet theory of the state to scrutiny and revision, but in doing so they also challenged the Soviet Union's imposition of a hegemonical structure on the world socialist system. The invasion of Czechoslovakia proved to be the only way possible to convince the Czechs of Soviet determination to maintain the monopoly of theoretical innovation. And in the aftermath of that invasion, the Soviet thoeretician, Lev Kovalev, in a *Pravda* article on 26 September 1968, enunciated the main features of the 'Brezhnev doctrine'. On the issue of sovereignty he said:

There is no doubt that the peoples of the socialist countries and the Communist Parties have and must have freedom to determine their countries' path of development. However, any decision of their's must damage neither socialism in their own country nor the fundamental interests of the other socialist countries nor the worldwide workers' mvoement, which is waging a struggle for socialism. This means that every Communist Party is responsible not only to its own people but also to all the socialist countries and to the entire Communist movement. Whoever forgets this in placing sole emphasis on the autonomy and independence of Communist Parties lapses into one-sidedness, shirking his internationalist obligations . . .

The sovereignty of individual socialist countries cannot be counterposed to the interests of world socialism and the world revolutionary movement . . .

World socialism as a social system is the common achievement of the working people of all countries, it is indivisable, and its defence is the common cause of all Communists . . .

Kovalev also made an important distinction between 'bourgeois' international law regulated by narrow adherence to state sovereignty and 'socialist' international law governed by class support for the principle of socialist internationalism:

Those who speak of the 'illegality' of the allied socialist countries' actions in Czechoslovakia forget that in a class society there is and can be no such thing as nonclass law. Laws and the norms of law are subordinated to the laws of the class struggle and the laws of social development. These laws are clearly formulated in the documents jointly adopted by the Communist and Workers' Parties.

This attempt to present a picture of socialist sovereignty as residing in the joint decisions of international communist conclaves met with a setback in 1975 when the Berlin meeting of ruling and non-ruling communist parties failed, at the insistence of the non-ruling Eurocommunist delegates, to endorse the Soviet concept of socialist internationalism as a principle impinging on the legal sovereignty of the state. The Soviets have been unable to reverse that ruling – or even to convene another summit since 1975.

Undeterred, the Soviets continued to insist on the supremacy of this principle in international relations within the socialist commonwealth – that is, members of both the socialist economic community, or Comecon, and the military alliance, or Warsaw Pact (the USSR, Poland, the German Democratic Republic, Czechoslovakia, Hungary, Romania and Bulgaria). Even here, however, Moscow has met with less than fulsome support. The Romanians from the very beginning refused to lend their imprimatur to Soviet-formulated principles of socialist internationalism. In the early 1980s, commensurate with both the downturns of

Soviet–American detente and the growing assertiveness of East European diplomacy in Europe as a result of the Helsinki process, several of the East European states – most notably East Germany, Hungary, Bulgaria and Romania – openly promoted the state rather than the class as the dominant actor in both international and intra-bloc relations. Thus the East Germans stopped attesting their loyalty to the principle of socialist internationalism, dropping the term altogether in official telegrams to Moscow on revolution anniversaries and other holidays. In June 1984, at an economic summit of Comecon heads of state (the first one the Soviets had succeeded in convening since 1971), the Soviet delegates and the Soviet press made repeated calls for closer integration (or *Sblizhenie* – drawing together) between member states, with some references even echoing the line – since discredited – enunciated by Brezhnev in 1976 at the 25th Party Congress that the 'process of gradual drawing together of socialist countries is now operating quite definitely as an objective law'.[7] The East European delegates almost uniformly called for greater attention to national differences; and the total absence from the final statement of any reference to *Sblizhenie* as a universal law reflects their ultimate predominance.[8]

Concurrent with the debates over socialist internationalism and integration have been efforts by some East European leaders to protect inter-European detente from the downturn in Soviet–American relations. In these efforts they have employed arguments about the role of 'small states' in international relations, saying that under current circumstances the 'small states' of Europe (whether socialist or capitalist) had the capability and the positive duty to bridge the gap between the superpowers. As stated by Matyas Szuros, the Hungarian Party Secretary responsible for foreign relations:

There are numerous examples to prove – and this is shown also by the experience of almost three years of work of the Madrid Conference as well – that we are dealing here essentially with a two-directional process: the great powers have the determining impact on events, and simultaneously, the role of small countries in bridging difference of views and developing rational and mutually acceptable compromises – altogether in fostering the continuity of East–West dialogue – is increasing.[9]

The Czechoslovak Party newspaper, *Rude pravo*, issued a harsh criticism of this 'revision' of Marxist–Leninist theory of international relations;

7 L. I. Brezhnev, *Report of the CPSU Central Committee and the Immediate Tasks of the Party in Home and Foreign Policy*, Moscow, Novosti, 1976, p. 9.

8 *Pravda*, 16 June 1984.

9 *Tarsadalmi Szemle*, no. 1, January 1984, as reprinted in Roland D. Asmus, *East Berlin and Moscow: The Documentation of a Dispute*, RFE Occasional Papers, No. 1, Munich, Radio Free Europe, 1985, p. 21.

and while the *Rude pravo* denunciation was published in Moscow, the subsequent Hungarian rebuttal appeared in the East Germany press.[10] Soon after, the First Deputy Head of the CPSU's Department for Liaison with Ruling Workers' and Communist Parties tried (without success) to put a halt to the argument by insisting that any categorization of the state by virtue of its size rather than its class basis was both 'artificial' and a 'deviation from Marxism–Leninism'.[11]

The succession from Chernenko to Gorbachev only further stimulated the debate, with some voices now being heard in the Soviet Union supporting the East European position. In March of 1985, during the debate which preceded the 30-year renewal of the Warsaw Pact, the Hungarian deputy foreign minister for Soviet bloc relations, in an article which once again was reprinted in East Germany, pointedly stated that 'the member states are independent and sovereign countries that, without exception, respect the principle of non-interference in each others internal affairs', adding that 'anyone in touch with reality will be cognisant of these differences and not see them as an "aberration".'[12] Even Gorbachev, who is regarded as the best hope for reform, conceded nothing to his bloc partners in his speech on the occasion of the treaty renewal. No mention was made of Soviet adherence to non-interference or the supremacy of state sovereignty over class relations, with the new Soviet Party chief choosing instead to state that 'relations are based on the full equality and comradely mutual assistance of sovereign states' who uphold 'the principle of socialist internationalism'.[13] Rakhmanin, in an attempt to limit the possibility of any but the most hard-line interpretation of Gorbachev's rather ambiguous remarks, bluntly wrote, again in a pseudonymous article, that East European states should not even attempt to revise the norms governing intra-bloc relations since 'on key international questions the foreign policy of the USSR and the Marxist–Leninist nucleas of world socialism is identical.'[14]

But it is at this point that other Soviet analysts, in apparent response, became engaged. Writing in the July issue of the Party's preeminent theoretical journal, the director of the Soviet Institute of the Economics of the World Socialist System countered Rakhmanin

10. *Rude pravo*, 30 March 1984; *Neues Deutschland*, 12 April 1984; *Novoye vremya*, 13 April 1984.

11 O. V. Borisov, 'Soyuz novovo tipa', *Voprosy istorii KPSS*, April 1984, pp. 34–49. Borisov is generally regarded as a pseudonym for Oleg Borisovich Rakhmanin, the First Deputy Head of this Department.

12 Istvan Roska, writing in *Nepszava*, as reprinted in *Neues Deutschland*, 4 March 1985.

13 *Pravda*, 28 April 1985.

14 Oleg Vladimirov, *Pravda*, 21 June 1985.

indirectly by saying that only by respecting the differing interests of other states can socialist internationalism ever be a really operative principle: 'Specific national and state interests cannot, of course, be ignored. That would not further the realization of our common international interests, nor would it strengthen the unity of the socialist countries'.[15] In the following month Nikolai Shishlin, a consultant to the Central Committee secretariat, added an even stronger comment to the debate on sovereignty v. socialist internationalism. He stated that 'Communists in power must be versed in the skill of harmonizing the national and international interests of the Socialist states.' And the only way to ensure such an approach, he says, is through 'unconditional respect for each country's sovereignty, a scrupulous attention to each other's interests'. However, almost as if he suddenly realized the bold implications of his statement, he then proceeds to qualify it by invoking the principle of socialist internationalism, which may, he continues, require at times 'certain sacrifices for the sake of the obligations of the alliance'.[16]

The role of the state as a unit subsidiary to the class in international relations between socialist states is unlikely, for mutually reinforcing theoretical and political reasons, to be revised in the foreseeable future. East European leaders cannot easily challenge the principle without appearing either to revise Marxist texts or challenge Soviet power. And the uneasy relationship between state sovereignty and class (party) supremacy is likely to shape the formulation of Soviet policy toward the capitalist and the socialist worlds as long as the Soviet Union protests its fidelity to Marxist–Leninist principles, as long as it exists in an international system dominated by competing standards of sovereignty, and importantly as long as the Party exercises supreme authority over the state in domestic affairs – the subject of the next section.

Relationship between State and Society

In national affairs, more than in international relations, it makes little sense to distinguish between 'the Party' on the one hand and 'the State' on the other in Soviet-type systems. While the two are organizationally distinct they are politically inseparable by virtue, not of their merger, but rather as a result of the state's total penetration by the Party. In dealing with the relations between state and society, therefore, it

15 O. Bogomolov, 'Soglasovanie ekonomicheskikh interesov i politiki pri sotsializme', *Kommunist*, no. 10, July 1985, p. 91.
16 N. Shishlin, *Novoye vremya*, 23 August 1985.

makes no sense to distinguish analytically between the state and the Party, since constitutionally, theoretically and politically, the USSR since Lenin's time has been a one-party state.

Whatever intentions Lenin may have had about putting into practice his utopian vision of the relationship between state and society as expressed in his *State and Revolution*, these were quickly forgotten when faced with Civil War and foreign intervention. Even in the early 1920s, when the revolution was not in imminent jeopardy, Lenin seemed unwilling or incapable of making the transition between pre-revolutionary requirements for conspiratorial organization and post-revolutionary needs for democratic participation. As early as March 1918, in a reply to Bukharin at the Seventh Party congress, Lenin sought to side-step the issue of the 'withering away of the state', saying: 'We shall have managed to convene more than two (Party) Congresses before the time comes to say: see how our State is withering away. It is too early for that. To proclaim the withering away of the State prematurely would distort the historical perspective.'[17]

The suppression of any significant theoretical discussion about the withering of the state and the gradual equating of the Party and the state occurred despite Lenin's increasing concerns about the growth of an oppressive bureaucracy. The programme of state nationalization of the means of production had swollen the ranks of the state bureaucracy by 1920 to 6,000,000 employees – at the very time when the mass exodus of the proletariat from the cities as a result of famine, disease and disorder threatened the very basis of the proletarian revolution.[18] Even the denationalization in 1921 of all but the 'commanding heights' of the economy under the New Economic Policy produced no discernible decline in the size of the bureaucracy. Lenin's frustration at being unable to deal with this problem led him in 1921 to characterize the Soviet Union as a 'workers' state with bureaucratic distortion'.[19] And a year later, at the last Party Congress he attended, Lenin admitted: 'If we take that huge bureaucratic machine, that gigantic heap, we must ask: who is directing whom? I doubt very much whether it can truthfully be said that the Communists are directing that heap. To tell you the truth, they are not directing, they are being directed'.[20] How ironic it was that Lenin should appoint Josef Stalin to the newly-created position of

17 V. I. Lenin, 'Speech against Bukharin's Amendment', *Collected Works*, vol. XXVII, Moscow, Foreign Languages Publishing House, 1960, p. 148.
18 This trend is the central thesis of Isaac Deutscher, *The Unfinished Revolution*, Oxford, Oxford University Press, 1969.
19 Lenin, 'The Party Crisis', *Collected Works*, vol. XXXII, p. 48.
20 Idem, 'Report of the Central Committee to the Eleventh Congress', *Collected Works*, vol. XXXIII, p. 288.

General Secretary of the Party in an effort to control the growth and oppressiveness of the State bureaucracy.

Although Lenin may have felt deep frustration at the growth of bureaucracy, many of the organizational and theoretical principles devised by him form the continuing backdrop of relations between the one-party state and society. Of all these principles two stand out: democratic centralism and the leading role of the Party. The former was originally devised by Lenin to serve as the basis for inner-Party organization; and it was envisaged the election of all leading Party bodies from lowest to highest, the subordination of the minority to the majority, and the duty of lower bodies to abide by the decisions of higher bodies. This has now become a key principle of organization between the state and society, and has been enshrined by the 1977 Soviet Constitution as the foundation for the structure of all state and societal inter-relationships.[21]

The second principle – the leading role of the Party – has long been established as the central feature of the constitution of all Soviet-type states, and Article 6 of the 1977 Constitution conveys the situation accurately:

The leading and guiding force of Soviet society and the nucleus of its political system, of all state organizations and all public organizations, is the Communist Party of the Soviet Union. the CPSU exists for the people and serves the people. The Communist Party, armed with Marxism–Leninism, determines the general perspectives of the development of society and the course of home and foreign policy of the USSR, directs the great constructive work of the Soviet people, and imparts a planned, systematic and theoretically substantiated character to their struggle for the victory of communism.[22]

The same Article concludes by cautioning that 'all Party organizations shall function within the framework of the Constitution of the USSR', and sets new constraints compared with the sweeping powers provided in the previous section. As a Polish author recently noted, the essence of systems of the Soviet type has always consisted in the fact that it has been the Party alone 'that enjoyed the real flight and real possibilities of defining its own *functions* within a more comprehensive system and its own *goals and strategies* ... it was the *only autonomous organization*, not subordinated to any of the remaining elements of that more comprehensive system, including the traditional institutions of the State, that is representative bodies, the government, and the courts of law.'[23]

21 *Constitution (Fundamental Law) of the Union of the Soviet Socialist Republics*, Moscow, Novosti, 1977.

22 Ibid., Article 6.

23 Wlodzimierz Pankow, 'The roots of "The Polish Summer": the crisis of the system of power', *Sisyphus Sociological Studies*, vol. III, Warsaw, Polish Scientific Publishers for

The autonomy and supremacy of the Party has not only been a feature of Soviet politics since the revolution, but even when the 'dictatorship of the proletariat' gave way to the stage of 'developed socialism', the theoreticians announced that 'increasing the leading role of the communist party (is) the objective requirement for the development of socialist society',[24] claiming that 'building a new society demands broader and stronger links between the party and the people.'[25]

Indeed, the party's leading role is seen as an inviolable principle – along with democratic centralism – for the construction to socialism. To deny this role, as Dubcek did in 1968 or Solidarity sought to do in 1980–1, is to deny – in Soviet eyes – the very commitment to the construction of communism. From Moscow's point of view the loss of central Party control, whether shed voluntarily or involuntarily, is tantamount to counter-revolution, since as is argued in the 1961 CPSU Party Programme: 'Unlike all previous socio-economic formations, communist society does not develop spontaneously, but as the result of the conscious and purposeful efforts of the masses, led by the Marxist–Leninist party.'[26] This mistrust of spontaneity is firmly rooted in both Russian political culture and in Lenin's own 'diagnosis' that the working class of its own free will is capable only of trade union consciousness. Such an attitude towards society poses great dilemmas for any leadership which bases its authority on the conviction that it is functioning in the true interests of all the people. It also poses practically insuperable problems for achieving any reform of the system, since, as discussed in the section below, by removing the possibility of conflict between state and society, the Soviet leaders have also in effect virtually denied that the relationship between the socialist state and the historical process is subject to the laws of dialectical materialism.

The State and the Historical Process

The Soviet Union and the key countries of Eastern Europe are now said to have entered the stage of 'developed socialism' characterized primarily by the complete state ownership of the means of production and the harmonization of the interests of all social classes and groups.

the Polish Academy of Sciences, Institute of Philosophy and Sociology, 1982, p. 34 (italics in original).

24 A. F. Yudenkov et al., eds, *Rukovodyashchaya rol' KPSS v usloviyakh razvitovo sotsializma*, Moscow, Mysl', 1979, chapter 1.

25 D. A. Keromov, ed., *Soviet Democracy in the Period of Developed Socialism*, Moscow, Progress Publishers, 1979, p. 38.

26 'Programma KPSS', *KPSS v rezolyutsiyakh i resheniyakh S"ezdov, Konferentsii i Plenumov TsK*, vol. VIII, Moscow, Politizdat, 1972, p. 301.

The state, which continues to be characterized as a 'state of the whole people', would not wither away in preparation for the final transition to communism, but instead would remain as strong as it was under the dictatorship of the proleteriat, changing only its social base to include other sections of society. Indeed, far from envisaging the gradual withering away of the state as the 1961 Party Programme had done, the 1985 Draft Party Programme specifically includes the following new formula: 'The key question of the Party's policy is *the development and strengthening of the Soviet socialist state* and the increasingly full revelation of its democratic, all-people's character.'[27]

This view, that the state apparatus will not, and need not, undergo transformation in the process of 'perfecting' socialist society, has been the subject of heated debates in Soviet theoretical journals and newspapers since the months preceding Leonid Brezhnev's death. Subterranean pressure for reform is a practically constant feature of Soviet politics, but this debate was apparently encouraged into the open by the speech Yuri Andropov delivered in April 1982 while Brezhnev was still alive in which he declared that 'the teachings of Lenin, like Marxism–Leninism as a whole, are a science; and like other sciences, they cannot tolerate stagnation.;[28]

At issue in the current debate is whether the party-state bureaucracy (and virtually all the literature makes no distinction between the two, seeing them as one single monolith) has not become so divorced from the society that far from being the major agent of historical transformation, it has become the major impediment to change. Some authors go so far as to suggest that the bureaucracy has developed all the features of a ruling class, and a class furthermore in conflict with all other, by definition exploited, classes in society. These authors believe that the necessity for a fundamental challenge to this bureaucratic distortion is necessary, because without it the very basis of socialism itself could be put in jeopardy.

The debate was also influenced by the need to determine and eliminate the root causes of the 1980–1 crisis in Poland. The standard Soviet response was to blame internal and external counter-revolutionaries, which in the Polish case meant the Catholic Church, the large devout and free-holding peasantry, and sections of the working class intelligentsia who were said to have been aided and manipulated by the Vatican, American trade unions, Radio Free Europe, and other external anti-Soviet agencies.[29] But other analysts, including many Polish

27 'CPSU Program (New Edition)', *Pravda*, 26 October 1985.
28 Yuri Andropov, 'Leninism: the inexhaustible source of revolutionary energy and creativity of the masses', *Pravda*, 23 April 1982.

theorists, saw the crisis as having its roots in a more general, systematic crisis of socialism brought about by bureaucratic distortion, corruption and abuses of power which although most evident in Gierek's Poland, exist everywhere. Writing in 1982, a leading Soviet proponent of reform, Anatoly Butenko, argued that deformation of socialism can occur anywhere when 'ownership of the means of production by the entire people is replaced by group ownership; the principle of planning, by spontaneity; the mechanism of democratic centralism, by bureaucratic centralism or anarchistic decentralism; when the bilateral ties of the managers and the managed . . . are reduced to relations of commanding from above. Incompatible with scientific socialism', Butenko stresses, 'are attempts to supplant the powers of the working people themselves with the exclusive activity of the state apparatus in the name of the working people, but not in their interests.'[30] A Polish sociologist came to the same conclusion about the roots of the crisis in Poland, although he chose to put it rather more bluntly:

Had the level of consumption been effectively linked to the labour contributed by each person . . . events could have taken a different course. But the logic of the system of power dictated another solution whereby the theoretical principle of 'to everyone according to one's work' was in practice replaced by the principle of 'to everyone according to one's positions in the system of power.'[31]

What is to be Done?

It is to be expected that any attempt at reform of the heavily bureaucratized party-state apparatus will have to be justified in terms of its consistency with Leninist precepts, especially in the USSR. It is through this perspective that another aspect of the debate which broke out in 1982, therefore, should be viewed. At the surface, the issue under discussion was the analysis of Lenin's response to the crisis which broke out in the Party in 1920–1. The workers and sailors who had supported Bolshevism had become disillusioned with the anti-democratic, centralized and anti-peasant policies of the phase of War Communism from 1918 to 1920. Lenin's primary reaction to the crisis in the Party and in

29 See esp. Ye. Bugaev, 'Strannaya Pozitsiya', *Kommunist*, no. 14, September 1984, pp. 119–26; R. Kosolapov, *Pravda*, 20 July 1984; idem, *Pravda*, 4 March 1983.

30 Anatoly Butenko, 'Socialism: forms and deformations', *New Times*, no. 6, 1982, p. 6.

31 Pankow, 'Roots of "The Polish Summer"', p. 43.

the country was to introduce the New Economic Policy, denationalizing all but the 'commanding heights', and reintroducing the market in agriculture and distribution. Moreover, the 1920s was a time of open political, cultural and intellectual activity, the likes of which were never again seen after the Stalinist clampdown. The question which has been raised, with contending answers, is: Was the New Economic Policy the true path of normal socialist development, with the preceding phase (and by implication the succeeding Stalinist phase) the temporary path imposed by expedience? Many of those in the Soviet Union who seek fundamental reform argue that NEP in fact is, in the words of one such reformer, 'the period of normal development'.[32] And furthermore, according to another, the lessons learned in the adoption of NEP have 'continued significance even today'.[33]

These voices of reform were all convinced that the Party leadership – in the 1980s as in 1921 – had the capability to correct any distortions, bureaucratic or otherwise which had arisen. Not all voices of change believe that the socialist party state is still capable of self-reform. Thus, in analysing the causes of the 1980–1 Polish crisis, Polish social scientists stressed that an accelerating factor in the crisis was the spectacle of obvious and blatant elite unwillingness, and then inability to deal with the systemic sources of the crisis: 'the existing system of power was incapable of self-correction even (or perhaps in particular) in the face of a grave social crisis. It was more and more evident that the system must be restructured. As it turned out, that restructuring had to be undertaken by social forces which remained as it were outside the system'.[34]

The state in socialist society, as has been shown, is not an issue confined in the socialist world to parlour debates, mid-term exams, or *rive gauche* cafés. It is part and parcel of the daily life of the elites, the party theoreticians, reformers and dissidents alike. Whether those seeking reforms will be able to stay within the system, or will ultimately either resume silence or join the ranks of the dissidents and emigrés, remains to be seen. On the resolution of this issue hangs not only the personal fate of a whole generation who have waited in the wings for the Stalin era finally to subside but also the institutional fate of one of man's greatest attempts to harness the power of the state to serve human

32 F. M. Burlatsky, 'Sovershenstvovaniye razvitovo sotsializma – vazhniy etap na puti k kommunizmu', *Voprosy filosophii*, no. 6, 1984, p. 25.

33 E. A. Ambartsumov, 'Analiz V. I. Leninym prichin krizisa 1921 g. i putei vykhoda iz nevo', *Voprosy istorii*, no. 4, 1984, p. 29.

34 Pankow, 'The Roots of "The Polish Summer"', p. 47. This view is shared by every other of the over 20 contributions to this special volume.

requirements. If they fail to dismantle the legacy of Stalinism this time, three full decades and five leadership transitions after his death, then it would appear that the prospects for any true legitimization of the role of the one-party state in socialist society will be permanently dimmed.

9

State-Making and Nation-Building

Anthony D. Smith

In the modern world only one form of political unit is recognized and permitted. This is the form we call the 'nation-state'. It is easy enough to discover. Nation-states have frontiers, capitals, flags, anthems, passports, currencies, military parades, national museums, embassies and usually a seat at the United Nations. They also have one government for the territory of the nation-state, a single education system, a single economy and occupational system, and usually one set of legal rights for all citizens, though there are exceptions. (In some federal systems, there may be citizenship rights for all members of the nation-state, but also communal rights for members of particular communities.)[1] They also subscribe, tacitly or openly, quietly or vociferously, to a single ideology which legitimates the whole enterprise – nationalism. Indeed, the whole system of states is built on its assumptions, even if its practice does not often conform to nationalist precepts.[2] We even call it the 'inter*national*' system.

At the same time, as has often been pointed out, there are actually very few genuine 'nation-states' today. If we mean by the term 'nation-state'

---

1 For example, in Catalonia and even more in Yugoslavia, see C. Bridges, 'Some causes of political change in modern Yugoslavia', in M. Esman, ed., *Ethnic Conflict in the Western World*, Ithaca, Cornell University Press, 1977.

2 There is, of course, a vast literature on nationalist ideology. Apart from the classic works of C. Hayes, *The Historical Evolution of Modern Nationalism*, New York, Smith, 1931, L. Snyder, *The Meaning of Nationalism*, New Brunswick, Rutgers University Press, 1954, and H. Kohn, *The Idea of Nationalism*, New York, Macmillan-Collier, 2nd edn, 1967, the more recent work of A. Orridge, 'A sequence of nationalism', in L. Tivey, ed., *The Nation-State*, Oxford, Martin Robertson, 1980, B. Anderson, *Imagined Communites*, London, Verso Books, 1983, and J. Breuilly, *Nationalism and the State*, Manchester, Manchester University Press, 1982, all pay attention to the varieties of nationalist legitimations of the state.

that the boundaries of the state's territories and those of a homogenous ethnic community are coextensive, and that all the inhabitants of a state possess an identical culture, then we will not be able to muster more than about 10 per cent of existing states as candidates for the title of 'nation-state'. Leaving aside tiny minorities, we may perhaps be able to include a few more, apart from states like Portugal, Greece, Poland and Somalia; Holland, Denmark and the two Germanies have small minorities, but are by now otherwise homogeneous, if we leave aside the immigrant workers. In other states – Sweden, Norway and Finland, for example – the Lapp and Karelian minorities do not, perhaps cannot, impair the cultural unity of the state.[3] Yet, this leaves a very considerable number, perhaps over half, with serious ethnic divisions which may spill over into antagonism, and another large group, perhaps a quarter of the total, in which a dominant culture-community must accommodate the demands of 'peripheral' *ethnie*, as in Britain, France and Canada, Romania and Bulgaria.[4] In the 50 per cent with serious cultural cleavages, it has not always been possible to contain the competing demands or meet the claims of rival communities. In India, Sri Lanka, Burma, the Philippines, Indonesia, Laos, Iran, Iraq, Turkey, Cyprus, Spain, Yugoslavia, Corsica (France), Ireland, Chad, Nigeria, Cameroons, Zaire, Zambia, Zimbabwe, South Africa, Uganda, Kenya, Sudan and Ethiopia, these divisions have at one time or another since 1914 erupted into overt violence and even warfare.[5]

There is something of a paradox here. In theory, we require our societies to assume a single shape. In practice, we are content with a formal declaration of intent, while our societies assume all manner of

3 For a classic statement of the argument, see W. Conner, 'Nation-building or nation-destroying?', *World Politics*, vol. 24, 1972, and in Europe, W. Connor, 'Ethno-nationalism in the First World', in Esman, *Ethnic Conflict*. On the Lapp, Karelian and other very small ethnic minorities, see the brief discussions in G. Ashworth, ed., *World Minorities*, vol. I, 1977; vol. II, 1978; vol. III, 1980: *World Minorities in the Eighties*, Sunbury, Middx, Quartermaine House.

4 In Canada, apart from Quebecois, Indians, Eskimo, Ukrainians, Poles and many others; in Romania, the large Hungarian *ethnie* in Transylvania, in Bulgaria, the considerable Turkish minority intent on preserving their identity, see Ashworth, *World Minorities*; J. Krejci, 'Ethnic problems in Europe', in M. Archer and S. Giner, eds, *Contemporary Europe: Social Structures and Cultural Patterns*, London, Routledge & Kegan Paul, 1978; and J. Krejci and V. Velimsky, *Ethnic and Political Nations in Europe*, London, Croom Helm, 1981.

5 There has been, to my knowledge, no comparative study of Third World separatisms and ethnic antagonisms, but I have found useful C. Anderson, F. von der Mehden and C. Young, *Issues of Political Development*, Englewood Cliffs, Prentice-Hall, 1967; T. Sathyamurthy, *Nationalism in the Contemporary World*, London, Frances Pinter, 1983; and V. Olorunsola, ed., *The Politics of Cultural Subnationalism in Africa*, New York, New York, 1972; cf. also R. Hall, *Ethnic Autonomy: Comparative Dynamics*, New York, Pergamon Press, 1979, for some case studies.

shapes. It is, of course, easy to write the whole business off as a case of Western myopia: we have equated the 'nation' and the 'state', because that is the form they took in the two historically influential societies – England and France – at the very moment when nationalism burst forth. In other words, Eastern Europe and the Third World have all been trying to imitate a rather singular model, whose ethnic homogeneity, like its parliamentary institutions, simply cannot be transplanted. They have been pursuing a Western mirage. To say that the only real state was a 'nation-state', and that the only realized nation was a 'nation-state', has not only thrown the geopolitical map into turmoil, it has entailed a fruitless and destructive quest for something unattainable outside a few blessed regions of the earth. And even in the West, the much-sought marriage of state and *ethnie* has not turned out to be all that happy and enduring.[6]

And yet, there is no question of turning back and re-erecting those rambling, polyethnic empires of which some anti-nationalists dream. It may be that the fault is all with nationalism, and that the problems only arise when ethnic homogeneity and cultural coextensiveness become desirable goals in themselves. The fact remains, and it is a central one to the whole of the modern era since the French Revolution, that the majority of educated and politically aware men and women are committed to 'nationalism' even if only tacitly, through exclusion and self-differentiation. They are no longer really aware of any other viable mode of culture and political existence. The assumptions of 'nationalism' have shaped their political horizons as much as those of 'development' have furnished their economic agenda. It may be that some of those assumptions were actually present even before nationalism made them explicit; but there is certainly no possibility of returning to a pre-nationalist era.

That being so, the practical question becomes one of reconciling, in the light of nationalist premisses, the often conflicting demands of state and nation. And the intellectual question becomes one of explaining the often intricate relationships between state and nation which the misleading omnibus term 'nation-state' is liable to obscure. This means in turn that we need to distinguish between 'state-making' and 'nation-building', and question those theories that claim that nations created states or the reverse; and ask ourselves whether, as I shall argue, they are formed most enduringly and fruitfully around some third unit of solidarity and community.

6 Indeed, our very terminology is Anglo-French (and Latin); see on this G. Zernatto, 'Nation: the history of a word', *Review of Politics*, vol. 6, 1944, and B. Akzin, *State and Nation*, London, Hutchinson, 1964, as well as the detailed study of terminology and

'Nation-Building' and Nation-Inventing'

The first move away from an exclusively Western and nationalist standpoint was taken in the early 1950s by the communications theorists. Their central idea was that of 'nation-building'. Unlike the nationalists, they did not hold that the nation was 'there' waiting to be discovered by a generation of nationalist Prince Charmings. The 'nation' had to be 'built', bit by bit. But the blueprint for the building remained firmly of Western origin. The goal was, after all, the 'national participant society' of the democratic Western states. And the manner of the building processes was also Western: social mobilization, linguistic assimilation and the use of the mass media and mass education. For Lerner the key was 'empathy': the formation of psychologically mobile personalities who had broken with tradition and were able to imagine, and desire, the new kind of participant society. For Karl Deutsch, cultural assimilation, as measured by language absorption, was the process *par excellence* that ensured the building of national units. While social mobilization uprooted peasants and artisans and propelled them into the larger towns, it was the standardization and inclusion of linguistic assimilation that turned this mobile but disunited mass into an educated 'public', who in turn would be bound to one another by the very density and homogeneity of the messages they received. But what neither Deutsch nor Lerner make clear is who sends these messages, in what they consist, to whom they are directed, or why they are sent at all. In other words, what is so patently missing in this approach is any real role for the state and state elites. Their presence is simply assumed throughout.[7]

There is a reason for this silence about the role of the state and its elites. Communications theorists were reacting to both the nationalist and anti-nationalist accounts of nation-forming. Common to both these

---

concepts by A. Kemilainen, *Nationalism; Problems concerning the Word, Concept and Classification*, Yvaskyla, Kustantajat Publishers, 1964. For the recent European disharmony, cf. P. Mayo, *The Roots of Identity*, London, Allen Lane, 1974.

7 D. Lerner, *The Passing of Traditional Society*, New York, Free Press, 1958, and K. Deutsch, *Nationalism and Social Communication*, 2nd edn, New York, MIT Press, 1966, are the main texts; but the collection of essays in K. Deutsch and W. Foltz, eds, *Nation-Building*, New York, Atherton, 1963, and the more recent expansion of his theories in K. Deutsch, *Nationalism and its Alternatives*, New York, Knopf, 1969, are fruitful. For appraisals, see Connor, 'Nation-building or nation-destroying'; A. D. Smith, *Theories of Nationalism*, London, Duckworth; New York, Harper and Row, 1971; 2nd edn, New York, Duckworth and Holmes & Meier, 1983, chapter 5; and idem, *State and Nation in the Third World*, Brighton, Harvester, 1983, chapter 1.

accounts was an interventionist and voluntarist view of history, that is, one which attributed to the deliberate actions of human beings the chances of building nations. For 'modernization' theorists (of which communications theory was one variant) such human intervention is largely superfluous; the processes of social development will in any case work themselves out and bring to fruition the potential for evolution that lies within. Hence the role of the state is simply to act as a handmaid of history, whose goal is a world of large-scale nation-states or regions.[8]

This is, in many ways, still the orthodoxy about both state-making and nation-building. It is clearly one that is profoundly Western and fundamentally endogenist. The socio-demographic processes which it charts lie within the 'society' concerned. The analyst is simply concerned to draw the lineaments of the new type of society out of the old, and to describe the ways in which this profound qualitative transition is accomplished by analysing such data as urbanization and literacy rates, indices of linguistic assimilation, the impact of the mass media, the rates of social mobility and the patterns of transport, mass education and voting.

Such data are, of course, useful. They tell us something about the manner and speed of the formation of national units – provided, of course, we have a clear idea of what we mean by a 'nation' in the first place. But they tell us nothing about the forces that impel people to seek to belong to 'nations' rather than any other type of unit. And, if one looks for a moment outside the West, this question becomes more than just academic. In the West, perhaps, one might concede that 'nations' grew up accidentally in the bosom of their respective states. But in the Third World, there are very few nations as yet; and the state is having to work hard at just keeping its various ethnic groups together, let alone 'build' a nation. And yet, 'nation-building' describes succinctly what Third World elites are trying to do. If anything, 'nation-building' is *the* basic Third World ideology and project, rather than a tool of analysis.

This is very much the conclusion which Marxists and others have reached. The question then becomes one of discovering the forces that make such a quest for nationhood universal in the Third World. For some, like Worsley and Amin, Third World nationalism is really a form of anti-colonialism, and presumably therefore a temporary one. The

---

8 On modernization theory generally, see S. Eisenstadt, *Modernisation: Protest and Change*, Englewood Cliffs, Prentice-Hall, 1965; and *Tradition, Change and Modernity*, New York, John Wiley, 1973; R. Nisbet, *Social Change and History*, Oxford, London, New York, Oxford University Press, 1969; A. D. Smith, *The Concept of Social Change*, London and Boston, Routledge & Kegan Paul, 1973; and A. Hoogvelt, *The Sociology of Developing Societies*, London, Macmillan, 1978; excessive endogenism and conceptual vagueness are the main targets.

small native bourgeoisies and intelligentsia have seized the apparatus of the colonial state, not only to use it for the tasks of 'development', but also to forge nations out of the many ethnic and regional communities which the colonial state has bequeathed them.[9] In this view, the state is first a target and then a base for revolutionary nationalism and the dominant classes who espouse it. Indeed, as Warren argues, Third World state elites drawn from the petite bourgeoisie have adopted a model of 'dependency' that fits well their basically nationalist ideals and goals. The 'distortions of development' are as real on the psychological plane (in the form of collective *atimia*) as they are on the economic level.[10]

But perhaps the most trenchant critique of communications theory comes from one who has adopted the basic framework of 'modernization'. Ernest Gellner argues that it is nationalism that invents nations 'where they do not exist', and that the reason for nationalism's ubiquity lies in the uneven development of modernization and industrialization. He agrees with Deutsch that social mobilization uproots traditional structures and that these are replaced by the forces of cultural assimilation, and notably language, in the expanding towns. He even agrees with Lerner about the need for a literate, participant society in an industrial age. Indeed, such a large-scale participant society in which everyone has become a literate and numerate citizen demands a mass, public, standardized and compulsory education system; and that in turn requires something the size of a state to sustain it. So one form of nationalism becomes loyalty to a linguistic homogeneous state.[11]

But there is another kind of nationalism. In the later stages of industrialization, when social communication is at its most intense, new

9 P. Worsley, *The Third World*, London, Weidenfeld & Nicolson, 1964 and S. Amin, *Class and Nation*, London, Heinemann, 1981; cf. also the more recent account in Sathyamurthy, *Nationalism in the Contemporary World*, in which 'nationalism' becomes subsumed in the struggle for 'national liberation' and anti-colonialism generally.

10 B. Warren, *Imperialism, Pioneer of Capitalism*, New York, Monthly Review Press, 1980, chapter 7 claims that 'dependency theories' express the nationalist aspirations of Third World petite bourgeoisies and intelligentsia; cf. also P. O'Brien, 'A critique of Latin American theories of dependence', in I. Oxaal, T. Barnett and D. Booth, eds, *Beyond the Sociology of Development*, London, Routledge & Kegan Paul, 1975, and on the concept of *atimia* (negative status in the international status order), J. Nettl and R. Robertson, *International Systems and the Modernisation of Societies*, London, Faber, 1968.

11 Gellner's early statement is in E. Gellner, *Thought and Change*, London, Weidenfeld & Nicholson, 1964, chapter 7; an amended statement appeared in E. Gellner 'Scale and nation', *Philosophy of the Social Sciences*, vol. 3, 1973, and a greatly expanded theory in E. Gellner, *Nations and Nationalism*, Oxford, Blackwell, 1983. There are important differences between the earlier and later statements, some of which are noted in A. D. Smith, 'Ethnic persistence and national transformation', *British Journal of Sociology*, vol. 35, 1984.

cleavages may appear. These are produced by the acute competition for scarce resources and facilities in the expanding towns, especially between the old-established denizens and the later arrivals. The trouble is that such conflicts may not only revolve around class issues. They may involve cultural differences. The two which cause most division are genetic and religio-cultural differences. Both are salient and both refuse to blur in the new linguistic state. Like ancient but hidden chasms, they open up in the fierce urban competition of late industrialization. And, if unchecked, they are likely to result in two new nationalisms on either side of the cultural divide, and hence two new nation-states. So the second, secessionist kind of nationalism is the result of the failure of industrialism to integrate everyone around a single culture, and it is responsible for all the new mini-states that have sprung up lately.[12]

But, again, we may ask: where does the state figure in all this? Its role seems to be that of a necessary adjunct and support, and in no way an initiator or even catalyst. The same is true of the recent 'centre-periphery' models of Hechter and Nairn, which are so influential today. In Hechter's analysis, the state, it is true, once possessed an initiating role: the British state, for example, in Tudor times incorporated Wales and later Ireland, and was enlarged by the union with Scotland in 1707. And today's renascent ethnic nationalisms in the Celtic fringe are again directed at the centralism of the bureaucratic state. But closer inspection reveals that, at least today, the 'state' is simply the form and agent of another larger force, an unevenly developing capitalist industrialism, which has turned the peripheral backlands into dependent economies and cultures and which, by its very embrace, keeps ethnic 'sectionalism' alive.[13] The state has a more important role in Nairn's account. Because the British state has remained 'patrician', Britain has not been able to take full advantage of industrial capitalism, and has therefore encouraged its expanding bourgeoisie since 1800 to seek foreign markets. Nationalism, therefore, began overseas, in the peripheral colonies seized by the British and French bourgeoisies. It began as a response by

12 Gellner, *Nations and Nationalism*, reviews these in chapter 6, but has difficulty over the roles of religion and ethnicity, the first admitted, the second more tacit. It is not clear whether he means to deny an important role to ethnicity in premodern eras, or indeed whether he thinks there is a real difference between *ethnie* and nations, an unexplored theme in his oeuvre.

13 M. Hechter, *Internal Colonialism: the Celtic Fringe in British National Development, 1536–1966*, London, Routledge & Kegan Paul, 1975, and his amended version, prompted by criticisms based on the differences between Scotland and Wales/Ireland, in M. Hechter and M. Levi, 'The comparative analysis of ethno-regional movements', *Ethnic and Racial Studies*, vol. 2, 1979; for some criticisms and studies of the Scottish case, cf. K. Webb, *The Growth of Nationalism in Scotland*, Harmondsworth, Penguin, 1977, and J. Brand, *The National Movement in Scotland*, London, Routledge & Kegan Paul, 1978.

elites in the colonies to capitalist imperialism. Since these elites had no other resources to fall back on, they appealed to the only thing they had: their masses, whom they 'invited into history'. Nationalism is therefore always populist, and it remains so, when it is exported back to Europe in the wake of decolonization to become 'neo-nationalism'.[14]

Again, however, the much-vaunted 'autonomy of the state' soon becomes obscured by the commanding autonomy of an unevenly developing capitalism and its bourgeois agents. This may be more faithful to the spirit of Marx, but it hardly tells us why the state has become so pivotal today, and how its role is related to the widespread appeal of nationalism. Or is this role another mask, this appeal another mirage? If nations can be 'invented', cannot states be 'made' and unmade, by other and more 'real' forces at work beneath the façade of history?

'State-Making' and Inter-State Systems

The underlying problem with all the above accounts is that the state has been seen simply as a place or arena in which other 'real' forces and processes are locked in combat. But the state is really far more than an arena. It does involve territory, but it cannot be simply reduced to a location. Its spatial quality is integral to its functions and agencies. Generically, the 'state' comprises a set of differentiated, autonomous and public institutions, which are territorially centralized and claim jurisdiction over a given territory, including the monopoly over coercion and extraction. In the past, it is questionable to what extent 'the state' was able to realize its claims beyond the immediate vicinity of the capital (if there was a stable capital); some of the great empires were really no more than loose coalitions of superordinate and subordinate realms, each with its own ruler and local institutions, usually in some form of tributary relationship with an overall monarch. Certainly, this was true of the early Mesopotamian and Chinese empires; and we find the pattern re-emerging whenever the dynasty is weakened and economic disaster undermines the delicate balance of bureaucratic controls over food production and communications.

What are the main functions of any centralized state? First and foremost, defence of the territory from external incursions, physical and cultural; hence some control over demographic movements (colonies,

14 T. Nairn, *The Break-up of Britain*, London, New Left Books, 1977, esp. chapters 2, 5 and 9; for general appraisals, cf. E. Hobsbawm, 'Some reflections on "The Break-up of Britain"', *New Left Review*, vol. 105, 1977, and A. D. Smith, *The Ethnic Revival*, Cambridge, Cambridge University Press, 1981, chapter 2, which also examines Hechter's model of 'internal colonialism'.

migrants, etc.) and new religious movements originating from beyond the state's domain. Second, conflict regulation within: the state as arbiter seeks to contain disruptive conflicts, especially between elites, but also between peasants and the towns over prices of crops and food. The *kudurrus* found in the fields of southern Iraq, and dating back to Kassite times, attests a conflict management role of determining boundaries of individual farms and fields through imperial grants, as does the succession of Sumerian and Babylonian law-codes, designed to ensure a unified order in and through which social interests could be pursued.[15] Third comes the imposition of a territorial order over and above the more usual (certainly in earlier times) kinship order. This involves the marshalling of manpower and resources according to territorial administrative divisions, and the inculcation, often through war over particular territories, of a sense of political community based upon shared and defended space. Of course, a polyethnic and often unwieldy polity like an empire may be hampered in this direction; but even large-scale empires like the Han under Wu-ti (140–87 BC) sought to homogenize originally culturally diverse populations (in this case, under Han Chinese auspices).[16] A fourth function is that of information control and transmission. Here, of course, the state usually has to fall back upon specialist literate classes, which in early times were usually priests and scribes. But the latter were early also attached to the bureaucracy, as in Pharonic Egypt of the New Kingdom, and were even trained by special government educational establishments.[17] Finally, there is a 'cosmic' function: the ruler as head of state also embodies (either as a promise, or in his very person) the essential link with sacred order beyond, from which all power, all fertility, all control over the elements, is deemed to flow. In his person, and in the smooth functioning of his government, pre-modern societies find the necessary assur-

15 On the *kudurrus* and law-codes in Sumer and Babylon, see G. Roux, *Ancient Iraq*, Harmondsworth, Penguin, 1964, pp. 224–5, and L. Oppenheim, *Ancient Mesopotamia*, Chicago, University of Chicago Press, 1964, pp. 123, 159, 286–7; state regulation, rather than any despotism founded on ecological necessity in river-valleys, as postulated by K. Wittfogel, *Oriental Despotism*, New Haven, Yale University Press, 1957, provided one of the main bases, along with defence from marauding desert tribes like the Amurru, for imperial unifications from Sargon of Akkad to Nebuchadnezzar. On all this, cf. M. Mann, *The Sources of Social Power: vol. I. From the Beginning to 1760 AD*, Cambridge, Cambridge University Press, 1986, for an excellent analysis.

16 For early China, see W. Eberhard, *A History of China*, 4th rev. edn, London, Routledge & Kegan Paul, 1977, chapters 2–6, and J. Meskill, *An Introduction to Chinese Civilisation*, Lexington, Mass., D. C. Heath, 1973, chapters 1–3; Wu-ti and other emperors also sought to keep out the Hsiung-nu at times.

17 On ancient bureaucracies, including New Kingdom Egypt, see W. Beyer, 'The civil service in the ancient world', *Public Administration Review*, vol. 19, 1959; and for Sumerian city-states, S. Kramer, *The Sumerians*, Chicago, Chicago University Press, 1963.

ance of an ultimate harmony with the cosmos, and hence of the minimum prosperity needed to assure food production and survival.[18] Whether, in these early days, states and rulers looked beyond this to what we might term economic development and redistribution is a moot point; there are some indications of an early concern with such redistribution, usually to prevent revolution or civil chaos, and perhaps we should add this to the generic functions of the state.[19]

When we come to the 'modern' or 'rational' state of early modern Europe and later, the scope and effectiveness of the state in performing these functions is immeasurably increased, but it is doubtful whether any really new functions are shouldered. If anything, one function, that of providing a link with the cosmos, is reduced, if not eliminated; or it would seem so. Instead, the other functions are subdivided and given wholly new meanings. Immigration controls become stricter, along with the growth of compact defensible territories, passport controls, currency controls and the like. Conflict regulation has turned into a vast array of law-codes, by-laws and regulations for dealing with every aspect, not just of 'law and order' concerns, but of relations between citizens and between the citizen and the bureaucracy. In the process, the numbers, scope, powers and efficacy of the bureaucratic agencies have multiplied. Similarly, control of information has spawned the rise of state systems of mass education, state-sponsored journalism and mass media, and state-controlled agencies of surveillance and information technology. The 'state as recorder and transmitter' has reduced the clergy and church in many societies to a side-show, as professional experts perform the earlier scribal functions in undreamt-of ways. And, quite clearly, the modern state has taken on a new welfare or developmental function as a central facet of its very *raison d'être*.[20]

Given this development from what Mann has called the 'despotic

18 The classic statement for the ancient Near East is H. Frankfort, *Kingship and the Gods*, Chicago, Chicago University Press, 1948; but cf. also R. David, *The Ancient Egyptians*, London, Routledge & Kegan Paul, 1982, for the position of the Pharoah in Egyptian religion and society.

19 M. Mann, chapter 4 in this volume, argues for this function, citing C. Renfrew, *The Emergence of Civilisation: the Cyclades and the Aegean in the Third Millennium B.C.*, London, Methuen, 1972, and, critically, E. Service, *Origins of the State and Civilization*, New York, Norton, 1975, for this early period. It certainly operated on a small scale in the temple-states of early Sumer (H. Frankfort, *The Birth of Civilization in the Near East*, New York, Anchor Books, 1954), but was far more difficult to organize over large-scale empires, as the rest of Mann's argument suggests.

20 On all this, see H. Jacoby, *The Bureaucratization of the World*, tr. E. Kanes, Berkeley and Los Angeles, University of California Press, 4th rev edn, London, Routledge & Kegan Paul, 1973, and of course M. Weber, eds, H. Gerth and C. Mills, *From Max Weber; Essays on Sociology*, London, Routledge & Kegan Paul, 1947; for an analysis of aspects of nineteenth-century European bureaucracies, cf. M. Anderson, *The Ascendancy of Europe, 1815–1914*, London, Longman, 1972.

power' of pre-modern states and empires, to the 'infrastrucutural power' of the modern state, we may now ask: how does the emergence of the modern 'rational' type of state with its infrastructural powers, affect the growth of nations? Can we not explain the ubiquity of nationalism as a response to, or expression of, this new type of state power?

This is very much the approach adopted by Breuilly and Tilly and his associates, when they search for the forces behind 'nation-building' in the context of Western 'state-making'. Broadly speaking, Tilly adopts a 'dualist' standpoint: there was an original, indigenous process of state-making, and nation-building, in Western Europe, and a derived, designed and externally imposed process outside. Had we asked in 1500 whether the modern state, as defined above, would have won out in the West over other political rivals like the city-state, feudal principality, theocracy or empire, we would have been thrown back on particular European contingencies for an answer. The fact that this peculiar modern form of rational and infrastructural state won out and became the norm across Europe (and later the world) was the result of several contingent factors like Western Europe's isolated geopolitical position at the time (unlike south-eastern Europe which fell within the orbit of – Ottoman – invasions); its relative cultural homogeneity (Christendom); its wealth through cities and trade; its social divisions of class (landed oligarchs versus peasants) rather than corporate kin groups (as in Africa); a decentralized political structure – and the perceived military and social superiority of the modern, centralized state, once it appeared (for example, in the Italian campaigns of the early Renaissance French kings from Charles VIII onwards).[21]

These were all factors that favoured the growth of modern states at the expense of their political rivals. But what turned a probability into a certainty was, first, the external environment, and second, the policies and will of certain elites. By the external environment, Tilly is referring to the inter-state system, both in its economic sense of a nexus of core capitalist states engaged in trade wars, and a system of absolutist states engaged in military warfare and diplomatic rivalries in Europe, especially since the Treaty of Westphalia in 1648.[22] By elites Tilly

21 C. Tilly, ed., *The Formation of National States in Western Europe*, Princeton, Princeton University Press, 1975, Introduction. Breuilly, *Nationalism and the State*, also starts from the growing separation of state and society in the sixteenth century, and posits the nationalist outlook (or 'argument') as a means of bridging the gulf and reintegrating society and state through solidarity and citizenship. This is certainly one source of nationalism's appeal (if not of its origins); but it also seems to presuppose an identity in 'society' which may be lacking or weakly felt, as polyethnic societies show, and nationalism therefore performs other functions for 'society' and 'culture' over and above the purely political realm.

22 Tilly, *The Formation of National States*, here leans on the analysis in I. Wallerstein,

means certain absolute monarchs and their chief ministers and generals, who succeeded, often in the face of determined opposition, in crushing rival centres of power within and staving off external interference, to create compact, solidary and fairly homogenous states able to take advantage of the technological revolutions that spread across the continent from the eighteenth century onwards. It was their policies and qualities of will and administrative skills that ensured the victory of the modern European state.

These same two sets of factors, the inter-state system and the policies and skills of certain elites, also shaped the state systems of the Third World. Only here, there was an extra element of design and imposition – by aliens. After each round of wars, and each treaty, more and more areas of the globe were divided up into 'compact states' by a few major European states – at the very moment when imperial greed could be sustained by a growing sense of national mission at home, and a growing acceptance of the efficacy and naturalness of the inter-state system abroad. There really did seem to be no alternative to the modern state. No other type of polity appeared to 'work' as well, in the sense of performing those reinterpreted and vastly expanded functions of state which were now, more than ever, felt to be its institutional preserve. Hence, the growth of popular conceptions of the modern state and what it was supposed to do accompanied and assisted the division of the globe into (colonial) 'replica' states.[23] Modern states could be, should be, and were, 'made'.

What about nations? After all, in Europe the presumption became one of national congruence. In the West, every state had its own nation, or so it seemed. So should not every nation have its own state? For the earliest nationalists, Herder and Rousseau, nations could get along quite well without their own states, so long as they kept fast to their cultures and lifestyles (preferably simple and agrarian, as in Corsica). But from Fichte onwards, a possessive theory of nationalism took root: to be a real nation you had to possess your own state (and, in Hegel's book, to have *had* your own state at some time).[24] But: if in Eastern Europe, the nation

---

The Modern World System, New York, Academic Press, 1974; cf. also Tivey, *The Nation-State*. On the military aspects, see M. Howard, *War in European History*, London, Oxford University Press, 1976.

23 Tilly *The Formation of National States*, conclusion; Smith, *State and Nation*; and R. Montagne, 'The "modern state" in Africa and Asia', *The Cambridge Journal*, vol. 5, 1952. On this nationalist imperialism, cf. J. Gallagher and R. Robinson, *Africa and the Victorians*, New York, St Martin's Press, 1963, and G. Lichtheim, *Imperialism*, Harmondsworth, Penguin, 1971.

24 On Rousseau, see A. Cohler, *Rousseau and Nationalism*, New York, Basic Books; on Herder, see F. Barnard, *Herder's Social and Political Thought*, Oxford, Clarendon Press,

was seeking for its own state, then what becomes of the theory that it is states that creates nations? And, more serious, what happens to those states that are unfortunate enough not to possess nations of their own? Can *they* create nations? In a world of invented states and state-making, can states that have no prior national content nevertheless fabricate nations?

This would certainly appear to be the result of the 'political action' school of state and nation formation. And it fits nicely with the recent emphasis upon the 'invented' quality of traditions and institutions – and of nations.[25] One could even combine the insights of the Gellner and Nairn traditions with those of Breuilly and Tilly's school: nationalism 'invents nations' and state elites create them. If the state elites are also nationalists, as so many of them are in today's Third World, then nationalism can be said to be creating nations by first making viable states which will form the matrix of the nations-to-be.

Patterns of Nation-Formation

At first sight, this is an attractive and convincing picture. Political mobilization and state-making, nation-building and -invention, all introduce an activist, dynamic element lacking in earlier accounts of state- and nation-formation, and appear to accord with the findings of much modern historiography of early modern Europe and the Third World.[26] In contrast, earlier accounts, most of them tinged with nationalist assumptions, appear wooden, deterministic and even mystical. The nation itself becomes a construct, and nationalism a mode of representation of history, a history that itself is being continually reinterpreted in the light of the constructs of 'nationalism'. The effect of this approach is to highlight the 'mythic' quality of the idea of the nation, and

---

1965. On early nationalism in general, see Kemilainen *Nationalism*, and S. Baron, *Modern Nationalism and Religion*, New York, Meridian Books, 1960; also H. Kohn, *Prelude to Nation-States: the French and German Experience, 1789–1815*, Princeton, Van Nostrand, 1967.

25 As the studies of national traditions in E. Hobsbawm and T. Ranger, eds, *The Invention of Tradition*, Cambridge, Cambridge University Press, 1983, demonstrate, though they also reveal that 'invention' can only take place within definite limits and requires rich materials from which to select and reinterpret.

26 Notably in Breuilly himself, but also the work of T. Ranger, 'White presence and power in Africa', *Journal of African History*, vol. 20, 1979, introduction and passim: A. Seal, *The Emergence of Indian Nationalism*, Cambridge, Cambridge University Press, 1968, and D. Beales, *The Risorgimento and the Unification of Italy*, London, Allen & Unwin, 1971, on sub-Saharan Africa, India and Italy, respectively.

the selective, distorting nature of the lens of nationalism as it seeks to reinterpret 'history' in the light of present collective needs.[27]

Unfortunately, these 'activist' and 'political' portraits of state-making and nation-building are not without problems. Two of these are particularly germane to our problem of the relationship between states and nation-building. The first is that, quite simply, there are more patterns of nation-formation than can be contained in the activist approach. The second is that a major problem, overlooked in these approaches, is the prior formation of ethnic communities which, in varying degrees, influence and condition the success of attempts to 'make states and build nations'. The two problems, of course, are not unrelated.

Let me start with the diversity of nation-forming patterns. We already saw that Gellner posited a distinction between early-industrializing integrative nationalisms based on mobility within a linguistic unit, and late-industrializing secessionist nationalisms based on 'counter-entropic traits' like colour and literate religion; i.e. those which refused to 'blur' in the assimilative pressures of industrial culture. Similarly, Tilly pointed to the historian's distinction, taken up in greater detail by Seton-Watson, between the 'old, continuous nations' of Europe and the new, designed or imposed nations of Asia and Africa.[28] In fact, we can isolate four main historical patterns or 'routes' of state-and-nation-formation:

1   *The Western*: where state and nation emerge *pari passu*, with dynastic and territorial states being built up around a definite ethnic core, to which other ethnic and regional groups and communities are successively attached by alliance, marriage, coercion and administrative intervention;

2   *The immigrant*: where small part-*ethnie* are beneficiaries of a state of their own, with or without a struggle, and they then seek to absorb and assimilate waves of new immigrants from different cultures into what becomes increasingly a territorial nation and a political community, as in America, Argentina and Australia;

3   *The ethnic*: where *ethnie* exists in varying degrees of completeness

27 On this 'lens', and for the museological concept of 're-presentation of history', see D. Horne, *The Great Museum*, London and Sydney, Pluto Press, 1984, which, despite its light-hearted emphasis on the ironies of European tourism, reveals the ideological intent of the way in which the European historical and artistic heritage is presented and understood.

28 H. Seton-Watson, *Nations and States*, London, Methuen, 1977, chapter 2; they include France, Britain, Holland, Spain, Sweden, Russia, and to some extent Poland and Hungary; cf. also Krejci and Velimsky, *Ethnic and Political Nations*. Seton-Watson would include many of the East European nations among the contrived and deliberate creations.

and self-consciousness prior to the advent of the modern, rational state and of nationalism, which then demands the 'up-grading' and transformation of these *ethnie* to fully-fledged nations replete with their own territories, economies, legal rights and education systems. This demand, in turn, gives rise to a drive for autonomy and statehood, as a means for creating the nation and giving it a protective shell;

4   *The colonial*: where a modern, rational state is imposed from above on populations which are divided into many different ethnic communities and categories, who band together to achieve independent statehood under the aegis of a state-wide nationalism, and then try to use this territorial state and its 'nationalism' to create a unified nation out of these divergent *ethnie*.

The above is not supposed to provide an exhaustive taxonomy of the historical routes to state-and-nation-formation (for one thing, it omits any reference to a whole group of, mainly Latin-American countries, where a semi-modern colonial state is imposed onto populations whom it fuses, in varying degrees, culturally and who share their culture with their rulers). Nor are its categories mutually exclusive. Given cases frequently combine elements from different patterns and routes at different periods in their historical trajectories.[29] Nevertheless, this inventory of routes does draw attention to the variety of ways in which states and nations have been created, and to the periods in which one or other mode of state-and-nation-formation was predominant.

Thus, prior to 1800, states and nations were created in tandem in limited areas of Europe and Japan, on the basis of prior dominant *ethnie*. After 1800 but before 1914, states were created, and later nations, on the basis of prior *ethnie* which sought to turn themselves into states and then nations. This was the classic era of self-determination, i.e. ethnic self-transformation, in Eastern Europe. Between 1914 and 1945, we find the apogee of national assimilation of immigrants to states which until the late nineteenth century had been based on fairly small settler communities. In this period, too, the state becomes an instrument for integration and social change on a large scale, rather than simply the patrimonial preserve of a ruling settler oligarchy. Finally, after 1945, the imposed alien state evokes an elite nationalism based on artificially constructed boundaries and territories. At the same time, it rouses a conflicting mass

29 Thus Poland and Hungary had elements of the 'Western' and 'ethnic' trajectories at different stages of their histories, as did Japan; Burma combined the colonial with an ethnic trajectory; South Africa also went through ethnic, colonial and immigrant phases, but now practises an ethnic policy within a racial colonialism (H. Adam, *Modernizing Racial Domination*, Berkeley and Los Angeles, University of California Press, 1971; W. de Clerk, *The Puritans in Africa*, Harmondsworth, Penguin, 1975).

ethnic nationalism, which may demand separation from the post-colonial state. Here the chances of conflict over basic loyalties and identities is greatest, with minority and peripheral *ethnie* competing with each other or with dominant and strategic core communities and their ethnically-inspired state elites, the concept of the 'state-nation' being in sharp opposition to that of the 'ethnic nation'.[30]

Ethnic Cores and Ethnic Pasts

The fact that there are more patterns and routes of state-and-nation-formation than previous accounts admit suggests in itself a need to amend the 'activist' approach, to give more prominence to the *order* or sequence of processes involved, and not just the static cleavages or the manipulative abilities of elites to influence events and create institutions. Nevertheless, these amendments could probably be incorporated without sacrifice of the particular dynamic or 'constructive' qualities of the activist approach.

The second problem, however, poses a more serious challenge to the 'reconstructive' approach. In all four patterns briefly outlined above, ethnicity not only played a vital part, but provided the point of departure for the first three of the four routes, and the opposition motif in the last. What I want to argue is that the central difficulties of both state-making and nation-building stem from the nature and intensity of ethnic ties and sentiments, and that lack of ethnic foundations and resilience can unmake states and dismantle nations as much as any inept elite activities or geopolitical calculations. While many processes and activities go into the 'making' of states and the 'building' of nations (both of which are ideological metaphors about large-scale abstractions and constructs) – economic development, communications, urbanization, linguistic standardization, administration – there are equally important questions of

30 There is, of course, much overlap between these four trajectories and periods; but it is interesting that in each case the state, and at least a regional inter-state system, is in place before the advent of the nation, though not of the *ethnie*. This is because nations, in the sense of territorial, legally and economically unified, and educationally homogenized, historic culture communities, even if they do not require states of their own, can most easily be created through state agencies and operations, once they have a core historic culture, i.e. an ethnic core. So that, for our purposes, the 'nation' becomes a territorialized, politicized, homogenized and economically unified *ethnie*, even if much of the 'historic culture' of that *ethnie* is 'reinvented' for present-day needs. Clearly, the 'nation' is a much more complex and abstract 'ideal-type' unit than any *ethnie*; that is why there are so many forms of nationalism, expressing the varying visions of 'the nation' entertained by nationalists at different times and in different milieux. For further elaborations, see Anderson, *Imagined Communities*, and A. D. Smith, *Nationalism*, A Trend Report and Annotated Bibliography, *Current Sociology*, 21, The Hague, Mouton, 1973, and idem, *Nationalism in the Twentieth Century*, Oxford, Martin Robertson, 1979, chapters 1 and 2.

meaning, identification and loyalty which 'make sense' of, and 'give purpose' to, otherwise unpatterned processes. The aspirations for identity, unity and autonomy that form the main ideological dimensions of nationalism undoubtedly confer that 'meaning' and 'purpose' on a gamut of modern processes engulfing individuals. But they do so only in virtue of prior meanings and purposes predicated of earlier communities of power and culture, i.e. territorial states and popular or aristocratic ethnic communities. All these communities are seen as having a past and a future, a history and a destiny, which is independent of individual aspirations, and yet subsumes their needs and desires. States can be said to have a 'history' and a 'destiny' only where the apparatus of state is associated with a particular dynastic line and set of fortunes; and its resonance will be greater if those fortunes and that pedigree can attract a larger following within a particular ethnic community, i.e. where the state becomes associated with a core *ethnie* which it protects and nurtures. Otherwise, it is the aristocratic and demotic *ethnie* whose past and future fortunes attract sympathy and solidarity and which are felt to possess a history and a destiny peculiarly their own. Because they have had a particular past, they form an identifiable unity, and hence can be conceived as having a destiny. Conversely, those without particular pasts can have no peculiar destinies, and therefore cannot become 'nations'. The history-less are destiny-less, and this becomes the central dilemma of state-making and nation-building today.[31]

If the last sentences paraphrase Hegel's 'theory of history-less peoples', then that is not only because Hegel at this point echoes the common nationalist position, but also because he has identified a crucial precondition of state-and-nation-formation in Europe and elsewhere.[32] Without subscribing to the notorious use made of his views by Marx and Engels, we may say that, if political leaders wish to create states and form nations under the appropriate social and technological conditions, they can only do so if the ethnic conditions are similarly favourable; and the more appropriate those ethnic conditions, the more likely are they to succeed in creating both states and nations. Conversely, the absence of such conditions creates a serious barrier to state-and-nation-formation.

31 For a study of premodern *ethnie* and their relationship to modern nations, see A. D. Smith, *The Ethnic Roots of Nations*, Oxford, Basil Blackwell, 1986, in which these types of *ethnie* and ethnic polities are explored; that such ethnic polities existed in Egypt, Japan and Judea cannot be doubted, although their unity and strength is far more debatable; cf. also Mann *The Sources of Social Power*, vol. I.

32 On this theory, see R. Rosdolsky, 'Friedrich Engels and das Problem der "Geschichtsloser Völker"', *Archiv für Sozialgeschichte*, vol. 4, 1964, Hanover, and I. Cummins, *Marx, Engels and National Movements*, London, Croom Helm, 1980. Nairn makes use of it in amended form to explain differences between Scottish and Welsh nationalisms, cf. Nairn *The Break-up of Britain*, chapter 5.

Not only does it remove the basis of cohesion necessary for political unities, it also creates rival bases for alternative unities and the chances of breakdowns of ethnically divided polities.[33]

Applying this argument first to early modern Europe, we must start from a set of factors that Tilly omits when he blandly asserts that Europe in 1500 was culturally homogenous. This might have been truer in the thirteenth century, but by 1500 dynastic states had begun to form around ethnic cores in England, France and Spain, to be followed shortly by Holland and Sweden. Even before, there had been ethnic polities in Hungary, Poland and Orthodox Russia, not to mention the ethnic diversities of Ireland, Wales and Scotland, of Brittany, Catalonia and Switzerland, at least some of which had political repercussions. Indeed, it is difficult to know whether the cultural differences between these ethnic regions was more or less marked in medieval than in early modern Europe. There were wide differences in ethnic cultures, despite the unifying bond of Catholicism, throughout the medieval era, and this 'ethnic mosaic' provided an important base for the subsequent consolidation of national states, first in western Europe, and later in central and eastern Europe.[34].

England provides one of the earliest and clearest examples of the indispensability of an ethnic core in state-formation. By ethnicity we mean here the sense of common historic culture and lifestyle. Thus an ethnic community becomes a named human population sharing common myths of descent, shared historical memories, a common culture, an association with a recognized territory, and a sense of solidarity.[35] On this definition, an English ethnic community which has

33 Ethnic unity does not, of course, guarantee the survival of strong states, as the Japanese case illustrates. But it does allow, perhaps encourage, their formation; in Japan, there were long periods of imperial, and Shogunal, rule, the periods of real breakdown and *daimyo* feudalism being fairly limited (the late Heian empire, in the late twelfth century; the end of the Kamakura Shogunate in 1334; the fifteenth and early to mid-sixteenth centuries, from the Onin War of the 1470s to Hideyoshi; see A. Lewis, *Knights and Samurai*, London, Temple Smith, 1974. Near-ethnic unity (Ainu tribesmen apart) clearly facilitated the various Shogunates, including the centralized Tokugawa feudal state.

34 On this 'mosaic', see H. Koht, 'The dawn of nationalism in Europe', *American Historical Review*, vol. 52, 1947; L. Tipton, ed., *Nationalism in the Middle Ages*, New York, Holt, Rinehart & Winston, 1972; and S. Reynolds, 'Medieval *origines Gentium* and the community of the realm', *History*, vol. 68, 1983, who argues that even early medieval Europe was divided into ethnic *regna* on the basis of common customs and myths of descent beneath the veneer of a Latinate Catholicism, even if the 'natures' of later universities did not carry the modern nationalist connotations we might expect; cf. G. Coulton, 'Nationalism in the Middle Ages', *Cambridge Historical Journal*, vol. 5, 1935.

35 For fuller discussions, see R. Schermerhorn, *Comparative Ethnic Relations*, New York, Random House, 1970; E. Burgess, 'The resurgence of ethnicity', *Ethnic and Racial*

emerged embryonically in Anglo-Saxon times and was enlarged by successive Danish and Norman cultural and social elements became stabilized and crystallized in the late fourteenth century, under the impact of external wars with Scotland and France and the growth of legal and linguistic unification.[36] By the late fifteenth century a myth of British history, first formulated by Geoffrey of Monmouth in the twelfth century, had taken root and became the basis for the dynastic and territorial claims of the Tudor state. The myth of Britain as the legacy of Brutus of Troy and his three sons, Locrinus (England), Kamber (Wales) and Albanactus (Scotland), soon provided a basis for claiming seniority and hegemony by England over Wales and Scotland; by the sixteenth century, the issue had provoked a series of polemical histories supporting or attacking Tudor claims to overlordship on the basis of an English priority over Welsh and Scots.[37] Conversely, Scottish attempts to refute the Brutus myth and the legend of King Arthur's domain were vital to preserve the independence of the Scottish crown. In both cases, the recovery of 'history', i.e. the use of selective memory and myth-making, helped to crystallize and reinforce nascent sentiments of ethnic community, and to prepare the ground for the use of state-making to create two nations under a single crown. As a result, union with Scotland was feasible, not merely for the bargains of interest which were struck to accommodate the Scottish bourgeoisie, but also because by 1707 the Scots and English were sufficiently confident of their sense of individual national identity to bring their fortunes together. In this, the Scots were in quite a different position from the Welsh or the Irish. For the latter, the recovery of a national identity was long postponed by the lack of a separate political framework within which ethnic sentiments could be articulated and expressed. On the contrary, forceful conquest

---

Studies, vol. 1, 1978; and Smith, *State and Nation*, chapter 4. Some of the theoretical and definitional controversies over 'ethnicity' are discussed in D. Taylor and M. Yapp, eds, *Political Identity in South Asia*, SOAS, London, Curzon Press, 1979, and A. D. Smith, 'Ethnic myths and ethnic revivals', *European Journal of Sociology*, vol. 25, 1984, and idem 'National identity and myths of ethnic descent', *Research in Social Movements, Conflict and Change*, vol. 7, Greenwich, Conn., JAI Press, 1984.

36 For a short account which dates an English nation to the period of Chaucer, employing a basically linguistic criterion, see Seton-Watson, *Nations and States*, chapter 2; cf. also J. Harvey, *The Plantagenets*, London, Fontana, 1967.

37 For details, see R. Mason, 'Scotching the Brut: the early history of Britain', *History Today*, vol. 35, 1985; the 'Brut' tradition of Geoffrey was purveyed by Caxton, Grafton, Holinshed, Parker and Foxe, not to mention Henry VIII's use of it in 1542 to assert his rights to sovereignty over Scotland; it was rejected and refuted by Scots historians from the opening paragraph of the Declaration of Arbroath (1320) to the *Scotichronicon* (1387) of Fordun and Boece's *Scotorum Historiae* of 1527; cf. H. Kohn, 'The origins of English nationalism', *Journal of the History of Ideas*, vol. 1, 1940.

had been followed by institutional dissolution and the loss of elites; memories were preserved mainly by itinerant bards or clergy among the peasantry in the more isolated and backward areas. So when the moment of ethnic revival came, it was under the impetus of nationalist ideas and an ideology inspired 'returning intelligentsia', and not of institutional elites based on former state agencies, like the judicial and educational systems. In this respect, the state-aspiring nationalisms of late nineteenth-century Ireland and Wales (the latter, more muted) resemble those of Eastern Europe; among Croats, Slovaks and Romanians, selective memories of ethnic polities persisted, but it needed a 'returning intelligentsia' to rework them into a mythology of nationality and a basis for acquiring statehood.[38]

In the French case, ethnicity also provided the foundation for effective statehood. The *regnum Francorum* gradually changed into a *Regnum Francie* under the later Capetians, at least in the northern and central feudal principalities, a process facilitated not only by the common Catholic heritage expressed in royal coronations and the early Frankish alliance with the papacy, but by the sense of Merovingian and Carolingian political unity. But this sense of earlier political unity was mainly articulated in the north; in Brittany, the Basque country, Languedoc and Provence, as well as Lorraine, quite different ethnic ties and sentiments prevailed up to and beyond the time of Henri IV. In many ways, the *regnum Francie* was imposed by military and administrative power onto the south, west and eastern principalities, where language and culture were quite different from the more puritanical, Frankish north.[39]

In other words, the French-speaking dynastic polity proved to be the instrument of modern state-making and nation-building. In their struggles with other feudal principalities and the unruly nobility, the French kings based on the Île de France were compelled to find ways of cultural integration in order to secure their administrative hold. Hence, Francis I, by the Edict of Villers-Cotterets in 1539, made French the sole official language, cutting such languages as Occitanian and Breton off from any institutional base. Similarly with religious uniformity;

---

38 For the Welsh and Irish cases, apart from Nairn and Hechter, see F. Lyons, *Culture and Anarchy in Ireland, 1890–1939*, London, Oxford University Press, 1979, and K. Morgan, 'Welsh nationalism: the historical background', *Journal of Contemporary History*, vol.6, 1971; on the bards and festivals in Wales, see P. Morgan, 'From death to a view: the hunt for the Welsh past in the Romantic period', in Hobsbawm and Ranger, *The Invention of Tradition*, which sets the Welsh revival in its romantic European context.

39 On the coronation ceremonies of the Carolingians and Capetians, see J. Armstrong, *Nations before Nationalism*, Chapel Hill, University of North Carolina Press, 1982; and for the growth of the Capetian domain, see Lewis, *Knights and Samurai*.

Louis XIV, by the Edict of Nantes in 1685, rescinded the statute of religious toleration shown to the Huguenots; while a century later, his Jacobin heirs proved to be equally intolerant of any regionalism or cultural federalism, suppressed the revolt of the Vendée in the west and promoted linguistic uniformity as a means of national, i.e. state-based consolidation. Such a policy would, however, have been doomed if, among the conditions producing a strong, centralized state, there had not been a high degree of ethnic cohesion in the north and centre of the polity, a cohesion that, in turn, was inspired by myths of Gallo–Roman and/or Frankish political origins and statehood.[40]

A similar interplay of state-making and nation-building can be discerned in some of the Mediterranean states. In Spain, memories of Roman and Visigoth unities over 'Iberia' were important factors in the goals of the Reconquista, and came to the fore in the late fifteenth-century trends towards state unification and religious purification. Both Reconquista and unification would have been impossible without either these general, if shadowy, political memories, and the stronger ethnic unities of Castile, Aragon and Catalonia. Of course, here the unification was less centralized, being founded on a union of two equal kingdoms, and faced with strong competing *ethnie* in the Basque country and Catalonia and in Portugal, which managed to secede. It was really only in the course of the sixteenth century with its quest for ethno-religious unity against Moors and Jews, and its new-found great power status, that a sense of Spanish ethnicity, harking back to earlier memories, emerged in the north and centre of the state; and only a prolonged contest with France under Napoleon was able to cement that sense of common ethnicity, albeit without submerging competing identities in Catalonia and Euzkadi.[41]

40 On Jacobin linguistic homogenization, see J. Y. Lartichaux, 'Linguistic politics during the French Revolution', *Diogenes*, vol. 97, 1977 and H. Kohn, *Prelude to Nation-States*. On the suppression of Breton aspirations, S. Berger, 'Bretons and Jacobins: reflections on French regional ethnicity', in Esman, *Ethnic Conflict in the Western World*. On political myths in late eighteenth-century France, see J. Barzun, *The French race: Theories of its Origins and their Social and Political Implications Prior to the Revolution*, New York, Columbia University Studies, 1932, and R. Herbert, *David, Voltaire, Brutus and the French Revolution*, London, Allen Lane, 1972; the conflict of mythologies which emerged fully during the period of the Revolution, mirrored the social cleavage and was given an ethnic interpretation. Again, a divided ethnic heritage weakens, at least temporarily, the fabric of the state; it was really only during the Third Republic that a strong state, and homogenizing education and military system, was able to integrate the various regions of France, see E. Weber, *Peasants into Frenchmen*, London, Chatto & Windus, 1979.

41 Seton-Watson, *Nations and States*, chapter 2, and W. Atkinson, *A History of Spain and Portugal*, Harmondsworth, Penguin, 1960; on Basque and Catalan ethnic nationalisms, cf. S. Payne, 'Catalan and Basque nationalism', *Journal of Contemporary History*, vol. 6, 1971.

In Greece, on the other hand, there were no competing *ethnie* to undermine a sense of Greek ethnicity. Yet the hiatus with classical antiquity engendered by the long-drawn out Slavic immigrations, and the equally long subjugation and fragmentation under the Ottomans, attenuated a lively sense of common ethnicity and ruled out the Western pattern of a state-making matrix of the nation. On the other hand, within the Greek *millet* trading and clerical elites had survived and prospered; the Phanariots had even succeeded in dominating much of the Ottoman administration, while the Patriarchate at Constantinople and the Orthodox Church in Greece and the Greek-speaking areas of Anatolia had kept alive some sense of religo–ethnic separation and of the great Byzantine past, at least in the towns.[42] It was from the more radical, less privileged sections of these elites and from the westernized, diaspora 'returning intelligentisa' that a nation-building ideology arose, which aimed at the capture of state power, at least in a part of the Greek-speaking, Orthodox world, which could serve as a base from which to 'rescue' a fallen Hellas and its downtrodden Hellenic peasantry and revive the former eras of glory. Of course, the recovery of at least one of these pasts, the classical, was greatly enhanced by Western classical scholarship, and by the sentimental philhellenism that swept Western Europe; less obvious, but perhaps more potent for most Greeks, was the selective memory carried by the clergy of the Byzantine past, from which both Phanariots and upper clergy traced an often tenuous biological descent and which they opposed to the cultural myth of Hellenic descent fostered by a secular, westernized intelligentsia.[43] As a result, Greek history in the nineteenth and early twentieth centuries was dominated by the conflict between two ideals of national identity and alternative myths of Greek origins and descent, each located in certain social classes and educational strata, and each seeking to capture and then use state power to promote Hellenism or Byzantinism at home and abroad. In law, education, commerce, agriculture and especially foreign policy, the consequences of this conflict of vision of Greek history were evident, and they contributed to the relative weakness of the Greek state and the erratic nature of Greek social development. A divided inner

---

42 L. Stavrianos, *The Balkans since 1453*, New York, Holt, 1961, and J. Campbell and P. Sherrard, *Modern Greece*, London, Benn, 1968. On the Byzantine past, see N. Baynes and H. Moss, eds, *Byzantium*, London, Oxford University Press, 1970, and Armstrong, *Nations before Nationalism*.

43 On this conflict of histories, see C. Frazee, *The Orthodox Church and Independent Greece, 1821–52*, Cambridge, Cambridge University Press, 1969, and Campbell and Sherrard, *Modern Greece*. On the Phanariot claims, see C. Mango, 'The Phanariots and Byzantine tradition', in R. Clogg, ed., *The Struggle for Greek Independence*, London, Macmillan, 1973.

sense of ethnicity was one factor that impeded the solidarity necessary for state-making and hence for nation-building; instead, these alternative ethnic interpretations reinforced the class conflicts in modern Greek society.[44]

In modern Israel, too, state-making is impeded by an enveloping but divided sense of common ethnicity. Again, there is a rich set of communal pasts from which to choose for models of a national utopia; but not so many of these have relevance to state power, since Jewry has been divorced from the exercise of power and state-making for the last 2,000 years.[45] Again, selective memories aligned to social class and educational stratum can fashion alternative regenerative visions for nation-building; a traditional, rabbinic prescription can draw sustenance from a genealogical myth of origins and descent traced from the priestly families of ancient Israel through the diaspora sages and scholars to the latter-day Eastern European Orthodox rabbis and their followers, while a secular, modernist myth looks across the two millennia of Jewish exile to the ancient commonwealth of peasants and herdsmen of Israel and Judah under the house of David.[46] But the division between Orthodox and secular images is not the only rent in the fabric of Israeli–Jewish ethnicity; there is also the parallel conflict between Ashkenazi and Sephardi Jewry, and the gulf between their respective outlooks and aspirations, which has resulted in periodic outbursts against the early *vatikim* from Eastern Europe.[47] In the case of

44 For the contribution of the intelligentsia to a Hellenic vision see C. Koumarianou, 'The contribution of the Greek intelligentsia towards the Greek independence movement, 1798–1821', in Clogg, *Greek Independence*, and R. Demos, 'The Neo-Hellenic Enlightenment, 1750–1820', *Journal of the History of Ideas*, vol. 19, 1958. On the effects of rival visions of the Greek past, see D. Dakin, *The Unification of Greece, 1770–1923*, London, Benn, 1972, and A. Pepelassis, 'The image of the past and economic backwardness', *Human Organization*, vol. 17, 1958; for other reasons for a weakened Greek state emanating from the underdevelopment of a semi-peripheral economy, see N. Mouzelis, *Modern Greece: Facets of Underdevelopment*, London, Macmillan, 1978.

45 On some factors holding diaspora Jewry together, despite the lack of territory and statehood, see Armstrong, *Nations before Nationalism*, chapter 7, and Ben Zion Dinur, *Israel and the Diaspora*, Philadelphia, Jewish Publication Society of America, 1969; also S. Baron, *Modern Nationalism and Religion*, New York, Meridian Books, 1960, chapter 7.

46 On these visions, see A Hertzberg, *The Zionist Idea, A Reader*, New York, Meridian Books, 1960, introduction; for the tensions generated on individual Jews in early nineteenth-century Germany, see M. Meyer, *The Origins of the Modern Jew: Jewish Identity and European Culture in Germany, 1749–1821*, Detroit, Wayne State University Press, 1967, and J. Katz, 'Jewry and Judaism in the nineteenth century', *Journal of World History*, vol. 4, 1958. A broader picture can be found in H. Sachar, *The Course of Modern Jewish History*, New York, Delta Books, Dell Publishing Co., 1958.

47 For a vivid portrait of these outbursts, see A. Oz, *In the Land of Israel*, London, Chatto & Windus, 1983; and the essays by Diskin and Peres and Shemer in D. Caspi, A. Diskin and E. Gutmann, eds, *The Roots of Begin's Success*, London, Croom Helm, 1984.

the Ethiopian Jews, the 'Falashas', intra-ethnic and religious divisions cross cut each other to some extent, and state authorities had to await religious approval over the vital question of who counts as an ethnic member, and hence a citizen of Israel. This is just one of many examples where, despite considerable bureaucratic centralization, ethno-religious factors, instead of providing a simple, ready-made Jewish base on which to form a strong state on the 'rational' Western model, as in the West itself, have by their internal fissures and ambiguities helped to weaken and impede centralizing drives towards state expansion and authority. There are, of course, several other impediments to state authority and jurisdiction, including the various legal legacies, the extreme version of proportional representation that produces an equally extreme multi-party system, and the influence of diaspora Jewish communities, especially in the United States. There are also factors that work towards greater state authority like the size of the country, the role of the army and education system, heavy urban concentrations and industrialization, and above all, the security problem and the general Arab–Israel confrontation. But, paradoxically, successive wars, though they may strengthen the military, have not enhanced state power in the same measure; and this may be attributed, in part, to ethno-religious divisions *within* a common *ethnie*, which as in the Greek case, find expression in party political conflicts.[48]

In this category, too, we should place a state that is often held up as a model of polyethnic society, Switzerland. In fact, the Swiss case tells us little about modern polyethnic states, since the ethnic core of the Swiss Confederation was for many centuries confined to a single Alemannic category. Moreover, Switzerland was built up in successive stages around the original three forest cantons of Uri, Schwyz and Unterwalden; it then attracted the richer city-states of the plains, Lucerne, Bern and Zurich, all German-speaking and Catholic at the time, before encountering in the sixteenth century its first linguistic test in Fribourg, and its first religious schisms in Zurich and Bern.[49] Moreover, the

---

For a more general picture of early Zionist aspirations and their later consequences, cf. A. Elon, *Israelis, Founders and Sons*, London, Weidenfeld & Nicolson, 1972.

48 For an analysis of some of these divisions and factors, see D. Segre, *A Crisis of Identity: Israel and Zionism*, London, Oxford University Press, 1980, as well as E. Gutmann, 'Religion and its role in national integration in Israel', *Middle East Review*, vol. 2, 1979, and the major comprehensive study of S. Smooha, *Pluralism and Conflict in Israel*, London, Routledge & Kegan Paul, 1978.

49 For a general history, see G. Thürer, *Free and Swiss*, London, Oswald Wolff, 1970; for the linguistic issue, see T. Warburton, 'Nationalism and language in Switzerland and Canada', in Smith, *Nationalist Movements*, and H. Kohn, *Nationalism and Liberty, the Swiss Example*, New York, Macmillan, 1957.

relative weakness of the Swiss state was both structural and deliberately contrived; it arose out of the original ideological impetus against the Habsburg governors and their centralizing interference, and out of the valley-canton system of self-rule, which has been jealously guarded ever since.[50] If more recently some measure of state centralization has seemed unavoidable, this is for economic and security reasons that emerge out of an already well-formed sense of common Swiss ethnic identity, which has integrated the various linguistic and religio-ethnic identities in different cantons and areas, even in the Jura. In fact, the Swiss have been enabled by the very length of their history, and the military successes of the Confederation, to establish and then take largely for granted a sense of common ethnicity in the face of external cultural and political threats; and this has allowed them to separate political representation in the cantons and central government from ethnicity and ethnic differences, which surfaced from time to time (Fribourg, Romansch, the Jura).[51]

State-Making in Polyethnic Societies

It is just this failure to separate ethnicity from politics that so bedevils the future of polyethnic states in Africa and Asia. Here, the common pattern was one of colonial conquest in which the alien power tended to categorize and classify the indigenous population in ethnic terms, and to incorporate different *ethnie* unequally into a divisive system of colonial power. Having first juxtaposed, and even divided, various *ethnie* within often artifically bounded colonies, the imperial powers then sought to rank members of different *ethnie*, not merely in terms of individual attainments or class position, but even more of ethnic origin. Indeed, whole communities were assigned to functional positions in the colonial hierarchy, as the concept of 'martial races' demonstrates.[52] As a result, from the outset indigenous territorial elites found it difficult to overcome their own and others' sense of ethnic identity, to forge a common

50 Analysed perceptively in J. Steinberg, *Why Switzerland?*, Cambridge, Cambridge University Press, 1976.

51 For A. Siegfried, *Switzerland*, London, Cape, 1950, it is the cross-cutting ties of region, religion and language that hold Switzerland together and prevent any one cleavage assuming too high a profile; but cf. the recent troubles in the Jura analysed by W. Petersen, 'On the subnations of Western Europe', in N. Glazer and D. Moynihan, eds, *Ethnicity: Theory and Experience*, Cambridge, Harvard University Press, 1975.

52 For this concept, see C. Enloe, *Ethnic Soldiers*, Harmondsworth, Penguin, 1980. For ethnic classifications by colonial powers in Africa, see C. Young, 'Ethnicity and the colonial and post-colonial state in Africa', in P. Brass, ed., *Ethnic Groups and the State*, London, Croom Helm, 1985.

front based on a territorial nationalism against the common colonial enemy. For a time, *ethnie* managed to put aside their rivalries to concentrate on the task of ridding the territory of alien whites and alien rule; but even during the process of opening up and capturing the apparatus of state, rivalries between aspirant members of different *ethnie* intensified and soon exploded in communal violence or military *coups*.

Given this general history, it is apparent that the task of both state-making and nation-building is likely to be far more difficult and complex than in Europe. For one thing, many European states had been in place before the advent of nationalism extolled the virtues of national congruence and coextensiveness. For another, the European states did not enter the economic race as late-comers, often endowed with poor natural resources and a low level of technical skills. Given the developmental nature of contemporary nation-building ideologies, i.e. a dual goal of creating nations and of ensuring self-sufficient growth, which are so heavily intertwined, any failure in performance for one goal is bound to diminish the chances in the other. There is, moreover, a commitment to a state-based and state-made nation. This means that not only will the often artificial colonial boundaries be rigidly retained, but only a nation created within and by the agencies of the state counts as a genuine nation, a conception that is the counterpart of state-based development strategies.[53]

In the light of these aspirations and constraints, the problems of polyethnic societies become even more intractable. Here we need to distinguish between those new states that have an ethnic core, and those that lack any. In the first category come some South-East Asian states and perhaps India; in the second, most African and some Middle Eastern states, apart from Egypt and Somalia.

The polyethnic or 'plural' states of South-East Asia – Burma, Indonesia, Malaysia – have a core *ethnie*, and thus resemble the Western European situation in the late medieval era. However, the time-scale and socio-technological situation is quite different. Incorporating Welsh, Bretons and Catalans was a long-drawn-out process, and the lack of communications, education and popular expectations, not to mention the much lower level of state power and intervention, made determined ethnic resistance much less likely.[54] In the later

53 On this conception in Africa, see B. Neuberger, 'State and nation in African thought', *Journal of African Studies*, vol. 4, 1977; for an early theoretical statement of the case for territorial nationalism, see C. Geertz, 'The integrative revolution', in C. Geertz, ed., *Old Societies and New States*, New York, Free Press,1963, and K. Silvert, ed., *Expectant Peoples: Nationalism and Development*, New York, Random House, 1963.
54 Though, in fact, Catalans and Bretons both revolted, the Catalans most seriously in 1640–52, see Atkinson *History of Spain and Portugal*, chapter 10.

twentieth century, however, the time scale has contracted and mass communications, transport, education and state intervention have all combined to create a much higher level of popular expectations, fed by the nationalism of competing elites. In such cases, Malay or Burmese national state-making and state attempts to create a Malay or Burman nation, are likely to encounter determined resistance from *ethnie* for whom the time-span of colonialism and post-colonialism has been insufficient to promote supra-ethnic integration. The absence of common wars against outsiders may also prevent movement towards a state-based national integration and hence a territorial nation. In those cases, such as Vietnam, where such wars have had to be fought, ethnic differences within the state have been more easily submerged.[55]

Perhaps the most complex example of the dominant-*ethnie* pattern of state-making and nation-building is provided by India. Divided into 16 regions and language groups, and with innumerable 'tribes' and *jati*, as well as different religious communities, India has tended to rest its unity upon the dominant Hindu and Hindi-speaking regions of northern and central India. In the important religio-ethnic divisions, Hinduism has proved a potent, if unstable, unifying bond, despite communal violence between Muslims, Hindus and Sikhs. But it has also proved tolerant of cleavages along linguistic and regional lines, like those between Marathis and Gujeratis, or Assamese and Bengalis. Nevertheless, Indian nationalism from Tilak and Aurobindo onwards, has drawn heavily on Hindu conceptions of Indian history which, though they contain few models of political unity apart from the northern Guptas, have assigned to the conquering Arya and their Vedic and Brahminic religion a unifying social and cultural role, which allows modern state-makers to operate and build the Indian nation out of its otherwise disparate parts.[56] Classical Hindu political models lend themselves to a federal conception which in turn allows a measure of ethnic

55 On the 'plural' societies of South-East Asia, see J. Furnivall, *Colonial Policy and Practice*, Cambridge, Cambridge University Press, 1948, for a classic statement, and F. von der Mehden, *Religion and Nationalism in Southeast Asia*, Madison, University of Wisconsin Press, 1963; on Burmese problems, J. Cadey, *A History of Modern Burma*, Ithaca, Cornell University Press, 1958, and for Malaysia, see W. Roff, *The Origins of Malay Nationalism*, New Haven, Yale University Press, 1967. On the links between warfare and ethnic consciousness generally, see Enloe, *Ethnic Soldiers*, and A. D. Smith, 'War and ethnicity', *Ethnic and Racial Studies*, vol. 4, 1981.

56 On Hindu influences in Indian nationalism, see R. Sakai, ed., *Studies on Asia*, Lincoln, University of Nebraska Press, 1961, and C. Heimsath, *Indian Nationalism and Hindu Social Reform*, Princeton, Princeton University Press, 1964; for the influence of Brahmin ideology and caste practise going back to post-Vedic northern India, see L. Dumont, *Homo Hierarchicus*, London, Weidenfeld & Nicolson, 1970, and R. Thapar, *A History of India*, vol. I, Harmondsworth, Penguin, 1966.

flexibility, suited to a country of so many *ethnie* subdividing the Hindu would-be nation. At the same time, both the centrifugal pressures and the British imperial legacy of unified administration operate, in opposite ways, to counteract the federalism of the constitution. It is significant that the Indian concept of their state is secular, and that Congress seeks to accommodate and represent every religious and regional group. And though more often caste, regional and religious cleavages and constituencies make themselves manifest in party factions, there remains a latent strain towards a strengthening of the centralized, bureaucratic state under effective prime ministers and cabinets.[57]

In India, unity is created and preserved, not through the Western route of 'state creating nation', nor through the East European process of '*ethnie* creating state which in turn moulds the nation'. Instead, a colonial trajectory operated in which a modern, bureaucratic state imposed from outside on diverse ethnic communities, has been captured by the elites in the northern and central Hindi-speaking and Hindu *ethnie*, who then seek to weld these communities together into a territorial nation by means of an overarching ethnic Hindu mythology and a series of interlocking institutions and cross-cutting allegiances. What makes the operation more feasible is not just the memory and legacy of British rule and an all-India civil service and communications, but the sentiments and ties of solidarity created by this selective Hindu mythology and a relative cultural homogeneity of the Hindi population in some northern and central provinces whose historical fate has been a shared experience for some centuries. Without these common bonds of ethnicity in a core area, 'India' would undoubtedly be a more precarious entity, and its creation even more doubtful. The tradition of strong states resting upon religio-ethnic cores in these northern and central areas contributes an important element to Indian state unity and to the chances of forging an all-India territorial nation.[58]

Several African states lack this ethnic core and religious tradition. True, some like Zimbabwe and Uganda, have (or have had) strong ethnic cores or ethnic polities. In both these cases, their dominance has been contested. In the Ugandan case, it was the British authorities who

57 On the cross-cutting alignments and the use of caste and region as party vote-catching constituencies, see S. Harrison, *India, the Most Dangerous Decades*, Princeton, Princeton University Press, 1960, and L. and S. Rudolph, *The Modernity of Tradition*, Chicago, Chicago University Press, 1967; see also Seal, *Emergence of Indian Nationalism*, for early Congress nationalism, and Sathyamurthy, *Nationalism in the Contemporary World*, for contemporary Indian political alignments.

58 On the effects of British rule, see A. R. Desai, *The Social Background of Indian Nationalism*, Bombay, Bombay Publishing Co., 1954; and of the Hindu mythology, see B. McCulley, *English Education and the Origins of Indian Nationalism*, Gloucester, Mass., Smith, 1966.

demoted the Bagandan kingdom and favoured other *ethnie* and their polities, especially the northern, Nilotic and Muslim communties and tribes. One cause of the subsequent political instability of the post-colonial state may lie here: in the consequent absence of an ethnic core, each ethnic community or group of communities vying for the dominant and strategic position the Baganda were compelled to vacate.[59] In Zimbabwe, British 'divide-and-rule' policies together with settler rule promoted cleavage between the Shona- and Ndebele-speakers, and parallel and rival nationalisms from early on, whose conflict is still unresolved. In both cases, the rise of the territorial state has served to intensify ethnic struggles for control over state policies and personnel; but, because ethnic nationalism was already so advanced and intense, further moves to consolidate and centralize the territorial state have been impeded and resisted, bringing guerrilla terror or a spate of military coups in their train. In neither case, has it yet been possible to begin the process of unitary 'nation-building', the justification and goal of independent statehood and the struggle for political control.[60]

Even greater difficulties attend the attempts of post-colonial states which lack a single ethnic core to 'make strong states' and 'build viable nations'. In 1960 'Nigeria' was a territorial expression for a system of federal, parliamentary rule devised by the British for a series of contiguous geographical areas and ethnic populations, who had never before lived in a unitary polity or shared a single religious or secular culture. Not only was there no pre-existing core *ethnie* or state; there were a large number of alternative cultures and histories from which models for 'nation-building' might be selected. Even the three largest *ethnie* only accounted for just over 60 per cent of the total population, leaving some fairly large and self-conscious *ethnie* (Efiks, Tiv, Ibibio, etc.) trapped in an impotent, minority status within the three main regions, and without any hope of their histories and cultures contributing to the creation of the new 'Nigerian' nation. The subsequent military coups, the Biafran war of secession and administrative redivisions have done little to improve their lot (the larger *ethnie* simply 'amass adminis-

59 A. Mazrui, 'Ethnic stratification and the military-agrarian complex: the Uganda case', in Glazer and Moynihan, eds, *Ethnicity*, and Young, 'Ethnicity and the colonial and post-colonial state'; a Marxist analysis of Aminism is presented in J. Saul, *The State and Revolution in East Africa*, London, Heinemann, 1979, but it neglects the ethnic issue.

60 There are, of course, other ethnic minorities in Zimbabwe, including Sotho, Karanga, Venda, Ndau, Xhosa and more, on which see P. Ucko, 'The politics of the indigenous minority', *Journal of Biosocial Science, Supplement* 8, 1983; but most of them are small and politically unimportant by comparison, and even so, government officials are chary of allowing too much cultural self-expression by such minorities, or of recognizing the Bushmen origin of many rock paintings and artifacts (very few Bushmen remain in Zimbabwe itself).

trative states' in order to secure a larger share of federal benefits for themselves), or to solve the problem of an absent ethnic core on which to base a concept of 'Nigerianness'.[61] At least in India or Burma, a significant and strategic proportion of the population belongs to an ancient ethnic culture with its own political traditions, and is able either to dominate or to envelop other *ethnie* within its cultural orbit. At least in Zimbabwe, and to a much lesser extent in Uganda, there was (and still might be) a basis for a would-be nation in the presence, albeit much challenged, of an ethnic core which could furnish the state-making personnel and institutions. But in Nigeria, Zaire, Ghana and possibly Kenya, where is the remotely acceptable ethnic core around which the institutions and personnel of a strong, bureaucratic state might form?

Perhaps it is this 'missing factor', of the many that might be cited, that so encourages authoritarian trends in the politics of many African and Asian states (like Pakistan, Iraq and Syria). Such states lacked the 'ethnic tranquillity' which comes from knowing that the bulk of one's (the state's) population, especially at the political centre, share a single culture and history, which in turn furnishes the myths, values, symbols and memories which the emerging state may 'take-for-granted' and promote in the efforts by state elites to maximize their control over the manpower and resources within their territorial domains. If a common ethnicity provides a 'language' and symbolism in which to express and spread bureaucratic controls by state elites jostling for power, then its absence threatens the very fabric of state power and the territorial basis of its jurisdiction. For the large ethnic populations who do not have any part in that language and sybolism, and in the common history from which they spring, the attempt by elites from any *ethnie* to wield state power and extend state control on the basis of their ethnicity, must appear alien and, given its novelty, illegitimate. In Western Europe this attempt to wield state power on the basis of a particular ethnicity was long-lived and tacit; it predated the era of nationalism and required no elaborations. Today, in Africa and parts of Asia, these attempts are of recent vintage and vociferous; they invite refutation and for the most part receive it, because by now every self-aware *ethnie* can and is making use of nationalist ideologies to further its ends. The overall result is a profound uncertainty in the very existence of many states, of a type unknown even in Western states threatened by recent ethnic autonomy

61 On the background to Nigeria's ethnic problems, see J. Coleman, *Nigeria, Background to Nationalism*, Berkeley and Los Angeles, University of California Press, 1958, and R. Sklar 'The contribution of tribalism to nationalism in Western Nigeria', in I. Wallerstein, ed., *Social Change, The Colonial Situation*, New York, John Wiley, 1966; on the war and military rule, see K. Panter-Brick, ed., *Nigerian Politics and Military Rule*, London, Athlone Press, 1970.

movements.[62] For, whereas in France or Spain, even the secession of Bretons and Basques, Catalans and Corsicans, would not cast real doubts on the existence of the Spanish and French nations (or their states), an ethnic secession in Africa and Asia (and that is how this uncertainty and refutation becomes manifest, as a problem of territorial boundaries) would immediately call the whole enterprise of nation-building through state-making into question. As yet, there is no 'Nigerian' or 'Zairian' 'nation'; to subtract any part of the population which is to make up this would-be nation would not only encourage other secessions, it would undermine the whole idea of such new, composite 'nations'.

For the central difficulty of 'nation-building' in much of Africa and Asia is the lack of any shared historical mythology and memory on which state elites can set about 'building' the nation. The 'nation' is not, as we see, built up only through the provision of 'infrastructures' and 'institutions', as 'nation-building' theories assumed; but from the central fund of culture and symbolism and mythology provided by shared historical experiences. Where, as in Nigeria, we have three or more such funds and histories, the problems of 'combining' them to create a 'Nigerian' political culture and political community become almost insuperable.[63]

This raises a further question. Does 'state-making' really require 'nation-building', where the latter means creating a unified 'territorial nation' out of the diverse *ethnie* and their homelands? Does Nigeria need nationalism? We could answer, as we argued at the outset: every state needs its nation, and every nation its state. That is to say, the contemporary world is a 'world of nations', and no unit claiming political sovereignty can evade the dictates of nationalism. The trouble is that for a state like 'Nigeria', creating the nation without an ethnic core, or with too many ethnic cores, is liable to be a self-defeating exercise. If we cannot completely evade the nationalist agendum, perhaps we can rewrite it?

62 For these movements, cf. A. Orridge, 'Separatist and autonomist nationalisms: the structure of regional loyalties in the modern state', in C. Williams, ed., *National Separatism*, Cardiff, University of Wales Press, 1982, and the essays in Esman, *Ethnic Conflict in the Western World*, and J. Stone, ed., 'Internal colonialism', *Ethnic and Racial Studies*, vol. 2, 1979.

63 Moreover, the differences between Christian Ibo and Muslim Hausa-Fulani are profound, while the Yoruba lay claim to descent from various medieval kingdoms. After their experience in India, the British colonial rulers evolved a system of 'indirect rule' in which the '*ethnie*' ('tribe') became the main unit of classification and differences were strengthened by unequal provisions, while in Zaire the Belgians, perhaps influenced by the growing cleavage at home, also began to classify in terms of *ethnie* and accentuate differences; see C. Young, *Politics in the Congo*, Princeton, Princeton University Press, 1965, and V. Turner, 'Congo-Kinshasa', in Olorunsola, *Politics of Cultural Subnationalism*; cf. M. Crowder, *West Africa under Colonial Rule*, London, Hutchinson, 1968.

In fact, this is being done in a number of ways. One is the 'immigrant' or United States way, another the 'autonomist' or Catalan way, a third the 'federal-nation' or Yugoslav solution. All are problematic, because all spring from the need to reconcile, in practice as well as theory, the conflicting demands of 'state-nation' and '*ethnie*-nation'. In the 'immigrant' model, which we touched on earlier, a relatively small or weak ethnic core, which assumed cultural primacy because it was 'there' first (where 'there' means in political control of the newly independent territory, before the influx of others), begins to build the institutions and norms of the modern state whose higher offices it at first monopolizes. Later, it admits waves of culturally alien immigrants whom it seeks to acculturate and even assimilate, turning what was originally an ethnic would-be nation into a territorial one. In the United States, as later in Canada, Australia and Argentina, the early and strategic English or Spanish creole *ethnie* transformed themselves into a broader political community in which non-English and non-Spanish white *ethnie* could achieve equal citizenship rights and social mobility.[64] Clearly, this is a solution that, though it still leaves problems about the relationship between ethnic cultures and the territorial political culture, could help to broaden the horizons of African and Asian 'plural states' by encouraging them to strive for the creation of political communities based on a larger 'political culture'. Unfortunately, it has two drawbacks in the African or Asian situation. The first is that none of the *ethnie* can advance an acceptable historical claim to cultural primacy, and so provide the basic ingredients of symbolism and mythology needed in any territorial nation. The second is that, unlike most immigrant societies, *ethnie* in African and Asian states are already territorialized and concentrated. They do not therefore mix physically or morally as do American or Argentinian *ethnie* and they continue to draw separate ethnic sustenance from their ethnic homelands, both in manpower and in ethnic culture. For these reasons, the immigrant model is likely to prove of limited value in Africa and Asia.

The 'autonomist' or Catalan model is also unlikely to appeal, since it presupposes the growth of a dual identity – Catalan and Spanish, Corsican and French, Scots and British. What Catalans, Corsicans and Scots have in the main wanted was maximum autonomy in the framework of

64 For the United States, see H. Kohn, *American Nationalism: an Interpretative Essay*, New York, Macmillan, 1961, and A. Greeley, *Ethnicity in the United States*, New York, John Wiley, 1974; on Canada, see J. Porter, *The Vertical Mosaic*, Toronto, University of Toronto Press, 1965, and idem, 'Ethnic pluralism in perspective', in Glazer and Moynihan, *Ethnicity*; on Argentinian and Brazilian nationalisms, see K. Masur, *Nationalism in Latin America*, New York, Macmillan, 1966; cf. also the essays in M. Mörner, ed., *Race and Class in Latin America*, New York and London, Columbia University Press, 1971.

the larger historical state into which they had long ago been incorporated. At a deeper level, Catalans, Corsicans and Scots want to find a framework in which they can reconcile two historic identities, one within the other like concentric circles of allegiance, both of which they deeply value. In former eras, such duality of allegiance posed few problems. In an age of possessive nationalism, it clearly must, and does, as the issue of conscription in the two world wars illustrated in the case of Quebecois, Flemish, Bretons and even Welshmen.[65] In 'normal' circumstances, the twin loyalties need not conflict in practice; ethnicity is treated as 'situational', that is, ethnic perceptions of 'who we are' and 'what we aspire to' change according to changing circumstances and perceptions of others – thus 'we' are Scots in England, and British when we go to France. But in situations of endemic conflict over scarce resources and decision-making, such as exists in most new states of Africa and Asia, this sort of concentric dual allegiance is fraught with difficulties. It is always on trial. There is always the pressure from state elites onto 'one's' *ethnie* through the allocation of resources, posts and services. There is always the competition for urban facilities and jobs which is viewed in terms of ethnic classifications inherited from the colonial powers (if not earlier). There is always the 'ethnic arithmetic' practised by governments who have accepted such criteria as the basic relevant ones for welfare and economic redistribution. Besides, once again, none of the larger circles of state/territorial allegiance is old enough to have attracted the devotion of more than a handful of the educated elites. Quite simply, 'Nigeria' cannot yet have the emotional attraction and symbolic potency of a 'France' or 'Spain'. Autonomism, therefore, while it too suggests a way forward for state-nations without ethnic cores in an age of nationalism, must await the growth of larger territorial loyalties which will effectively compete with ethnic ties.[66]

This leaves the 'federal-nation' or Yugoslav way. In Yugoslavia, the *ethnie* (all six of them) have been promoted to national status; or rather, their claims to constitute nations in virtue of an historic culture, territory and polity, have been accepted and turned into the corner-stone of the Yugoslav constitutional and ideological edifice. Contrary to African fears of 'Balkanization', the Yugoslavs themselves have made a virtue of national individuality and used it to build up a 'Yugoslavism' in which

65 For these 'concentric circles of allegiance', see Coleman, *Nigeria*; for the ethnic reactions to conscription in the Wars, see A. Marwick, *War and Social Change in the Twentieth Century*, London, Methuen, 1974. For the Basque case, in particular, see M. Heiberg, 'Insiders/outsiders: Basque nationalism', *European Journal of Sociology*, vol. 16, 1975.

66 Of course, a politically dominant *ethnie* may enforce its power, as with Kikuyization in Kenya; see D. Rothchild, 'Ethnic inequalities in Kenya', in Olorunsola, *Politics of Cultural Subnationalism*. But that is not the same as inducing dual loyalties.

national self-determination, like self-management, becomes the hall-mark of the Yugoslav way of political existence.[67] Of course, here too there is something present in the Yugoslav context for which there is no parallel in Africa or much of Asia: a common ideological-political system (non-aligned communism) and common memories of a loose ethnic kinship among the Yugoslav tribes (with the exception of the Muslim community which is now asserting a separate status) that have lived in a single area of south-east Europe, the old Roman province of Illyria, for centuries, have boasted glorious kingdoms and fallen under lengthy foreign rule,[68] so that, despite deep conflicts and differences, especially between Croats and Serbs, their histories have fallen within a common orbit and common problems, which have thrown them together.

In the African context, no such common orbit can be said to exist, and certainly no interrelationship of histories. True, there was a common, if varied, experience of Western colonialism and slavery and racism; and a corresponding sentiment of the dignity of Blackness and the 'African personality'.[69] But the lives and horizons of Nigerians can in no sense be said to have interacted with those of Tanzanians until very recently. Within Tanzania or Nigeria, too, the ethnic categories and communities now incorporated in the British-carved states often had little relationship to each other in pre-colonial days; so that there is not even any over-lapping characteristic, be it in family system or language or religion or institutions, which marks these communities off from neighbouring ones.

And yet, the Yugoslav model of recognizing *ethnie* as nations in a federal constitutional context offers real hope for the consolidation of

67 On the African fears of Balkanization, see B. Neuberger, 'The African concept of Balkanisation', *Journal of Modern African Studies*, vol. 13, 1976. For an argument equating African 'tribes', i.e. *ethnie*, with East European nations, see W. Argyle, European nationalism and African tribalism', in P. Gulliver, ed., *Tradition and Transition in East Africa*, London, Pall Mall Press, 1969, and 'Size and scale as factors in the development of nationalist movements', in Smith, *Nationalist Movements*.

68 For the Yugoslav case, see G. Schöpflin, 'Nationality in the fabric of Yugoslav politics', *Survey*, vol. 25, 1980, and A. Djilas, 'Communists and Yugoslavia', *Survey*, vol. 28, 1984; there was also an 'Illyrian' movement in the early nineteenth century, cf. Stavrianos, *The Balkans since 1453*.

69 On African history and the legacy of slavery and colonialism, see I. Markovitz, *Power and Class in Africa*, Englewood Cliffs, Prentice-Hall, 1977, and A. Ajayi, 'The place of African history and culture in the process of nation building in Africa south of the Sahara', *Journal of Negro Education*, vol. 30, 1960; on the consequent Pan-African move-ment and Negritude, see I. Geiss, *The Pan-African Movement*, London, Methuen, 1974, and C. Legum, *Pan-Africanism: a Short Political Guide*, London and Dunmow, Pall Mall Press, 1962, and in the context of colour nationalism, Smith, *Nationalism in the Twentieth Century*, chapter 4.

the state and the authority of its institutions. It solves, at a blow, the problem of primacy, and assures each community of potential equality of treatment. Of course, the Yugoslav experiment was born out of a war of resistance which overrode ethnic differences; and there have since been considerable tensions between Serbs and Croats, in particular. Yet, there has been broad acceptance of the principle of national equality, and of a Yugoslavia composed of equal nations, which might well provide a model for the more intractable 'state-nation' conflicts in Africa and Asia, even if the minimal unity of Yugoslavs is lacking in the new states.

As these last 'polyethnic' cases make clear, the absence of an ethnic core around which state elites can unite populations and build nations makes even the persistence and unity of the state uncertain. There are, it is true, a number of forces, both inter-state and domestic, which contribute to the maintenance of state power in general in Africa and Asia, and of these particular states in their present boundaries. There have, in fact, been few successful secessions or forcible revisions of post-colonial boundaries: one thinks of Bangladesh, Singapore, the divisions of Germany and Korea, the Indonesian incorporation of East Timor and the secession of Anguilla. There have been other failed movements of secession, especially Biafra, and some current ones like those of the Tigre and Eritrea, the Mizos and Shan. Yet, the state system and state boundaries since 1945 have held remarkably firm, despite continual pressures from ethnic movements.[70]

At the same time, nationalism too has proved remarkably tenacious. Hence the ever-present problem of 'national congruence', making states and ethnic nations coextensive. Without an ethnic core, there is no place from which to start the process of 'nation-formation'. The state has nothing to work on. *With* an ethnic core, there remain severe problems in reconciling other ethnic identities with that formed around an ethnic core as it has been transmuted into a territorial nation. *Without* an ethnic core, there is the much more intractable difficulty of creating an identity in the first place out of quite disparate ethnic materials. The polyethnic states of Africa, in particular, reveal the inner contradictions of the nation-state system most acutely, and the theoretical and practical shortcomings of our approaches to state-making and nation-building. To summarize our main conclusions:

1　In the past, successful states have been built up around a dominant ethnic core, especially in early modern Europe;

70 For some reasons for this state of affairs, see A. D. Smith, *State and Nation*, chapter 7, and idem, 'Ethnic identity and world order', *Millennium*, vol. 12, 1983.

2 In the past, *ethnie* aspiring to become full 'nations' have found it necessary to seek autonomy and independent statehood, and then use the state apparatus to transform themselves into citizen nations;

3 In the modern era, an era of nationalism, statehood can only be legitimized in terms of the 'nation' and nationalism, and states must therefore be seen to be 'nation-building';

4 In an era of nationalism, states which have a divided ethnic core and rival ethnic pasts are generally weaker and less well-developed than their ethnically secure counterparts;

5 In an era of nationalism, states which lack clear-cut ethnic cores (or have a multiplicity of contenders) are severely handicapped in their chances of both effective state-making and nation-building;

6 In an era of nationalism, the length and manner of ethnic incorporation by a modern state is crucial for ethnic tranquillity and concentric loyalties; if independent statehood coincides with ethnic arousal, 'immigrant' or 'autonomist' solutions are of limited relevance for polyethnic states;

7 Because state institutions can only be effective for nation-building where their homogenizing, territorializing and mobilizing trends do not stir up ethnic antagonisms (which, in an era of nationalism, is very unlikely), the prospects for effective state-making and nation-building in plural states are bleak, and perhaps the only hope is a 'federal-nation' model which turns *ethnie* into equal nations and reduces state power correspondingly, and hence the chances of a political community and 'territorial' nation;

8 As long as the nation is accepted as the sole norm of government and statehood, and as long as 'national congruence' is part of the nationalism's agenda, states without ethnic cores will tend to resort to authoritarian regimes to mask the disunity consequent on the absence of ethnic identity and history.

10

Patterns of State-Building in Brazil and Argentina

J. G. Merquior

The political results of independence in Spanish and Portuguese America were very different. Historians often contrast the unity maintained by the vast former Portuguese colony, Brazil, and the Balkanization of its larger Spanish counterpart, where four vice-royalties in 1800 were replaced by 17 countries by 1824, at the close of 15 years of tough independence wars. Now the River Plate province went through a far less protracted struggle (emancipation from Spain was definitely achieved in 1816, five years before Mexico's and eight before Peru's); yet somehow the ex-vice-royalty of the Plate reproduced the fragmentation pattern of the Spanish American whole: by mid-century, it was conspicuously divided into four nations (Argentina, Paraguay, what is now Bolivia and the Banda Oriental or Uruguay), with the first, largest and most important of such states – Argentina – still uncertain about the boundaries of two defining elements of statehood, territory and central power. Indeed, civil strife over the national issue was still going on in the 1870s, well after the primacy of Buenos Aires over the other provinces had been secured (1861) and alliance with the Brazilian empire had defeated López in the long and costly Paraguayan war (1865–70). On the other hand, the federative claims made in Brazil at the time no longer posed any real threat to national unity.

This chapter will examine the divergent political paths of post-colonial Argentina and Brazil in their efforts at state-building. In describing each national political process in turn, I shall try to make use of three key variables: the economic context, the pattern of centre/periphery relations, and the nature of the power elite. Besides sketching a few general conclusions, I shall roughly indicate how the historical experience of both countries in their state-building stage has conditioned their subsequent sociopolitical evolution.

For Carlos Castello Branco.

The Long Centrifugal Pull: Argentina from Independence
to 1880

In the River Plate region, as in Brazil and most other areas of Latin-America, the demand for independence sprang from elite discontent with increasingly unprofitable links with the Iberian metropoles. The colonial economy in Argentina was but an entrepôt. The merchants of Buenos Aires did not trade the country's products; they rather imported consumer goods for a market stretching to the Andes in exchange for precious metals. The city's great asset was the revenue from the silver mines of Potosí, controlled by Buenos Aires since the Bourbon reforms of the vice-royal system in the late eighteenth century. However, on the eve of the uprising against Spain (May 1810), the proportion of mining revenues in Buenos Aires's overall income, which in the 1790s amounted to four-fifths, had dwindled ten-fold; and the remaining trickle was appropriated by the crown in order to pay for war in Europe. Therefore, Buenos Aires looked for foreign trade to make up for its losses. But as commerce with Spain was also hard hit by the Napoleonic wars, the *porteño* (the inhabitants of the Buenos Aires region) merchants turned to free trade. When Madrid tried to reassert its control after the Bourbon restoration, a stronger class of local merchants marched towards independence.

Free trade meant British trade. Thanks to their ownership of capital and shipping, Britons came to dominate Buenos Aires's commerce; local wealth shifted to landowning and especially cattle-breeding. Until independence, land exploitation had been far from central. But from the second decade of the century, the province of Buenos Aires thrived on the disarray of richer cattle areas like the fluvial provinces of the west, torn by secession wars, and the Banda Oriental (Uruguay), plagued by revolution and Portuguese invasion. At the same time, though, the *porteño* elite was heavily taxing the other provinces, again as a way of off-setting the loss of mining revenue. This spelled much trouble ahead. Indeed the centrifugal forces in Argentinian politics were long fuelled by the fight for customs control between the port monopoly of Buenos Aires and the anti-monopoly claims of the littoral eastern provinces, Santa Fé, Entre Ríos and Corrientes.

All the interprovincial feuding took place within the framework of a moribund economy. Markets for the two staples of Argentinian cattle-raising, hides and salt beef (the latter sold to the slave plantations of Brazil and Cuba) did not expand. The real linkage with the world economy, wool exports, only became important in the 1840s. So the scramble for profits between the capital region and the littoral provinces remained a zero sum game; it was also a power contest in a society which, without being rigidly stratified, was starkly polarized. Nowhere in Argentina was there a middle class, urban or rural. When Buenos Aires, after independence, tried to make the littoral provinces submit, they hit back and crushed the capital's troops at Cepeda (1820). In desperation Buenos Aires turned for help to the *estancieros* (ranchers) of its own countryside – but in the process had to sacrifice the liberal, modernizing politics of the enlightened *porteño* elite, best embodied in the short-lived presidency of Bernardino Rivadavia (1826–7). War for independence followed by repeated secession brought about a conspicuous militarization of politics; by 1830, it became also obvious that the autonomy (let alone the hegemony) of Buenos Aires could hardly dispense with *caudillo*-led forces. Yet *caudillismo* in turn meant a generalized ruralization of power bases.[1] On the strength of their estates (many held on lease from the state) and of their armed bands, the *estancieros* tied the former *mestizo* (racially mixed) nomads of the pampa – the gauchos – to their land; and the *caudillos* were as a rule wealthy landowners whose valour had been proved, often against the Indians, at the head of rural militias. Under one of them, Juan Manuel de Rosas, the landowning class eventually prevailed over the independence elite – the merchants, bureaucrats, intellectuals and officers who had vanquished Spain.

The Rosas era (1829–32, 1835–52) was sheer governmental terrorism – a Hobbesian response to dismemberment and lawlessness. Though a relative of the opulent Anchorena family, Rosas was a self-made *estanciero*. Born in 1793, he was just ten years younger than Bolívar. Politically he emerged as a rescuer of the capital, then led the 'federal party', the rural foe of Rivadavian 'unitarianism', the centralist liberalism of the *porteño* bourgeoisie. As has been pithily remarked, 'the Rosas state was the *estancia* writ large';[2] – a coarse patrimonial autocracy which bullied its subjects as though they were the *peones* of the hacienda. Like his contemporary, Andrew Jackson, Rosas consolidated his reputation by fighting the redskins on the frontier; his Desert Campaign of 1833 stretched the territory of Buenos Aires down to the south of Río Negro. Yet whilst Jackson depatricianized the American presidency, Rosas 'feudalized' the infant republic in the pampa. Socially, the settlement of new lands was closer to the Norman conquest than to the

---

1 Cf. Tulio Halperín Donghi, *Revolución y Guerra: formación de una elite dirigente en la Argentina criolla*, Buenos Aires, Siglo Veinte Uno, 1972.

2 John Lynch, 'The River Plate republics from independence to the Paraguayan War', in Leslie Bethell, ed., *The Cambridge History of Latin America*, vol. III (from independence to c. 1870), Cambridge, Cambridge University Press, 1985, p. 640.

American pattern; land grants rewarded military rank. The root of the difference lay in social structure: homestead democracy in Jacksonian American contrasted with a crude clientage system in Argentina in which land ownership was kept in far fewer hands.

The long inability of the Argentinian state to get a grip on its 'normal' national territory engendered a paradoxical situation, resembling the fate of conquering nomad tribes in the history of Islam. Once victorious, that is, masters of Buenos Aires, federal factions tended to turn centralists – just as the triumphant Muslim tribes founded urban-based dynasties. Thus the Rosas regime, born of the defeat of *porteño* unitarianism, nevertheless continued to impose the monopoly of the port of Buenos Aires. This annoyed European commercial interests as much as the littoral provinces; hence naval blockades on Buenos Aires by France (1838–41) and by France and Britain (1845–7) followed. These blockades had more than one effect. Several cattle-ranchers who were harmed by the interruption of trade dumped livestock on the Buenos Aires market. The ensuing cheap meat lowered the cost of living and helped Rosas to control the urban population. But the slump brought about by blockades also goaded many *estancieros* into rebellion. As modern historians note, by 1840 Rosas no longer represented the landowning class. The regime's sustained military effort went against the interests of its ranching basis. Enlistment pushed up wages in a labour-hungry rural economy, thereby blocking growth despite a potential for expanding trade. The cost of the army bred inflation, and inflation ate the income of the Buenos Aires bureaucrats. Last but not least, it compelled the dictator to tighten the fiscal screws on the River Plate trade; this reinforcing the hated monopoly of the capital's port. Eventually, a revolt of the littoral state of Entre Rios, allied under General Urquiza to Brazil and to Rosas's enemies in Uruguay, overthrew his rule.

In his account of the *Beagle* voyage Darwin narrates his meeting in Patagonia (during the Desert Campaign) with General Rosas. The young naturalist was appalled by the cruelty of the extermination of the Indians but he was also impressed by Rosas's personality and thought it possible that he would use his influence to give Argentina 'prosperity and advancement' – a hope which Darwin himself, in the second edition of his journal, seven years before the dictator's downfall, found miserably disappointed.[3] We need not agree with him on both scores. The despotism of Rosas, a violent but hard-working tyrant, secured order in the pampa long enough for the ranch economy to allow sheep farming,

3 As recalled by Mr G. J. Tee in his letter to the *Times Literary Supplement* 7 May 1982.

the basis for the export boom which so enriched Argentina. On the other hand, there was little advancement and still less freedom. Bigot Rosas was as autocratic as his Voltairean counterpart, Dr Francia of Paraguay (1814–40): he muzzled the press and neglected education altogether; he scorned intellectuals and their talk of 'improvements'.

Still more germane to our problem, Rosas's institutional legacy was almost nil – a point stressed by John Lynch in his great biography.[4] But his successors did little better. Urquiza, the main victor of Rosas's regime, was made 'provisional director' of the Argentine Confederation (Rosas himself had ruled only as governor of the province of Buenos Aires, albeit endowed with the 'suma del poder público'). In 1853 a new republican constitution, devised by Juan Bautista Alberdi (1810–84), enshrined three main principles: bourgeois liberalism, Rivadavian meliorism, and a keen concern to balance central authority and provincial rights. Alberdian federalism also provided for a *Zollverein* by abolishing interprovincial tariffs and it nationalized the capital's customs income – precisely the move that had shattered unitarian power two decades earlier. Nevertheless, Buenos Aires and the provincial *caudillos* did not share a sense of national unity. Urquiza established a rival capital in Paraná, strove to bypass the Buenos Aires port and eventually tried militarily to subdue the *porteños*. He failed in this latter at the battle of Pavón (1861). Halting the confederation forces at Pavón made room for compromise. The Buenos Aires governor Bartolomé Mitre, soon to become supreme allied commander in the Paraguayan war, accepted the 1853 federal constitution and was elected president of the whole nation. Argentina had finally become Argentina. The successive administrations of Mitre, Domingo Sarmiento and Nicolás Avellaneda (1862–80), pledged the country to unity as a framework for progressive liberty and wholesale modernization, opening the doors to the big immigration waves of the end of the century. 'To govern is to people', wrote Alberdi. School teacher Sarmiento, one of Spanish America's greatest writers, was a liberal humanist from the hinterland. 'What are Rosas and Urquiza?' he asked. His reply came filled with contempt: 'Cowboys.' Avellaneda was Sarmiento's minister of education. In the 1860s, this liberal outlook saw itself utterly denied in López's Paraguay – the realm of unabashed autocracy, running an increasingly militarized rural economy; this was dangerous as the provincial *caudillos* in Argentina looked on Paraguay as an alternative model to *porteño* hegemony.[5]

Political unification was much helped by the long boom which trans-

4 John Lynch, *Argentine Dictator: Juan Manuel de Rosas 1829–1852*, Oxford, Oxford University Press, 1981.

5 Lynch, 'The River Plate Republics', p. 670.

formed Argentina into a major foodstuff supplier, a leading exporter of meat and grain. British investment built in the pampa the largest railway network in Latin America to allow beef exports. Nevertheless, the tasks facing the newly unified state were quite daunting. 'National government had to build the state almost out of nothing', wrote José Luís Romero; it was necessary to establish in space and in law, the jurisdiction of the provinces, as well as to settle the thorny issue of their relations with Buenos Aires; provincial armies had to be disbanded; the national mail and the national customs set up; and so on and so forth.[6] Yet by 1880, despite the impact of world depression, the new Argentinian state was able to resist the secessionist revolt of . . . Buenos Aires. For the capital, having led unification under Mitre in the 1860s, resisted the 'national' solution in the 1870s. Sarmiento's administration ended with new challenges to federal authority. Avellaneda was backed up by an alliance of the interior provinces and the 'autonomy' party in Buenos Aires, although then was forced to govern from another town, Belgrano. Thus the capital port re-enacted its own separatist history at the close of the state-building years. This time, however, even with a divided army, the state was strong enough to curb the centrifugal pull once and for all.[7]

State-Building in Imperial Brazil (1822–89)

The state which helped Urquiza defeat Rosas in the battle of Caseros, in February 1852 – imperial Brazil – differed from both Argentina and Uruguay in that it had by then achieved permanent political unity on a colossal territorial basis. Historians and social scientists keep wondering about what made this possible. After all, from independence (1822) to the middle of the nineteenth century, Brazil witnessed eight major regional revolts, half of them with clear secessionist intent. In the 1830s northern oligarchs like Pernambuco's Holanda Cavalcanti seriously entertained the idea of splitting up the empire into at least two separate countries; in the 1840s, with a fierce revolt against the crown going on in Rio Grande do Sul, the Brazilian side of the River Plate region, foreign travellers thought that the disintegration of Brazil was just a matter of time. What 'glue' kept Brazil united?

Unlike her Spanish-American neighbours, Brazil had a slave economy; black slaves manned the cash crops of sugar and coffee in northern and southern plantations. Naturally enough, there have been

6 José Luís Romero, *La Experiencia Argentina*, Buenos Aires, Editorial de Belgrano, 1980, p. 77.
7 The point is underscored in Oscar Oszlak, *La Formación de Estado Argentino*, Buenos Aires, Editorial de Belgrano, 1983.

scholars who insist that slavery was the main reason for unity. They argue that the division of the former colony might have undermined the social structure and that fear of slave rebellion was rife.[8] Yet the elite groups who felt most threatened in this were *not* prominent amidst those who insisted on national unity. A better answer seems to lie in politics. For the second big difference which set late colonial Brazil apart from her Spanish-American neighbours was the presence of the Portuguese court in Rio de Janeiro. Initially a refugee from Napoleonic invasion, the king remained until 1820. Brazil was even upgraded from colony into 'united kingdom' in 1815, one year before the completion of independence in the River Plate countries. When John VI eventually returned to Lisbon, his son took over, first as prince regent and then as emperor. It is often assumed that monarchy maintained unity, and hopes along these lines were doubtless in the back of the *libertadores'* minds. San Martín, the Argentinian independence leader, thought that only a throne would prevent anarchy in post-colonial Hispanoamerica. Bolivar himself, trying hard (if in vain) to avoid the break-up of the former vice-royalties, wanted presidents to be kings in all but the name. Brazil, it would appear, realized a widespread aspiration, and for the rather impressive spell of six decades (1822–89). Yet why was this only possible in Brazil?

The answer, it has been claimed of late, is that Brazil, unlike most other Spanish-American countries, had a *national* political elite. In fact, there was at least one other remarkable instance of unity *cum* stability: Chile. But Chile was far smaller – in fact, it was a land island whose population was huddled together in a fertile central valley between the formidable Andes barrier and the coastal range; it never knew regional challenges to Santiago,[9] where a civilian oligarchy ruled through a strong presidential system from 1833 to 1891. Therefore size and diversity made the case of the Brazilian state truly unique.

Modern research, notably by José Murilo de Carvalho,[10] has shown the imperial political elite to have been chiefly composed of magistrates whose training in civil law made them adept at upholding the interests and prerogatives of the monarchy. Instead of belonging to the motley crowd of lawyers, Rousseauian priests and ambitious warriors who

8 Cf. Emilia Viotti da Costa, 'The political emancipation of Brazil', in A. J. R. Russell-Wood, ed., *From Colony to Nation, Essays on the Independence of Brazil*, Baltimore, Johns Hopkins University Press, 1975.

9 On this point, see Claudio Véliz's Canning House lecture, 'Continuities and departures in Chilean history', London, The Hispanic and Luso Brazilian Council, 1981.

10 José Murilo de Carvalho, *A Construção da Ordem: a elite política imperial*, Brasília, Editora da Universidade de Brasília, 1980; and also idem, 'Political elites and state building: the case of nineteenth-century Brazil', *Comparative Studies in Society and History*, vol. 24, 1982.

surrounded the Spanish–speaking *libertadores*, the Brazilian empire-builders had a common educational and professional background: they were nearly all alumni of Coimbra, and shared the experience of having served as agents of the crown in several places, both metropolitan and colonial – a circulation that imbued practical skills and widened mental horizons. By contrast, Spanish-American leaders had been to local universities of a predominantly theological orientation. Most importantly, creoles were excluded from the higher posts in Spanish America's bureaucracy; this exclusion from participation above the humble level of the *cabildos* (the local administrative bodies) eventually meant that the elites which won independence and sought to build states had a far less comprehensive practical knowledge of rule and administration. Except for a few *libertadores*, those who had won independence outside Portuguese America lacked any larger view of things, and this reflected a rather parochial experience. Neither life nor training had educated them for a consistent concern with state authority.

Moreover, the Braganza throne in the tropics reproduced the basics of Portuguese political elite training: it taught the next generations of politicians and high civil servants in only two non-provincial law schools (in São Paulo and Recife), both intended to be not just technical but *hautes écoles*;[11] and it circulated its high officials widely throughout the empire[12] before entrusting them with top positions in cabinet, in the strategic State Council or in the no less prestigious senate, whose members for life were chosen by the emperor from a list of elected names. 'The specificity of the Brazilian case', writes Carvalho, 'was . . . the presence of a national political elite, that is, of an elite that could aggregate the interests of the dominant groups and protect them through the mediation of state power.'[13] In social origin the bureaucratic makers and upholders of the centralist empire were by no means very different from their opponents, the leaders of regional, centrifugal movements; in terms of professional and ideological socialization they were. A national elite, they thought, of course, in national rather than regional categories.

Furthermore, their unitarian strategy made much sense in view of the country's economic situation during the nineteenth century. The average growth rate remained pretty low. Exports were never very large. The domestic sector suffered from the low productivity of agriculture; poor roads and the distance of natural waterways from economic centres made transport expensive, and this prevented producers from taking

11 Carvalho, *A Construção da Ordem*, chapter 3.
12 Ibid., chapter 5.
13 Carvalho, 'Political elites and state building', p. 390.

advantage of the national market. Sustained development presupposed infrastructural facilities such as roads and railways, but the modesty of its fiscal resources did not allow the state to provide them. Fiscal revenues derived mainly from imports (some 60 per cent of state income by 1860); only some 16 per cent came from taxes on exports,[14] which, as indicated, were far from highly profitable anyway. The vast size of the country and the lack of transport integration invited fragmentation. Understandably, therefore, a highly centralized state was in order. But this also created a vicious circle: by practically monopolizing whatever there was by way of taxes, the state left too little for provincial and local authorities to invest so as to generate wealth by improving trade and production on a more significant scale.[15]

There was of course another reason for the imperial elite to maintain unity through centralism. The Brazilian ruling class was well aware of the costs of *disunity* in the rest of post-colonial Iberoamerica – and more than determined to forestall them. There is a substantial amount of historical evidence to justify this claim. For our purposes, however, what is worth stressing is precisely the long-lived elite consensus on territorial unity and the need for an effective central authority. Thus a significant state was preserved, and even expanded. True, the state was not robust enough to prevent the Rothschilds from having their own way in its loans, nor to cope with the prospect of armed confrontation (which it had the sense to avoid) with the world imperial power when it came to ending the slave trade – which Britain wanted to abolish both for humanitarian reasons and to shield the sugar output of her own West Indies from Brazilian competition.[16] But in broad terms the Braganza state in the South Atlantic was along with Chile by far the strongest in all the continent.

But limitations on state 'strengths' are again worth stressing. The very strata that were so keen on statehood lived in dire need of the state. For in Brazil the state did not only protect the overall interests of a propertied class, it also procured jobs and status in conditions of chronic upper-class unemployment. The stagnation of the sugar economy in the north, the near monopoly of trade by foreigners in the main towns and in general the persistent undevelopment of the country as a whole pushed many scions of the upper class into the bureaucracy, and hence into

14 Cf. Richard Graham, 'Brazil from the middle of the nineteenth century to the Paraguayan War', in *The Cambridge History of Latin America*, vol. III, p. 767.
15 For all this paragraph's argument, see Nathaniel H. Leff's conclusions in his *Underdevelopment and Development in Brazil*, vol. II: *Reassessing the Obstacles to Economic Development*, London, Allen & Unwin, 1982, pp. 126–8.
16 For a careful analysis of the struggle over the slave trade, see Leslie Bethell, *The Abolition of the Brazilian Slave Trade*, Cambridge, Cambridge University Press, 1970.

politics. Up to the middle of the century, the massive majority of cabinet ministers were civil servants. Until the very end of the regime, the bureaucracy – overwhelmingly concentrated in national rather than local jobs – cost the state 60 per cent of the budget. As a proportion of the national population, the Brazilian bureaucracy was then bulkier than the American one. Nó wonder social-minded liberals like the abolitionist, Joaquim Nabuco, could write epigrams on a slave society whose officials were in turn 'the government's serfs'.

By the third quarter of the century, the 'state serfs' could behave as masters in the 'house divided' that was Uruguay (which, in the mid-1820s, the nascent empire had been unable to wrest from Argentina, the resulting stalemate having led Britain to impose the creation of an independent buffer state); they could help decisively to topple a super-*caudillo* like Rosas or wage an implacable war on the Paraguayan 'Prussia' of López – but they were not able really to reach the periphery of their own state. The central government, in the well-known quip of a lucid conservative statesman, Viscount Uruguay, was all head, with neither arms nor legs. Nevertheless, no regional, let alone local, powers were able to defy, in any constant or consistent way, the short-armed centre, no matter how small an undertaking it was, or how remote from the web of daily relations in the recesses of a country that was still, to a large extent, a vast social and economic archipelago.

Thus the state, though without a deep range or a high degree of penetration, could block developments it did not like. Significantly, the power elite often proved capable of acting against powerful sectors of the dominant class. Viscount Rio Branco, heading the longest cabinet (1871–5) in the whole reign of Pedro II in the wake of victory in Paraguay, freed all the future children of slaves in the teeth of staunch opposition from the coffee-planters of three key provinces, Rio, São Paulo and Minas. The supporters of Rio-Branco's bill in parliament were a coalition of civil servants and north-eastern landowners (by then the slave percentage in the labour force in the sugar counties of Pernambuco had already fallen to something around 15 per cent[17] – but the fact that in the early 1870s, at the time of the first census, the total number of slaves also amounted to just 15 per cent of the ten million souls of the empire did not bar the wrath of planters in the centre-south, where the slave force was concentrated).

In a sense, the state elite was closer to its own class at the outset than towards the end of the regime. At the beginning the coffee boom was a

---

17 Not least because there had been a substantial transfer of slave labour force from the declining north to the coffee-booming economy in the south: cf. Evaldo Cabral de Melo, *O Norte Agrário e o Império*, Rio, Nova Fronteira, 1984, pp. 21–56.

major factor in the triumph of centralism over the centrifugal trends unleashed during the Regency (1831–40). The Conservative Party was born in the process, its first leaders coming from Minas, the court itself, the coffee economy of the Paraíba valley in the Rio province and, last but not least, Coimbra University: Vasconcelos, Olinda, Eusebio, Itboraí and Uruguay, Paraná. These were the founding fathers of the Brazilian version of the Iberian 'centralist tradition', to quote Claudio Véliz's illuminating if controversial label.[18] Their party was dominated by an alliance of magistrates and *fazendeiros* (large landowners), sometimes the same politician evincing both attributes.

Yet wise historians like Sergio Buarque de Holanda have cautioned against assuming heavy landowner influence over the political system from the start; this influence was only acquired later, in the so-called Old Republic (1889–1930).[19] More microscopic analysis of the articulation of agrarian interests is confirming this point. For instance, it is a well-known fact that Pernambuco and Bahia – two provinces where sugar production was most important – were well represented within the cabinet. But, Evaldo Cabral de Melo's well-researched study of the relations between government and the northern agricultural exporters at the end of the empire has shown that, far from responding to the landowners' wishes, the sugar policy of the central government, even under a northern prime minister like Viscount Sinimbu, actually *countered* the planters' interests in favour of Rio speculators and incompetent British capital – and this, ironically enough, at a time when the sugar syndicate in Recife was dominated by party cronies of Sinimbu.[20] Overall, there was no constant let alone effective agrarian lobbying during the empire. What the crown bestowed upon the *fazendeiros* was titles – and hence status, rather than power.[21]

However, one should not exaggerate the state's autonomy from the landed class. For if the landowners did not cut much ice with the state, no imperial government ever went as far as trying to change the economic model. From a Gerschenkronian perspective, there was a glaring absence: there was no genuine attempt to embark on structural development by fostering industrialization and import-substitution; no Prussian- or Japanese-type 'revolution from above' was ever suggested. Free trade – meaning low tariffs to benefit the agro-export economy and the consumption of the upper class – went unchallenged until the end.

18 Claudio Véliz, *The Centralist Tradition of Latin America*, Princeton, Princeton University Press, 1980.
19 Sergio Buarque de Holanda, *História Geral da Civilização Brasileira*, vol. II, O Brasil Monárquico, V, São Paulo, Difel, 1972, pp. 283–6.
20 Cf. Cabral de Melo, *O Norte Agrário e o Império*, pp. 157–87.
21 Cf. Buarque de Holanda, *Historia Geral*, p. 285.

Even the most centralist among the Conservatives were orthodox economic liberals.

What about the *political* Liberals? Did they represent a substantial alternative for the polity or the society? Did they ever come close to forming a counter-elite? Let us look at their social background. Liberal politicians tended to be either landowners, too, or (at first) priests and (later) lawyers or journalists; like the conservatives, there was a great deal of overlapping between these other occupations and various degrees of entrepreneurial landowning. But when landowners (and quite often slave-owners), Liberals often came from depressed or peripheral economic sectors: the old mining areas of Minas, the towns of pre-coffee São Paulo, the sugar counties in the north, and the cattle-ranching of the Brazilian pampa in the far south. For a long time (until the 1860 elections), the Liberal programme was pre-eminently a mildly federal one: their main requirement was a modicum of provincial and local autonomy in justice and administration. Moderate Liberals, some of them later to turn Conservative, were vocal and active in forcing the abdication in 1831 of the first emperor, Pedro I, a constitutional monarch who became increasingly authoritarian and surrounded by his fellow Portuguese. During the ensuing Regency the Liberals sponsored legal reforms introducing habeas corpus and the jury system as well as enlarging the powers of justices of the peace – a local squirearchy of sorts. The Liberal minister of justice, later elected regent, Diogo Feijó, a priest from São Paulo, created a National Guard inspired by the French model established under Louis Philippe. The most extensive device of patrimonial domination in Latin America, in a modern expert appraisal,[22] the Guard replaced an unreliable army as the main instrument of despotic power in the hands of the elite.

From the late 1830s, as a Conservative reaction reasserted the centralist regime, especially in the judicial sphere, the Liberal Party merely claimed the devolution of some provincial power. It was only in the last decades of Pedro II's reign, after much political realignment, that liberal opinion as a whole (rather than the party of that name) stood for both full federalism and the extension of individual rights. The main drive behind serious Liberal agitation, except for abolitionism in the 1880s, remained the power hunger of regional oligarchies. This explains why Liberal solidarity was often strangely missing. The northern 'Liberals' did not stir when their southern comrades rose against the central government in the early 1840s; and Liberal São Paulo and Liberal Minas stood idle when Liberal Pernambuco staged the last provincial

22 Fernando Uricoechea, *The Patrimonial Foundations of the Brazilian Bureaucratic State*, Berkeley, University of California Press, 1980.

revolt in 1848. The Liberal Party was not even consistent on matters of constitutional principles. It voiced the greatest indignation in the small but free press when the emperor, using his 'moderating power', removed the mainly Liberal centrist coalition (the Progressive League) in 1868; but it did not mind benefiting from the same monarchic prerogative to return to office ten years later.[23] In their own ambivalent way, many Liberals accepted the authoritarian and oligarchic nature of the imperial state. Not surprisingly, the regime was able to make room for them by reforming the government-controlled electoral system so that the opposition could have a larger share of MPs. Together with measures trying to discourage the presence of provincial factions in parliament, this was the main institutional novelty introduced by the coalition government led by the Marquis of Paraná. His 'conciliation' politics (1853–8), coming in the wake of victory in the Plate, lent a moderate and progressive hue to the spell of greater prosperity created by the world boom, the rising price of coffee and the capital released by the end of the slave trade.

The Legacy and its Transformation

The growth of the state, as a body of regulations and as a set of social apparatuses, is an ongoing world-wide process, necessitated by the very nature of modern society. By 'state-building' we generally mean just the preliminary stage of such *statification* (to use Weber's wording): the *rise* of state, that is, state-*building* as, literally, the state in the *making*. That implies chiefly the emergence of a central power possessing effective control of the means of coercion, continuous sovereignty over a given territory and the ability to levy taxes regularly, together with a stable judicial system.

By these criteria the Brazilian empire had by, say, 1860 built a state, whereas Argentina was still groping at a structure of central authority with effective territorial and institutional reach. If, in Ernest Gellner's celebrated dictum, legitimacy is indeed sovereignty recollected in tranquility, the state under Rosas in the 1840s, Urquiza in the 1850s or even Mitre in the 1860s was not yet fully legitimate on a national scale. By the turn of the century, Argentina was an instance of completed but belated stateness. This much has been acknowledged by political scientists with a taste for comparative studies.[24] Though in Argentina the struggle for

23 As recalled by Francis Lambert, 'The Cortes and the king: constitutional monarchy in the Iberian world', Institute of Latin American Studies, University of Glasgow, 1981.

24 For a good recent example, see Hélgio Trindade, 'A Construção do Estado Nacional na Argentina e no Brasil (1810–1900): esboço de uma análise comparativa' (mimeo), 1984. Trindade holds a political science chair at the Federal University of Rio Grande do Sul in Porto Alegre.

independence left far less scars on economy and society than in Mexico, and the degree of political instability throughout the following decades was certainly not higher than in Peru or, again, in Mexico, the long after-life of *caudillo* politics since emancipation from Spain did reflect a protracted, chequered genesis of the national state. *Caudillismo* in itself was, of course, the nadir of institution-making. Rosas refused even to discuss a constitution; his victors found it very hard to apply that of 1853. National disunity – the long centrifugal pull – went hand in glove with political instability and low institutionalization; and, all three actu-ally postponed successful statification until the last third of the century. In Brazil, on the other hand, several factors – the circumstances of independence, the distance and weakness of separatist foci, above all, perhaps, the centralist determination of a national elite – made statifica-tion quicker and easier.

Let us now look at the two patterns with the help of Michael Mann's perceptive distinction between two dimensions of state power: *despotic power* (the range of actions which the state is able to undertake without regular negotiation with civil society groups) and *infrastructural power* (the state's capacity actually to penetrate society and implement political decisions).[25] Imperial Brazil was patently an instance of a rather high level of despotic power combined with a middle-to-low level of infra-structural power, mainly on account of the state's poor extractive capacity and lack of entrepreneurial activities. In Argentina, by contrast, as soon as the age of *caudillo* rule was over (i.e. in the 1860s) and there came a time for 'national organization', the most lasting and significant advances in stateness were achieved along the infrastructural dimen-sion: the state set up, or helped to set up, extensive networks in educa-tion, transport and urban facilities. Nothing similar, on a comparable, nation-wide scale, was ever attempted by the more despotic, ingrained Brazilian state during the empire – or, for that matter, in the next regime, the Old Republic.

What happened to their respective legacies – belated stateness and imperial pattern – in their political evolution after the 1880s? The first point to be made is that for all her priority in state-building, Brazil was considerably later than Argentina when it comes to *nation*-building in the well-established political sociology sense of the word. For nation-building to obtain, the existence of the state as a central source of authority is not enough: there must also be the growth of an active citizenship in the democratic sense; a citizenship, that is, as a living principle or legitimacy, meaning, as it has meant since the French Revolution, general civil and political equality under the law. Now

25 M. Mann, 'The autonomous power of the state', chapter 4 in this volume.

nationhood in this political sense was achieved in Argentina with president Sáenz Peña's electoral reform bill of 1912. Its immediate effect was the supersession of oligarchic Liberal rule – the historical successor to *caudillo* autocracy in the pampa. In Brazil, however, though the first republican constitution (1891) got rid of census democracy (the disqualification of the illiterate), the widespread practice of electoral fraud and the unabashed political filtration of access to Congress (even after the election) made a mockery of universal male suffrage. The secret ballot and the judicial vetting at elections as an impartial referee system were introduced in the early 1930s (by Mauricio Cardoso's electoral code and the Weimar-like 1934 constitution); but the beginning of their continuous practice had to wait until 1946, as against 1916 for Argentina.

This lag in nation-building was related to the different levels in the dynamics of integration of each agro-export model into the North Atlantic world economy between 1880 and the Depression. The pastoral agro-export economy of Argentina dealt with staples – wool, meat, grain – obviously far more needed than coffee, the luxury key produce in the Brazilian plantation system. The American Civil War disrupted cotton exports from the American South to the great benefit of Argentinian wool sales, and she seldom ceased to profit from the Atlantic trade at a bulk and a pace unrivalled by agrarian Brazil. From the end of interprovincial strife up to the First World War, oligarchic domination prevailed under the continuing export bonanza. Patrician rule held sway over an immigrant country where nearly one-third of the population by 1914 was foreign-born – double of the proportion in the United States. The growth rate was a real *Wirtschaftswunder*: GDP grew 5 per cent per year between 1860 and 1914. The Alberdian republican formula read: civil freedom for all, political liberty for just a few. Such were the ground rules of the Argentinian polity in the halcyon days of her 'conservative order'.[26] Yet its very prosperity created an urban society incomparably more sophisticated than the social landscape of the *caudillo* age. The upper class of Beunos Aires's Paris-like streets and English-like clubs was much wealthier than its continental counterparts, and Argentina was the first country in Latin America to boast a numerous and cultured middle class.

Furthermore, beneath its pastoral pattern of agro-exports the country had swelling towns (and a macrocephalic capital), *but practically no peasantry*. Cattle-ranching was not labour-intensive, and wheat was often grown by disenfranchised foreign colonists. Like Brazil, and

26 Natalio R. Botana, *El Orden Conservador: la política argentina entre 1880 y 1916*, Buenos Aires, Sudamericana, 1977.

unlike Mexico or Peru, Argentina no longer possessed a sizeable amount of Indians (though getting rid of them took from 1830 to 1880); unlike Brazil, however, she had no rural masses either. In the long run, such a situation could but favour the workers. Without the handicap of a 'reserve army' from the countryside, whose very availability pressed wages down, the bargaining power of the urban workers was considerably strengthened (in a still longer run, of course, it turned out to be less of an advantage, for it deprived the urban lower classes of a potential rural ally). Understandably, when the workers, in the Belle Époque, started unionizing and turning leftwards, the oligarchy thought it clever to pre-empt social challenges by co-opting middle-class dissent. Landowners from the littoral, the old rural bourgeoisie of backward provinces untouched by the long export boom, and educated town-dwellers were all claiming a share in political power. Soon these groups formed the Radical Party, and stirred uprisings in 1893 and 1905.

Now Sáenz Peña believed, like Disraeli in 1867, that if the bulk of the urban masses were enfranchised they would not rock the boat. In a sense, however, Sáenz Peña's dreams of controlled democracy resembled the first rather than the second British Reform Bill: for, given the illiterate contingent and the large number of foreign workers, his 1912 reform still excluded half the adult males from the vote. This was crucial because, as it turned out, the working class remained outside the party system, notably during the years of radical rule, from 1916 to 1930.[27] The great radical leader, Yrigoyen, was at first sympathetic towards the workers, since he had no intention of losing any part of the popular vote to the Conservative forces. But when the big strike wave of 1918–19 aroused a red scare, he was as harsh in repression as another famous former left-winger, Clemenceau. After that rising wages in the 1920s, and unemployment in the 1930s further undermined the union movement and its search for a political outlet. Thus when Perón entered the stage, in the mid-1940s, he could easily mobilize a working class that, for all its being now 90 per cent literate and native, had still to find proper channels of industrial and political representation.

Even before Depression made itself felt in Argentina the oligarchy began to refuse the consequences of its own democratic reform. The triumph of radicalism dislodged the former elite, signalling the rise of professional politicians of middle-class origins and the likelihood of a state-steered economy – two prospects loathed by the pampa's patricians and their *laissez-faire* 'conservative order'. Little by little,

27 Best examined in David Rock, *Politics in Argentina, 1880–1930: The Rise and Fall of Radicalism*, Cambridge, Cambridge University Press, 1975.

party politics became anathema for the right. In 1930 the military, also much indisposed towards 'politics' and politicians, toppled old Irigoyen, putting an end to the radical republic. The army had been engineered by the liberal fathers of the national organization period to cope with López's militarized Paraguay and curb the power of the *caudillos*. Now it nipped democracy still in its teens. But the military themselves were in two minds. Some of them, under General Justo, favoured a Conservative restoration and a return to the pre-1912 system. Others longed for a new, corporate state. The Conservative centurions prevailed. They enacted a batch of social legislation, tried to win over many politicians (including right-wing radicals) in the vain hope that the political class and the party system would obligingly go back to the fraudulent, pre-Sáenz Peña kind of elections, and, last but not least, disgraced themselves by signing a commercial treaty with Britain (the Roca–Runciman treaty, 1933). The treaty had been urged by cattle-raisers lest the newly adopted British system of imperial preference should block Argentina's access to her main beef market. But it gave Britain excessive privileges in trade, exchange and investment. Argentina became a kind of Sixth Dominion, though British investment never actually resumed after the First World War. Argentinian nationalism began to simmer.

After the Second World War American farming, under the umbrella of the Marshall Plan, kicked Argentinian grain out of most of its traditional European markets. No wonder ill feelings towards the Anglo-Saxon world became even stronger. Building on them, a thoughtful colonel, Juan Perón, elected in 1945, nationalized the railways, sought to redirect the economy towards industrialization and managed to improve not only the lot of the workers but also their share in the national income; this was all financed by post-war trade surpluses (1946–8). In 1951 he was re-elected with 70 per cent of the vote, despite an austerity programme imposed by the abrupt end of the export boom. Up to then his rule had been a modern *caudillismo*, a mass clientelistic politics in which the 'new state' vision of his corporatist fellow-officers merged with the 'controlled mobilization' and the *Führerprinzip* of European fascism. Perón's rhetoric spelt an authoritarianism not traditionalist but 'revolutionary'. Its result was to be a powerful if demagogic alliance between the military, the 'national bourgeoisie' and a working class paternalistically pampered (Evita's *descamisados*) as a *plebs* rather than respected, as in the Keynesian West, as an independent estate of the realm. As growth receded this unstable, unpolitical coalition began to crack; the pampa's Caesar went 'radical' and decided to take on the landed class and the church. Two years later, the navy bombarded his presidential palace and Argentina entered on almost three decades of dramatic political instability (17 presidents and 9 coups since 1955).[28] Once more, the institutions had been extensively damaged and the state enjoyed no real national, i.e. all-class authority.

According to the distinguished Argentinian political scientist Guillermo O'Donnell, the trouble with the modern state in his country is that it has been too much 'colonized' by civil society. Social groups encroached upon the state, projecting their conflicts onto the institutions and thereby splitting and weakening state power. This may sound paradoxical in view of the commonplace identification of repressive cycles with 'strong' states; yet sociologically these two things can be vastly different from each other. For instance, the British state in the 1950s or 1960s was conspicuously more consensual and less muscular than Franco's state in Spain, yet its 'infrastructural power' was much greater. Authoritarian states are not necessarily the most authoritative ones; this is not liberal wishful thinking but a sound sociological remark. O'Donnell further suggests that the very strength of the 'popular sector' in the de-Perónized politics of 1955–73 gave the national (industrial) bourgeoisie a strategic ally, enabling the urban upper class to challenge more effectively the hegemony of the rural oligarchy.[29] Moreover, the very fact that the country's main exports, meat and grain, were also the chief components of the Argentinian diet induced a pact between the national bourgeoisie's defence of a home market and the interest of the urban masses in avoiding consumption reductions entailed by export price rises.

At any rate, one thing is sure: a praetorian Argentina (1955–83), a country where political decay seemed insurmountable and periodical military intervention unavoidable, political life never allowed room enough for continuity in economic policy. The contrast with Brazil could not be greater. In Argentina de-, re- and then once again de-Perónized, it was as though the old fragmentation of state power reproduced itself, except that whilst in the past the strife was between provinces, now it took place between warring social forces: the different sectors of the bourgeoisie, the army, the unions, the technocrats, the political class, and, of course, the student guerrillas. But the outcome

28 For an analytical survey of the political process leading from electoral reform to the fall of Perón, see Peter H. Smith, *Argentina and the Failure of Democracy: Conflict among Political Elites, 1904–1955*, Madison, University of Wisconsin Press, 1974. A good account of Argentinian politics since then can be found in Eduardo Crawley, *A House Divided: Argentina 1880–1980*, London, Hurst, 1985.

29 Cf. Guillermo O'Donnell, 'Estado e Alianças na Argentina, 1956–76', in Paulo Sérgio Pinheiro, ed., *O Estado na América Latina*, Rio, Paz e Terra/CEDEC 1977, and also idem, *Modernization and Bureaucratic Authoritarianism: Studies in South American Politics*, Berkeley, University of California, 1973.

was basically the same as under Rivadavia, Rosas or Urquiza: a permanent weakening of the state (despite its growing hold on the economy) because of *persistent political civil war*. Aestheticians used to say that for art to work there must obtain a minimum of 'aesthetic distance' from reality. For a state to work there must also be some 'political distance' from society. In pre-Alfonsín Argentina, for all the sabre-rattling and martial posturing, there never was such a distance – hence the military's desperate appeal, in 1973, to the aged Perón and his worn-out populist witchcraft. Naturally enough, this began to falter even before his death, and it could not survive in the unsure hands of Isabelita, his widow and heiress in the Casa Rosada.

The extraordinary length of the Argentinian political crisis is often referred to as an *institutional* disease. But in fact the Argentinians, the most literate and best educated of all peoples from Iberian stock, have a more than reasonable grasp of the right meaning and role of most modern political institutions, and a fairly long tradition thereof. Take their political parties, for instance: whilst in Brazil most parties have been rootless and ephemeral, the Argentinian party system is older and better grounded than the Italian and even the French ones, at least in their present forms. Therefore the root of the problem in modern, authoritarian Argentina seems to have been not a lack of institutions but a long deficiency in political culture – in the way most influential groups value, and hence react to, the 'rules of the game', that is, the normal mechanisms of representative democracy. (To say this does not, of course, in itself explain *why* Argentinian political culture had that particular character.)

What about modern, authoritarian Brazil? During the Old Republic, the archcentralism of the Brazilian state was largely dismantled. There was a Jacobin, statist wing among the first republican generation, which was comprised of Comptian positivists. They were widely influential within an army which had been much enlarged since the Paraguayan war and whose officers often felt snubbed by the imperial establishment.[30] But the new power elite to emerge after the collapse of the monarchy was a political class composed of lawyers with a clear landowning background rather than of bureaucrats. The new leaders were in this way more class representative than the state-builders of the empire had been. They calmly proceeded to establish the federation as a prop of the main economic interests of the major provinces; hence followed the

---

30 Cf. J. G. Merquior, 'The politics of Brazilian positivism', *Government and Opposition*, vol. 17, Autumn 1982. On the military mind at the dawn of the Old Republic, see Paulo Mercadante, *Militares e Civis: a ética e o compromisso*, Rio, Zahar, 1978, pp. 51–77, and Edmundo Campos Coelho, *Em Busca de Identidade: O Exército e a Política na Sociedade Brasileira*, Rio, Forense Universitária, 1976, pp. 34–96.

early, majestic succession of presidents from coffee-rich São Paulo (1894–1906), the nearest thing Brazil had to a Whig oligarchy. It was only when export prices fell that the coffee barons, needing the helping hand of the Union, stooped to sharing power and had to make room (as in 1906) for politicians from cattle-raising Minas, thereby establishing the famous marriage of 'coffee-and-milk', with power supposedly alternating between Minas and São Paulo. This unwritten alliance, in turn, had to weather throughout the 1920s growing urban dissatisfaction, continuous electoral fraud, and young Turk-like agitation within the army. Shortly before the 1929 crash, the *paulista* rulers, instead of imitating Sáenz Peña, chose to keep the system of oligarchic rule and to break the ruling coalition by denying Minas its turn to hold the presidency. Thus the power elite was divided when its economic basis in agro-exports was hurt by the onset of the Depression. Thanks to its division, more than anything else, a leader from a peripheral state, the *gaucho* Getulio Vargas, stepped in, in the name of nation-wide discontent (1930).

In Argentina, the impact of the 1929 crash was as we saw a conservative backlash; in Brazil it sounded the hour of Bonapartism. A crafty politician, Vargas was put into the position of mediator between the democratic counter-establishment and its urban constituency, the weakened landed classes, the army's young Turks (*tenentes*) and, as the decade unfolded, the local communists and fascists. An authoritarian moderniser who was also a virtuoso compromiser, Vargas wielded a mild form of *Führerprinzip*; but he avoided the popular mobilization later relished by Perón as much as any true implementtion of his officially corporatist state.[31] Above all, he fully restored the centralist thrust of the Brazilian state, to the point of burning provincial flags. His dictatorship – the 'New State', 1937–45 – also gave a new impetus to 'infrastructural power' through the creation of a truly national modern bureaucracy and the launching of a core of heavy industry. With Vargas, two key aspects of the Brazilian state tradition were revived: over-centralism and state aloofness from class-rule.

The liberalization of 1945 and the 1946 constitution gave Brazil 18 years of limited democracy, roughly tantamount, in political terms, to the Argentinian experiment of 1916–30. It was in the main a period of party politics in a liberal–populist mould.[32] Thus at long last the despotic dimension of state power was, to a fair measure, contained. In

31 For a shrewd short discussion of the ideological temper of Vargas's Estado Novo, see Vamireh Chacon, *Estado e Povo no Brasil — as experiências do Estado Novo e da democracia populista*, 1937–64, Rio, José Olympio, 1977, pp. 40–58.

32 For the history of the period, see Thomas E. Skidmore, *Politics in Brazil, 1930—64: An Experiment in Democracy*, New York, Oxford University Press, 1967.

the infrastructural dimension, however, state power remained highly centralized. The breakthroughs in industrialization during the bold Kubitschek administration (1956–61), shortly after the sad end of Vargas's constitutional return to office, were undertaken by a neo-Bismarckian state which, while inviting the collaboration of foreign capital, was very keen on harnessing resources for investment under its own financial and planning control. Significantly, it was Kubitschek's chief planner, Roberto Campos, who masterminded the centralist streamlining of the economy from 1964 to 1967, following the military take-over. The 1964 breakdown of democracy seems better explained by a historist analysis of the internal socio-political situation rather than by causes exogenous to the polity: government instability, the disintegration of the party system, virtual paralysis of legislative decision-making; equivocal attitudes on the part of President Goulart, not least with regard to his own succession; the threat of an ill-defined agrarian reform; military concern with government-blessed sergeants' mutinies; and mounting radicalism on both the right and the left. And all of this was compounded by soaring inflation and, of course, by the haunting ghost of the Cuban revolution.[33]

It is easy to see this 'second republic', which in the early 1960s became plagued by an economic downturn, as bound to fail, a prey to growing political mobilization and bourgeois reaction. This is easy but misleading – a blatant case of the 'tyranny of hindsight'. For the truth is that the democratic decades did on the whole perform quite honourably on economic and political grounds. The average yearly growth (7 per cent) was remarkable. As for politics, it was becoming increasingly less clientelistic and more socially representative. Democracy was maturing, not degenerating, when civilian leadership started to fail.

Many, however, still wonder whether the pattern of modernization and development in twentieth-century Brazil is not bound to reproduce the excessive centralism of the state-building age; this is worrying once it is remembered that over-centralization was associated with a high level of 'despotic power'. Of course the two-decade experience, just finished, of modernizing authoritarianism,[34] which put the country into

33 The political deadlock has been exceedingly well analysed in Wanderley Guilherme dos Santos, *The Calculus of Conflict: Impasse in Brazilian Politics and the Crisis of 1964*, PhD dissertation, Stanford University, 1974.

34 For the history of the post-1964 period, see Peter Flynn, *Brazil: a Political Analysis*, London, Benn, 1978, pp. 308–522 (up to 1977), and Ronald M. Schneider, *The Political System of Brazil: Emergence of a 'Modernizing' Authoritarian Regime, 1964–1970*, New York, Columbia University Press, 1971. Early 1970s assessments are contained in Alfred Stepan, ed., *Authoritarian Brazil – Origins, Policies, and Future*, New Haven, Yale University Press, 1973, 1973; mid-1970s ones in Riordan Roett, ed., *Brazil in the Seventies*, Washington, American Enterprise Institute for Public Policy Research, 1976. Outstanding

the league of the ten biggest industrial economies, seems to support such an impression. Yet one should, I submit, resist it. For those who think that, after the simple import-substitution stage, the mixed model of 'deepened' industrial growth, based as it is on state economy plus multinationals, requires the eclipse of democracy still have to prove their case. First of all, 'deepening' itself is a controversial premise.[35] Furthermore there are instances, like Venezuela or, most tellingly, Brazil herself from 1974 to 1979, where industrial expansion on the above mentioned basis has been accompanied either by fully-fledged democracy (Venezuela) or at least by undeniable (no matter how controlled) decompression leading to conspicuous liberalization (Brazil under Geisel and then Figueiredo).

When the Brazilian military rule began in 1964 few observers realized that the Castello Branco government was not just a triumph of reaction but also a form of neocapitalist, technocratic reformism[36] which was intent on sustained growth and modernization. No doubt it was also a centralizing reformism, for the military had always been one of the most centralist groups within Brazilian society. The fiscal system in particular reflected clearly the overbearing primacy of the nominally federal government. The state enhanced its extractive powers enormously; but it was the *central* state which, on the grounds of securing developmental breakthroughs, kept the lion's share of all the major taxes, leaving just crumbs to states and counties. And because centralism was once again rampant along the 'despotic' axis, two large imbalances were deepened rather than mitigated. First, the gap between the wealth of regions, so visible in the contrast between rich south and poor north-east, widened – especially as the result of a drought of biblical length. Second, the chasm between, on the one hand, the upper echelons of society and the expanded middle classes and, on the other, the poverty of the masses, which often amounts to sheer destitution, remains; the rise of an in-

---

attempts at conceptualizing the 'system' include Candido Mendes de Almeida's essays on the first (Castello Branco) military presidency in *Dados*, no. 1, 1966, and nos 2–3, 1967; Helio Jaguaribe, 'Political strategies of national development in Brazil', 1968, repr. in Irving L. Horowitz et al., eds, *Latin American Radicalism*, New York, Random House, 1969; Fernando Henrique Cardoso, *O Modelo Político Brasileiro*, São Paulo, Difel, 1972; and Celso Lafer, *O Sistema Político Brasileiro*, São Paulo, Perspectiva, 1975, pp. 71–128.

35 For two well-known critiques, see José Serra, 'Three mistaken theses regarding the connection between industrialization and authoritarian regimes', in David Collier, ed., *The New Authoritarianism in Latin America*, Princeton, Princeton University Press, 1979 and, in the same volume, Albert O. Hirschman, 'The turn to authoritarianism in Latin America and the search for its economic determinants'.

36 A remarkably perceptive exception was Candido Mendes.

dependent union movement in the industrial heartland sprang from the labour aristocracy of São Paulo but this did not do much for the peasants or for (an important newcomer) the rural proleteriat (*boia-frias*) linked, in centre-south farms, to new ventures in agro-export such as the soya boom. The social face of 'despotic' centralism was indeed an ugly one, the cold mask of too uncaring a society. The demographic explosion compounded the problem; population growth, far more than capital-intensive modern technology, largely offset the remarkable job-creation of the 'Brazilian miracle' which was at its peak from 1967 to 1973.

Centralism, however, was politically half-hearted. The new regime issued an up-to-date, Gaullist constitution (1967), but proferred no new political formula and cared little about new symbols of legitimacy. Its economic plan, predicated on financial discipline in order to widen and strengthen economic development, implied a compromise, underwritten by the state, between different sectors of the wealthy classes as well as a temporary demobilization of the masses. Now to some analysts, not necessarily Marxist, this blend of upper class entente and popular de-mobilization constituted a parafascist intervention. Others, mindful that historical fascism involved precisely mass mobilization, prefer to call it a new, bureaucratic–military brand of authoritarian domination.[37] Certainly the hardening of military rule around 1969–70, during the guerrilla flare-up, lent more scope and consistency to authoritarianism, even if state violence in Brazil never reached the sad levels of the Southern Cone countries. Yet even before 'decompression', experts on authoritarianism such as Juan Linz were describing the Brazilian case as an authoritarian 'situation' unwilling to institutionalize its hierarchic and coercive elements.[38] The trouble with the authoritarian regime was that it refused to see itself, as such, as a regime, instead of a temporary (however prolonged) response to the self-destruction of the democratic polity.

That is also why liberalization came after all so smoothly. There was no externally induced collapse of armed rule, as in Greece in 1974 or Argentina in 1982. The foreign relations of authoritarian Brazil were if anything successful. Tension with Argentina because of Brazilian deter-mination to build the great Itaipú dam across the Paraná river led, through skilful diplomacy, to compromise and agreement (1972 and 1979). Without a collapse of the technocratic-military order, liberaliz-ation (the *abertura*) was even more gradual and incremental than in

37 For the 'parafascist' thesis, see Gino Germani, *Sociología de la Modernizacíon*, Buenos Aires, Eudeba, 1969; for the 'bureaucratic–military' thesis, see Juan Linz, 'The future of an authoritarian situation on the institutionalization of an authoritarian regime: the case of Brazil', in Stepan, *Authoritarian Brazil*.

38 Linz, 'The future of an authoritarian situation'.

Spain – but the absence of an institutional paradigm for consolidating illiberal rule was an important negative precondition in the return to democracy. From the outset the reluctant state elite sought no further validation than whatever legitimacy can be born of lasting economic success. As a keen analyst of the Brazilian scene, Ludovico Incisa, a diplomat and a political scientist, surmised by 1973, as long as the system went on delivering the goods (at the impressive growth rate of 11 per cent a year) there was little reason to expect real change.[39] Conversely, as soon as, after 1981, growth rates plummeted amidst inflation and the toll of the giant foreign debt, technocratic praetorianism had nothing to oppose to the nemesis of its own, rather naive economism.

Conclusion

Brazil has, in the opinion of the political scientist Bolivar Lamounier, a liberal democratic tradition both in institutions and political culture. What seems to be missing in her history is rather the practice of representative democracy, involving its normally high degree of mobilization, its mass parties and their regular alternation in office.[40] The New Republic, inaugurated in 1985, does not seem destined to lag behind Alfonsin's democracy south of the River Plate. In fact, despite all the differences in their social and political evolution, both countries came increasingly to share many key aspects of their recent past as well of their painful but by no means grim present. The long recurrence of a stop–go, or boom–bust, patern of growth eventually led both nations to undergo wild levels of stagflation. This has had decisive political and not only economic effects. Each country has been taught the futility of attempting to re-enact the facile 'social contract of inflation' which transferred income to industrialists (without taxing the farmers) by means of easy credit and overvalued currency since this had spectacular inflationary and growth-inhibitory results. Both have learned that wild inflation, by eating up wages and still more by precluding growth and therefore employment, is indeed the 'cruellest of all (modern) taxes'. A huge debt, the prospect of slower growth, the pitfalls of unseasoned democracy: the two republics do face a common problematic.

39 Ludovico Garruccio (alias Ludovico Incisa di Camerana), 'L'Egemonia militare in Brasile. Le alternative e il nuovo modello politico', in Garruccio, ed., *Momenti dell'Esperienza Politica Latino-Americana — tre saggi su populismo e militari in American Latina*, Bologna, Il Mulino, 1974, p. 251.

40 Bolivar Lamounier, 'Apontamentos sobre a questão democrática brasileira' in Alain Rouquié, B. Lamounier and Jorge Schvarzer, eds, *Como Renascem ad Democracias*, São Paulo, Brasiliense, 1985, p. 106.

Their current leaders *seem* to be learning from history. In Argentina, 40 years of political instability (praetorianism in Huntington's sense) forced the country's elites and interest groups to realize the value of civic consensus. The state, in their view, is no longer up for grabs, and therefore should not once more reproduce the old propensity to disunity and fragmentation. In Brazil, 20 years of demobilization ended up in the only industrial economy in the world which has no decent welfare state. While Argentina, in order to exorcize the ghost of statelessness, must now stick to a badly needed civic code, Brazil, in order to curtail the despotic side of its own strong state, cannot but sign a long overdue social contract – although no one can tell in advance how this could work without much economic centralism. One thing is certain: anything short of both these two goals ought to be deemed unworthy of both the promise and the reality of two splendid national spaces.

While in Argentina president Alfonsín's rule bravely turned against inflation and brought the military to book for their brazen violations of human rights, in Brazil the New Republic under José Sarney also wages war on inflation no less boldly if in better conditions (that is, in a spell of growth recovery) and seems determined to bridge the huge social gaps of the country and to promote a long needed agrarian reform. No wonder both rulers enjoy today unheard-of rates of popular support and national as well as international respect.[41]

41 This chapter was already printed when three important recent works came to my attention: vols IV and V of the *Cambridge History of Latin America*, ed. Leslie Bethell, Cambridge, Cambridge University Press, 1986, covering the period from 1870 to 1930; and Emilia Viotti da Costa's *The Brazilian Empire — myths and histories*, Chicago, University of Chicago Press, 1985, where chapter 8 contains one of the finest discussions of the social background of the fall of the monarchy in 1889.

11

Supranationals and the State

Susan Strange

For most of the last century people of many nationalities and a variety of political persuasions have been wishing, hoping, predicting – and sometimes even working – for the withering away of the state. Yet the state remains. It still looms large on the horizon of every individual life. It does not look like disappearing any more quickly in the next 50 years than in the last 50. And while the world economy has become ever more closely knit together, and while cheaper and easier transport and communications have created the beginnings of what one might reasonably call a world society, the international political system with which students of international relations have been mainly concerned has remained fundamentally unchanged. It still consists of a society of territorial states whose governments are united in their proclaimed deference to the principles of sovereignty and autonomy. True, its membership has grown very substantially. There were hardly more than two score states at the beginning of the century. There could be four times as many before its end. Yet the principles of the system have changed only very little. The exercise of political authority by its members is still for the most part bounded by territorial limits (or to be more precise, in view of the extension of authority to exclusive zones at sea, by cartographical limits). And the exercise of that authority requires the acquiescence (if not the formal recognition) of other similarly recognized political authorities. Between these authorities, the system allows both for conflict and for cooperation. Despite nearly a century of effort to limit the one and to nurture and extend the other, these attempts have not been nearly as successful as the idealists and internationalists have hoped. The essentially anarchic quarrelsome society of states has not fundamentally changed.

The argument presented in this chapter is an attempt to offer an explanation (or perhaps a political explanation) for the persistence of the state as *the* – or at least as *a* – major entity in the international political system, and for its continued enjoyment (in most cases) of predominant political authority within its own territorial limits. It will suggest and try to explain a paradox. For while the authority of the state has been under attack from two different directions, at the hands of two different kinds of supranational or transnational entities, at the same time both of these supranational entities have also been busily contributing to the power and authority of the state.

The situation I propose to describe can best be understood by analogy. In a large and powerful river, where the river is broad and the water is shallow, sandbanks appear. At the upstream end, the river will tend to erode the sandbank. At the downstream end, it will tend to build them up. Occasionally, some sandbanks will be washed away. New ones will appear. But the simultaneous process of erosion and deposition will go on all the time. That, so it seems to me, is just what has happened to international society, to what Bruce Miller calls the world of states; and what is still happening at the hands of the two major kinds of supranational entity that we observe in the world today, to wit, international organizations and transnational corporations. Both are building up the sandbank of state power at the same time as, in other ways, they are eroding it.

It has to be added that the deposition of new powers with the state – like the silt or sand to the sandbanks – has been substantially aided by two historical phases that have directly or indirectly affected all the states in the society of states. Or rather, one should say four phases since each – both wars and slumps – have occurred twice in living memory: there have been two world wars – and, indeed a long-drawn-out 'cold war' with some especially acute periods – and two world economic depressions.

All these systemic changes – like changes in the state of the river itself as when a spring flood might wash down an extra quality of silt from the hills above – have tended vastly to increase the powers of the state, regardless of the political ideology professed by its government. This is a commonsensical point often lost sight of by students of comparative politics or comparative sociology. They become so interested in the many queer ways in which societies and political systems differ from one another that they sometimes overlook the ways in which their behaviour is strikingly similar. (In truth, they should not be called comparative studies at all but contrastive, for they concentrate on the contrasts not the comparisons.) It is a tendency easily corrected by attention to international studies, and particularly to world history, both political, economic and societal.

In our own times, for instance, Franklin Roosevelt was elected to balance the budget and restrain federal power. Yet the increase in federal spending and taxation and the proliferation of federal agencies had never before been so great as under the New Deal. At the same time, across the Atlantic, the increase of state power under the National Socialist government of Germany as compared with the Weimar Republic was powered with the same economic forces of slow economic growth, credit scarcity and consequent unemployment that occasioned the New Deal. And more recently, President Reagan when elected promised to reduce the power of the federal government and to turn the rising tide of state spending. Yet he has presided over fiscal deficits that broke all previous records, and (despite some peripheral deregulation) over an increase in the powers of some key agencies like the Federal Reserve Board and the Comptroller of the Currency and over more protective intervention on behalf of uncompetitive American industries than had been seen for many years. Nor is he alone. Notwithstanding the wave of deregulation in certain limited sectors started by the United States, it seems that the 1980s have witnessed an extension of the powers of all states over everyday life – over prices, wages, imports, credit, educational systems and factory conditions for instance – as states have struggled to respond to the vicissitudes of international debt, shrunken markets and rising unemployment.

As for wars, it must be obvious that the powers assumed by governments at war over the life and death of individuals, over how much people eat (and drink), over where and how they work, over where they may and may not go and what they may and may not say were all vastly enhanced in the First World War, never entirely abandoned after it. They were once again enhanced during the Second World War. Yet while wars and slumps tend to reinforce state power in a cyclical manner, international cooperation has tended to increase both secularly and cyclically. It tends to increase steadily as technical imperatives make adaptive cooperation (as in the organization of transborder railways, air transport, telegraph or radio systems) more necessary. And it tends to increase in a mildly cyclical pattern in the aftermath both of wars and of world economic depressions. After the First World War, the League of Nations, the International Labour Office and the Permanent Court of International Justice were established, each breaking new ground in the scope, the size and the aspirations of international institutions to supplant or restrain the power of the state in the world system. After the Second World War came the United Nations organization extending its concern for the preservation of peace and international order to a wide range of economic and social issues, including the preservation of human rights, the ending of colonialism and the assertion of common standards in all sorts of areas of state policy.

Though it was far less marked, we can also see a similar reaction to world depressions. In the mid-1930s, the major states in the international monetary system laid a new basis of restored order in the Tripartite Agreement of 1936. Too late, the Bruce Commission three years later recommended that the League of Nations set up permanent machinery for international economic cooperation. Today, too, in a similar reaction to economic disorder and uncertainty, there are signs of a shift in opinion towards genuine monetary reform – as distinct from the phoney 'reforms' of the 1970s – and towards some strengthening of the machinery for managing the world economy.

Much more powerful, and certainly more apparent, has been the secular trend towards the internationalization of markets and of production. The growth of transnational corporations – the misnamed 'multinationals' – has so undermined the coincidence that used to prevail between state borders and economy borders that everyone today is aware of the effects this has had on the capacity of states to order and manage their national economies. The globalization of business – and the powerful response of enterprises, public as well as private, to it – constitute the second great eroding force on the power of the state. It is if anything intensified by the sharpened competition between enterprises for shares in a world market shrunken by world depression.

No wonder then that the onset of the second world economic depression has tended to revive academic interest in the perennial question of the twentieth century: is the state gaining power or losing it? The debate has intensified of late not only among sociologists but also in other branches of social science. Those economists still concerned with the real world (and not lost like so many of their fellows in a world of mathematical abstractions) are currently engaged in a series of discussions revolving around the relation of political authority to market forces. The whole question of fixed and floating exchange rates, for instance, which was thought by the late 1970s to have been a closed issue, has been reopened. There is discussion of the costs and benefits of protection by various means. And there are great debates ranging from the deeply philosophical to the abstruse and technically complex about the role of money and the machinery for its management and about the management of the credit-creating institutions, both banks and near-banks.

Political scientists, too, are showing a rather marked lack of agreement among themselves as to whether the state is or is not growing in power. The central theme chosen for the triennial world congress of political scientists in Paris in July 1985, was 'The changing state and its interaction with national and international society'. But predictably, whilst some discounted the extent of fundamental change, and others insisted upon it, the great majority were uncertain and hedged their bets. As one of them put it:

There is no clearcut answer to the question of whether the state's competence is widening or withering ... the foreseeable future is likely to be one of states limping along, muddling through as it were, buffeted by internal and external forces that leave the norms, habits and practices relevant to their capacities for cooperation hovering endlessly on the brink of transformation yet managing to persist through time.[1]

It has to be said that the current uncertainty and confusion of the political scientist is evidently greater in the United States than in Europe, and greater too among the international relations people who have been interested in international organizations than in those who have been interested in, for example, other branches of the subject such as strategic studies or foreign policy analysis. The reason in both cases is that the exaggerated expectations of a few years ago have now been replaced by chilling disillusion. The Americans in the 1950s and 1960s exaggerated the power of the US government to solve the problems of the domestic economy and society and to dominate and shape the international system. The so-called behavioural revolution in the social sciences swept through the universities like an epidemic, replacing attention to the state and the realists' 'world of states' with attention to systems and to the quantitative analysis of systems. The violence of the reaction that set in in recent years was one which Europeans and many other non-Americans found somewhat surprising.

Similarly, enthusiastic students of international organization were once apt to exaggerate the changes in state behaviour likely to be brought about when governments agreed – often for mixed and contradictory reasons – to set up new intergovernmental institutions like the United Nations, the European Economic Community or the Organization of Petroleum Exporting Countries. Now that the limitation of each of these have been so often demonstrated that they are undeniable, there is growing disarray to be seen among the theorists who seek to find general theories to explain the growth and the decline of international 'regimes'. All this is very different from the prevailing academic opinion 50 years ago – and perhaps suggests that ordinary people should exercise some caution in paying too serious attention to academic opinion. Then, Harold Laski was writing scornfully about the pretensions of the state, its boundaries 'instinct with difficulty rather than implicit with

1 J. N. Rosenau, 'The state in an era of cascading politics, wavering conceptions, widening competence for weathering change' (mimeo), IPSA XIII World Congress, 1985.

meaning'.[2] He poured scorn on its moral pretensions in the light of immoral behaviour and revelled in his own acumen in seeing the social skeleton and class structures beneath the flesh of political constitutions. His thoughts on international relations outlined in *A Theory of Sovereignty* were not too different from those of a contemporary, David Mitrany, still remembered as the father of functionalism – the notion that the habits of cooperation developed by technocrats in adaptive international organizations would slowly transform the behaviour of states towards each other in 'more political' matters. Yet even while they were writing in the mid-1930s there was hardly a state – China was the major exception – in which the hold of government over society and economy was not stronger than it had been before the world depression.

My purpose, however, being to shed some small ray of light on the current confusion, the next question is how best to demonstrate my contention that states are being sustained by two prevailing groups of supranational entities even while they are also being undermined by them. One way would be simply to give a selection of illustrative evidence of the ways in which this is being done. That seems to be unsatisfactory because it may be said that circumstantial evidence can always be selected that will back a particular argument. So, though examples will be useful, they will perhaps be more convincing if set in a broader historical perspective of change in the international political economy. By this means it is easier to identify the shifting bases of the power and authority of states – which are both social and economic – and thus the ability of both political institutions and economic enterprises to either reinforce and sustain or to challenge and diminish that power and authority.

Broadly speaking, it may be said that, looking back over the past millennium, two changes relevant to the state have taken place. There has been a change in the basis of state wealth, and therefore power, from land and labour to capital and knowledge – including in 'knowledge' not only technology but also other kinds of information. And in the last century or less, there has been a change in structural power which from being contained within the state now spills out far beyond its frontiers, returning in some respects to an earlier pattern in which supranational institutions – the medieval church in Europe, for example – enjoyed certain kinds of structural power over secular governments whose authority was territorially bounded.

Let us take first the change from land and labour as the basis of state power to capital and knowledge. The argument is simple. The exercise

2 H. J. Laski, 'International government and national sovereignty' in *Problems of Peace*, London, Geneva Institute of International Relations, 1927, p. 289.

of political authority consumes resources. Though by imposing order it may make possible or easier the production of resources by others, the rulers and their servants, including generals and judges, are not themselves productive. Authority therefore has to tax the economy; it has to extract resources from society in order to support itself. In a preindustrial economy with limited transport systems and therefore limited opportunities for trade, the major source of wealth was agriculture, with hunting perhaps contributing some marginal resources.[3] The land is necessary for the production of food and other crops; and manpower – labour – is necessary both to cultivate the land and to provide the means of military force to acquire more land.

All the great empires of the ancient world, therefore, were built by the acquisition of more land by military conquest. Once built, great empires could exploit the manpower of their dominions to supplement their own resources of military manpower with auxiliaries, whether voluntarily recruited or compulsorily conscripted. The state in each case also enhanced its ability to tax the products of the land and therefore to increase the resources it could dispose of for political purposes, whether this was building pyramids or road systems or organizing elaborate games and entertainments.

With certain differences, the economic basis of political power was still the same in medieval Europe as it had been in the ancient world. Weaker states and a more insecure political system meant a sharing of the power to tax the resources produced by land and labour. Security systems became more localized. There was no *Pax Romana*. Feudal lords therefore exacted resources from the land which gave them political power. So too did the church and the great religious orders – the first capitalist enterprises whose ability to accumulate capital and invest it in long-term land improvement was not limited by the mortality of the individual. Between rulers, wars were fought for land and the rulers who could muster the largest military forces were those with command and authority over the largest feudal pyramid of landed barons and their vassals. And besides conquest there were the other means of acquiring land. As the old farming saying has it, there are three ways to acquire land: patrimony, matrimony and parsimony. Between rulers, therefore, the pursuit of daughters bringing substantial dowries of taxable land was a recognized form of interstate rivalry. And disputes over patrimonial rights and succession were a common cause of conflict and insecurity within and between states up until the eighteenth century.

---

3 Hunting in northern Europe would soon have ceased through the depletion of species to be a useful source of scarce protein in winter if everyone had been free to do it. Hence its restriction, backed by political power, to members of a ruling class.

In this pre-industrial economy, only a very few states were able to exploit the possibilities of commercial exchange successfully enough to find in trade a secure basis of political power. Trade had to be highly profitable to provide the resources sufficient to stand up to states built on resources of land and labour. For a time the city-states of Italy aided by more advanced technology were able to exact enough tax from their traders and artisans to pay *condottieri* for their defence. But as the invasion of Italy by Charles VIII of France in 1494 showed only too painfully, no alliance of city-states was strong or firm enough to resist such a large territorial state coming from outside. Only Venice, sustained by sea power, proved less vulnerable. And it was only other ports with similar sea power and similar opportunities for accumulation through sea trade – towns such as Hamburg, Antwerp, Genoa, and later London – which were able to acquire power in the world of states by exploiting trade as well as land and labour.

The nineteenth century can be seen as the period of balance – halfway between the old political economy which gave power to states with command over land and labour and the new political economy of today and of the future which gives power to states with command over capital and technology. In the nineteenth century and more or less until the First World War, the majority of the working population even in the most advanced industrialized countries still worked on the land. The productivity of agriculture was therefore still a major determinant of wealth which an efficient state machine could extract by taxation. And since mercenaries (like the *condottieri* before them) had been shown to be no match for armies imbued with nationalist fervour, rightly preferring to run away and live to fight another day, the European states now depend on their manpower to provide them with large conscript armies. But already technology in weaponry was proving more decisive. The French *poilus* overrun at Sedan in 1870 by a better equipped Prussian army were mown down again at Verdun in 1916, once again outclassed by more advanced military technology (tanks, poison gas, Big Berthas).

And in the world beyond Europe, the domination of Europeans over non-Europeans was achieved not only through their advanced technology and therefore ability to conquer and rule, but also through their control of credit. Wealth gave them the ability to grant or to withhold the capital which even then was vital to other states with undeveloped economies which they hoped to modernize and make more productive. Tsarist Russia, for example, with more men and more land than France, was yet the junior partner through her dependence on French credit and French (and other foreign) technology. The Ottoman Empire, similarly, was vulnerable to European states less because of military weakness – it performed well enough in the Dardanelles encounter after all – than because of its debts and its dependence on foreign capital. Other debtors like Egypt and Morocco actually lost their autonomy through dependence on foreign loans which they could neither repay nor service. And across the Atlantic, the domination exercised by the United States over Central America and the Caribbean at the turn of the century was only partly due to the superior naval power exhibited in the Spanish American war; it was also the result of the ability to lend capital to indigent or incompetent governments.

If 'parsimony' is taken as a synonym for capital accumulation, it has certainly replaced matrimony as a useful tool of interstate relations and as a means of increasing power and influence over others. As late as the post-1945 period, the British Dominions, as they were then still called, were still looking to Britain to supply capital for development. Only when those hopes proved empty did the old imperial links weaken and break. By then, too, it was obvious to all that the one state still able to supply capital to others was the United States of America. It was the only state to come out of the war with an economy vastly stronger and more productive than it had had at the beginning, apart from India which was divided, poor and populous, and the neutrals like Sweden and Switzerland which were small and cautious. American domination of Western Europe, Latin America and the whole world market economy rested predominantly on its power to offer long-term loans or investments to countries whose appetite for imports to build, or rebuild, their economies vastly exceeded their capacity to earn foreign exchange by producing for export.

By 1945, however, another major change had taken place in the relative importance of the four factors of production – land, labour, capital and technology – as bases for the power of states. The United States was ahead of all others in producing an atom bomb. If the Russians, the Germans or the Japanese or the Chinese had got there first, the outcome of the war and the post-war world would have been very different. And it was a military advantage achieved by recruiting a small, multinational band of rather pacific-minded scientists, not by any of the conventional sources of military might.

Hiroshima and Nagasaki, then, were a turning point in the evolution of states. For these terrible explosions left the United States with a brief monopoly of atomic weapons of destruction sufficiently threatening to balance the power of the only other victorious state still able to keep large numbers of what now became 'conventional' forces under arms. The opportunity costs of doing so must have slowed Soviet economic recovery and consequently widened the gap still further between American and Soviet GNP. By the end of the 1950s, and as demonstrated in the Cuban crisis of 1962, the monopoly had effectively become a duopoly, as the Soviet Union matched the American power not only to make nuclear weapons but to deliver them with intercontinental ballistic missiles.

The significance of this for the world of states was clear enough; armies, as traditionally understood, had become less important in the competition of states than technical superiority in the development of new destructive weapons. For thousands of years, armies had been necessary to conquer and to occupy territory – in order to acquire land. Now land was not so necessary to power, and the power to destroy cities in seconds was a more powerful threat than that of invasion, occupation and annexation. States, including the superpowers, still behaved as though land were the chief base of state power. John Foster Dulles's policy of containment aimed to confine the USSR within its territorial limits; and the Soviet Union in 1956, in 1968 and in 1981 fiercely resisted any internal challenges from Hungarians, Czechs and Poles that would have weakened its occupation of East European territory. But this was more because, as always, internal social cohesion was a necessary condition for the exercise of external power than because a territorial empire was a source of power and wealth.

By 1984, with Ronald Reagan's announcement of a Strategic Defence Initiative (SDI), the shift of interstate competition from competition for land to competition for technology became yet more pronounced. Whoever could first devise a defensive system against the delivery of nuclear warheads would enjoy a monopoly of immunity. The balance of nuclear power aptly described by the acronym MAD (Mutual Assured Destruction) would be gone, and the threat to survival posed by the proliferation of nuclear weapons among an ever-growing number of middle and even small states (like Israel or Spain) would have been averted. The dangers and uncertainties opening up before us as a result of SDI becoming more than a pipedream are matters of continuing debate, not least for the Europeans whose long experience of interstate conflicts have taught them that peace is often just as much in jeopardy when a major state is materially weakened as when one suddenly perceives itself as materially stronger.

The shifting of interstate competition to technology has a very direct bearing on the question before us: how do supranational entities add to or subtract from the power of states? The point is that neither international organizations nor transnational corporations occupy land. But both do dispose of technology, and that, together with their disposition over capital, is the major reason why in any study of states, the relation of a state to either international organizations or transnational corporations must make up an important part of the analysis.

It would not be so necessary to emphasize the point by setting it in a longer historical perspective if the conventional wisdom in the study of international relations had not been so slow to take the point. Textbooks still take an essentially territorial view of the bases of state power and the focus of interstate competition. Yet as long ago as 1968, Robert Gilpin, observing the importance attached by General de Gaulle to the organization and application of science in France, had written:

Just as the nation-state with its superior organization and resources, supplanted the city-state and feudal society after 1500, so today the organization of political life is being transformed by the role of science in human affairs. Increasingly, international politics will be dominated by large-scale political entities with substantial scientific and technological resources at their disposal.[4]

Gilpin's argument was that only the two superpowers still had the scientific and technological resources to enjoy full economic, military and political independence. Western Europe was caught between them and faced three dangers: that US corporations would pre-empt decision-making power over European industrial development; that the United States would control all the defence-related industries; and that there would be a continued brain drain westwards across the Atlantic which would rob European countries of their capacity for autonomous innovation. He ended by quoting a British European Movement report on European cooperation published in 1965 which wrote prophetically:

The conclusion forced upon us is that the European countries must pool their efforts if they wish to play a continuing part in world economic development. Otherwise, it will not be many years before they are so far behind the United States and the Soviet Union in advanced industrial fields that relatively they will have fallen to the level of underdeveloped countries.[5]

Just 20 years later, Dr W. Dekker, president of Philips, was repeating the warning. The *Untergang des Abendlander* predicted by Spengler would after all be their fate if European countries failed to realize that the only things they could achieve in the field of industrial innovation were the things they could achieve together. Referring to the world market for micro-electronics, he said:

If we wait too long for a European initiative, the result could be that we, in Europe, lose the battle [i.e. with the US and Japan]. Believe me, I am European enough to wait for the last possible moment and literally do everything possible

4 Robert Gilpin, *France in the Age of the Scientific State*, Princeton, Princeton University Press, 1968, p. 4.
5 United Kingdom Council of the European Movement, *European Cooperation in Advanced Technology*, Report of a conference, July 1965, p. 4, quoted in Gilpin, *France in the Age of the Scientific State*, p. 458.

to prevent that happening. If Europe is neither willing nor able to develop its own unique economic structure ... industrial innovation will pass Europe by.[6]

The scramble by Mitterand to get EUREKA, a rival research programme to SDI, off the ground and by other European governments to exert a counterforce pulling scientists and corporations back from contracting to work for the US programme, were further indications of the importance attached to SDI.

If Gilpin was somewhat ahead of the times with the book on French science policy, he was somewhat behind with a later and better-known one, *US Power and the Multinational Corporation: The Political Economy of Foreign Direct Investment*.[7] That is to say, he was the initiator for many readers of the notion that big transnational corporations were inimical to the interests not only of developing countries but also of developed ones. Beware, he told his fellow-Americans, of the example of the British who allowed so much of their wealth to be poured into foreign investments that their own industrial base degenerated and went into irreversible decline. This was the exact complement of a view of transnational corporation activity being propounded throughout the Third World, and at UNCTAD and the United Nations, and expounded by André Gunder Frank, Johann Galtung and a host of Latin-American *dependencia* writers. All of them saw the large foreign corporation as a threat to the autonomy and often the welfare – broadly defined – of the less developed countries.

It is my contention that both Gilpin and Galtung et al. were right – and that both were also wrong. They were both right in perceiving the power exercised in the system by TNCs, through their influence on the structure of production by the disposition of capital and of technology. It was true, as Gilpin said, that US electronic or clothing firms, for instance, that relocated production abroad either in what Michalet has called 'relay affiliates' or else in 'workshop affiliates'[8] were taking jobs from American workers and reducing manufacturing production in the United States. It was also true, as the *dependistas* said, that TNCs often kept control over research and development and used the proceeds of their sales in LDCs to finance more research and development. But it seemed to stretch credibility to accept both views. Could it be that

6 Dr W. Dekker, 'The importance of innovation on the economic structures of Europe', Paper delivered at a *Financial Times*-Institute for Research in Multinationals conference, Munich, April 1985.

7 New York, Basic Books, 1975.

8 C. A. Michalet, *Le Capitalisme mondiale*, Paris, Presses Universitaires de France, 1976. A relay affiliate was one which reproduced the production process developed for the TNC's own home state. A workshop affiliate was one in which part of the process was 'farmed out' by the parent company to an enterprise in another country.

TNCs were both undermining the power of the US for the benefit of the rest of the world, and that they were also undermining the power of the LDCs for the benefit of the US? That paradox could only be true if it could be argued that the TNCs were both a help and a hindrance, both antipathetic and sympathetic to the interests of both their home countries and their host countries.

That, essentially, is my argument: that there is a symbiosis between state and transnational corporation from which both benefit, that they are allies as well as competitors or opponents. That is why the one-sided interpretation of the role of transnationals put forward by Gilpin for the United States and by Galtung, UNCTAD and others for the developing countries is behind the times. It is denied everyday by the ever-increasing structural power of the United States to which US corporations have markedly contributed, and by the ever-increasing collaboration of foreign corporations in the industrial development of at least some developing countries.

That this should be so – and I shall suggest in a moment where the evidence for it is to be found – should not surprise anyone with some historical perspective. Take the relations between church and state from say the thirteenth to the eighteenth centuries. All the arguments over papal authority, and over the respective domains of canon and secular law, and all the use of 'ultimate weapons' by both sides – excommunication by the church, dispossession and death by the prince – bear witness to a perennial conflict between them. Yet both were well aware of the useful support forthcoming from the other. For the state, the church would legitimize the social order, sanctifying with divine blessing 'the station in life to which it has pleased God to call us', legitimizing foreign policy aims in the world beyond Europe, and anathematizing people whom the state regarded as dissidents as well as people whom the church regarded as heretics. For the church, the security necessary to communication between bishops and religious orders, the extension of the faith to the heathen, and resistance to the inroads of Islam on Christianity all required the cooperation of the state. It was only over the rights to tax and the rights of property that the really serious conflicts arose between the state and church, just as today it is over the same issues (in different disguise) that state and corporation come into conflict with each other. For the rest, now as then, it often suits both to pretend that each is totally opposed to the other. *Le Rouge et le Noir* was about a contest already obsolete when Stendhal wrote it, just as Disestablishment was a dead issue when Granville Barker wrote *Waste*. In the same way, political leaders continue to inveigh against the wickedness of the multinationals, and corporate executives to castigate the restrictions and the excessive nationalism of governments in public, while each – big business and big governments – is in the other's pocket in private.

The best illustration of this symbiosis is to be found in the multitude of joint production arrangements, one of which is almost certain to figure in the financial press on any chosen day of the week. The foreign corporation agrees to provide the technology, to open up access to the coveted export markets and to help arrange the finance; while the host state or one of its major state enterprises guarantees a preferred place in the domestic market, a good share of the output and the profits, freedom to repatriate them and in many cases a slice of the equity. It is by these means that so much of the world's manufacturing capacity has moved from north to south, from developed to developing countries. It could not have been done without the collusion of the multinationals. It was the Japanese corporations (and their banks) which helped put South Korean manufacturers – ships, steel, shoes and cars – on to Asian export markets. It was United States corporations that built up Mexico's industrial capacity. It was French companies that made possible industrial development in, for example, the Ivory Coast, just as it was the Germans in Brazil and the British in India.

All these newly industrializing countries (NICs) have found an easier and quicker way to gain access to the technology required for rapid industrialization. Japan's method of buying patents wholesale seems cumbersome and slow by comparison. As a result the great issue of the 1960s – nationalization – is rarely mentioned. As Edith Penrose pointed out many years ago, it was unnecessary and wasteful to buy 51 per cent (let alone 100 per cent) of a company if by buying 5 per cent of the shares a state could gain access to the information needed to negotiate a better bargain whether over profits, wages, exports or training.[9]

The big issue today is taxation. A good example of how crucial it is can be seen in Indonesia. From barely a dozen in 1973, the number of multinationals with regional headquarters in Manila rose in ten years to over 375. But when Indonesia was obliged to seek IMF help to service its debts, a condition of the $9.7 billion package was that the government reduce its fiscal deficit and tax the multinationals. Over 200, mostly but not all American, very promptly moved their offices elsewhere.[10] The moral of the tale is simply that big business and big government are now competing as tax authorities. One exacts tax by using coercive power – the *mafias* and religious authorities do the same

9 E. Penrose, '"Ownership and control": multinational firms in less developed countries', in G. Helleiner, ed., *A World Divided*, Cambridge, Cambridge University Press, 1976.

10 *International Management*, January 1985, p. 9.

– while the other exacts tax by 'internalizing the market' as the business school literature has it; in other words, by taking the tax out before the profit is declared instead of afterwards. The effect is the same, inasmuch as state and corporation then take political (i.e. non-market, non-profit-maximizing) decisions as to how and on whom the proceeds should be spent.

As for the international organizations, the ways in which these supranational entities sustain the state is rather different. The similarity of their role with that of the TNCs is only that their sustaining effect has been, on balance, far more effective than their undermining effect. For a great many new states in the world, recognition as members of the United Nations has been the major basis of their claim to legitimacy. For a start, it is necessary to make the point that international organizations fulfil these three functions in the world of states: adaptive, strategic, and symbolic. That is to say, they are sometimes set up in order to allow autonomous political authorities bounded by territorial limits to benefit from the economic opportunities offered by new systems of transport, communications or commerce. Thus, they must agree to adopt standard practices or rules and to resolve differences before they can make use of new techology, whether it is the electric telegraph or the communications satellite. In each case, states have been careful never to let the powers of an international bureaucracy extend beyond what is strictly necessary for the system to be workable. Alternatively, international organizations have been set up by a state or group of states essentially as tools of foreign policy. The cost is small, the PR effect is great, and the achievement (whether it is the administration of Marshall Aid by the OEEC in the 1950s, the coordination of allied forces by NATO or the Warsaw Treaty Organization or the prevention of default and ending of a debtors' profligacy by the IMF) is very much more impressive than anything that could be achieved through the exercise of bilateral diplomacy by the rich and strong acting on the poor and weak. Finally, some of the best-known international organizations in which the highest hopes reposed have turned out to be primarily symbolic. As Conor Cruise O'Brien, writing about the UN's Congo operations in 1960, once described it, they are 'ritual drama'. They express an aspiration; they acknowledge, as by genuflexion, a moral principle; and they profess faith in the reality of a society of mankind – but without accepting for one moment the costs of putting any of these highminded objectives into practice. It is only necessary to think of the UN's record on human rights, on sanctions, on genocide, on child welfare and wildlife to see that this is so.

Given that many international organizations fulfil more than one of these functions at the same time, this way of looking at them explains better than looking at the subject or issue-area of their operations – trade, money, security or whatever – why it is that some international organizations do appear to exercise an influence on states while others have reached an impasse of tedium and irrelevance from which even those most moved by their symbolism cannot save them. Those that are primarily symbolic in function have had least effect on state behaviour. Those that serve some powerful state's strategic purpose – counting the preservation of an open market system and the property rights of corporate capital as a strategic purpose – have had most effect on state behaviour. But the effects are uneven, as in any political system. The rulers do not abide by the rules they impose on the ruled. Just think of the fiscal profligacy practised by the United States with such impunity and the costly demands made by the IMF on Indonesia. And the organizations that are primarily adaptive do somewhat modify state behaviour, but only within strict limits set by the state's own definition of its national interest.

The result is that generalization about international organizations and their relation to states is increasingly impossible; a general theory is a chimera. Organizations are polarized between those which are irrelevant and dispensable, and those which serve an important political purpose. On their side, states too are polarized. International organizations have been fairy godmothers to weak and small states that posed no threat or that offered no tempting prize to more powerful neighbours. But they were little use to Hyderabad or Goa, to Nepal or Tibet, to the would-be nation-states like Biafra, West Irian, Kurdistan or the Polisario. They were of enormous legitimizing value to Tuvalu or Zimbabwe, to Bangladesh, or to the mini-states of the Caribbean. They are useful tools for strong states and useful sanctifiers and benefactors for small ones. Some, like the World Bank, can offer access to capital and technology which otherwise would be more costly or more inaccessible; state powers are thereby reinforced. Once again, a symbiosis is apparent. The fact that the Finance Minister of Upper Volta can spend up to half his working days receiving visiting aid missions from a galaxy of multilateral organizations and some bilateral donors when he should be putting his country's finances in some sort of order is just one indication of the mutual interest shared by the IMF and its 'victims', by the World Bank and its mendicant dependants.

Broadly speaking, it is the middle powers whose attitude to international bureaucracies is understandably ambivalent. They are too big to need either the sanctification or the largesse of international organizations but too small to be able, alone, to muster either the capital resources or the scientific and technological ones to keep up with the great continental superpowers. This, and not simply age and a sclerotic alliance of conservative interests opposed to change (as described by Mancur Olson[11]) is part of the reason for the weaknesses of the European Community and the European dilemma as perceived by industrialists like Dr Dekker. So acutely do the industrialists of Europe perceive the vulnerability of their home states to American and Japanese domination in advanced technologies that they have actually formed an association which, in conscious imitation of inter-governmental ones, they call the Group of 22. The 22 are the leading European TNCs like Siemens, Philips, Nestlé, Thyssen, Olivetti, Unilever, Ciba-Geigy and Volvo. Their purpose is to create a new industrial *élan* in Europe by funding new joint ventures in advanced technology, by combining research efforts and by influencing governments to act more positively – for all the reasons explained by Dr Dekker.

This is but one more illustration of a significant new phase in the development of the international political economy in which the association of corporate enterprises is becoming more like the association of political authorities – international organizations – and in which the competition between states for market shares, for capital and for technical leadership is becoming more and more like the competition of corporations for those very same objectives. It is hardly to be wondered at that, as these two global chess games merge with one another, there should be both more cooperation and more conflict between the two groups of players.

11 See M. Olson, *The Rise and Decline of States*, New Haven, Yale University Press, 1983.

Contributors

Peter Burke is University Lecturer in History at the University of Cambridge

Patricia Crone is Lecturer in Islamic History at the University of Oxford.

Colin Crouch is University Lecturer in Sociology at the University of Oxford.

Karen Dawisha is Professor of Politics at the University of Maryland.

Clive Gamble is Lecturer in Archaeology at the University of Southampton.

Ernest Gellner is Professor of Social Anthropology at the University of Cambridge.

John A. Hall is Senior Lecturer in Sociology at the University of Southampton.

Michael Mann is Reader in Sociology at the London School of Economics and Political Science.

J. G. Merquior was Professor of Political Science at Brasilia University until 1982.

Anthony D. Smith is Reader in Sociology at the London School of Economics and Political Science.

Susan Strange is Professor of International Relations at the London School of Economics and Political Science.

Index

Abbott-Seagraves, B., 40
aboriginal society, 30, 33, 35, 37, 51
absolutism, 179–80
Adams, J. C., 192
Adams, R. McC., 56, 58
Africa, state-making in, 255–9
African tribes, 52, 54
agriculture
   development of, 30–2
   effect of, 42
   and state power, 128–31
Akkermans, T., 207
Alaev, L. B., 82
Allen, J., 27
alliance systems, 32–4, 39–42, 47
Ambartsumov, E. A., 226
Amin, S., 232–3
Ammerman, A. J., 31
AMP (Asiatic Mode of Production),
   80–91, 95–107
Amsden, A., 170
Anderson, P., 81, 88, 93, 100–1, 180
Andropov, Y., 224, 226
Anquetil-Duperron, A. H. and Marx,
   93
Arabs
   and egalitarianism, 74–7
   as a tribe, 54
Arendt, H., 2, 211
Argentina, 124, 264–9, 276–88
Aristotle, 139, 143
Aron, R., 4, 5

Asia, state-making in, 253–4, 257,
   259
Asia Minor, city states in, 148
Asiatic Mode of Production see AMP
Asmus, R. D., 218
Australia, prehistory of, 35–8, 47
   see also aboriginal society
Austria, 186, 188, 198–9, 205–6, 210
authoritarianism, 18, 19, 38, 115–16
   see also despotism
autonomy
   in city states, 139–40, 143, 150,
      153
   in Europe, 162
   loss of, 23, 40, 41–6
   and state power, 15, 109–36, 235

Badie, B., 4
Bahro, R., 212
Bakunin, M. A., 99
Balazs, E., 151
bands as precursors of tribes, 50–1,
   54, 56–7, 64–5
Barbour, V., 145
Baron, C. and Florence, 138
Baron, S. H., 102
Barzun, J., 248
Beaton, J. M., 36
bedouin, 55
Belgium, 188–9, 193, 205
Belgrade declaration, 216
Bender, B., 32, 34, 36

Bendix, R., 115
Berend, I. T., 192, 197
Berger, S., 248
Bertelli, S., 140
Bethell, L., 272
Beyer, W., 236
Bicchieri, M., 29
Biebuyck, D. P., 49, 53
Binford, L. R., 31
Birdsell, J., 35
Blau, P., 29
Bloch, M., 143
Bogomolov, O., 220
Bonaparte, Louis and Marx, 121–2
Borisov, O. V., 219
Botana, N. R., 278
Bottomore, T., 200
Bowdler, S., 36
Boyd, A., 202
Bradley, R., 40
Brazil
    democracy in, 278, 282–4
    economy of, 271–2
    political elite in, 270–6
    slavery in, 270, 273, 276
    state-building in, 269–88
Brevilly, J., 228, 238–40
Brezhnev, V. I., 216–17, 218, 224
British European Movement, 229
bronze metallurgy, 27
Brown, J. A., 27, 33, 34
Brown, K., 150
Brown, T., 202
Buarque de Holanda, S., 274
Buenos Aires, 265–6, 268–9
Bukharin, N., 221
bureaucracy *see* state power
Burke, P., 162, 137–53
Burkhardt, J., 17, 138–9
Burlatsky, F. M., 226
Burns, R. I., 150
Butenko, A., 225
Butlin, N., 36
Butzer, K., 32

Cabral de Melo, E., 274
Cahen, C., 160

Cannon, A., 28
capitalism, 133, 175, 179, 180, 198,
    234–5
    and development of communism,
        79, 94, 99
    end of, 4–5, 6–7, 214
    industrial, 234
    and the state, 10, 16, 19, 155–68
    threats to, 7–8
capitalist democracies, 113–15
capstone government, 157
Carneiro, R. L., 28
Catalonia, city states in, 147
Catholicism, 245
    see also church, political role of
caudillismo in Argentina, 266, 268,
    277, 278
cemeteries, data from, 27
centralization and state power, 126–
    32, 285–6
'centre–periphery' models, 234
Chacon, V., 283
chambers of commerce, 191
Champion, T. C., 29
Cherry, J. F., 23, 27
chiefdoms, 28, 57, 60, 65
Childe, V. G., 11, 24–6
Chile, 270, 272
China, 16, 113, 157–8, 167
    cities in, 151–2
    see also Maoism
Chinese empire, 16, 235–6
church, political role of, 181–6,
    192–3, 202, 208, 301
Cingvla, V. I., 29
city-states, 137–53
    in Asia Minor, 148
    autonomy of, 139–40, 143, 150,
        153
    in Catalonia, 147
    and *contado*, 140–1
    in France, 143–5, 147
    in Germany, 146–7
    in Greece, 73, 148–9
    in Mesopotamia, 149
    model of, 140–2
    in Netherlands, 145

in northern Italy 138–46, 149
in Switzerland, 145–6
see also Sumer
Claessen, H. J., 27, 38, 57
Clarke, D. L., 40
class struggle, 7–8, 122, 125, 130
Clastrex, P., 127
Coe, M. D., 31, 63
Cohen, G. A., 79
Cohen, M. N., 31
Cohen, R., 38, 45, 71
cold war, 185
Cole, D. P., 54, 55
colonial states, 242, 252–3
Colson, E., 48
communism, 79, 178
in France, 183
communist manifesto, 88, 92
communist parties, 214, 216, 220–3
complexity and state development,
28–9, 32–4, 37–41
Conkey, M. W., 34, 36
Connor, W., 229
consociationism, 178, 187–9, 206–7
contado, 140–1, 144–5, 148
corporatism, 183–4, 186, 204–9
see also neo-corporatism
Cowie, T., 40
Creveld, M. L. van, 129
Crone, P., 12, 31, 48–77
Crouch, C., 177–210

Damas, D., 29
Darwin, C. and General Rosas, 267
Darwinism, 9
Dawisha, K., 211–27
defence and the state, 120–1
Dekker, W., 299–300, 305
democracies, power in, 113–15,
173–4
Denmark
economic development in, 196–9,
205–6
labour movements in, 196–7
social infrastructure in, 174
despotism, 113, 116, 118, 126, 132
in Brazil, 277

in China, 113
in Roman empire 113
in Russia 113, 130–1
Deutsch, K., 231
developed socialism, 210–27
developmental spiral, 37, 41–2
DeVore, I., 29–30
Diakonoff, I. M., 56, 58, 61–2
diffusion, 105–6
Djilas, M., 213
Dole, G. E., 52, 54
Dollinger, P., 147
domestication, 26–7
Donghi, H. D., 266
Dulles, J. F., 298
Dyson-Hudson, N., 52

Earle, T., 27
Eastern Europe and USSR, 216–20,
223, 224–5
Easton, D., 51
education, role of, in economic
development, 170–1, 174
Edzard, D. O., 56, 58, 61–2
egalitarianism, 61, 73–7
Egypt, 16, 57, 67
Eisenstadt, S. N., 51, 112, 128, 134
Elvander, N., 196
Elvin, M., 85, 156
Engel, D. W., 129
Engels, F., 4, 73, 82–5, 87, 90, 92–4,
98, 244
Ericson, J. E., 27
Eridu *see* Sumer
Eskimo society, 32
ethnic minorities, position of, 114
ethnie, 229, 241–63
Europe and the state system, 18
Europe, medieval
autonomy of cities in, 162
economy of, 161–5
infrastructure in, 164–6
see also Eastern Europe; *individual
countries*
Evans, G., 60
Evans-Pritchard, E. E., 51, 54, 55

Falkland Islands, 124
farming societies, 30–1
fascism, 7, 178, 184–5
federal nation, 260–2
Feller, R., 146
Fernea, R. E., 85
feudal state, 115
feudalism, 79, 119, 133, 154–5, 179,180
finance as basis of state power, 296–7
Finer, S., 8, 133
Finland and church power, 186, 201–3, 205–6
Finley, M., 148
Flannery, K. V., 28, 31, 38, 45
food production *see* agriculture
Foster, B., 61
Fowler, W. W., 139
Fox, A., 193
Foxon, A., 40
France
  city-states in, 143–4, 147
  communism in, 183
  corporatism in, 209–10
  economic development of, 191, 199, 205
  ethnicity of, 247–8, 258
  investment in, 174
  labour movement in, 183–5, 191, 199, 201
  political power of the church in, 182
  science in, 299
Frank, A. G., 300
Frankfort, H., 149
Freidel, D., 40
Freistadte *see* Germany, city-states in
Fried, M. H., 27, 56, 65, 68–9
Friedman, J., 29, 33
Friedrichs, C. R., 146

Gadd, C. J., 58, 60–1
Galenson, W., 197, 203
Gallie, B., 4
Galtung, J., 300

Gamble, C., 22–47
Gargallo, G., 138
Garrison-Estebe, J., 144
Garruccio, L., 287
Geary, D., 7
Geertz, C., 151
Gelb, I., 58, 59, 62, 63
Gellner, E., 39, 49, 54, 76–108, 129, 169, 172, 233–4, 241
Germani, G., 286
Germany
  city-states in, 146–7
  corporatism in, 205–7
  despotic power in, 110
  economic policy of, 174
  labour movements in, 8, 201
  microcorporatism in, 178
  political power in, 200–1
  see also Prussia
Gerschenkron, A., 127
Gibbon, E., 167
Gibson, M., 57
Giddens, A., 111, 117, 129–30
Gillett, M., 191
Gilpin, R., 299–300
Giner, G., 184
Giner, S., 173
Godelier, M., 51, 101
Goethe, J. W. von, 87
Goody, J., 13
Gorbachev, M., 219
Graham, R., 272
Gramsci, A., 212
Grant, M., 148
Great Britain
  corporatism in, 205–6, 208–9
  economic policy of, 174, 194–5
  ethnicity of, 245–7
  labour movements in, 193–4
  political power of church in, 187
  secessional nationalism in, 234
Greece
  city-states in, 148–9
  ethnicity in, 249–50
  nation-building, 249–50
  prehistory of, 24
Griffeth, R., 151

Grootings, P., 207
group 22, 305
Grunebaum, G. E. von, 54
Guemple, L., 32
guilds
  in Austria, 198–9
  in Denmark, 196–7
  in France, 190–2
  in Germany, 200–1
  in Scandinavia, 197
  in United Kingdom, 193–4
Guilherme dos Santos, W., 284
Gumplowitz, L., 9, 110, 126

Hall, J. A., 1–21, 154–76
Hapsburg empire, 185–6
  see also Austria; Portugal; Spain
Hardiman, N., 209
Hayden, B., 28
Hayward, J. E. S., 182
Hechter, M., 234–5, 247
Hegel, G. W. F., 85, 239, 244
Heidenheimer, A. J., 201
Helander, V., 203
Held, D., 2, 9
Helm, J., 48, 51, 52
heterogeneity, 29
Higgs, E. S., 30
Hindess, B., 86
Hinds, M., 74–5
Hintze, O., 9–10, 110–11
Hirst, P. Q., 86
Hobson, J. A., 4–5
Hoge Raad van Arbeid, 188
Homo sapiens sapiens, origins of, 22
  in Australia, 35
Hopkins, K., 9, 126
Hough, J., 213
House of Lords, 180
Huang, R., 157
Humphrey, C., 100
hunter-gatherers, 22–47

Ibish, Y., 76
Ibn Khaldun, 100, 158–9
Ikung campsite *see* aboriginal
  society

IMF *see* international organizations
immigrants and state formation,
  241, 259
imperial state, 115
imperialism, 5
Inalcik, H., 150
Incisa, L., 287
India
  and Marx, 100–1
  nation-building in, 254–5
Indonesia and IMF, 302, 304
industrial capitalism, 234
industrial revolution and state
  power, 130
industrialization, effect of, 168–72,
  179
inflation, effect of, in Latin
  America, 287
infrastructural power, 237–8, 277
  in Argentina, 277
  in China, 157–8
  in Denmark, 174
  development of, 113–19, 132–5
  in medieval Europe, 164–6
Ingham, G. K., 198
Ingold, T., 32
internal order, maintenance of,
  120–1
international organizations, 131,
  290–3, 298, 301, 303–5
internationalization of markets, 292
Ireland, 201, 205, 209
Islam
  cultural unity in, 158–9
  economic development in, 159–
    60, 167
  egalitarianism, 74–7
  land tenure in, 160
  law, 149
Israel, state-making in, 54, 250–1
Italy
  city-states in northern Italy,
    138–46
  corporatism in, 205, 209
  economic development in, 192
  fascism in, 185
  labour movements in, 184

Italy (*cont.*)
  political power of the church in,
    184, 192

Jacobsen, T., 60
Jacoby, H., 2
Jansen, J. J., 57
Japan
  city autonomy, 150
  ethnic unity in, 245
  and feudalism, 119
  microcorporatism, 171
  protectionism by, 126
  role of the state in, 171
Java and Nikiforov, V. N., 98–9
Jessop, B., 7
Jochim, M. A., 34
Johansen, L. N., 178
Johnson, G., 40, 44–5
Jones, A. H. M., 148
Jones, E. L., 25, 164, 168
Jones, R., 35

Kalahari society, 30, 41
Kammer, 198, 201
Kant, E., 10
Kautsky, J. H., 104, 129–30
Keynes, J. M., 4
Khazanov, A. M., 55, 56, 70, 106
Khruschev, N., 216
King, L. W., 58
kinship, 48–9, 51, 59
Kirchoff, P., 58
Kohn, H., 228, 240, 245–6, 248, 259
Komoróczy, G., 61
Korpi, W., 178
Kovalev, L., 217
Kovalevsky, M. M., 94–6, 100, 108
Kramer, S., 63, 236
Kreisi, H., 208
Kristensen, O. P., 178
Kristiansen, K., 24
Kuhnle, S., 187, 197
Kus, S., 28

labour movements, 179
  in Argentina, 279
  in Austria, 189–201

in Belgium, 189
in Denmark, 196–7
in France, 183–5, 191, 199, 201
in Germany, 8, 201
in Great Britain, 193–4, 199
in Italy, 184
in Norway, 203
laissez-faire, 154, 175, 180, 189, 194
  see also market economy
Lamberg-Karlovsky, C. C., 27, 46,
    61, 63
Lambert, F., 276
Lamounier, B., 287
land tenure in Islam, 160
Landes, D., 192
Lange, P., 209
Langton, M., 30
Lapidus, I., 159–60
Lartichaux, J. Y., 248
Laski, H., 293–4
Lattimore, O., 119, 124, 155
law, Islamic, 149
law, respect for, 154–5
Leach, E. R., 39, 85
Leacock, E., 30, 41
Lee, R. B., 29–30, 41
Leff, N. H., 272
Lehmbruch, G., 178, 188, 205
Lenin, V. I., 4–5, 83, 211, 214,
    221–3, 225–7
Lerner, D., 231, 233
Lévi-Strauss, C., 91
Lewis, A., 245, 247
liberty
  in city states, 139
  and economic development,
    168–75
Lijphart, A., 187
Linz, J., 184, 193, 286
Lipinski, E., 58
Lipset, S. M., 183, 184, 187, 189
literacy and state power, 118
Lorwin, V., 191, 201
Lourandos, H., 36
Lukas, G., 212
Lutheran church *see* church,
    political role of

Luxemburg, R., 5
Lynch, J., 266, 268

McAdams, R., 23
Macassan traders, 37
McFarlane, A., 166
MacGuire, R., 28–9, 32, 39
MacIver, R. N., 112
McKibbin, R., 7
McNairn, B., 25
Machiavelli, N., 140–1, 146
Maier, C. S., 177, 191
Mallowan, M. E. L., 63
Man the Hunter, 29–30
Mann, M., 8, 16, 109–36, 155, 163,
    166, 167, 237, 244, 277
Maoism and AMP, 102–3
Marcuse, H., 212
market economy, 180
markets, internationalization of, 292
Martin, D. A., 183, 184, 186, 187
Marx, K., 3–5, 81–5, 96, 100–1,
    111, 121, 214, 244
Marxism
    and AMP, 83–6, 93–8
    in France, 199
    and peace, 4
    and theory of the state, 6–9,
        109–10
    and tribalism, 106
    and Wittfogel, 83–5
Marxism–Leninism, 211–27
Maschke, E., 20
Mason, R., 246
materialism, 104–7
Meliksetov, A. V., 102–4
mercenaries, 141
Merquior, J. G., 9, 173, 264–88
Mesoamerica, 27, 31, 68
    see also Mexico
Mesopotamia, 23, 37, 56, 63, 116,
    117, 149, 235
Mexico, formation of, 23
Michalet, C. A., 300
microcorporatism, 174
Middle East, 149–50
    tribes in, 54–5, 57

Middlemass, K., 209
Middleton, J., 52
Miliband, R., 6
militarism, 110–11, 124, 126–32
military control, range of, 129
'military Keynesianism', 128
military organization, 9
military power, 8–10
Mill, J. S., 2, 213
Millard, A. S., 191, 200
Miller, D., 43
Milward, A. S., 192, 196
Mitrani, D., 294
mobility, 42, 44
Moeller, B., 146
Molitor, M., 208
Moore, B., 169–70
Morgan, L. H., 24, 56, 73, 85, 92–8
mortuary data, 27
Morwood, M. J., 36
Moscati, S., 148
Muller-Jentsch, W., 208
multinationals *see* transnational
    corporations
Mulvaney, D. J., 37
Mundy, J. H., 144
Murilo de Carvalho, J., 270–1
Musil, A., 54
Muslims *see* Islam
Myers, A. R., 163

Nairn, T., 234–5, 244, 247
nation-building, 231–5
nation-states, 228–30
nationalism, 6, 228–63
    by secession, 233–4
negotiator, 42–3, 46
neo-corporatism, 178, 197, 205–7
neolithic revolution, 26, 30, 37
Netherlands
    city-states in, 145
    consociationalism in, 188, 195–6
    corporatism in, 205–7
New Economic Policy (Soviet
    Union), 226
Newly Industrializing Countries
    (NIC), 170–5, 302

Nicholas, D. M., 145
Nigeria, state-making in, 256–8, 261
Nikiforov, V. N., 78–108
nomadic style model, 30
nomads, 55, 56, 69–73, 158
see also bedouin
Norway, 201–3, 205–6

O'Brien, Conor Cruise, 303
O'Connell, J. F., 35
O'Donnell, G., 281
Olsen, M., 15, 305
Oppenheimer, F., 9, 126
Oppenheimer, L., 236
O'Shea, J., 34
Ostrovityanov, Y., 102
Oszlak, O., 269

Palaeolithic period, 36
Pankow, W., 222, 225, 226
Papua New Guinea, pottery trading, 27
Paraguay, autocracy in, 268, 280
Parker, D., 144
parliament and European development 163
'parliamentary parenthesis', 177, 181
Parsons, T., 120
pastoralists, 54–5
Paters, G., 181
Peebles, C., 28
Peel, J. D. Y., 2
Penrose, E., 302
Peterson, N., 30, 33
Phear, J. B., 96
Pirenne, H., 145
Plekhanov, G. V., 95
Pocock, J. G. A., 2
Poggi, G., 180
Poland, 224–6
see also Eastern Europe
polis, 66, 139, 148
'political space', 177–210
political units, 53

polyethnic societies, state-making in, 252–63
Polynesian chiefdoms, 65
population growth, 26, 31, 36
Portugal
economic development in, 192–3, 210
fascism in, 185, 193
political power of the church in, 184
pottery, trade in, 27
Poulantzas, N., 6–7, 110, 122, 132
praxis, 214
pre-capitalist modes of production, 86
prehistory and state development, 23–8
Price, T. D., 33, 34
Protestantism *see* church, political role of
Prussia, 126, 198
see also Germany
pyatchik, 78, 88, 94

radiocarbon dating, use of, 23, 31
Rakhmanin, O. B., 219
Ranki, G., 192, 197
Rappaport, R., 38
Ratzenhofer, 110
Reagan, R., 291, 298
reductionism and theory of the state, 109–10, 112, 117, 120, 134
Reichstadte *see* Germany, city-states in
religion and the state, 182–204
Renfrew, C., 28, 31, 38, 46, 126, 237, 278
Rerum Novarum (1891), 183, 188
Reynard, J. D., 183, 191, 192
Rhee, Song Nai, 149
Roberts, J. M., 23
Rock, D., 279
Rokkan, S., 147, 183, 184, 187
Roman empire, 9, 126–7, 155–6
Rome
as city-state, 148

and the empire, 9, 155
Romero, J. L., 269
Roosevelt, F. and New Deal, 290–1
Rosas, General J. M. de, 266–8, 276
Rosdolsky, R., 244
Rose, R., 181
Rosenau, J. N., 293
Rosenberg, H., 200
Roska, I., 219
Ross, A., 36
Rousseau, J. J., 146, 239
Roussel, D., 73
Roux, G., 236
Rowlands, M. J., 29, 33, 38, 40
Rowley, Conwy, P., 33
Russell-Wood, A. J. R., 270
Russia *see* Soviet Union
Rüstow, A., 110

Saad, E. N., 151
Sablov, J. A., 27, 46
Saggs, H. W. F., 62
Sahlins, M. D., 27, 30, 45, 50–2, 56–7, 65–8
Sakharov, A., 212
Saul, S. B., 191, 192, 196, 200
scalar-communication stress, 40, 41, 44–5
Scandinavia and the church, 186–7
Schapera, I., 50, 51
Schmitt, C., 110
Schmitter, P. C., 205
Schrire, C., 30
Sellin, V., 192
Seminov, Y., 80, 90–1
Serra, J., 285
Service, E. R., 27, 28, 38, 56–7, 62, 64, 68, 126, 237
Seton-Watson, H., 241, 248
Sevilla, E., 173, 184
Sforza, C., 31
Shalev, M., 178
Shanin, T., 98, 143
sheep, 26, 27
Shennan, S. J., 27, 29
Sheridan, A., 32, 34

Shishlin, N., 220
Shorter, E., 191
Sismondi, J. C. L. S. de, 138–9
Skalnik, P., 27, 38, 57
Skiling, G., 213
Skocpol, T., 10, 11, 14, 111
slavery
  in Brazil, 270, 273, 276
  and the city-state, 148
Smith, Adam, 2, 154, 167–76
Smith, Anthony, 228–63
Smith, D., 19
Smith, P. H., 281
social class and state organization, 3–4, 111
social cohesion and religion, 13
Social Darwinism, 9, 110, 174
social evolution, 19–20, 24, 27
social revolution, 10–11
societies and states, 16–17
Soffer, O., 36
Southall, A. W., 54, 55
Soviet model of development, 171–2
Soviet Union,
  constitution of, 222
  despotic power in, 113, 116, 131
  fascism in, 185
  foreign policy, 215–20
  industrialization, 170–2
  state organization 211–27
Spain
  economic development, 192–3
  state-building in, 248, 258
Spencer, H., 2–3
Spencer, R., 126, 128
Spencer, W., 150
Spengler, 299
Spitaels, G., 189
stäands, 181–2
staatslehre, 183
Stalinism, 226–7
ständestaat, 189–90, 196–201
Stanner, W. E. H., 35
State
  authority in, 38
  basis of strength, 181

State (*cont.*)
definition of, 112
functions of, 120–2
necessity for, 119–20
numbers of, 289
origins of, 22–47
political power of, 289, 305
and prehistory, 23–8
and religion, 182–203
as a territorial unit, 122–5, 128–9, 134
theory of 6–17, 214
two-dimensional model, 111
withering away of, 1–6, 289–90
see also city-states; colonial states; imperial state; nation-states
state elites, 15, 112–13, 125, 135, 238–9, 240, 243
in Brazil, 270–1, 273–6
in China, 157
state formation, 241, 259
state-making, 235–63
in Africa, 255–9
in Argentina 264–9, 276–88
in Asia, 253–4, 257, 259
in Brazil, 269–88
in India, 254–5
in polyethnic societies, 252–63
state power
and agriculture, 128
and autonomy, 15, 109–36
centralization of, 126–32, 285–6
change in the basis of, 294–5
definitions of, 112–16
and industrial revolution, 130
and literacy, 118
and militarism, 125–32, 295
origins of, 119–25
and technology, 294, 296–8
and transnational corporations, 13, 289–305
see also despotism; infrastructural power
Stephens, J. D., 198
Sterbalova, A., 102
Stern, S. M., 149
Steward, J. H., 27, 49

Stewart, D., 168
Strange, S., 289–305
Strategic Defence Initiative (SDI), 298, 300
Streeck, W., 208
Sumer
conquest of, 149
fishing in, 64
law codes of, 236–7
organization of, 60
prehistory of, 57–9
religion in, 60–3
superpowers
influence of, 124–5
and nuclear weapons, 16
Sweden, 174, 197–8, 205–6
see also Scandinavia and the church
Switzerland
city-states in, 145–6
consociationism, 187
corporatism of, 205, 207
nation-formation in, 251–2
structure of, 195
Syria and tribes, 53
Szuros, M., 218

Talos, E., 186, 198–9
Tapper, R., 54
Tato, M., 23
taxation, 163, 303
technology as state power, 294, 296–8
territorial centralization, 122–5, 129
Third World
nation-building in, 232, 239
and transnational corporations, 300–2
Thorner, D., 149
Tilley, C., 43, 111–13, 191, 238–40, 245
Tkachev, P. N., 90, 99
Tocqueville, C. A., 164
trade, 27, 296
transnational corporations (TNC), 290, 292, 298, 300–3

Troxlar, F., 198
tribal social structure and L. H.
Morgan, 92
tribal state, 50
tribalism and Marxism, 106
tribe
biological basis of, 48–50
concept of, 48–55
and egalitarianism, 61, 73–7
and evolution of the state, 55–68
organization in, 48–9
tribes, African, 52, 54
East African, 51
Indian, 74
see also nomads
Trindale, H., 276
trinitarianism, western and eastern,
78
Trotsky, L., 5, 212
Tucker, R. C., 85
Turkey, 27
Tylor, E., 24

Uganda, state-making in, 255–6
unilinealism, 80
United Kingdom *see* Great Britain
United States
and corporatism, 14
economic policies of, 175
and military power, 17
urban revolution, characteristics of,
25
Uricoechea, F., 275

'vacuum theory' of the city state,
152
Vargas, G., 283
Vatican *see* Italy, political power of
the church in
Veliz, C., 270, 274
Ventura, A., 143
Viotti da Costa, E., 270

Vladimirov, O., 219

Waddington, C. H., 32
Wade, R., 170
Waley, D., 140
war
causes of, 4–6
end of, 2–3
and the state, 8, 9–10
and state power, 291
Ward, W. A., 57
Warner, W. L., 52
Warren, B., 233
Warsaw pact, 217, 219
see also Eastern Europe and
Soviet Union
Weber, M., 9, 110–12, 130, 137,
153, 156, 162, 236
Western Europe and technology,
298–300, 305
White, G., 170
White, J. P., 35
White, L., 17
Whittle, A., 29
Wiener, M. J., 195
Wiessner, P., 41
Wilensky, H., 178
Williamson, P. J., 184, 192
Windmuller, J. P., 188, 207
Winkler, H. A., 179
Wittfogel, K. A., 82–5
Wobst, H. M., 28, 34
Wolin, S., 110
Worsley, P., 233
Wrigley, A. M., 169

Yoffee, N., 23, 37, 38
Yugoslavia, 260–1

Zasulich, V., 97
Zimbabwe, 256
Zvelebil, M., 34, 38